Joachim Eibach
Fragile Families

Joachim Eibach

Fragile Families

Marriage and Domestic Life in the Age of Bourgeois Modernity (1750–1900)

Translated by
Alissa Jones Nelson

DE GRUYTER
OLDENBOURG

Original edition: „Fragile Familien. Ehe und häusliche Lebenswelt in der bürgerlichen Moderne",
De Gruyter: Berlin/Boston 2022.

ISBN 978-3-11-221514-2
e-ISBN (PDF) 978-3-11-108170-0
e-ISBN (EPUB) 978-3-11-108215-8

Library of Congress Control Number: 2023940523

Bibliographic information published by the Deutsche Nationalbibliothek
The Deutsche Nationalbibliothek lists this publication in the Deutsche Nationalbibliografie;
detailed bibliographic data are available on the internet at http://dnb.dnb.de.

© 2025 Walter de Gruyter GmbH, Berlin/Boston
This volume is text- and page-identical with the hardback published in 2023.
Cover image: Joseph Hartmann: Forstmeister Wilhelm Heinrich Seyd und Familie
(1845); Hessisches Landesmuseum, Darmstadt .
Printing and binding: CPI books GmbH, Leck

www.degruyter.com

No question about it.
For Anna, Ferdinand, and Luise

Acknowledgements

This book on the history of the family has its own long history. The story actually begins in the summer of 1983, when I rather coincidentally stayed with Antonio Alfonso Alves and his family in the village of Padornelos in northern Portugal. Life in their house and among their family was conducted in a very different way than I was familiar with. Over the course of my academic career, I subsequently got involved in various research topics. The history of the home and the family came to the fore in 2001, with my inaugural lecture at the University of Giessen, where Sonja Finkenzeller supported me in acquiring research materials and teaching. My exploration of this topic took off in 2008, at the German Historians' Conference (*Deutscher Historikertag*) in Dresden, where I co-founded the working group "The House in Context" (*Haus im Kontext*) with Inken Schmidt-Voges. My 2011 article on the open house ("Das offene Haus") became a widely cited text and opened the door to further research. This work was granted a generous framework by means of the Sinergia project "Doing House and Family," a research project which was approved by the Swiss National Science Foundation in 2014 and which I led for four years, along with Sandro Guzzi-Heeb, Jon Mathieu, and Claudia Optiz-Belakhal. This spark of inspiration also ignited my doctoral students Maurice Cottier, Arno Haldemann, and Eric Häusler. Fruitful collaborations on 'domestic spheres' and 'open houses' then arose with Margareth Lanzinger and Raffaella Sarti as well.

    The fact that I was able to sit down and write this book all at once, chapter by chapter, with focused attention after years of preparation, must be attributed to the Covid-19 pandemic that took hold in the spring of 2020. The virus has certainly wreaked havoc around the globe, but it also provided favorable circumstances in which I could write this book, thanks to the deceleration and domestication of everyday life. I also received very helpful advice and references to significant self-narratives – sometimes at conferences, sometimes in passing – particularly from Norbert Furrer, Frank Hatje, Kaspar von Greyerz, Peter Paul Bänziger, Margareth Lanzinger, and Matthias Ruoss. Frank Hatje has been a fount of information and a reliable discussion partner on all questions concerning the history of the Hamburg couple Ferdinand and Caroline Beneke. Mr. Erhard Franke, a retired cantor, unexpectedly contributed details from the church records in the Saxon municipality of Hartenstein concerning the journeyman printer Friedrich Anton Püschmann's milieu. The process of researching the photographic material for this book also precipitated valuable contacts with researchers who were previously unknown to me. In this respect, I would like to thank Jan Arni, Li Gerhalter, Bernadette Hagenbuch, Urs Held, Karin M. Hofer, Matthias John, and Nikola Langreiter, as well as the Wienerberger company, the Paula Modersohn Becker Foundation in Bremen, and the Otto Modersohn Foundation in Fischerhude.

Many students at the university of Bern have shared and continue to share my enthusiasm for diaries as a source of family history. My student assistants have provided invaluable support in developing the sources for this project: I am grateful to Amanda Kaufmann, Maximilian Lederer, Lisa Linder, Lena-Sophie Margelisch, and Maria Schmidlin. For their understanding of the importance of collegiality, I would like to thank Heinzpeter Znoj, Tobias Haller, Thomas Späth, Christian Büschges, and certainly not least Julia Richers. When my motivation flagged during the writing process, Paul Klee's "Ungeheuer in Bereitschaft" shook me awake. In the end, the interdisciplinary seminar with Yahya Elsaghe on Thomas Mann's *Buddenbrooks* has not resulted in the hoped-for book chapter, and these ideas are still percolating, waiting for an appropriate publication. Jon Mathieu read and commented on the entire manuscript within a few days. Three anonymous peer reviewers endorsed the manuscript very favorably, for which I am grateful. I would also like to thank Alissa Jones Nelson for her beautiful translation. Last but not least, the well-read pianist Rudi Spring offered praise for the musicality of the title. Each fragile family has its own rhythm.

Finally, I am grateful to Anna Heier-Eibach for many things, not least her healthy disinterest in my research, which continues to be very refreshing after many years. Yet there is more of her in this book than she knows, and perhaps even more than the author himself realizes...

Contents

Chapter 1
Fragile Families? Stylish Staging and Everyday Disorder —— 1

Chapter 2
Research and Sources —— 6
        The Family – Past and Present —— 6
        Contexts: The Family, House and Home, and Domesticity —— 10
        People: Actors, Subjects, and Habitus —— 14
        Self-Narratives: Beyond *Bürgerlichkeit* —— 17
        Initial Questions —— 20

Chapter 3
Love and a House of His Own: The Peasant Ulrich Bräker Seeks a Wife —— 22
Toggenburg, Switzerland (1754 – 1798)
        The Literary Peasant —— 23
        Courtship and Matchmaking in the Village —— 25
        Rationality and Marriageability —— 30
        A Precarious Married Life —— 34

Chapter 4
Pious Everyday Life in the Bailiwick and the Patrician Milieu:
Henriette Stettler-Herport —— 38
Bern, Switzerland (1771 – 1789)
        Self-Formation and a Pietist Record of the Soul —— 40
        Household Management —— 49
        Marriage Politics Among the Urban Elite —— 55
        Marriage as Hierarchy and Companionship —— 58
        House vs. Family: Two Models of Living Together —— 61

Chapter 5
Bourgeois Marriage and Open Domesticity:
Ferdinand and Caroline Beneke —— 68
Hamburg, Germany (1805 – 1816)
        The Bourgeois Romantic Subject —— 69
        The House and Household —— 74
        Why Caroline? The Complications of Finding a Partner —— 80
        Marriage Beyond Stereotypes —— 89

Vulnerable Love and Volatile 'Gender Characters' —— 96
The Domestic Sphere as a Social Relay —— 100

Chapter 6
The Parsonage as Labyrinth: Ursula and Abraham Bruckner-Eglinger —— 104
Basel, Switzerland (1819–1833)

Sociability and Self-Accusation —— 106
An Unexpected Yet Predictable Proposal of Marriage —— 107
The Perfect Household as Chronic Overload —— 109
Emotional Care Relationships —— 117
Domestication or 'Open House'? —— 122

Chapter 7
A Traveling Journeyman's Home: Friedrich Anton Püschmann —— 127
Stollberg, Germany, and on the Road (1848–1856)

The Craftsman's Honor, Bourgeois Values (*Bürgerlichkeit*), and Leisure Time —— 129
Collective Domesticity Among Young Men —— 133
The Journeyman's Travels: Variable Accommodation and No Privacy —— 137
Limited Marriage Prospects: The Barmaids and the Young Lady —— 143
The Family as an Emotional and Supportive Community —— 146
Open Domesticity in a Small-Town Context —— 149

Chapter 8
Marital Crisis and Social Decline Among the Petite Bourgeoisie: Barbara and Johann Baumgartner —— 153
Krems and Vienna, Austria (1870–1885)

From Naïve Girl to Sought-After Marriage Partner —— 154
Matchmaking and Marriage in a Small Town —— 157
Logbook of a Married Couple in Crisis —— 162
Female Labor and Precarious Familial Support —— 171
The Absence of Visiting Culture and the Presence of Gossip —— 175
A Modern Couple —— 178

Chapter 9
Growing Up Among the Proletariat:
Friedrich Engels' Report and Adelheid Popp —— 181
Manchester, England (1845); Inzersdorf and Vienna, Austria (1869 – 1902)
        Engels' Report on the Slums in English Cities —— 182
        The Female Subject's Emancipation from the Precariat —— 186
        Migrant Families and One-Room Domesticity —— 192
        Co-Presence in Chambers and Bedsits —— 197
        Another Family Model? —— 201

Chapter 10
From a Bourgeois Family to an Artists' Marriage:
Paula Becker and Otto Modersohn —— 206
Bremen and Worpswede, Germany, and Paris, France (1892 – 1907)
        Liberal Habitat and Cultural Capital —— 207
        The Letter-Writing 'I' and the Diary-Keeping 'I' —— 211
        Family and Art: Between Familiarity and Departure —— 215
        Engagement: A Culinary Course and 'Social Magic' —— 223
        The Chosen 'Family' as Sacred Friendship —— 228
        Marriage as a Crisis-Ridden Communion of Soulmates —— 231
        Family Trust and the Desire for Freedom —— 242

Chapter 11
The Family: Decline or Resilience? —— 245
        Thomas Mann's *Buddenbrooks* —— 245
        Matchmaking and Society —— 247
        Relationship Patterns and Gender —— 251
        Small Rituals and Time-Outs —— 256
        Work and Leisure —— 258
        Habitat as an Actor —— 260
        Between Privacy and Openness —— 262

List of Figures —— 265

Bibliography —— 267

Index of Persons —— 287

Index of Subjects —— 291

Chapter 1
Fragile Families? Stylish Staging and Everyday Disorder

At first glance, we see a bright, harmonious world. The painting by the German portraitist Joseph Hartmann (oil on canvas, completed in 1845) depicts a nineteenth-century bourgeois family in a Biedermeier interior.[1]

Fig. 1: The Forester Wilhelm Heinrich Seyd and Family (1845), by Joseph Hartmann.
Source: Hessisches Landesmuseum, Darmstadt, Germany

The forester Seyd, upon whose living room the viewer's eye falls, has achieved a tasteful prosperity alongside his wife and three children. While a forestry official's social position was not exactly the pinnacle of Olympian middle-class aspirations,[2] it did offer financial security and the chance to establish a refined domestic environment. This painting makes a statement. The clothes worn by the various family members are neat and clean. Sunshine falls through the open window into the domestic interior. No servants or visitors disturb the family idyll. The fact that the young daughter is teasing the family dog poses no threat to this domestic peace,

---

[1] For further details on the painter, see Zeeb, "Hartmann, Joseph, (1812)"; on the family as motif, see Hammer-Tugendhat, "'Familie! Familie?'"; on the depiction of the family in Biedermeier, see Lorenz, *Das deutsche Familienbild*, esp. 139–40; see also Dorgerloh "Beseelung der Bilderscheinung," 434; Koschorke et al., *Vor der Familie*, 21–28.
[2] Krünitz, "Forst-Bediente," *Oekonomische Encyklopädie* 14 (1773): 525–30, available at: www.kruenitz1.uni-trier.de.

although the older son seems to take this as an opportunity to admonish his younger brother. The gender hierarchy is also depicted in this scene. The mother holds her pretty little daughter lovingly on her lap, and the two face each other. The two sons, on the other hand, are dressed like adults. Elevated above the family, somewhat set apart, stands the father in his dark coat, stuffing his pipe and wearing a serious expression. Nevertheless, the family is united around the living-room table, and the viewer discerns no conflicts or difficulties.

In this and many other paintings from the same period, the bourgeois nuclear family is staged as a moral and civilizational achievement. Thus in Georg Wilhelm Friedrich Hegel's *Elements of the Philosophy of Right* (*Grundlinien der Philosophie des Rechts*), published in 1820, marriage – the central familial relationship – is also understood as "the immediate ethical relationship."[3] Liberalism, which was the dominant political strain at the time, also argued along Hegel's lines. In terms of natural law, the liberals referred to a general "moral law" and to "the idea of the dignity, indeed the sanctity of marriage, which prevails everywhere among civilized [...] peoples." Thus the family was considered "the foundation of all noble human and civic life, all human and civic happiness."[4] Of course none of this was designed to be gender-neutral, but was primarily intended as a "society of independent housefathers."[5] Conservative critics such as Wilhelm Heinrich Riehl, on the other hand, were extremely displeased by the new understanding of the family that Hartmann and other painters depicted – the privatized, bourgeois nuclear family, without servants, conspicuously dressed up, neither down-to-earth nor "old German." Riehl saw no morality or sanctity here, but rather a decline in morals and a fatal dissolution of traditional domestic family ties; he regarded the new urban middle class as the driving force behind these changes and held them responsible accordingly.[6]

Historically well-informed readers need not be told that the Elysian world in miniature advertised in Hartmann's portrait was anything but secure in the year in which the painting was created. This was a time of rampant poverty. A great famine would occur in Europe the very next year, causing widespread hunger, and revolution would follow three years later. Shortly thereafter, in the 1850s, the period of high industrialization began in Central Europe, and the upheaval in-

---

[3] Hegel, *Elements of the Philosophy of Right*, p. 200: https://archive.org/details/elementsofphilos0000hege/page/n5/mode/2up; see also Hegel's understanding of marriage in Gestrich et al., *Geschichte der Familie*, 381–82.
[4] All quotations taken from Rotteck, "Familie, Familienrecht (natürliches)," 386–87.
[5] Gall, *Von der ständischen*, 27.
[6] Riehl (*Die Naturgeschichte des Volkes*) refers to "das neue städtische Bürgertum": see 145–65, esp. 145, 150, 153–59.

stantiated by these changes also directly affected family life and relationships. In reality, precarious living conditions prevailed in many places across Europe. Friedrich Engels was one of the first to describe this in his *The Condition of the Working Class in England*, the German edition of which also went to press in 1845.[7] Even prior to industrialization, the bourgeoisie – who enjoyed having their portraits painted as much as certain painters enjoyed propagating this family ideal, which was synonymous with a certain lifestyle – constituted a social minority. Nevertheless, this family model remained extremely appealing for decades, and well into the twentieth century. *Bürgertum* did not simply come to an end after its 'heyday' in the nineteenth century.[8] The question of whether the children and grandchildren of the people who participated in the 1968 anti-bourgeois student movements (known as 'the 68ers'), children who take ballet or piano lessons, have in fact returned to the bourgeois habitus need not be addressed here.[9] Rather, the point is that hardly anything in the beautiful family scene depicted in Hartmann's oil painting appears to be insecure or endangered, and that important aspects of domestic and family life together thus remain hidden from view.

The subject of this book is families – which, on closer inspection, turn out to be fragile. But what does 'fragile' mean in this context, and why were families fragile in the nineteenth century? In English, as in other languages, this adjective refers to something that is both valuable and endangered. The *Oxford English Dictionary* offers "easily broken or damaged" and "thin or light and often beautiful" as definitions of the term. In German, the standard *Duden* dictionary provides the meanings "zerbrechlich" and "zart," with the synonyms "feingliedrig" and "grazil." In French, the *Larousse* dictionary gives us "peu stable, éphémère, précaire." For some historians, this term will immediately call to mind Arlette Farge's classic *La vie fragile*, which describes the precarious living conditions faced by the lower classes in Paris during the eighteenth century.[10] Fragility also implies impor-

---

[7] Engels, *Condition of the Working Class*. On the stages of industrialization, see Wehler, *Deutsche Gesellschaftsgeschichte*, 3:66–84; on the development of housing conditions in Germany, see Reulecke, *Geschichte des Wohnens*; von Saldern, "Im Hause."
[8] See Budde, *Blütezeit des Bürgertums*; see also Kocka, "Das europäische Muster," 10; Hettling and Hoffmann, *Der bürgerliche Wertehimmel*; Dejung et al., "Worlds of the Bourgeoisie," 2; on the middle class after 1945, see Budde, *Bürgertum nach dem bürgerlichen Zeitalter*. Note on the text: single quotation marks indicate relevant terminology and indirect citations, while double quotation marks indicate direct citations.
[9] See the discussion of the new middle class in Bude et al., *Bürgerlichkeit ohne Bürgertum*; see also Reckwitz, "Wie bürgerlich ist die Moderne?."
[10] Farge, *Das brüchige Leben*. In German, the term is used in more formal language; in English, it can also be found in colloquial language and even pop songs, for example in the line: "Precious and

tance and significance: the higher the discursive pedestal, the farther one can potentially fall in one's everyday life. In this sense, the home and the family were fragile long before the advent of middle-class modernity. In the time of Martin Luther and the Reformers, all of Christian society had its roots in the home, and the 'domestic estate' was supposed to be a pious haven – a church in miniature.[11] Marriage was almost indispensable for anyone who wanted to acquire social status, prestige, or property in the early modern period. Additionally, marriage and the family were inscribed as legal institutions. As laws were gradually liberalized from the revolutionary period onward, the voluntary principle – in cases of both marriage and divorce – became increasingly valid. In practice, however – even in the nineteenth century – it was clear that other actors both within and outside the family, as well as government bodies and authorities, frequently had a say in decisions regarding marriage.[12] Moreover, prior to the advent of liberalism, Pietism and Romanticism had already placed an enormous emphasis on familial inwardness (*Innerlichkeit*) and familial love, thus elevating these concepts to a programmatic status and providing new discourses that also shaped the relevant actors' experiences and practices. The early modern 'working couple' (H. Wunder) was replaced by the 'loving couple' (Trepp) and the middle-class 'educated couple' (R. Habermas). Nevertheless, it is not clear what actually became of the working couple after 1800, or whether the household did in fact continue to be a site of work – for women as well as for men – even in the era of middle-class modernity.[13] This normative discourse – which had a concrete effect on upbringing and education, for example, as well as on a particular 'moral' habitus – placed higher expectations on the family. While classic works on family history written in a characteristically emancipatory style take for granted the functional release and liberation of the modern family around 1800, one can also observe a new focus on the home during the period of transition (the so-called *Sattelzeit*).[14] Thus in some re-

---

fragile things need special handling" in Depeche Mode's song "Precious" (2005), or in Sting's "Fragile" (1987).
11 Luther referred to this as 'der häusliche Stand.' See Th. Kuhn, "Das Haus"; see also Roper's classic 1995 text, with the apt title: *The Holy Household.*
12 For an overview, see Ehmer, "Ehekonsens"; more recently, see Haldemann, *Prekäre Eheschließungen*; on divorce, see Blasius, *Ehescheidung in Deutschland*; Arni, *Entzweiungen.*
13 Ågren, *Making a Living*; this is the guiding question behind the "Gender and Work" research project at Uppsala University, led by Maria Ågren: www.gaw.hist.uu.se/what-is-gaw/research+project/.
14 Mitterauer and Sieder, *Vom Patriarchat zur Partnerschaft*, esp. 100–02; for a more cautious approach, see Gestrich, *Geschichte der Familie im 19. und 20. Jahrhundert*, 69–71; on the importance of the domestic sphere, see Eibach, "Das Haus in der Moderne", 22–25, esp. 29; on the current state of research generally, see Eibach and Lanzinger, *The Routledge History of the Domestic Sphere.*

spects, house and home took on increasing importance as a familial sphere, a social context, and a stage on which to interact.

This book seeks to look behind the familial façade and examine the muddle of everyday domestic life. The actors I consider here come from a variety of contexts, including but not limited to the prototypical middle class. It would be nearly impossible to write the middle class out of any history of the family. However, one desideratum of such research is to bring other families into the narrative as well. The actors in this book do not appear in their Sunday best, but rather in everyday clothes. They experience crises and conflicts, face challenges, and sometimes seem hopelessly overwhelmed. The first research question is a fairly simple one: Who did what, how, and with whom? It is important to take our starting point not from the nuclear family ideal, but rather from domesticity (*Häuslichkeit*) as a multifaceted sphere of real interaction, which included not only parents and their children, but also other groups of people.[15] This approach enables us to explore socialization from the inside out. For in this everyday disarray, domestic relationships do indeed reflect general developments. Close connections existed – and still exist – between the family, the domestic microcosm, and society more broadly.

---

[15] For a recent take on the concept of the domestic sphere, see Eibach and Lanzinger, *The Routledge History of the Domestic Sphere*; on the striking discrepancies between norms and "self-definitions" on the one hand and "actual practices" on the other, see R. Habermas, *Frauen und Männer des Bürgertums*, 11.

Chapter 2
Research and Sources

The Family – Past and Present

One way or another, we all have a family history – and as a rule, each family history seems special, unique, and alien to those on the outside. Moreover, we gain personal experience in partner relationships that lead to marriage or continuous cohabitation – and later perhaps to separation – just as we do in parent–child or sibling relationships. Seen from an insider perspective, the familiar ways in which we deal with our families – whether or not these are pleasant – are very much our own. Seen from the outside, they may seem strange: sometimes romantic, sometimes tragic, sometimes comedic, and often with a tendency toward the dramatic. In the present as well as the past, whole armies of experts have tried to impose or establish order in families: politicians and lawyers, mediators and psychiatrists, psychologists and educators, historians and sociologists, not to mention advisors among one's friends and relatives. All of these people are primarily concerned with determining what happens in families in the first place, as well as how family relationships can be improved. The body of literature on the family is enormous and continues to grow steadily. This is true in the present, and it was also true in the past. Clergymen and judges in matrimonial courts in the early modern period lamented what they saw as widespread 'evil housekeeping' (*Übelhausen*) and pursued the goal of Christianizing family relationships, which in practice often meant simply preserving 'domestic peace.'[1] Advisors to rulers and monarchs, Enlightenment thinkers and Pietists, liberals and Romantics, restorationist conservatives after 1945, the communards among the 68ers, and gender theorists have all developed their own ideas about and new conceptions of the family. From this vast sea of discourse, the interested reader can draw two conclusions: first, what happens in the domestic–family sphere is important across epochs up to the present day; second, the family as an institution is historically mutable.

Contrary to many predictions, the family has survived. Nevertheless, it is obviously fragile and not easily defined. Every society negotiates anew what 'family' actually means. This realization indicates that historians are unconvinced by any claims that the family represents an anthropological constant. If we consult the

---

1 Schmidt-Voges, *Mikropolitiken des Friedens*; see also Westphal et al., *Venus und Vulcanus*; on control over the household and housekeeping, including recommendations for further reading, see Schläppi, "Logiken der Subsistenz."

handbooks on the sociology of the family, we encounter a definition that is valid across most societies: "the female–male dyad with one or more children is typical of families and is designed to achieve permanence based on joint economic activity."[2] In the dry terminology of systems theory, the modern family figures as a functionally differentiated "socially specialized system with a specific logic of meaning and action."[3] Accordingly, the family's basic functions include biological reproduction and the socialization of the next generation; in addition, certain patterns predominate when it comes to roles and forms of cooperation. On the one hand, social rationalization processes do indeed affect family life; on the other hand, the central function imputed to the contemporary family is the "psychological and physical regeneration and stabilization of all its members (young and old)."[4] Such a worldly description would have seemed strange to the sixteenth-century Reformers, who understood and promoted marriage and family as 'God's primary order' on earth.[5] All the above-mentioned characteristics of the family have been and continue to be instantiated differently in different cultures, and a closer look reveals major normative distinctions, and particularly differences in everyday life. Anyone who operates on the basis of an overly narrow, one-sided concept of the family will soon come across unexpected variations not only in the plural reality of the present, but also as one steps backwards through history. At any rate, the fragile family in the modern period has a lot to do with emotion. Modern families are long-term communities of care. Here 'care' means feelings of responsibility, communication based on mutual trust, and the expectation of material support. Moreover, emotions – as relevant research has found – are historically variable and culturally shaped. The family produces and teaches a certain understanding of feelings, but it is also a sociotope in which these feelings – by no means only positive ones – are acted out directly and continuously.[6]

In fact, even the early modern period was characterized by highly variable forms of living together under one roof, for both demographic and economic reasons. In recent decades, the family in Europe has gone from a socially and morally

---

2 Hill and Kopp, "Familiensoziologie," 9.
3 Nave-Herz, "Der Wandel der Familie," 2.
4 Nave-Herz, "Unkenrufe," 992, 994.
5 H. Wunder, "*Er ist die Sonn'*," 67. On relevant discourse during the Reformation, see Burghartz, *Zeiten der Reinheit* and "Zwischen Integration und Ausgrenzung"; on the house and home, see T. Kuhn, "Das Haus im Protestantismus"; on marriage discourse in the premodern era generally, see Schnell, *Sexualität und Emotionalität*.
6 On the mutability of feelings, see Frevert, "Defining Emotions," and *Mächtige Gefühle*, 8–14; on communication based on trust, see Frevert, *Vertrauensfragen*, esp. 15–17; on love and family, see ibid., pp. 8, 212–14; on the modern family as an emotional sphere, see Opitz-Belakhal, "A Space of Emotions."

binding institution to an optional way of life.[7] The legal and social deregulation of marriage and the family has led to a diversity of lifestyles. In addition to the enduring family model in which two parents raise their biological children, we can also observe other relationship patterns: single parents with children, patchwork families, 'living apart together,' households in which married children live with their parents, and rainbow families. In practice, it is the perceptions of the people in a particular family that determine who is considered a member of the family and who is not.[8] The normative framework in which family relationships are negotiated has undoubtedly become broader and more liberal. In this context, the increased divorce rates in Western societies from the mid-1960s to the early years of the new millennium could be understood as a symptom indicating a crisis of the family. Yet this would be a superficial diagnosis, for two reasons: First, such a diagnosis underestimates the fragility of marriage even in the heyday of the morally entrenched middle-class model of marriage, when marital crises were hidden from public view and divorce was a 'no-go.' Second, the fact of divorce paradoxically points to a harmonious life together as the marital ideal, which in particular cases does not or ceases to find sufficient resonance in everyday marital life. Many divorced people marry a second or even a third time. Even around 1900, when divorce rates were already soaring, finding happiness within the nuclear family (*Kleinfamilienglück*) remained a central goal in most people's lives, according to numerous diaries written by members of the middle and lower classes.[9] Additionally, despite the vast plurality of lifestyles today, Europe-wide surveys show that the model in which a family is made up of two parents and their children remains attractive.[10] On the whole, sociologists of the family tend to argue that the family is not currently experiencing a new kind of crisis, but is – and a historian would add: once again – experiencing a phase of accelerated change. The family community has never been secure or untroubled, except perhaps in the realms of psychological need or sacred memory.

The household and the family are among the topics that each generation of historians addresses with a new emphasis. Nor is this surprising. Years ago, Max Weber established that changes in our ideas about cultural values (*Kultur-*

---

[7] See Schneider, "Familie in Westeuropa," 21; on the changes since the nineteenth century, see the cursory treatment in Wienfort, *Verliebt, Verlobt, Verheiratet*.
[8] On this concept, see Widmer, *Family Configurations*; see also the inspiring approach in J. C. Kaufmann, *Schmutzige Wäsche*.
[9] Bänziger, *Die Moderne als Erlebnis*, 387. On modern marriage's first crisis period around 1900, see Arni, *Entzweiungen*.
[10] Hill and Kopp, *Familiensoziologie*, 272; Nave-Herz, "Unkenrufe," 993–94; on the ongoing modern discourse on the family in crisis, see Koschorke et al., *Vor der Familie*, 12–14.

wertideen) influence the questions we ask. In this sense, it is striking that many of the received ideas about the history of the family were formulated against the backdrop of changes in the family that were seen either as desirable or as signs of crisis. This was already true in the nineteenth century, when the modern approach to history and the social sciences emerged. Wilhelm Heinrich Riehl in Germany and Frédéric Le Play in France evoked the patriarchal 'whole house' or 'stem family', which was threatened with extinction in the face of the social dynamics that industrialization set in motion.[11] Around 1900, in the context of the emerging critique of historicism, social scientists discussed the phenomenon of domestic economy all the way back to antiquity. Against the backdrop of the restorative mood after 1945, Otto Brunner was concerned with the reassertion of the bourgeois family and its concept of parental dominance as well as the rejection of state claims to regulation, arguing for the continuity of patriarchal rule in the 'Occident' from the ancient 'oikos' to the eighteenth century.[12] In contrast, quantitative approaches to social history from the 1960s onward discussed the tone-setting theories of modernization and soberly constructed different models of the family throughout European history, which they then described as a "household" or a "coresident domestic group."[13] With reference to comparable phenomena in the history of the premodern family, Peter Laslett warned against dramatizing "the deviations from the norms of family life that are so often deplored at present," namely extramarital cohabitation, marital separation, and homophilie.[14] Michael Mitterauer and Reinhard Sieder's emancipatory proposal in their 1982 book *The European Family: Patriarchy to Partnership from the Middle Ages to the Present* (first published in German in 1977 as *Vom Patriarchat zur Partnerschaft*) constituted one of the foremost arguments refuting the notions of the large family and of people marrying young in preindustrial times, which were widely accepted and associated with conservative family policy at the time.[15]

Since the 1990s, of course, cultural-historical research on the family has also found itself in a changing political environment. While Karin Hausen's now-classic 1976 article on the construction of quasi-natural "gender characters" in the nine-

---

11 Riehl, *Die Naturgeschichte des Volkes*; see also Burkart, *Familiensoziologie*, 13; on Le Play, see Wall, "Ideology and Reality."
12 Brunner, "Das 'ganze Haus'"; see also see Weiß, "Otto Brunner und das Ganze Haus"; on research developments in Germany after 1945, see Hahn, "Trends der deutschsprachigen historischen Forschung."
13 Laslett, "Introduction," 1.
14 Laslett, "Die europäische Familie," 41.
15 Mitterauer and Sieder, *Vom Patriarchat zur Partnerschaft*; see also Rosenbaum, *Formen der Familie*.

teenth century[16] stood on its own in the German research landscape for quite some time, the liaison between microhistory and feminist-inspired concepts of gender led to an upswing in research on the history of the family from around 1990 onward. As the influence of the French Annales school waned, the pioneering works that provided an orientation to the field increasingly came from Britain. As a rule, these texts primarily relied on court records or self-narratives.[17] In German-language research, the subsequent wave of scholarly work also referred to judicial records and self-narratives as bases on which to write the history of the family as a history of gender, with female actors.[18] Certainly the fact that the successes of the women's movement, the dynamic rethinking of the family as a form of relationship beyond the patriarchal model, and the upswing in cultural-historical research on the family coincided is no accident. As a result of the aforementioned developmental shifts, research on the history of the family has since become established, institutionalized, and differentiated in multiple directions.

Contexts: The Family, House and Home, and Domesticity

Anyone who wants to write a history of everyday life, of that which is seemingly self-evident, cannot exclude the family as a topic, and family life is usually – if not always – situated in homes or domestic contexts.[19] The focus on forms of domestic cohabitation enables us to reconstruct historical societies from the inside out, combining micro and macro perspectives. We must also acknowledge that, while external processes certainly had an impact on the home and the family, the reverse was also true: far-reaching transformations have begun and continue to begin in the domestic sphere. I will briefly illustrate this point with four examples. First, the inception of the Enlightenment as a social phenomenon was inextricably linked

---

[16] Hausen, "Die Polarisierung der Geschlechtscharaktere"; see also Hausen, "Der Aufsatz über die 'Geschlechtscharaktere.'"
[17] Roper, *Das fromme Haus*; Davidoff and Hall, *Family Fortunes*; on research in England particularly, see Vickery, *The Gentleman's Daughter*, and *Behind Closed Doors*; Tosh, *A Man's Place*; see also the summaries in Shoemaker, *Gender in English Society*; Maynes, "Class Cultures."
[18] On court records, see: Möhle, *Ehekonflikte*; Burghartz, *Zeiten der Reinheit*; Arni, *Entzweiungen*; Schmidt-Voges, *Mikropolitiken des Friedens*; Lanzinger, *Verwaltete Verwandtschaft*; Haldemann, *Prekäre Eheschließungen*; on self-narratives, see: Budde, *Auf dem Weg*; Trepp, *Sanfte Männlichkeit*; R. Habermas, *Frauen und Männer*; B. Kuhn, *Familienstand*; Saurer, *Liebe und Arbeit*.
[19] For an overview of the history of the house and the home, see Sarti, *Europe at Home*; Eibach and Schmidt-Voges, *Das Haus*; for a micro-historical perspective, see Hochstrasser, *Ein Haus*; Schillig, *Hausgeschichten*; for a recent take on the history of the self-evident, see Eibach, "The Everyday Life."

to gatherings of reading societies as well as to informal meetings of learned men and women, both of which took place in private houses. For Christopher Clark, such domestic gatherings of aristocrats, public servants, and commoners – including Jews, as in the Berlin Wednesday Society – for the purpose of reading and discussion were a central factor in the emergence of modern civil society.[20] Second, the genesis of middle-class society is a standard topic in university seminars on history and sociology, but how did this happen in concrete terms? Social relationships arose and continue to arise not least out of marriage relationships. Based on his research on a village in Württemberg, David Sabean has shown that in the transformative phase from the eighteenth to the nineteenth century, relationship patterns shifted in such a way that the number of marriage and godparent relationships established within the compass of the wider family circle increased significantly. Contrary to all the theories of modernization, kinship did not lose its importance, but proved to be an important factor in shaping new social milieus in middle-class society.[21] Third, socialization in the home and within the family played and continues to play a primary role in learning and practicing a particular habitus. The model of middle-class, and specifically bourgeois marriage was based on gender roles that were passed on to the children.[22] The early modern household, with its familiarized domestic labor, and also the later working-class family, in which both women and men pursued gainful employment outside the home, necessitated different arrangements and allocations than the middle-class family. Last but not least, such arrangements always involved a small claim to power in everyday life. The informal power exercised by the 'housemother' in everyday life in the early modern period was greater than the patriarchal legal framework would suggest.[23] The extent to which nineteenth-century practices in the home and the family correspond to the dichotomous construction of middle-class gender roles remains an open question.

The great potential of historical research on the family can be seen in the ways in which it connects to very different theoretical concepts. Thus family communication can be analyzed with reference to Niklas Luhmann's systems theory, as a self-referential system or as a subsystem that interacts with other subsystems,

---

20 Clark, *Preußen*, 295–99. On the emergence of the middle-class audience, see the classic work by J. Habermas, *Strukturwandel der Öffentlichkeit*, 107–16.
21 Sabean, "Social Background," and "Kinship and Class Dynamics."
22 On this practice, see Budde, *Auf dem Weg*; Trepp, "Anders als sein 'Geschlechtscharakter,'" "Männerwelten privat," and *Sanfte Männlichkeit*; R. Habermas, *Frauen und Männer*.
23 See H. Wunder, "*Er ist die Sonn'*."

such as the school, the economy, or the sciences.²⁴ With Pierre Bourdieu we can trace the ways in which a person's 'habitus' is permanently imprinted by the 'habitat' of the home, since "Bourdieu de facto [...] locates the primary genesis of habitus in the family environment."²⁵ One can view the house, or indeed the apartment or other dwelling as a social space endowed with a specific culture and atmosphere. In nineteenth-century sources, this was referred to as 'domesticity' (*Häuslichkeit*). Over the course of the 'spatial turn' and the 'material turn,' the house can be understood as an actor, influencing relationships and sensibilities.²⁶ Undoubtedly one's place of residence and the associated spatial arrangements, with their rules of access and visibility, play a major role in one's relations with the social environment.²⁷ Industrial housing with standardized rental units represents a relatively recent phenomenon historically. The family's everyday environment is situated in a spatial context – a fact which has yet to be sufficiently addressed in cultural-historical research on the family. Meanwhile, theses on the genesis of the modern family as an intimate group with emotionalized relationships in a historically novel private space separated from the outside world, as well as the formation of separate, gender-specific spheres – women in the home, men in public – are controversial and open to debate.²⁸

The history of the family is something of a grab bag: the variety of topics across the spectrum of international research seems inexhaustible.²⁹ So what more can one expect from a new book on the history of the family? My aim in this monograph is to reconstruct the history of the home and the family in the era of middle-class modernity on the basis of significant examples from a variety of milieus. At the same time, it is important to take into account the cultural he-

---

24 Nave-Herz, "Der Wandel der Familie," and "Unkenrufe"; see also Luhmann, *Die Gesellschaft der Gesellschaft*.
25 On Bourdieu in this vein, see A. Lenger et al., "Pierre Bourdieus Konzeption des Habitus," 23; on the home, habitat, and lifestyle, initially with a structuralist approach, see Bourdieu, "Das Haus," and *Die feinen Unterschiede*, chap. 3.
26 See Gieryn, "What Buildings Do," which takes up the concepts introduced by Bourdieu and Anthony Giddens; on things as 'actants,' see Latour's (*Eine neue Soziologie*) actor-network theory.
27 For more on this concept, see Eibach, "Das offene Haus," and "Das Haus," 25–27; for a revealing example focusing on the history of the door, see Jütte, *The Strait Gate*.
28 See Hausen, "Öffentlichkeit und Privatheit"; Vickery, "Golden Age of Separate Spheres?"; Tosh, *A Man's Place*; Flather, "Space, Place, and Gender"; Sarti, "Men at Home"; and more recently Opitz-Belakhal, "A Space of Emotions."
29 For an overview of these topics, see Gestrich, *Geschichte der Familie im 19. und 20. Jahrhundert*; Gestrich et al., *Geschichte der Familie*; on English social history, see Maynes, "Class Cultures"; on kinship, see Sabean et al., *Kinship in Europe*; on house and home, see Eibach and Schmidt-Voges, *Das Haus*; on the 'domestic sphere,' see Eibach and Lanzinger, *The Routledge History of the Domestic Sphere*.

gemony of the bourgeoisie from the end of the eighteenth century, as well as to extend the focus to other contexts that have received little attention thus far. The starting point for all of this is the current *communis opinio* in the relevant literature: that the modern family emerges out of the transition from the old, estate-based society to middle-class society. Yet perhaps it would be a mistake to take the great changes that took place around 1800 – which unleashed the modern family, so to speak – as our point of departure.[30] It may also be that continuities existed between the early modern and the modern periods, or that transformational shifts affected the family more or less continuously: the Enlightenment and Pietism, liberalism and Romanticism, the period of high industrialization from 1850 onward, and ideas about reform that characterized the turn to the twentieth century. Innovative and restorative phases may follow each other dialectically, and the phrase '*the* modern family' may ultimately prove to be a gross oversimplification. In any case, changes in the family and in domestic life provide delicate instruments with which to measure historical developments. In processes of exchange with the outside world, new forms of relationships were repeatedly negotiated and put to the test in everyday domestic life.

While it is true that this book focuses on marriage as well as parent–child and sibling relationships, the history considered here is not reduced to the nuclear family. Taking as our starting point the 'diverse household' and the 'open house' at the end of the early modern period, the social aspect of the domestic sphere takes on new weight after 1800.[31] In legal terms, the modern family is undoubtedly constituted differently than the 'house' in the context of estate-based society. Nevertheless, narrowing our focus to the nuclear family would entail overlooking certain people who were present in the domestic sphere even after 1800: other relatives and servants, so-called 'nightly lodgers,' personal and family friends (*Hausfreunde*), guests and other visitors. In addition to permanent co-residence, we must take into account the fact of temporally variable co-presence in the domestic sphere. Historical research on the house and the home has identified long-term trends toward increasing intimacy and privatization.[32] Only by focusing

---

[30] For further details, see Eibach, "Das Haus," 19–22; on continuities, see Eibach and Lanzinger, *The Routledge History of the Domestic Sphere*; on the periodization of the history of the family, see Mathieu, "Temporalities and Transitions."
[31] On the early modern period, see Tadmor, "The Concept of the Household Family," and *Family and Friends*, here 20; on the 'open house,' see Eibach, "Das offene Haus"; more recently see Sarti et al., "Open Houses." Maurer (*Die Biographie des Bürgers*, 518) argues that the middle-class family in the eighteenth century was a type of "large household family."
[32] For further details on the stages of development, see Kaspar, "Das mittelalterliche Haus"; Heyl, *A Passion for Privacy*; Spohn, "Verdichtung und Individualisierung"; for an overview, see Sarti, *Eu-*

on concrete domestic practices can we venture to make more precise statements on the subjects of privacy and intimacy versus openness and accessibility.

My focus in this book is on 'doings and sayings' – that is, everyday practices and perceptions. Within the framework of this praxiologically informed approach, the behavioral patterns evinced by actors in social spaces are particularly relevant. It is all about the ways in which people conceptualized and practiced family and domesticity: both the customs and the exceptions, as well as the routines and rituals that shaped interaction.[33] Perhaps it is no coincidence that in the German-speaking world, even in the nineteenth century, the word 'Haus' (which can refer to both house and home) was still used in the sources both alongside and as an alternative to the term *Familie* (family).[34] Both as a building and as an imagined space, the house has the power to create identity – a sense of belonging. We can think of houses as a person's 'second skin.' At the same time, we must be wary of creating an overly fixed preconception of the house. All the actors I consider in this book changed their place of residence at least once, and some did so several times.

People: Actors, Subjects, and Habitus

As I have made clear above, my focus here is on actors in their everyday domestic lives, as well as authors who reflected subjectively on themselves and their close social relationships, because the source material for this book consists of self-narratives. This raises certain questions about conceptual categories. From its earliest days, the new cultural history was concerned with identifying the 'faces in the crowd.' Additionally, the 'doing gender' approach offers a second point of reference in its understanding of gender differences as performance and as the result of social interactions in everyday life.[35] Historical processes always involve actors of all genders, each with their own histories, but as such, their socio-cultural contexts

---

rope at Home; see also the contributions in Reulecke, *Geschichte des Wohnens*; for a classic in the field, see Ariès and Duby, *Geschichte des privaten Lebens*; more an up-to-date treatment, see Eibach and Schmidt-Voges, *Das Haus*.

33 On everyday interaction rituals, see Goffman's pioneering work in this field (*Interaktionsrituale*); on definitional questions in research on ritual, see Stollberg-Rilinger, *Rituale*, esp. 7–17; on the 'performative turn,' see Martschukat and Patzold, "Geschichtswissenschaft."

34 On the history of these terms, see the recent contribution by Mathieu, "Domestic Terminologies."

35 See the influential conceptualization of this topic in Butler, *Das Unbehagen der Geschlechter*, 190–208; see also the overview in Opitz-Belakhal, *Geschlechtergeschichte*, 27–30.

are obviously also influential. Of course the process of determining the relationship between an actor and their context – whether structure, discourse, or system – is the issue at the heart of multiple theoretical approaches. Recently scholars have been discussing the 'return of the subject,' although not in the sense of the subject as a 'heroic individual' who acts autonomously and is fully aware of his or her thoughts and actions.[36] Such heroic subjects have constituted a fixed point in the Western master narrative since classic works on the Renaissance, and they found much resonance in nineteenth-century historical scholarship. The return of the subject is a different thing: it involves a revised understanding of the subject. In contrast to the concept of the actor, in this approach female and male subjects are granted more nuances with regard to their agency – that is, their own scope for action and patterns of interpretation are taken into consideration.[37] Perhaps the following simile will illuminate this concept: like actors in a play, the characters have a script that includes dialogue and staging directions, but at the same time they are free to interpret, subvert, rewrite, or expand this script.

Andreas Reckwitz's *The Hybrid Subject* (*Das hybride Subjekt*) offers an attractive theoretical approach to understanding subject cultures in the modern period. Throughout this work, Reckwitz's conceptualization of the subject refers back to Bourdieu's notion of habitus and to Foucault's 'technologies of the self.'[38] Thus, in contrast to the ideas canonized in the traditional humanities, the subject is "created, trained, and stabilized in everyday practices," not least in "the practice of personal and intimate relationships."[39] According to Reckwitz, modern subjects do not act or think uniformly or without contradictions, but rather hybridly, combining and coupling various codes that have different cultural origins – in other words, different patterns of meaning. This aspect may be difficult for readers unfamiliar with the theoretical discourse of cultural studies to digest, but the concept will become clearer as this book progresses. One could just as well refer to lived "multiple cultural belongings."[40] In concrete terms, this means (for example) that bourgeois men and women gladly strove for order and morality and rejected excess, but at the same time incorporated aspects of the Romantic subject's crea-

---

[36] Here I take up Fabian Brändle's apt formulation in Jancke and Ulbrich, "Vom Individuum zur Person," 21, which in turn carries on previous research by Dülmen (*Die Entdeckung des Individuums* and *Entdeckung des Ich*).
[37] Füssel, "Die Rückkehr des 'Subjekts,'" 151; Deines et al., *Historisierte Subjekte*; on *The Practice of Everyday Life*, see De Certeau.
[38] Reckwitz, *Das hybride Subjekt*, 23, 25, 29, 41, 45, 54, 71–72, 166–68.
[39] Ibid., 29.
[40] Medick, "Einführung," 181; see also Reckwitz, *Das hybride Subjekt*, 31–34; with reference to Reckwitz's praxiological approach, see Böth, "'Ich handele,'" 254.

tive and aesthetic individuality. However, Reckwitz constructs the bourgeois subject as the ideal-typical antithesis of the Romantic subject, and Romanticism as a countermovement to the dominant bourgeois mindset – an approach which is questionable in some respects, even at the level of periodization. Nevertheless, over the course of the nineteenth century, the bourgeois subject is then free to adapt Romantic subjectivity – in more moderate forms – to his or her own patterns of thought and behavior.[41]

Hybridity as a key concept calls to mind postcolonial theory, but Reckwitz's analysis of hybrid relations in modern subject cultures is concerned with European–Western cultures from the eighteenth century onward. The period from the end of the *ancien régime* to around 1900 figures in his approach as the subject order of the middle class, and specifically the bourgeoisie, which is then superseded by the era of the white-collar subject and, from the 1960s, by the postmodern subject culture that is still taking shape today. Only the subject order of middle-class modernity is of interest to us here. Those aspects of everyday life and self-perception which Reckwitz defines as fields of practice for bourgeois subjectivity are not new in and of themselves. At issue are the working professional subject's autonomy, practices of self-formation, and the ways in which the middle class demarcates itself in relation to both the amoral aristocracy and the lower classes. Typical aspects of the bourgeois struggle for sovereignty include an affinity for education and self-reflection. Constitutively important factors in the shaping of the bourgeois subject include the practice of personal, private, and familial relationships: marriage, family, and friendship.[42] This is true for women as well as for men. Thus domestic practices are not simply one more aspect of what it means to be bourgeois, but rather a decisive factor in the production of the bourgeois subject. Reckwitz understands this subject as a "subject of intimacy" and emphasizes the "formation of the bourgeois sphere of intimacy" or "the bourgeois culture of intimacy."[43] Accordingly, the bourgeois ideal of marriage and family, following the model of friendship, is considered "for the most part an exclusive, 'private' practice *à deux*," with children and servants relegated to the background.[44]

Reckwitz's subjects share some aspects in common with Bourdieu's habitus, although Bourdieu more strongly emphasizes social class as a factor in lifestyle. For both authors, the habitus – defined as "the embodied schemata" or "the social

---

[41] Reckwitz, *Das hybride Subjekt*, 213–14.
[42] Ibid., 145–51. On the formation phase of the German middle class, see Maurer, *Die Biographie des Bürgers*; on the question of the continuing effects of these relationships on postmodernity, see Reckwitz, "Wie bürgerlich ist die Moderne?," 175–76.
[43] All quotations taken from Reckwitz, *Das hybride Subjekt*, 145–47.
[44] Ibid., 153, italics original; see the overview in the section on pp. 151–66.

made body" – is an actor's enduring disposition. According to Bourdieu, it is inert – that is, endowed with certain powers of persistence.⁴⁵ Subjects are constituted in the habitat of the home and the family, and conversely, home and family are the field on which the bourgeois habitus is played out. The self-narratives which constitute the sources for this book refer to both cultural formations and individual interpretive authority. In what follows, the "subject" – or colloquially, the personality – who wrote the primary source is always introduced at the beginning of each individual chapter, but in general I prefer the term "actor."⁴⁶

Self-Narratives: Beyond *Bürgerlichkeit*

Self-narratives enable us to explore everyday life in the home and the family, as well as personal relationships and subjective reflections on such relationships, in ways that hardly any other types of sources allow. Here I understand "self-narrative" in the broader sense of "writing about one's own life."⁴⁷ Diaries are particularly relevant here, but I also consider letters and, in two cases, autobiographies. Once again, this raises the question of the relationship between a predetermined script and personal interpretive power, between discourse and experience, and between genre conventions and one's own subjectivity. There is no question that even a diary is written with preconditions, and the contexts in which such texts were written changed considerably over the course of the eighteenth and nineteenth centuries. The act of writing regularly about oneself and one's life could serve very different purposes: as a confession and an examination of one's conscience before God, as a chronological documentation of one's life for posterity, or as a purely secular orientation of the fragile ego to itself and its social environment. It is not only printed diaries that have addressees; unedited and unpublished diaries have them too: God the Father in heaven, the family and posterity, or one's own mirror image as the 'alter ego.'

---

45 Bourdieu and Wacquant, *An Invitation to Reflexive Sociology*, 223 and, 127; on the question of persistence, see A. Lenger et al., "Pierre Bourdieus Konzeption des Habitus," 24–25; on its application to class society in France, see Bourdieu, *Die feinen Unterschiede*, esp. chs. 3 and 5.
46 In the chapter titles, I always mention the main author of the personal narrative by name; in contrast, I only mention their spouse if he or she can really be grasped as a subject.
47 Jancke and Ulbrich, "Vom Individuum," 12, also 17–19; for more on self-narratives, see: Brändle et al., "Texte zwischen Erfahrung und Diskurs"; Messerli, "Der papierene Freund"; Baur, "'Sich schreiben'"; Kormann, *Ich, Welt, Gott*; Piller, "Private Körper"; Hämmerle, "Diaries"; von Greyerz, "Observations"; Hatje, "Aus dem Leben," and "Tagebücher und Korrespondenzen"; Böth, "'Ich handele'"; on autobiography in the eighteenth century, see Niggl's programmatic text (*Geschichte der deutschen Autobiographie*).

These self-narratives, which became more numerous from the eighteenth century onward, constitute a medium of subject formation: a 'technology of the self' in Michel Foucault's sense, and subsequently in Reckwitz's understanding as well. Foucault has outlined specific mechanisms that go beyond simple commands and prohibitions, such as "certain modes of training and modification of individuals" that we can trace back to Greco-Roman antiquity. He postulates two overarching precepts when it comes to practices such as confession, composing a letter to a confidant, or writing a diary: "to know yourself" and "to take care of yourself."[48] The connection between introspection, writing about oneself, and self-formation is constitutive of diary writing, which in the Christian tradition functioned primarily as an examination of one's conscience. The goal of the exercise is to purify and to better oneself. Again, the question of whether one prioritizes the self-constraint aspect of the practice or the quasi-free power of disposition exercised by the writing subject is a matter of emphasis. Such 'technologies of the self' also have a history. Thus Foucault identifies a relevant shift in the eighteenth century: "From the eighteenth century to the present, the techniques of verbalization have been reinserted in a different context by the so-called human sciences in order to use them without renunciation of the self but to constitute, positively, a new self."[49] Both the roots of this genre as a religious, introspective practice and the goal of purifying the self remain palpable in the modern period. Nevertheless, keeping a diary in the nineteenth-century middle-class milieu – in terms of both content and habitus – no longer meant the same thing as it had during the Enlightenment or in the context of Pietism, when the genre was already flourishing.[50] After 1800 it was no longer an issue of renunciation, but rather of personal development.

Independent of the considerations of Pietism, pedagogization, or Romanticism, the purpose of writing a regular self-narrative, as well as the narrative's intended addressee(s), may well change over the years – or even from entry to entry. Unlike dossiers and official minutes and records of proceedings in the context of the marital justice system, these personal sources contain more than just legally relevant statements. The appeal of diaries as a source for the history of the family lies precisely in the fact that the content is not entirely determined by contexts and genre conventions. Instead, the reader always encounters chance discoveries and surprising effects, and it is precisely what the reader notices in passing that may turn out to be important. Sometimes the options available to the author in the con-

---

48 Foucault, "Technologies of the Self," 18 (first quotation) and 20 (second and third quotations).
49 Ibid., 49.
50 On the diary's relevance to the "pietistic conception of the subject," see Gleixner, *Pietismus und Bürgertum*, 394; on the following, see Bänziger, *Die Moderne als Erlebnis*, 21–27.

text of diary-writing conventions circumvent the author's actual intentions. For example, Ursula Bruckner-Eglinger, a pastor's wife who lived near Basel, usually mentions her husband, Adam Bruckner, in a very affectionate and respectful manner; however, on May 1, 1832, after a marital dispute about her son Eduard's future education, she notes with a hint of irony: "Now that night my husband was sorry & he began to take the necessary steps; but he had been so exhausted by his running & racing, that after staying in the church for two hours, he contracted a severe cold and was not at all well when he came home."[51] As another example, in 1816, after many years of financial insecurity, the Hamburg-based lawyer Ferdinand Beneke hoped to be appointed legal advisor to the council of the so-called elders (*Oberalten*). In his diary, he had frequently complained about cronyism and patronage in his city, yet his father-in-law was one of these influential *Oberalten*. Beneke "leaves the selection of the most capable [...] to God and to conscience"; at the same time, he considers his chances against other candidates, not least because the eligible voters have good relations with his father-in-law. A few years earlier, he had made fun of the same group of senior officials and called them "a herd of old oxen."[52]

Diaries contain more information than their authors realize or desire. For a history of the family as a history of the self-evident, diaries as well as letters are an excellent source.[53] Nevertheless, one should be under no illusions that such self-evident matters have been reported without a filter. Taboos exist, and certain things are not interesting to the writing subject, even though they may be quite exciting from our perspective today. Thus it is often the relationship between spouses that remains somewhat nebulous, unless the self-evident daily routines of such relationships are disturbed by a temporary separation, a crisis, or other uncertainties. Nevertheless, the perspectives presented in diaries and other personal testimonies offer fascinating insights into hidden areas of the history of the family. Family histories are particular, but they are not random. The challenge lies in distilling that which is not a matter of chance. A micro-historical approach that analyzes several families and different domestic contexts over a longer period of time, rather than making selective reference to a single case study, offers opportunities for new insights.

I have undertaken extensive, time-consuming research for this book in libraries and archives. While numerous diaries from the period around 1800 and the final third of the nineteenth century have been preserved, there is a dearth of ma-

---

51 Bruckner-Eglinger (ed. by Hagenbuch), May 1, 1832, p. 511.
52 Beneke, *Tagebücher*, January 5, 1816, vol. 3.2, p. 350 (first quotation); May 5, 1807, vol. 2.2, p. 457 (second quotation).
53 On letters as a source genre, with further references, see Dobson, "Letters."

terial from the middle decades of the century. The self-narratives I ultimately selected, which are particularly rich in content, represent a roughly equal number of male and female authors. In order to counteract the striking overrepresentation of the middle class in research on this topic, I took care to refer to self-narratives from different milieus when I compiled the source material. Diary writing was a decidedly middle-class preoccupation, but it was not only educated, proppertied people who kept diaries. This book brings together the perspectives of people in rural society, the urban patrician class, the educated middle class (*Bildungsbürgertum*), the working class, skilled craftspeople, and artists. The sources are drawn from various regions and confessional traditions in German-speaking Central Europe and are roughly – though not perfectly – evenly distributed over the decades of the period under consideration. My selection of sources owes much to disinterested advice I received from colleagues working on similar topics.[54] In this respect, the configuration of the source corpus has been more than merely an individual research project; it is the result of professional discourse at conferences as well as informal conversations over a cup of coffee.

Initial Questions

Theory is one thing, but what really matters is what happens 'on the field.'[55] How did families arrange and experience their everyday disarray? On a general level, the following initial questions arise as a cursory summary: Which actors interacted with each other in the home and within the family, and in what ways? Starting with matchmaking, can we observe a change in the concepts, practices, and patterns of relationships over the long nineteenth century? How are marriage, the history of the family, and history in general related to one another?

With regard to international research, it helps to recall a few points. The dichotomy between a romantic 'love marriage' and a status-based 'marriage of convenience' is subject to contrary interpretations.[56] The classic theses in the history of gender concerning the shaping of specific gender roles and 'separate spheres' for the sexes as part of the transition to middle-class society offer points of depar-

---

[54] See the acknowledgements section at the end of this book.
[55] A piece of wisdom from the soccer field, precisely formulated as follows: "Grau ist alle Theorie – maßgebend is auffen Platz." This oft-quoted remark is attributed to Adi Preißler, a player for Borussia Dortmund who was active in the 1950s. See https://gutezitate.com/zitat/266304.
[56] Cf. Borscheid, "Geld und Liebe"; R. Habermas, "Spielerische Liebe"; Trepp, "Emotion und bürgerliche Sinnstiftung"; Wienfort, *Verliebt, Verlobt, Verheiratet*, 20–21; Saurer, *Liebe und Arbeit*, 21–23; Reckwitz, *Das hybride Subjekt*, 161–62.

ture.⁵⁷ Academic research has long been interested not only in marital relationships, but also in parent–child and sibling relationships.⁵⁸ In the course of the transformation from an estate-based to a middle-class society, family and kinship relations took on added significance.⁵⁹ The traditional, accepted understanding of the nineteenth century as the 'golden age' of the private sphere is no longer sacrosanct, but the shift from the 'open house' of the early modern period remains unexplained.⁶⁰ What were the essential components of this emphatically idealized domesticity? Starting in Western Europe, the urban middle class had been inventing a certain habitus and lifestyle since the eighteenth century – one that made bourgeois men and women recognizable as such and had much to do with the presentation of the home and the family.⁶¹ In harmony with Reckwitz, we can speak of a bourgeois subject culture that conspired with the aspirational morality of the loving family.⁶² Yet here we encounter our first problem: love, like morality, is fragile.

---

57 Hausen, "Die Polarisierung der Geschlechtscharaktere," and "Der Aufsatz"; Davidoff and Hall, *Family Fortunes*; for a critical perspective on 'separate spheres,' see Vickery, "Golden Age of Separate Spheres?"; Shoemaker, *Gender in English Society*; and more recently Joris, "Gender Implications."
58 On sibling relationships, see Johnson and Sabean, *Sibling Relations*; Davidoff, *Thicker than Water*; Ruppel, *Verbündete Rivalen*; Labouvie, *Schwestern und Freundinnen*; and more recently A. Kaufmann, "Gel(i)ebte Geschwister"; on childhood, see Budde, *Auf dem Weg*; Jarzebowski, *Kindheit und Emotion*.
59 See particularly Sabean, "Kinship and Class Dynamics."
60 A classic but conceptually unclear text on this topic is Ariès and Duby, *Geschichte des privaten Lebens*; see also Perrot, "Introduction"; Tosh, *A Man's Place*; on the 'open house' in the nineteenth century, see Eibach, "Das Haus," and "From Open House to Privacy?"; on the public aspects of the private sphere, see Mettele, "Der private Raum"; Trepp, *Sanfte Männlichkeit*; R. Habermas, *Frauen und Männer*; Vickery, *The Gentleman's Daughter*, and *Behind Closed Doors*.
61 See Kocka's ("Das europäische Muster," 17–18) definition of *Bürgerlichkeit*; see also Budde, *Blütezeit des Bürgertums*, 13–14; for a global perspective, see Dejung et al., "Worlds of the Bourgeoisie," 2 and 9, on gender and the family, see ibid., 11; see also Hettling and Hoffmann, *Der bürgerliche Wertehimmel*.
62 Reckwitz, *Das hybride Subjekt*, 29, 111, 118–19; on the persistence of these issues into postmodernity, see Reckwitz, "Wie bürgerlich ist die Moderne?"

Chapter 3
Love and a House of His Own: The Peasant Ulrich Bräker Seeks a Wife

Toggenburg, Switzerland (1754–1798)

As a peasant's son, Ulrich Bräker was part of a milieu from which very few self-narratives have been preserved. In his life story, which he began writing in the early 1780s and addressed to his children, he declares: "All of our friends and blood relatives are impecunious people, and I have never heard anything different about any of our ancestors."[1] As far as he knows, no one from the Bräker family line has ever attended university. This peasant, born on December 22, 1735 in a remote hamlet in the Toggenburg region of St. Gallen, Switzerland, sees no cause for ancestral pride. Yet since the goal of presenting his life story is to recommend modesty and righteousness to his children, this is not a disadvantage. On the contrary, he understands "honest and upright" poverty, which does not require a person to beg, as a virtue.[2] The 'poor man in Toggenburg' – as he is presented in the title of the very first complete edition of his self-narrative, published in 1789 – makes no effort to conceal his destitution, nor does he dally with merits that are not properly his to claim. Having taken on considerable debt, his father, Johannes Bräker – a peasant who owned eight cows and also tried to make ends meet as a day laborer and a gunpowder maker – had to sell his house and his farm in 1754 and move with his wife and eight children to the settlement of Wattwil, where the family lived as tenants. Oppressive debt and worry over the family's daily subsistence would remain the central theme of Ulrich Bräker's existence as well, from his youth until his death in September 1798. Although he succeeds in building a farmhouse prior to his marriage by going into debt, like his father he would never manage to live the life he struggled for – that of an independent farmer. Apart from an interlude as a recruiting officer's servant and a Prussian mercenary conscript at the beginning of the Seven Years' War, Bräker laboriously sup-

---

[1] Ulrich Bräker, *Lebensgeschichte und Natürliche Ebentheuer des Armen Mannes im Tockenburg* (*The Life Story and Natural Adventures of a Poor Man in Toggenburg*; hereafter cited as: *Lebensgeschichte*), 364–65; on Bräker's chronology and biography, see Bräker, *Sämtliche Schriften*, 5:1024–29; Böning, *Ulrich Bräker*, and "Der lesende Bauer"; Wegelin, *Ulrich Bräker*; and the contributions in Messerli and Muschg, *Schreibsucht*. Bräker's diaries only begin in 1768, a few years after his marriage; see Bräker, *Sämtliche Schriften*, vol. 1.
[2] *Lebensgeschichte*, 365.

ports himself by producing saltpeter to make gunpowder, working as a yarn merchant, weaving cotton, and subsistence farming in his native valley. Part of the social history of this place is the fact that its population grew continuously over the course of the eighteenth century, which meant that traditional agriculture was no longer sufficient to earn a living. This forced people in these rural areas to move into the proto-textile industry or to take up other occupations. In addition to linen weaving, cotton production became increasingly important in Toggenburg beginning in the middle of the eighteenth century. The settlement of Wattwil, where the young Bräker lived, would be home to more than 4,000 inhabitants by the 1820s.[3]

The Literary Peasant

Ulrich Bräker wrote more than just an autobiographical text – he also wrote notes on the weather, stage plays, commentaries on Shakespeare, and last but not least, diaries. There is no doubt that this 'literary peasant' – a man who belonged to the lower agricultural class, who attended school as a child for only a few weeks each winter, and who had acquired his knowledge as an autodidact – is an unusual, perhaps even a sensational case. Yet his situation is no coincidence. The young Bräker's pietistic upbringing initially encourages him to read the Bible and various other edifying texts. His further reading is also an effect of the Enlightenment's stated aim of conveying its utilitarian thinking, its moral precepts, and its economic reform projects not only to the educated upper classes, but also to the impoverished rural population.[4] Perhaps in no other country in Europe can the diffusion of Enlightenment ideas in rural contexts be better traced than in Switzerland. The schoolmaster in Wattwil, Johann Ludwig Ambühl, 'discovers' Ulrich Bräker, and the latter is admitted to the Toggenburg Moral Society of Lichtensteig in 1776. Bräker thus has access to a library, participates in 'enlightened' conversation, and becomes part of the formative 'public' invoked by Immanuel Kant in his famous 1784 essay "What Is Enlightenment?" as a prerequisite for the movement's efficacy. Thanks to a letter from the pastor in Wattwil, the Zurich publisher Johann Heinrich Füßli hears about Bräker and eventually publishes his life story in 1789. As a 'hybrid subject' in Reckwitz's terms, Ulrich Bräker combines aspects of Pie-

---

3 Hans Büchler, "Wattwil," hls-dhs-dss.ch/de/articles/001387/2016 – 11 – 23; Büchler, "Toggenburg," hls-dhs-dss.ch/de/articles/007642/2017 – 03 – 16/.
4 See Gerber-Visser, *Die Ressourcen des Landes*; on the Enlightenment in Switzerland more generally, see Zurbuchen, *Patriotismus und Kosmopolitismus*.

tism and the Enlightenment with the experiential horizon of rural society, which he had taken as a given throughout his childhood and his youth.

In contrast to pietistic diaries, which served the purpose of continuous introspection,[5] Bräker's intention in writing his autobiography is to take preliminary stock of his life, which he then presents to God as praise, to his children as instruction, and to the reading public as a form of knowledge.[6] Do these confessions mirror Rousseau's in *Les Confessions*, which was written at about the same time? Yes – and no. In publishing an autobiography in the 1780s, the peasant's son finds himself in the very best company. At the beginning of the preface, Bräker castigates his own "vanity" and "addiction to writing" (*Schreibsucht*). Nevertheless, he mentions the "manifold transgressions" committed over the course of his life only as a secondary motivation for writing.[7] One of the last chapters in the book is explicitly titled "My Confessions."[8] For long stretches of the text, however, what seems more important to the author of this account is the "innocent joy [...] and extraordinary pleasure" of reviewing the various stages of his life – above all "the days of my youth."[9] The charm of Bräker's text lies in the characteristic style of authentic naïveté in which he reports it, as well as the constant obstinacy (*Eigensinn*) displayed by the actor,[10] whom Bräker the author refers to as "Uli Bräker." At the same time, this author certainly bows to the expectations of enlightened moral discourse and gives his readership hints about his education in passing, when he mentions contemporary authors such as Lavater, Goethe, and Jung-Stilling, or makes allusions to the Bible and to antiquity. He employs the genre of autobiography to clothe his experiences in a discursive mantle, with a hint of mischief as well. Thus Bräker repeatedly refers to his (future) wife Salome as "my Dulcinea,"[11] alluding to the mistress and supposed noblewoman (who actually originates from the peasant milieu) in Miguel de Cervantes' *Don Quixote* – thereby positioning himself as a Don Quixote. Bräker seeks to offer what he sees as an honest portrayal of his life within the framework of particular linguistic and moral conventions. As

---

[5] For details on the principles of pietistic diary-writing, with further references, see the examples of Henriette Stettler-Herport and Ursula Bruckner-Eglinger in this volume.
[6] *Lebensgeschichte*, "Vorrede des Verfassers" (Author's Preface), 363–64. On the special conditions of Bräker's authorship, see the contributions in Messerli and Muschg, *Schreibsucht*, esp. Bürgi, "Das Reisen."
[7] All citations taken from *Lebensgeschichte*, 363.
[8] *Lebensgeschichte*, 515. In any case, Bräker is not interested in any comparisons between his work and Rousseau's: see 514.
[9] Both citations taken from *Lebensgeschichte*, 363.
[10] See the application of Alf Lüdtke's concept to marriage in Haldemann, *Prekäre Eheschließungen*.
[11] *Lebensgeschichte*, 474 ("Dulcinee") and 525.

a deeply religious man with a pronounced awareness of sin, who is simultaneously sympathetic to the ideas informing the French Revolution, he must strive for truth – in other words, for the unvarnished rendition of his life, including his 'transgressions.'[12] Naturally this is a subjective truth. Moreover, in certain sections the text is strikingly laconic.

Courtship and Matchmaking in the Village

Ulrich Bräker's 'natural adventures' (the *natürliche Ebentheuer* of the original German title) provide insights into the processes of courtship and matchmaking in the village milieu. His family's enforced move from an isolated farmstead to the settlement of Wattwil proves to be a stroke of luck for 18-year-old Ulrich. Now he has opportunities to get to know people of his own age, 'boys' as well as 'girls.' Contact between the sexes takes place in public, under the auspices of strict social control, thus finding expression in glances, facial expressions, and teasing. Bräker mentions encounters with the opposite sex at group games on his free Sunday evenings and at the fair. Writing about one particular woman, he notes: "in church, I looked at her more than at the pastor."[13] The next step in a courtship is an invitation to share a glass or two of wine at the village inn, followed by escorting the girl to her front door. The essential third step in initiating a relationship is entering the house itself, and more precisely an intimate meeting between the couple in a private chamber, most often in her bedchamber. The function of the watchful 'village eye' is performed by the neighborhood women in particular. As Bräker remembers: "The entire neighborhood, and especially the women, gawked at my face wherever I went or stood, as if I were an Icelander. 'Ha ha, Uli!,' they would say, 'So you've worn out the kid's shoes.'"[14] More important than the control exercised by the neighborhood public, however, is the way in which the couple's parents react to their courtship. As Bräker makes clear, marriage without parental consent is conceivable under certain circumstances – namely, when the couple is financial-

---

12 Thus at the end, Bräker insists: "I can testify before God that I wrote the pure and honest truth"; see *Lebensgeschichte*, 514.
13 *Lebensgeschichte*, 408.
14 *Lebensgeschichte*, 406. On the neighborhood as a space of female communication, see Capp, *When Gossips Meet*; on the function of the neighborhood in terms of social control, see Eibach, "Das offene Haus," 626–28; on the history of the neighborhood more generally, see Wrightson, "The 'Decline of Neighbourliness' Revisited"; on control over matchmaking, see Lischka, *Liebe als Ritual*, 133–35.

ly independent – but it is not feasible for him. This issue plays an important role in his story.

When Bräker is 20 years old, he develops a liaison with the neighbor's daughter, Anna Lüthold[15] (whom he calls 'Ännchen'), which lasts several months. The process by which the couple gets to know each other follows the stages outlined above. In line with Erving Goffman, one can speak of rituals of interaction: from the first shy exchanges of glances in public, at the market and at church, to nights spent together in her chamber; in retrospect, Bräker considers these "certainly not only the most blissful, but also the most blameless nights of my life!"[16] This relationship between Ulrich Bräker and Anna Lüthold – so warmly recollected and described – is interesting and significant in several respects. Throughout the account, it is not the single young man who takes the initiative, but rather the woman, who is about three years older than he is. She literally takes him by the hand and asks him to buy her a glass of wine. She invites him to her home. She makes him wait, and she determines when the time is right to exchange kisses and engage in other physical contact.[17] Yet the view through the keyhole that Bräker's account affords his readers reveals nothing out of the ordinary. In both Protestant and Catholic milieus, young people's courtship practices – *Kilten* and *Fensterln* – often led to 'bed courtship,' in which the couple spent the evening or the night together. In this context minor sexual practices were not only permissible, but common; sexual intercourse, however, was forbidden until the couple had made a mutual promise to marry.[18]

This episode, set in 1755, has all the emotional ingredients to enable us to speak of love – at least as far as the initially shy farmhand and saltpeter producer Bräker is concerned. We can do so even with the knowledge that emotions such as love are historically and culturally shaped, and moreover that they were subject to different social framing around 1750 than they are today.[19] Uli feels irresistibly drawn to Ännchen and seems hardly able to control himself, reacting physically to her presence and unable to stop thinking about her. He himself describes his feelings

---

15 See the entry on Anna Lüthold in Bräker, *Sämtliche Schriften*, 5:950.
16 *Lebensgeschichte*, 413. On rituals of interaction, see Goffman, *Interaktionsrituale*; on matchmaking and marriage practices, see van Dülmen, "Fest der Liebe"; Lischka, *Liebe als Ritual*; von Greyerz, *Passagen und Stationen*, 141–59.
17 *Lebensgeschichte*, 403–4 and 411–13.
18 H. Schmidt, *Dorf und Religion*, 177 and 202; Beck, "Illegitimität," esp. 122 and 138–40; Shorter, *Die Geburt der modernen Familie*, 124–26 and 147–49; cf. the overview of the state of the field in Guzzi-Heeb, *Passions alpines*, chap. 4; see also Guzzi-Heeb, "Sexuality and Intimacy," and *Le sexe*, chap. 9; on this debate, see also Lischka, *Liebe als Ritual*, 245–47 and 290–92; see also Hardwick, "Sexual Violence and Domesticity."
19 See Frevert, "Defining Emotions," and *Mächtige Gefühle*, 8–14.

for her as "love," "delight," and "sweet pleasure."[20] For him, Ännchen's appearance – or more precisely, her habitus – is one of the most attractive things about her. He describes her as "a beautiful, slender, kind child, in the loveliest *Zürchbietler* costume!"; as "the best, most honest girl"; and at the same time, as "almost my height, so slender and handsomely proportioned that it gave [me] pleasure."[21] As far as he is concerned, her allure cannot be separated from her deportment and her appearance – an example of "the social made body."[22] That is why, even thirty years later, Bräker is still defending the young Anna Lüthold against her less-than-stellar reputation in the village.

Bräker writes this account of his life only a few years after two widely read romance novels of the day were published: Rousseau's *Julie ou la Nouvelle Héloïse* (1761) and Goethe's *Werther* (1774). This is certainly well before the heyday of literary Romanticism, and yet – in this epoch of *belles lettres*, at the beginning of literary modernity – it is already possible to speak of love as a subjective experience in a new way.[23] It is hard to deny that Ulrich Bräker is familiar with the emotion and the style of communication that we today commonly refer to as 'love,' even before the advent of modern literature. Furthermore, the milieu in which this episode takes place is certainly not what we commonly refer to as the educated middle class (*Bildungsbürgertum*). Is it possible that the young Bräker fell for his Ännchen only in retrospect, because he may have read Rousseau or Goethe in the meantime? This is unlikely – Rousseau is rarely mentioned in his writings, and Goethe only once.[24]

Ulrich Bräker describes his own story-self, the young farmhand Uli, as "a fool" whose "head was full of crickets."[25] Some of the details in his depiction of his re-

---

20 In the original German: "Liebe"; "Entzücken"; "süsse Wohllust"; *Lebensgeschichte*, 404–5, 408, and 411. On the debate over the emergence of the 'love marriage' and the theory of a 'sexual revolution' beginning in the mid-eighteenth century, see Gestrich et al., *Geschichte der Familie*, 486–88.
21 *Lebensgeschichte*, 403 and 409. The *Zürchbietler* costume was a style of dress worn in the rural region around the city of Zurich.
22 Bourdieu and Wacquant, *An Invitation to Reflexive Sociology*, 127.
23 See Luhmann, *Love as Passion*, 26, albeit from a different theoretical point of view; Reckwitz, *Das hybride Subjekt*, 224–30; Trepp, "Emotion und bürgerliche Sinnstiftung"; Saurer, *Liebe und Arbeit*, 47–63; briefly Wienfort, *Verliebt, Verlobt, Verheiratet*, 20–21.
24 See the index of persons in Bräker, *Sämtliche Schriften*, 5:933 and 964; Bräker mentions Goethe's *Werther* in his life story at one point, not with reference to love, but to suicidal thoughts ("des jungen Werthers Mordgewehr" or "the young Werther's murder weapon") he had as a result of his debts: 502. On the influence Bräker's reading material had on his reflections, see Böning, "Der lesende Bauer," esp. 64; see also Guzzi-Heeb, *Le sexe*, chap. 9.
25 *Lebensgeschichte*, 405 and 402.

lationship with his neighbor's daughter correspond to Niklas Luhmann's sketch of modern love as "a deviation from normal social controls," a process which society "nevertheless tolerated as a sort of disease."[26] Among the factors that prompt Bräker to write his life story, a pronounced sense of individuality is certainly not the least important. Yet the peasant's son is not one of those elites who have left class restrictions behind – those whom Luhmann, Anthony Giddens, and many others identify as the forerunners when it comes to implementing a new symbolic code of love in eighteenth-century Europe. Here we have a case of romantic love before the Romantic era. This is more than a passing fancy for Uli Bräker, and so he puts his relationship with Ännchen to the test by proposing marriage. At this point, however – if not in fact before – the social environment of the family and the village once again makes itself unmistakably felt. Moreover, the young Bräker knows the accepted rules of matchmaking. In the second half of the eighteenth century, these were defined not only by the legislature and the ecclesiastical courts, but also and significantly by the couple's families. For the betrothed couple's parents and other relatives, marriage was primarily a resource with which to build and maintain social networks.[27]

While Uli's mother encourages the 19-year-old to make contact with their neighbor's daughter, Anna Lüthold, his father is strictly against it, for moral as well as social reasons. Anna's stepfather runs a bar: "Ännchen's stepdad was a reckless publican; he didn't care who came and drank his *Brenz*."[28] *Brenz*, or brandy, was the cheap everyday alcohol that poor people enjoyed, and the Bernese pastor and writer Jeremias Gotthelf would later strongly condemn its consumption.[29] Bräker's father not only rails against "this damn brandy nest" and the "dissolute girl" who comes from that house,[30] but openly states that his eldest son had better marry a peasant's daughter, "a good peasant's girl." He should work and pray diligently, and then he will become "a man in the field."[31] When we consider all this bluster, it seems quite likely that Johannes Bräker has not gotten over the disgrace he had suffered only a year before: the social degradation of giving up his debt-ridden farm. Only those who managed their own farms as independent farmers could be said to have achieved the desired goal for people of his class – a goal which could also be accomplished by marrying into the right family. From this perspec-

---

26 Luhmann, *Love as Passion*, 26. On the following, see Giddens, *Wandel der Intimität*.
27 See most recently Haldemann, *Prekäre Eheschließungen*, chap. B 2.2.
28 *Lebensgeschichte*, 408.
29 See Gotthelf's story *Wie fünf Mädchen im Branntwein jämmerlich umkommen. Eine merkwürdige Geschichte*.
30 *Lebensgeschichte*, 409.
31 *Lebensgeschichte*, 410.

tive, personal inclination and other emotions had to be subordinated to the priority of acquiring and securing social status. Thus we see that Ulrich Bräker never seems to have asserted his feelings for Anna Lüthold as an argument against his father's authority. The fact that he ignores his father's scolding, breaks off the acquaintances his father arranges with other women, and continues to meet his Ännchen in secret speaks to the strength of his affinity for her. Yet the young Bräker is not blind to the economic issues at stake. At the time of the *ancien régime*, there were many cases in the nearby canton of Bern in which couples who wanted to marry managed to persevere and, despite parental objections, to be heard before a higher court and so achieve their desire.[32] However, Bräker never seems to have considered this option. Here matchmaking and marriage are coupled with ideas about honor in several respects. Thus he ambiguously explains to his 'girl,' who is three years older than he is:

> You have no idea how much it hurts me, but you can see that we couldn't stand it much longer and keep our honor. And I just can't consider marriage right now. I'm still too young; you're even younger [sic], and neither of us has a penny to our name. Our parents would not be able to help us create our little nest; we would become beggars.[33]

Spurred on by one of his father's acquaintances, who turns out to be somewhat dubious, Bräker concocts a plan to leave the valley and the hopeless economic situation facing him there, to make his fortune working abroad, and to return after a few years "loaded with honor and possessions," ready for marriage.[34] Bräker does not explicitly mention the extent to which he has definitively agreed upon this plan with his Ännchen, but he suggests that he has. Ultimately this is an attempt to bring together the elements of love, honor, and financial independence, with a view to securing their livelihood in the long term.[35] But despite Bräker's best-laid plans, this couple's story would turn out differently. After Bräker leaves Wattwil in September 1755, at the age of 19, his father's acquaintance abandons him with a recruiting officer in Schaffhausen, in exchange for money. Bräker does indeed experience some "adventures" during this period, ending up as a Prussian conscript in Berlin and finally deserting the army a year later, during the Battle of Lobositz.

---

32 See the findings in Haldemann, *Prekäre Eheschließungen*.
33 *Lebensgeschichte*, 418.
34 *Lebensgeschichte*, 416.
35 On the so-called *Heiratsgutmechanismus* (marriage property mechanism) in the transfer of farms, see Breit, *"Leichtfertigkeit,"* 60–66; H. Schmidt, *Dorf und Religion*, 182; on the importance of property for family relationships in the early modern period more generally, see Lanzinger, "Spouses and the Competition for Wealth."

After making his way home to Toggenburg at the end of October 1756, he meets an acquaintance on the bridge outside the village and learns that his Ännchen is now spoken for; Anna Lüthold married Ulrich Bräker's cousin Michel Bräker, a farmer, on March 23, 1756. Seven months after the wedding, she has already given birth to a child – this was also a sanctioned custom even in the Reformed Protestant regions of Switzerland, provided the couple had made a mutual promise to marry before they first had sexual intercourse.[36]

According to Bräker's account, the emotional interactions he had enjoyed with Anna – the increasingly intimate physical contact that took place between Uli and Ännchen – were reciprocal. Once again, this was no game for him, but perhaps it had been more so for her.[37] In any case, her marriage to the farmer Michel Bräker, who was one year older, was in keeping with the rulebook for their milieu, which quite unromantically associated marriage with the prospect of a secure livelihood and social advancement.

Rationality and Marriageability

Uli Bräker is deeply disappointed, but he recovers quickly. Despite his still-precarious economic situation, this soldier – who has returned from abroad, carries himself with a military bearing, maintains his hairstyle, and goes around in his Prussian uniform, which constitutes his "entire fortune" – seems to have been an attractive apparition in the valley. As he himself says, "My looks had quite improved."[38] There follows a period in which he makes various acquaintances with single women from Toggenburg or the neighboring region of Appenzell. For him, all of these relationships are subject to the dual concerns of mutual inclination and the question of marriageability. In the long section "My Confessions" and elsewhere, Bräker mentions – not without pleasure, and incidentally without any pietistic framing – a certain Lisgen von K.; the daughter of a Catholic widow, by the name of Marianchen; and also Kätchen, Mariechen, Ursel, and a wealthy woman named Rosina. Things get serious with a 'girl' who catches his eye while he is conducting his saltpeter trade, which takes him from farm to farm, and also in church: Salome Ambühl. She is slightly less than a year older than he is and possesses the

---

36 *Lebensgeschichte*, 469. On the biographical information, see Bräker, *Sämtliche Schriften*, 5:918 and 950; see also H. Schmidt, *Dorf und Religion*, 177; Beck, "Illegitimität," 122.

37 On premarital relations as an ambivalent game between the sexes, see R. Habermas, "Spielerische Liebe."

38 *Lebensgeschichte*, 519.

desired attribute of being a peasant's daughter.[39] After a phase of mutual observation, 22-year-old Ulrich relatively quickly lets it be known that he intends to marry her. She is probably expecting this, and yet it does not seem to spark any euphoria or other strong emotion in her.

From the very beginning, this sober relationship with Salome Ambühl develops in a completely different way, as a counter-example to his love affair with Ännchen. Moreover, this contrast is intentional on the author's part. The woman he is courting sets two conditions for her consent to the marriage: First, Bräker must give up his dirty trade in saltpeter (the saltpeter required to produce gunpowder was extracted from urine deposits in stables) and instead trade in yarn. As a form of start-up capital, she offers him money for this. Bräker is thus persuaded to change his profession. Salome Ambühl's second condition for saying yes to Bräker is expressed as a question: "But where [will we] keep house and reside?" She is not satisfied with a rented apartment, and she lets him know this in no uncertain terms: "'in my lifetime, I won't accept anyone who doesn't have his own house'!"[40] Bräker acquiesces to this demand as well. Both conditions – a clean trade and homeownership – closely correspond to ideas about status and the symbolic capital of honor in the peasant milieu. So it is unsurprising that the potential bride asserts these conditions and that the suitor responds positively, despite the fact that he had previously been unable to attain either goal. When Ulrich Bräker decides to buy a plot of land on the Hochsteig near Wattwil as the place to build a house of his own, she once again offers financial assistance. Bräker's father, who has no objections to this match, also agrees to support him. In 1761, during a period of relative economic prosperity, Bräker finally succeeds in building a house. He achieves this goal by means of his income from the yarn trade, supplemented by assistance from his family and hers, as well as from neighbors – and also by taking on debts, from which he will never manage to free himself. In the same year, after a considerable gap of four years since they first became acquainted, the couple weds.

With remarkable candor, the ageing Ulrich Bräker confesses in his text: "since it was in fact purely political motivations which prompted me to marry her, I did not feel that tender inclination toward her which one is accustomed to call love." Salome Ambühl was "by far the most suitable" (*die tauglichste*) wife for him. Making direct reference to central Enlightenment tenets, he adds: "my reason recog-

---

39 *Lebensgeschichte*, 473; for further biographical information on Salome Ambühl Bräker, see *Sämtliche Schriften*, 5:910.
40 In the original German: "Aber wo hausen und hofen?"; "in meinem Leben nehm' ich keinen, der nicht sein eigen Haus hat!"; both citations taken from *Lebensgeschichte*, 476.

nized that no one could be more useful to me."⁴¹ This woman's social status, origins, and family speak in her favor – even in retrospect – which gives him hope that they can achieve the economic security necessary to establish a household. The young Bräker is also impressed by his bride's education. In contrast to his relationship with Anna Lüthold, we learn little about the ritualized courtship practices in the relationship between Uli and Salome, apart from the fact that they write letters to each other on the days when they do not see each other. Since her letters to him are in verse, Bräker 'the literary peasant' believes he has found "in her an excellent poet." However, it turns out that his "mischievous Dulcinea was a master of deception": in fact, she can neither read nor write, and her letters are written by a "trusted neighbor."⁴² From the beginning, a contentious relationship develops between the two, which he attributes not least to her lack of understanding for his interest in poetry and literature, at the expense of time spent working and acquiring material goods. The two would never become an 'educated couple' (*Bildungspaar*).

Bräker's juxtaposition of love and reason – his intense 'inclination' for Ännchen and his 'useful' marriage to the stern Salome – may seem like a literary construction. Yet this is not an anachronistic reading of the text. Bräker makes this distinction in the text himself, with an eye to his implied readership. Moreover, if the contrast were merely a literary topos, then the author could have left it at that. Instead, his history with Ännchen repeats itself as part of his budding relationship with Salome, the woman who would eventually become his wife. Furthermore, Uli Bräker's liaison with a woman named Kätchen in Herisau, in the Appenzell region – which was not coincidentally located outside his home valley, and therefore beyond the village eye's field of vision – is also astonishing in its spontaneous emotionality. They meet for the first time by chance, on the road to Herisau; according to Bräker's account, they are "soon walking arm in arm [...] singing and joking around." Once they arrive in town, she does not want him to accompany her home, hoping to avoid trouble with her parents. Instead they arrange to meet at an inn, where Bräker waits an hour for her. In order to avoid arousing suspicion, Kätchen, who turns out to be "the daughter of a respectable merchant and about 16 years old," appears with one of her little sisters on her arm. The innkeeper provides a room where the couple spend a few hours alone in "sweet, tender, but blameless intimacy," as Bräker tellingly puts it.⁴³ Uli is so impressed by the young woman that he extends his stay in Herisau by several days, until he runs

---

41 All citations taken from *Lebensgeschichte*, 480.
42 All citations taken from *Lebensgeschichte*, 480.
43 *Lebensgeschichte*, 520–21.

Fig. 2: Ulrich Bräker and Salome Ambühl. Source: Bernisches Historisches Museum, Bern, Switzerland

out of money. Their farewell is tearful. She then writes him a letter, to which he does not respond, thus ending the relationship. Even in his "Confessions," Bräker is unable to say exactly why he does this. Yet he suggests that the merchant's daughter is too young and also socially out of reach for a peasant's son in his early twenties who is looking for a marriage partner. He cannot imagine "that I could ever hope to possess her."[44] Many of Ulrich Bräker's stories do not end well. Twenty years later, still married to Salome, Ulrich will once again visit his "Herisau treasure," whom he clearly cannot forget any more than he can forget Anna Lüthold. In the meantime, Kätchen has become an innkeeper's wife in Herisau, but she lives "in very poor circumstances," married to "a brutal and ludicrous man" who soon goes bankrupt. She is the mother of ten children. The reunion be-

---

[44] *Lebensgeschichte*, 521.

tween these two married people extends "late into the night" and ends with them exchanging kisses.⁴⁵ She dies four years later, at about 40 years of age. Bräker mourns for her.

A Precarious Married Life

Ulrich Bräker does not undertake this review of his life without intent; he makes clear references to the contemporary discourse on virtue, and his purpose is to offer moral instruction to his children and to the reading public. His accounts of Ännchen and Kätchen on the one hand, and Salome on the other, describe types of courtship and matchmaking as well as models of relationships between the sexes. Ultimately, however, the story of the search for the right path to a good marriage does not end well in Bräker's case. In other words, the experiential reality that Bräker devotes himself to working through in his self-narrative proves to be more complex than a simple theory of types. It is not only 'housekeeping' (*das Hausen*), which in the eighteenth century combined the goal of economic stability with domestic morality,⁴⁶ but also everyday married life that remains precarious for Bräker. He cannot in good conscience sell his audience the story that his own real-life marriage to Salome Ambühl was exemplary, and so he makes no attempt to do so – although he does point out certain advantages in her personality. Both directly and indirectly, Bräker formulates criteria for an ideal marriage in his description of his own. He admits that had he followed his wife's strict principles, he probably "never would have gotten into that labyrinth" of debt.⁴⁷ Nevertheless, early on he is brought to the realization that "our souls were simply not compatible."⁴⁸ Instead, their marriage is characterized by strife from beginning to end, as she rebukes, criticizes, exposes, and attempts to dominate him, even "when I tell her a hundred times that yelling is useless."⁴⁹ In contrast to the misery of his own marriage, he mentions a friend's marriage, which is based on agreement and mutual understanding, and in which differences of opinion are clarified in

---

45 *Lebensgeschichte*, 522. Further biographical information on Kätchen (Käthchen) of Herisau has not been found; see Bräker, *Sämtliche Schriften*, 5:944.
46 Sabean, *Property, Production, and Family*, 102–7; Beck, "Frauen in Krise," esp. 150–56; on housekeeping in general, see Schläppi, "Logiken der Subsistenz."
47 *Lebensgeschichte*, 524.
48 *Lebensgeschichte*, 474. On the following, see esp. 524–28.
49 *Lebensgeschichte*, 528.

"a loving way."⁵⁰ Certainly Ulrich Bräker's marriage to Salome Ambühl is based neither on companionship nor on mutual inclination, although he wishes for both and recommends both to his readership. Yet he does emphasize his bond with his wife, and the marriage produces no fewer than seven children. At times the enterprising Salome takes over the yarn trade from him. Together they constitute a 'working couple,' as was characteristic of married couples in the early modern period.⁵¹ Unfortunately Salome's perspective on the situation has not been handed down, so we have to rely solely on his judgment. Salome Ambühl would certainly not have enjoyed reading or hearing about this published account of their everyday marital life as riven with one crisis after another.

Linguistically as well as factually, the alliance between these spouses – oriented as it is toward 'fitness' and 'usefulness' – is linked to the house in essential ways. As we have seen, during their courtship the peasant's daughter makes 'keeping house and residing' (*Hausen und Hofen*) within her own four walls a condition for her consent to the marriage. Only once the house is built does the wedding take place. Bräker refers to his bride as "the house's young ornament" and to his wife as the other "half of the house."⁵² In 1792 Bräker builds an extension onto the house on the Hochsteig for his son Johannes and Johannes's wife.

Although this investment puts him even further in debt, the parlor in the new extension, where his beloved daughter-in-law resides, becomes a "place of refuge" for Bräker, the literary "free spirit," who seems to be increasingly isolated in the village as well. He also takes shelter there from "Xanthippean winter storms" – a literary reference to Socrates's wife and a metaphorical reference to his own wife's temper.⁵³ Despite this refuge, everyday married life seems to have become unbearable to him in his old age. Although the possibility of divorce as a solution to broken marriages was offered to French and Prussian subjects for the first time under revolutionary law in France and the 1794 General State Law (*Allgemeines Landrecht*) in Prussia, respectively, it took time for this legal principle to be implemented socially, accompanied as it was by a radical secularization of the concept of marriage.⁵⁴ Moreover, the Helvetic Republic did not introduce a corresponding di-

---

50 *Lebensgeschichte*, 525. Both this example and Bräker's ideas of a good marriage call into question the assumption that "loveless marriages" were the norm in the early modern period, but see Shorter, *Die Geburt der modernen Familie*, 78; cf. H. Wunder, "*Er ist die Sonn'*," 262–66.
51 H. Wunder, "*Er ist die Sonn'*," 266.
52 In the original German: "junge Hausehre"; "Haushälfte"; *Lebensgeschichte*, 476 and 524. On the woman who embodies the honor of the house, see H. Wunder, "*Er ist die Sonn'*," 267.
53 *Lebensgeschichte*, 523 (first citation); Bräker, *Tagebücher*, entry titled "Relation u. Beschluß des J.1792," 3:390 (second and third citations); see also Böning, *Ulrich Bräker*, 187–88.
54 Blasius, *Ehescheidung in Deutschland*, 27–30.

Fig. 3: Bräker's House with the Extension, Hochsteig, near Wattwil, by Heinrich Thomann. Source: Toggenburg Museum, Lichtensteig, Switzerland

vorce law. In the early modern period, the ecclesiastical marriage courts permitted 'separation from bed and board' – not to be confused with a formal divorce – only in cases of serious offenses or rampant domestic violence. Instead, pastors and ecclesiastical courts were tasked with reconciling quarrelsome spouses and thus protecting marriage as a sacrament or a quasi-sacred institution.[55] On March 22, 1798, Bräker left his home and his farm, declared bankruptcy, and found lodgings with friends and patrons in St. Gallen and in Zurich before eventually returning, ill and penniless, to his family and his wife – who was not amused – a few months before his death.[56]

In the history of the family, the period around 1800 – with its structural shift from an estate-based to a modern class-based or bourgeois society – is considered to be the epoch of transformation that first gave rise to the modern family. Yet the story of Ulrich Bräker's courtships, matchmaking, and marital life seems surprisingly modern in some respects, despite the fact that he was a peasant's son from Wattwil in the remote valley of Toggenburg and lived under the *ancien régime*. He clearly knows and experiences love, whether this is defined as an emotion, a symbolic code, or an intimate form of communication 'in the private chamber.' When he reaches a marriageable age, he pursues a series of acquaintances and liaisons under the ambivalent auspices of emotional attraction and convenience with re-

---

[55] For further details, see Beck, "Frauen in Krise"; Eibach, "Der Kampf um die Hosen"; on Bern, see H. Schmidt, *Dorf und Religion*, 251–53.
[56] See Bräker, *Tagebücher*, entry titled "Auswanderung," March 22, 1798, 3:728–30; see also Böning, "Der lesende Bauer," 213–14.

spect to a potential match. He also seems to have experienced something like attraction at first sight, which is not in fact coincidental, but relates to the woman's habitus – her social performance. His relationship with the woman who would become his wife also begins when the insecure Bräker notices her stern "Amazonian face."[57] Thus we see that love is not a concept invented by the intellectual elite or the aspiring middle class.[58] Nevertheless, Bräker's decision to marry Salome Ambühl is essentially determined by rational considerations that were typical of the peasant milieu. This provides a contrast to a 'love marriage' – as such relationships were depicted and propagated, particularly in Romantic fiction around 1800 – the model which would eventually rise to become the new North Star in the bourgeois firmament. Yet when it comes to the issues of love and status in the earthly realms of bourgeois reality, the problems and considerations that went along with finding a partner in that context seem to have been very similar to those in rural Toggenburg.[59] The dominant demeanors of the two most important women in Bräker's life stand in striking contrast to the patriarchal context. In the premarital relationship between Ännchen and the shy Uli, the initiative lies entirely on Anna Lüthold's side. Later Salome Ambühl sets the terms for entering into the marriage. Ultimately the peasant's son Ulrich Bräker does not manage to achieve his aim of finding a companion in his everyday domestic life who can provide both a secure livelihood and intimate affection.

---

57 *Lebensgeschichte*, 473.
58 In addition to the literature already cited, see Edward Shorter's older, much-discussed thesis on the 'sexual revolution' at the end of the eighteenth century: "The great surge of sentiment begins earlier in the cities than in the countryside, and sooner among the middle classes than the lower;" Shorter, *The Making of the Modern Family*, 61. Cf. on the current state of the field, Guzzi-Heeb, *Le sexe*, chap. 9: "Bilan: les nouveautés du XVIIIe siècle"; Guzzi-Heeb, "Sexuality and Intimacy."
59 R. Habermas, "Spielerische Liebe"; Trepp, *Sanfte Männlichkeit*, and "Emotion und bürgerliche Sinnstiftung"; see also the chapter on Ferdinand and Caroline Beneke in this volume.

Chapter 4
Pious Everyday Life in the Bailiwick and the Patrician Milieu: Henriette Stettler-Herport

Bern, Switzerland (1771–1789)

Our second study focuses on a family that was part of the political and social elite in the city-state of Bern at the end of the *ancien régime*. Henriette Herport, born on April 7, 1738, was the daughter of one of Bern's Grand Council (*Großer Rat*) members and was linked to the patriciate by birth as well as by family connections – as were her husband, Rudolf Stettler, who was seven years her senior, and their eight children. Her parents' marriage in 1737 is remarkable in that it only came about after her mother, Margaritha Im Hoof, filed a paternity suit against Johann Anton Herport, Henriette's unwilling progenitor and later father.[1] Henriette spent her formative years in the French-speaking town of Morges, where her father was a bailiff; when she was just 8 years old, her father encouraged her to keep a regular diary as a means of cultivating self-discipline. In 1771, as a 33-year-old woman married to the bailiff Rudolf Stettler, Henriette would once again take up diary writing, thus producing a detailed record of her everyday life and concerns.[2] Perhaps the fact that this was the same year she moved with her husband and children to the official residence in the Bernese bailiwick of Frienisberg reminded her of the habit she had begun during her childhood in just such a 'bailliage.' The position of bailiff was very well remunerated and was a highly sought-after career for many of the Bernese patrician progeny.[3] Frienisberg, which was located approximately 15 kilometers northwest of Bern, was a bailiwick with high revenues, and Rudolf Stettler would continue his career there even after the end of his six-year term. In 1786 he became a member of the Small Council (*Kleiner Rat*), and in 1792 he was appointed Bern's envoy to the Federal Diet of Switzerland (*Tagsatzung*).

Henriette Stettler-Herport was writing her diary at a time when educated Europeans viewed the Swiss Confederation as a haven of freedom, an idyllic place

---

1 Schnegg ("Tagebuchschreiben als Technik") offers the best introduction to Henriette Stettler-Herport; see esp. 107–8.
2 Henriette Stettler-Herport, *Journal de mes actions*, Burgerbibliothek Bern, FA Stettler 12 (1–5), hereafter cited as: *Journal*, vol. number, date of entry. See also Christoph Zürcher, "Rudolf Stettler," in *Historisches Lexikon der Schweiz*, hls-dhs-dss.ch/de/articles/007212/2016–09–28/.
3 Dubler, "Landesherrschaft und Landesverwaltung," 449.

where one could pursue a 'natural' lifestyle. However, Switzerland in the second half of the eighteenth century was certainly not the 'Other' in Europe's midst in every respect.[4] Both the manorial context in which Henriette lived and the fact that she kept a regular diary demonstrate aspects of life and lines of connection that can be generalized beyond the Swiss Confederation's borders. During the period of the *ancien régime*, Switzerland was a country with no princes and no powerful landed aristocracy, but it was by no means a country without established authority. As a bailiff, Rudolf Stettler personified urban rule over rural subjects in the largest city-state north of the Alps. In terms of culture and lifestyle, the eighteenth-century Bernese patriciate took its cue from the French nobility. In the era of the Enlightenment, Switzerland was an important site of the European *République des Lettres*. Additionally, the Pietist and Revivalist movements that had been so influential in both England and Germany since the end of the seventeenth century also had a major impact on Switzerland and had attracted a large following.[5] When it comes to the genesis of the new middle class (*Bürgertum*), it is clear that they did not emerge from a social *tabula rasa* at the turn of the eighteenth century, but that they had precursors among and roots in the old urban elite (*Stadtbürgertum*). In this respect, the socio-cultural connections with the emerging middle class in Swiss cities are striking.[6] We can safely assume that the new ideas about marriage and the family were also received in the educated milieu of Bern's elite circles and those who were close to the council.

Henriette Stettler-Herport's *Journal de mes actions*, which she kept from 1771 until the end of 1789, provides insight into two different households: until 1777, it records rural manorial life at the official residence of a bailiwick in the Swiss *Mittelland*; and for the years following the family's move to Bern at the end of 1777, it gives us a glimpse into everyday family life in the context of convivial culture in the city-state's capital. Furthermore, like many patrician families in Bern and many wealthy bourgeois families in German cities, the Stettler-Herports owned a country estate in addition to their main residence in the city: a house in Kirchberg, near Burgdorf, 24 kilometers northeast of Bern, which the family regularly visited during the summer. Despite all this, as a source for the history of the family and domesticity (*Häuslichkeit*), Henriette Stettler-Herport's diary has not yet received any scholarly attention.

---

4 On this topic more generally, see Holenstein, *Mitten in Europa*.
5 On the Enlightenment in Switzerland, see Zurbuchen, *Patriotismus und Kosmopolitismus*; on Pietism in Basel, see Hebeisen, *Leidenschaftlich fromm*; T. Kuhn, "Basel"; on Bern, see Dellsperger, *Die Anfänge des Pietismus*.
6 See Gall, *Vom alten zum neuen Bürgertum*, and *Stadt und Bürgertum*; Maurer, *Die Biographie des Bürgers*; on *Bürgertum* in Switzerland, see Tanner, *Arbeitsame Patrioten*; Sarasin, *Stadt der Bürger*.

Self-Formation and a Pietist Record of the Soul

For connoisseurs of the history of devotional movements, the fact that a woman kept a diary in the eighteenth century is not surprising. In both style and motivation, Henriette Stettler-Herport's diary perfectly aligns with the demands for religious introspection which are typical of female self-narratives, including those stemming from the respectable Pietist elite (*Ehrbarkeit*) in Württemberg.[7] Since the end of the seventeenth century, both the city of Bern and the Bernese countryside had been centers of early Pietism in Switzerland. In addition to her aforementioned upbringing under her father's influence and the imprint her childhood made on her, as well as her move to the countryside as a married woman, another reason for this patrician Bernese woman to take up diary writing again after so many years was probably her knowledge of Johann Caspar Lavater's *Secret Diary* (*Geheimes Tagebuch*), published by a Leipzig publishing house in 1771. She herself mentions reading a diary written in German, in which the author strives to offer a moral examination of his behavior as a stimulus for the reader, although she does not explicitly mention Lavater, a theologian based in Zurich who would eventually visit her and her husband in Frienisberg in April 1777.[8] Both the purpose and the goal of Henriette Stettler-Herport's diary are clear: she hopes to spiritualize her everyday domestic life and perfect her character with reference to Christian morality by systematically logging her sins, transgressions, and problems in an ongoing written confession to God. She repeatedly describes both her everyday life and her personal demeanor as deficient and in need of correction. For this reason the content of her diary is by no means evidence for the thesis that many women found in Pietism "a bit of outer liberation along with the inner."[9] As Brigitte Schnegg has pointed out, this diary can well be understood as a "technology of the self" in Foucault's sense.[10] Nevertheless, this does not mean that the diary entries present nothing more than an attempt at continual self-conditioning. For example, in a kind of preface written at the beginning of 1772, Stettler-Herport formulates a set of guidelines for her daily life on the basis of 16 "Régles Générales," focusing on spiritual edification, reading sacred texts, and practicing piety with re-

---

[7] Gleixner, *Pietismus und Bürgertum*, 119–23 On the following, see Dellsperger, *Die Anfänge des Pietismus*, and "Der Pietismus in der Schweiz"; see also Mettele, *Weltbürgertum oder Gottesreich*, 195–97.
[8] *Journal*, vol. 2, December 15, 1771. On Lavater's visit, see vol. 4, April 11, 1777. See also Schnegg, "Tagebuchschreiben als Technik," 115.
[9] Dellsperger, "Der Pietismus in der Schweiz," 609.
[10] See Schnegg, "Tagebuchschreiben als Technik des Selbst."

gard to her marriage, her family, housekeeping, and educating her children.[11] However, the diary records repeated deviations from this ideal daily routine which the realities of daily life often generate, and which torment – or, in more modern terms, deeply depress – the religious 'I' in the entries. In an account of "my usual way of life" written after the family moved to the city of Bern, the author no longer makes any attempt to force her everyday life to fit within a rigid daily schedule of pious discipline. Instead, she soberly and realistically records her daily routines and notes her desire for better order "in household matters."[12]

Henriette Stettler-Herport's five-volume diary offers scholars who research the family a window onto a domestic routine defined by tightly interwoven norms and routines, as well as disruptions and dissonances. Until early 1773, she consistently writes in French. The entries alternate between French and German over the subsequent years, until the author ultimately switches to German entirely. Events that occur outside the domestic sphere – such as, in retrospect, the 1755 Lisbon earthquake or Emperor Joseph II's visit to Bern in July 1777 – are rarely mentioned.[13] Instead, the entries revolve entirely around the self, the subject, and her relation to God, as well as to a microcosm that consists of her husband and her children, servants and visitors, relatives and friends. The following observations and analysis are primarily based on volumes 3, 4, and 5 of the diary, dating from the time when regular entries resumed, on New Year's Day 1772. From that time until the beginning of October 1772, the Bernese bailiff's wife writes in her diary almost daily. At that point she decides to keep her entries brief in the future and to leave out trivial matters, because otherwise she will never reread her entries, and a failure to do so will ultimately be no help in her goal of "advancing on the path of virtue."[14] Over the subsequent years, Sundays in particular become days for taking stock of her life in her diary. In times of crisis, her entries often become more frequent and longer. Overall, however, her recordkeeping becomes more irregular. The author blames her reluctance to write not only on her monotonous daily routine, but also on her health problems, as well as her "in-

---

11 *Journal*, vol. 3, 1772, "Régles Générales pour l'emplois que je propose de faire, de mon tems tout les jours."
12 In the original German: "im Hauswesen"; *Journal*, vol. 5, January 18, 1778. According to Gleixner (*Pietismus und Bürgertum*, 130), the Pietist concept of a diary as a "dialogue with God" also serves "to compare religious aspirations with reality, which not infrequently leads to the expression of religious despair."
13 *Journal*, vol. 2, December 28, 1771; vol. 4, July 17, 1777.
14 In the original French: "m'avancér dans le chemin de la vertu"; *Journal*, vol. 3, October 1, 1772.

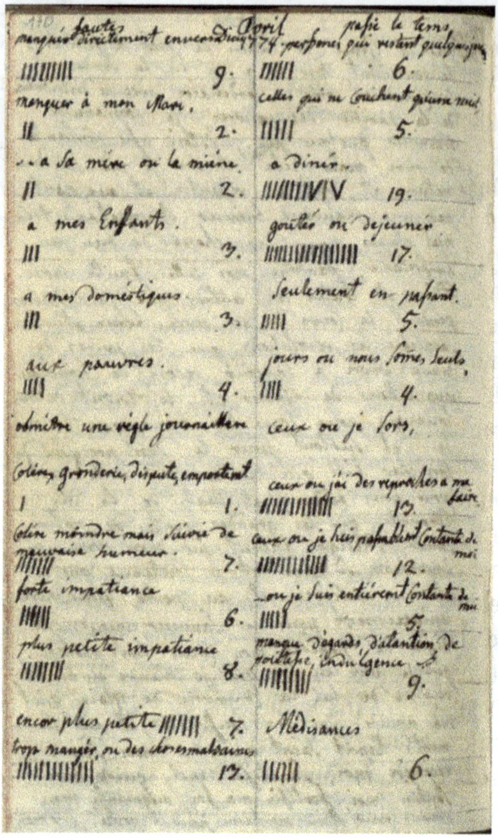

Fig. 4: Henriette Stettler-Herport's Tally Sheet of Transgressions, Pastimes, and States of Mind, April 1774. Source: Journal de mes actions, Burgerbibliothek Bern, FA Stettler 12.4

dolence and despondency."[15] There is no evidence to suggest that she read aloud from her record of the soul, either within the family circle or at Pietist gatherings.

Here we have a remarkable analogy between the macro- and the micro-world, between Enlightenment-era regional surveys commissioned by governments and the scrutiny of the soul: on both levels, counting and tabulation processes became common practice in the late eighteenth century. At least, this is what Stettler-Herport's diary suggests. At the beginning of 1722 she began to keep tally sheets in addition to her narrative entries – first monthly, and then semi-annually. These were lists of her sins, transgressions, and bad habits, but also of the visits she paid and

---

15 *Journal*, vol. 5, August 1, 1779.

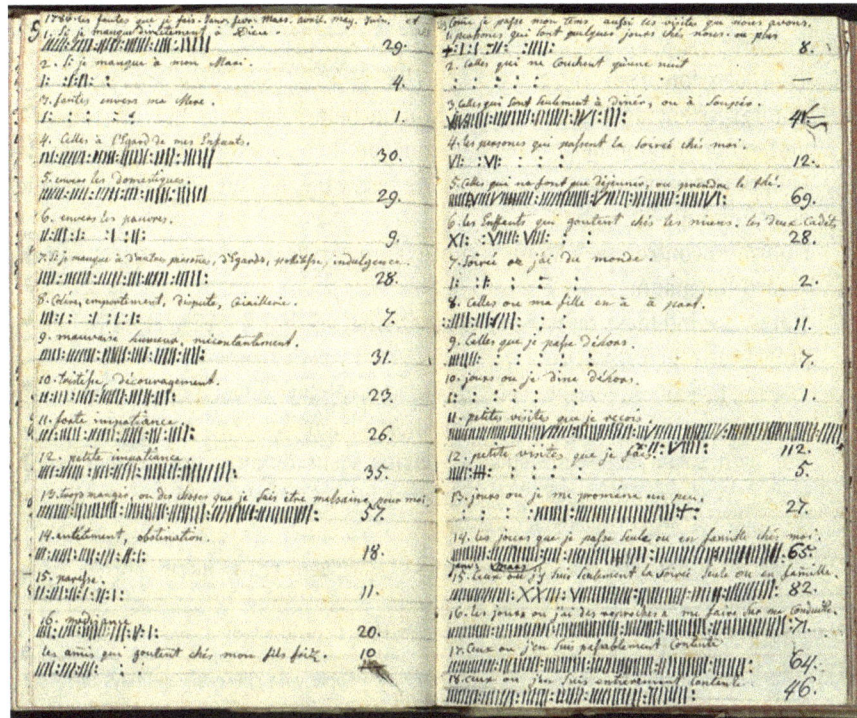

Fig. 5: Henriette Stettler-Herport's Tally Sheet of Transgressions, Pastimes, and States of Mind, January–June 1786. Source: Journal de mes actions, Burgerbibliothek Bern, FA Stettler 12.5

received.[16] Both individual sins and certain visiting practices apparently stood in the way of her pious self-image – that is, of her subject formation. Beyond the purpose of compiling a "tabular record of sins,"[17] the diary contains an impressive documentation of visiting practices – first at the bailiwick in Frienisberg, and then from 1778 onward at the Stettlers' house in the center of Bern as well as the family's country estate near Burgdorf.

---

16 The first tally sheet is found in vol. 3, after the "Régles Générales" and before the entry for January 1, 1772.
17 This is an apt term found in Schnegg, "Tagebuchschreiben als Technik," 118. On the Pietist take on subjectivity, see also Mettele, *Weltbürgertum oder Gottesreich*, 205.

The rubrics of Henriette Stettler-Herport's tally sheets can be generally categorized as follows:
1. Transgressions against God;
2. Transgressions against her fellow human beings (such as her husband, her mother or her mother-in-law, her children, her servants, and poor people);
3. Failure to comply with various rules for everyday life (such as eating too much or eating unhealthy food);
4. Failure to control her emotions (for example, *colére* and *impatiance*) and disregard for manners;
5. States of mind (days on which she is satisfied vs. days characterized by self-reproach or a bad mood);
6. Visiting practices (whether for visits of several days, involving overnight stays; for meals or formal dinners; or for short visits);
7. Her own social behavior (such as paying visits or attending soirees, taking walks, and spending days or evenings at home, whether alone or *en famille*).

Table 1: Record of Transgressions, Visits, and States of Mind; Bern, first six months of 1786

My transgressions		How I spend my time, and our visits	
1. My offenses against God directly	29	1. People who spend several days or longer with us	8
2. My offenses against my husband	4	2. Those who spend just one night	0
3. Transgressions against my mother	1	3. Those who come only for a meal or for dinner	41
4. Those concerning my children	30	4. People who spend the evening with me	12
5. Against the servants	29	5. Those who come only for lunch or for tea	69
6. Against the poor	9	6. Children who have a snack with my two youngest	28
7. My offenses against other people, regarding consideration, politeness, forbearance	28	7. Evenings on which I have guests	2
8. Anger, rage, quarrelling, nagging	7	8. Those on which my daughter has [guests or] goes out	11
9. Bad temper, annoyance	31	9. Those I spend out [of the house]	7
10. Gloom, despondency	23	10. Days when I go out for dinner	1
11. Extreme impatience	26	11. Short visits paid to me	112

Table 1: Record of Transgressions, Visits, and States of Mind; Bern, first six months of 1786 *(Continued)*

My transgressions		How I spend my time, and our visits	
12. Mild impatience	35	12. Short visits I pay to others	5
13. Eating too much or eating things that I know are not good for me	57	13. Days on which I take a little walk	27
14. Obstinacy, stubbornness	18	14. Days I spend alone or with the family at home	65
15. Laziness	11	15. Those on which I am alone or with the family only in the evening	82
16. Slander	20	16. Days on which I reproach myself for my behavior	71
[17.] Friends who have a snack with my son Fritz	10	17. Those on which I am fairly satisfied	64
		18. Those on which I am quite satisfied	46

Certain aspects of this account are worth considering in more detail. Over the years, the categories become more numerous and more differentiated. One striking aspect is the juxtaposition of the lists of individual errors in behavior and emotional issues on the one hand, and domestic visiting practices on the other. Henriette Stettler-Herport perceives the amount of time spent on visits and visitors as a major problem. This is because the more visitors come, the less time she has to spend on edifying reading, educating her children, and her efforts to spiritualize everyday life in her home. Consequently, from her point of view, there is no *caesura* here; it is all about "how I spend my time, and the guests [who spend time] with us."[18] Visitors often arrive unannounced, thus upsetting her tight daily schedule. Such a pious economy of time played a major role in many Pietist diaries.[19]

It is no secret that Pietism and other eighteenth-century Christian reform movements played a significant role in the history of the home and the family.[20] The Reformation had already laid strong groundwork in the domestic sphere. For both Martin Luther and Heinrich Bullinger, the home was a church in miniature, the "location of ideal and real piety," and the foundation which would ensure

---

18 In the original French: "Comme je passe mon tems et le monde que nous avons"; *Journal*, vol. 5, heading of the table for the second half of 1786, right-hand side.
19 Gleixner, *Pietismus und Bürgertum*, 127.
20 See the overview in Gestrich et al., *Geschichte der Familie*, 371–73.

the success of the Reformation's project of Christianizing society.[21] The doctrine of "proper Christian housekeeping" was subsequently propagated in sermons and tracts. In this way, eighteenth-century Pietism merged seamlessly with the Reformers' ideas, although from the perspective of Philipp Jacob Spener and other leading Pietists, these ideas had not yet been realized in the world of daily life. Many questions about what a 'pious family's' everyday life looked like in practice remain open. Moreover, the scholar who approaches the history of the family on the basis of personal diaries as sources must also consider the history of subjectivity. Therefore, even when we take into account the pietistic obligation to confess in self-narratives, it is still worth analyzing the ways in which Henriette Stettler-Herport constitutes herself as a subject in the process of writing.[22]

Indeed, this Bernese Pietist's self-reflections turn out to be remarkably modern in some respects, despite the fact that her primary goal is to be able to say with conviction, one day in the not-too-distant future: "I am a true Christian."[23] As the reader progresses through the diary, they are presented with an actor who has a markedly hybrid subjectivity.[24] Henriette Stettler-Herport is not only a pious Christian; she is also the wife of a council member and a public official, as well as a patrician with family and social connections. Her discourse draws on key Enlightenment concepts – such as 'morality,' 'virtue,' and 'reform' (*Besserung*) – at important points in the diary. Moreover, some of the domestic and familial ideals she presents presage notions of the family that would become common in the new middle-class society. Her central problem seems to be reconciling these different cultural identities. As she herself dejectedly observes after mentioning many upcoming, troublesome visits: "Oh, if only I weren't such a twisted creature! – I am made up of so many contradictions, indescribable and inscrutably strange; oh, I always hope for improvement."[25] Such expressions vary both linguistically and contextually, and so they do not come across as a rehearsed, predefined script.

The diary, which is not intended for publication, documents the writing subject's confrontation with a world that is unbearable to her in some respects. On the one hand, she notes her desire for retreat, silence, and domesticity. On the other

---

21 T. Kuhn, "Das Haus im Protestantismus," 726. For the following citation see ibid., 730; see also Gestrich, "Ehe, Familie, Kinder," 507.
22 Gleixner (*Pietismus und Bürgertum*, 394) remarks: "The Pietist concept of the subject is essentially based on the practice of writing and self-interpretation in various pietistically shaped genres"; see also ibid. 251 and 267.
23 *Journal*, vol. 5, January 10, 1779.
24 As mentioned in previous chapters, see the approach in Reckwitz, *Das hybride Subjekt*; linked to this, see Böth, "'Ich handele.'"
25 *Journal*, vol. 5, August 2, 1778.

hand, she writes, "I must see many people, go out often, otherwise people would say that I am strange, unkind, melancholic, and I don't know what else."[26] After the years she spent in the remote country bailiwick, this patrician woman experiences her return to the social life of her hometown not as a liberation, but as an imposition. The convivial pleasures of this world provoke an inner conflict. Yet the people in her immediate family environment seem to have fewer issues with these pleasures. After attending a ball at a hotel in Bern with her mother, Henriette Stettler-Herport notes, "This ballroom is beautiful, splendor and vanity hold sway there; I will not go there often, as I myself find no pleasure in splendor and vanity."[27]

The authorial 'I' constantly operates on the meta-level of introspection, but at the same time also perceives this tendency toward self-reflection as a problem: "in which many things seem to me to be quite burdensome, morose, and sad, [and I] worry about them and grieve, but they are really only trifles and do not merit the slightest contemplation."[28] The writer also provides concrete details about her social, health, and – in modern scientific language – psychological problems. The portrait of the author in the first volume of the diary shows a slender, petite person. Yet this woman manages a large manorial household every day. Between the ages of 19 and 39, Henriette Stettler-Herport gives birth to eight children, three of whom do not survive infancy. She repeatedly suffers from headaches and stomach ailments, and she has trouble sleeping. By the end of her fourth decade, she complains of hearing problems, and later also of problems with her vision. Her medical options are limited. She tries twenty different remedies for her stomach complaints, none of which work.[29] Following a recommendation she receives, she puts bacon in both ears for six days, but this does not improve her hearing.[30] Even in her early years at the bailiwick, she describes her state of mind with adjectives such as 'cold' or 'frigid' (*kaltsinnig*). Although self-reproach and self-dissatisfaction are a constant problem – one which she records in her tally sheets – she also experiences particularly acute depressive episodes, the onset of which she fears: "Oh, that I would not fall back into that cold indifference."[31] At the same time, the writing subject also repeatedly records moments of joy, particularly fol-

---

26 Ibid., January 4, 1778. See also ibid., July 29, 1781.
27 *Journal*, vol. 5, January 2, 1778.
28 *Journal*, vol. 5, January 4, 1778.
29 *Journal*, vol. 2, review of 1768.
30 *Journal*, vol. 5, August 5, 1781.
31 In the original German: "o wann ich nur nicht wieder in die kaltsinnige gleichgültigkeit falle"; ibid., July 26, 1778. See also the entries for December 25, 1776; January 4, 1778; December 24, 1778; and August 22, 1779.

lowing days spent in smaller social circles, not least after spending time alone with her husband and children.

Fig. 6: Henriette Stettler-Herport (artist unknown). Source: Journal de mes actions, Burgerbibliothek Bern, FA Stettler 12.4

According to her tally sheets as well as her narrative entries, Henriette Stettler-Herport recognizes her eating habits as a particular problem. Among those of her personal transgressions which do not refer to people in her social environment, the category of "eating too much or eating unhealthy things" (*trop manger ou choses malsaines*) always contains the most tally marks – not infrequently 10–20 per month. Could we identify this as an eating disorder or as depression? A psychiatrist, with their diagnostic perspective, would probably have fewer scruples about doing so than a cultural historian would. In any case, in these contexts it is worth noting the 'sayings' – that is, the contemporary vocabulary and the intellectual repertoire available to the actor. In addition to pious commands in favor of moderation, the author's good intentions with regard to the conduct of her life also refer to the human capacity for reason, and thus to an Enlightenment idea: when it comes to "too much food, is it possible that a rational creature can be so dependent on its mouth?"[32] Once again, from a very modern, up-to-date perspective, she sees a connection between her eating habits, her fragile body, and the fluctuations in her state of mind. She undergoes seltzer-water cures to improve her health – sometimes along with her husband and her daughter. Here Pietism and the Enlightenment come together in her efforts to subject her own life to systematic control, to an optimization that is both purpose-driven and value-rational. Her intention to control her affect as well as the rigid discipline to which she subjects herself through her fixed daily routine both support this. Henriette Stettler-Herport's diary documents a radical self-experiment in shaping one's habitus.

Household Management

The Stettler-Herports' domestic life shifts between the demands of their class and the social order on the one hand, and a desire for privacy within the family circle on the other. In this sense, what we have here is two different and in fact competing concepts of domesticity. Let us first take a look at the house and home. The diary tells us more about the spatial arrangements of the official residence in Frienisberg than about the family's townhouse in Bern or the *campagne* in Kirchberg. The bailiwick's official residence is located in a former monastery.
In fact, Bernese bailiffs' official residences were typically situated in old castles or monastery buildings. Over the course of the eighteenth century, these residences were structurally modernized, which led to a stricter separation between the official rooms and the bailiff's family's living quarters, as well as the differentiation of various spaces according to function – such as the kitchen, living rooms, and sleeping quarters.[33] Precisely when this division of the rooms took place in Frienisberg is unclear. Rudolf Stettler still uses the official bailiwick reception room on the ground floor to read sermons to his family, and presumably also to the servants, on Christmas Day 1774.[34]

The servants' sleeping quarters are located in the outbuildings. The monastery's large premises offers no shortage of rooms. The *chambre à manger* – equipped with a stove and used as a parlor and a common room – and the sleeping quarters were probably located on the first floor, which could be heated easily, and later perhaps also on the second floor. Nevertheless, not every member of the family has their own room. After Bernhard Albrecht ('Brechtli') is born in

---
32 *Journal*, vol. 3, 1772, Introductory Resolutions, item 11. On Pietism and pathology, see Ernst, *Krankheit und Heiligung*.
33 See the concise overview in Schweizer, "Die Landvogteischlösser."
34 *Journal*, vol. 4, December 25, 1774.

Fig. 7: Official Residence of the Frienisberg Bailiwick (Bern), c. 1670. Source: Bernisches Historisches Museum, Bern

1774, there are four children to care for; the parents share a bedroom, the two youngest children are quartered in the "children's rooms," and 4-year-old 'Frizli' sleeps in a room with Henriette's cousin, who visits for several months to help with the household chores and childcare. The couple's 16-year-old daughter, also called Henriette, has a room to herself.[35] However, the bailiff's wife uses the bedroom she shares with her husband as her personal chamber during the day. In Henriette Stettler-Herport's life, 'ma chambre' or 'meine Stube' is an important, frequently mentioned retreat, which she uses to read, to pray, to write letters or to write in her diary, to take a relaxing footbath, or to offer her children edifying lessons. As she notes, "At the moment I find more pleasure when I am alone in my room."[36]

The bailiff's seat also includes agricultural lands, a bakehouse where bread is distributed to the poor, several barns, and a horse stable. The diary often mentions the bailiwick's agrarian surroundings. The whole complex resembles a manor. In the winter months pigs are slaughtered, and in the summer up to 70 harvesters are

---

35 Ibid., August 14, 1774.
36 *Journal*, vol. 3, August 12, 1772. See also the entries for January 29, 1772; July 6, 1772.

employed to work the hay and grain harvests – a fact which the diary's author notes with a hint of pride.[37] The proceeds earned from working the land constitute part of the bailiwick's income. In addition, there are also rabbits and chickens.[38] Some of the visitors go hunting with the bailiwick's gamekeeper. The pious author of the diary notes that fortunately, her husband is not a hunter.[39] In 1772 a garden with terraces and a *cabinet* is laid out for the family to enjoy in their leisure time.

Who made up the staff at this 'whole house' in the Frienisberg bailiwick? After the family moves to the bailiwick's official residence in November 1771, the 'housemother' notes who needs to be cared for in the new household. In addition to her own growing family, there is the collector (*reçeveur*) responsible for the bailiwick's finances, a Mr. Salchli; five female servants (*servantes*); and seven male servants or farmhands (*valets*). There are also two more farmhands who do not eat with the household.[40] The number of servants fluctuates, however. On New Year's Day 1775, the family presents gifts to seven servants.[41] Among the servants, tasks are divided according to gender: the men are valets, coachmen, hunters, and later a tutor, as well as several farmhands on the estate in Kirchberg; the women work as cooks, chambermaids, and children's maids – at times each child has their own maid. After the family moves to Bern, the household staff is reduced to one cook and four maids. The tutor, who continues to work for the family, lives on one of the townhouse's upper floors.[42] The collector and the tutor sometimes accompany the married couple to church services or on a walk. In terms of co-presence, other close relatives sometimes spend weeks or months with the family at the official residence. Henriette Stettler-Herport's mother-in-law, 'Madame la Banderette,' has her own room, shares in much of the family's social life, dines with them at the table (except at breakfast), reads to the children, and goes to church with the family. Her relationship with her daughter-in-law is not always the

---

37 *Journal*, vols. 3 and 4; on harvest work, see the entries for June 13, 1772, and August 13, 1775; on animal slaughter, see the entries for February 13, 1772; January 30, 1774; and January 14, 1776.
38 *Journal*, vol. 3, August 26, 1772.
39 Ibid., July 30, 1772. On the following, see the entry for March 29, 1772.
40 *Journal*, vol. 2, review dated November 6, 1771. Whether the family and the servants engaged in table fellowship remains unclear. For all the necessary criticism, Brunner's concept of the 'whole house' with regard to the staff beyond the nuclear family in the premodern era touches on an important aspect; for further research on this topic, see Hahn, "Trends der deutschsprachigen historischen Forschung."
41 *Journal*, vol. 4, January 1, 1775.
42 *Journal*, vol. 5, January 18, 1778; January 31, 1779. On the following, see vols. 3 and 4; January 22, 1772; and December 25, 1775.

best, as Henriette Stettler-Herport documents in her diary entries and tally sheets.[43]

The housemother's relationship to the servants is dominated by issues of work and morality. After the family moves into the "well-built" townhouse with several floors, which they share with the servants, and in which the kitchen is very "smoky," the position of cook – the first of whom is "entirely unskilled" – has to be filled several times.[44] She mentions the servants with whom she has a more personal relationship – such as the maid, Marion, or the children's maid, Elseli – by their first names. One of the issues domestic rule entails is keeping a watchful eye on the servants' behavior and morals. Several times Henriette Stettler-Herport reports that she has had to mediate conflicts among the servants, and she confesses: "I do not treat them with as much leniency, kindness, and friendliness as I should."[45] In her record of sins, there are many lines regarding misconduct with respect to the servants over the years. Here and there she notes the servants' illnesses or an evening prayer offered with them. However, offenses against discipline and morality ultimately outweigh reliable work and personal commitment. Thus 'das Mädeli' (the girl), although she was "dear" and "served well," is sent away for keeping "bad, licentious company" and visiting "lewd places" under the "pretext of dancing."[46] Furthermore "Jean," who was "such a good personal servant," is also dismissed with a heavy heart after several years of service due to his "vice of drunkenness," despite the fact that "we" will never again "find one who possesses all his good qualities."[47]

Such a large household, involving approximately 12–20 people at any given time, requires oversight and organization. This task, which resembles managing a business, falls to the housemother. According to the diary, Rudolf Stettler hardly ever gets involved in this respect. Thus his wife has a lot to do. She coordinates the housekeeping, hires and directs the servants, makes purchases in Bern, settles payments and bills, arranges the laundry in the clothes presses, and so on. In addition, she brings up the children and undertakes her duties as the bailiff's wife, which I will discuss below. As early as the beginning of 1772, her diary offers one telling sentence with regard to her role as head of the household when she discusses

---

[43] *Journal*, vol. 3, March 17, 1772; October 31, 1772; review of 1771. Henriette's father-in-law, Johann Rudolf Stettler, held the prestigious office of Venner (a high office in Bern); throughout the diary she records her mother-in-law, Johanna Catharina Stettler-Wyttenbach, as 'Madame La Bandrette' or 'Frau Venner,' indicating a certain distance.
[44] *Journal*, vol. 5, January 18, 1778; see also several other entries for the year 1778, *passim*.
[45] Ibid., January 4, 1778. See also vol. 3, January 26, 1772; November 15, 1772; January 8, 1775.
[46] *Journal*, vol. 5, December 24, 1782 (all citations).
[47] *Journal*, vol. 4, July 26, 1774.

the precepts for an ideal daily routine in Frienisberg: "After breakfast I will go to the kitchen, give my instructions for lunch (*le dinér*), and lay out all the necessary items."[48] Even after moving to the city, this patrician wife does not do the cooking and cleaning herself, but has servants to do these tasks for her. Her husband's official role means that his wife does not contribute to the family income directly, in contrast to women who performed agricultural or craft work. Nevertheless, there is certainly enough for her to do in the household.[49] The diary provides information on the principles of pious economic management. On the one hand, this concerns the general duty to keep her house in order (*tenir mon Ménage en ordre*), while on the other hand, it calls for a life of thrift and moderation (*vivre avec économie et sobrieté*).[50] After the family moves to Bern, Henriette Stettler-Herport once again emphasizes and elaborates on her guidelines for 'housekeeping': she begins to rise before 7 o'clock in the morning in the winter months "for the sake of order and industriousness in household affairs," "which I and my indolence find quite difficult." Everything is very expensive, but "we have six children, and we want to keep house as well as possible for their sake." Supporting the poor is also important, as is managing one's material goods in a way that is "equally removed from stinginess and from wastefulness," and thus, with God's help, "to allocate our income wisely."[51] It is worth noting that the key term in this maxim – 'housekeeping' (*Hausen*) – is understood in an economic sense, as is typical in the eighteenth century.[52] For Stettler-Herport, pious household management also includes doing good for one's neighbors and, if possible, working with one's own hands.[53]

One of the key terms in Stettler-Herport's *Journal de mes actions* is the word 'travail' (work), which she uses well over one hundred times. Yet the author does not always make clear what she means by 'work' or what her concrete role in the labor process is. Primarily, however, 'work' refers to domestic practices, the most time-consuming of which are mainly doing the shopping and both the large and small laundry. After a day of shopping – which was certainly not a leisure pursuit – taking care of the purchases and putting them away, and thereafter settling the

---

48 *Journal*, vol. 3, "Régles Générales," 1772, item 5.
49 On paid and unpaid work in the household, see Whittle, "A Critique of Approaches to 'Domestic Work'"; Zucca-Michelletto, "Paid and Unpaid Work."
50 *Journal*, vol. 3, 1772, Introductory Resolutions, item 14.
51 *Journal*, vol. 5, January 18, 1778 (all citations).
52 See Beck, "Frauen in Krise," 150–56; Sabean, *Property, Production, and Family*, 107; Schläppi, "Logiken der Subsistenz."
53 *Journal*, vol. 3, 1772, Introductory Resolutions, item 14. On Pietism and the value of work, see Mettele, *Weltbürgertum oder Gottesreich*, 68.

bills, could take up to two days.[54] For larger laundry items, she hired women to do the laundry and the ironing, who came to the house and were paid a daily wage. If the weather was bad over a long period of time, as it was in the summer of 1772, then washing the larger laundry items at the bailiwick could take up to two weeks, from sorting and soaking the laundry to drying, ironing, and putting everything away.[55] For Henriette Stettler-Herport, the word 'travailler' meant not only giving instructions, shopping, and paying the bills, but also activities in which she herself lent a hand directly. One such task was treating the animal products resulting from the slaughter of livestock on the farm, which in January 1774 involved four pigs, took one week, and made her very tired.[56] Other tasks included sorting larger laundry items and clothing, and knitting in the evening. As was characteristic of early modern practices around work and social life, the term 'work' also occurs in the context of chit-chat: "After supper we chatted and worked."[57] In contrast to social duties, the housemother does not perceive her "small household tasks" as a burden.[58]

As outlined above, one of the central research questions in this book relates to the spouses around whom domestic relations revolve: first, the motivations for and practices involved in matchmaking; second, the relationship between husband and wife, particularly concerning hierarchy and companionship; and third, the question of the genesis of separate spheres for men and women, and modern gender roles. Eighteenth-century piety movements emphasized not only the individual's role – individual feelings and perceptions, and one's personal relationship to God – but also the importance of marriage and family as a model for the Christian transformation of everyday life.[59] Studying Henriette Stettler-Herport's diary, however, also demonstrates that the discursive horizon of Pietism by no means explains everything. Moreover, these examples of cohabitation – how the spouses, the children, and the other people in the households in Frienisberg and Bern live and work together – enable us to consider which aspects of the Pietist patrician context may presage the model family of the bourgeois era.

---

54 *Journal*, vol. 4, December 11, 1774. See also vol. 3, April 29, 1772.
55 *Journal*, vol. 3, April 17– May 1, 1772.
56 *Journal*, vol. 4, January 30, 1774.
57 *Journal*, vol. 3, March 13, 1772; see also entry for September 23, 1772.
58 In the original French: "petites ocupations de ménage"; entry for March 17, 1772. This follows the remark: "j'ai eu le rare bonheur, de passér la journée suivant mon Gout."
59 See Gestrich, "Ehe, Familie, Kinder," 507; Gleixner, *Pietismus und Bürgertum*, 119 and 210–12.

Marriage Politics Among the Urban Elite

Upon taking up her diary again, Henriette Stettler-Herport reflects back on the match made between herself and the commission clerk Rudolf Stettler in 1755, followed by their wedding in February 1756. At the time of their marriage, she is 17 years old and he is 24. The Herport and Stettler families are distantly related, although the two bloodlines only meet as far back as the sixteenth century, so we cannot speak of a 'cousin marriage' in this case. In her view, the starting point for their relationship, which leads to marriage after only a few months, is nothing less than mutual love: "We loved each other tenderly."[60] Her father, Councilor Herport, is initially against this union for his only daughter, but eventually agrees to meet the suitor in person, to see whether their mutual inclination (*inclination reciproque*) is serious and enduring (*sérieuse et durable*). On New Year's Day 1756, Rudolf gives Henriette a gift, which can be understood as a promise of marriage. A few weeks later, Henriette's father sends Rudolf a written declaration approving the match, thus providing the necessary parental consent. The marriage is then a matter for the two families to settle. Contracts are exchanged, and the bride's dowry is set. After the wedding, which takes place in a village near Bern, a large dinner is laid on for family and relatives at the bridegroom's house, and the following day another meal takes place at the bride's parents' house. Remarkably, this concise report makes no mention of divine will or of any influence exercised by a congregation of the pious and the converted – in contrast to the typical Pietist roadmap for finding a spouse. The bride and bridegroom persistently work together, in mutual love and appreciation, to earn her father's approval. The married woman who writes an account of all this at the age of 33 does not fail to thank her God. However, the story of the matchmaking and of her happy day (*jour heureux*) seem rather worldly on the whole.[61] She makes no mention of the bridegroom's religiosity or his outlook on life. At the same time, the love match between Henriette and Rudolf clearly followed the principle of social endogamy within Bern's patrician elite, which is not necessarily a contradiction. After the fact, Henriette does not say why Rudolf Stettler was attractive to her. Yet it is no coincidence that he came from a socially commensurate parental home and had good prospects

---

60 In the original French: "nous nous aimions tendrement"; *Journal*, vol. 2, December 28, [1770]. On 'cousin marriage,' see Sabean, "Social Background to Vetterleswirtschaft," and "Kinship and Class Dynamics"; Johnson and Sabean, *Sibling Relations*.
61 *Journal*, ibid. (all citations). On matchmaking in Pietist circles in Basel, see Hebeisen, *Leidenschaftlich fromm*, 254–64; on Württemberg, see Gleixner, *Pietismus und Bürgertum*, 215; on the topic in general, see Gestrich, "Familie, Traditionsstiftung und Geschichte," 505–6.

for an administrative career. Thus the social or worldly-material aspect of the match may have played a role in this marriage from the beginning.

A few years later, when suitors begin to vie for the hands of her daughters Henriette (b. 1758) and Anna Maria (b. 1772), Mrs. Stettler-Herport becomes more explicit on the topic of the qualities a suitable husband would have to bring to the match. She asks God for an honest man and a good Christian (*honetthomme et bonn Chrétien*) husband for her eldest daughter.[62] However, steadfast faith and a pious life are not her only criteria. The prerequisite for marriage remains mutual consent, and also affection between bride and groom. In 1776, when a lawyer from among their distant relations asks for Henriette's hand in marriage, her mother is taken with the prospect and attests that he has a favorable demeanor, an excellent character, and good opinions. But when her 18-year-old daughter does not return his affection and declares that she prefers to remain free (*restér libre*), since another equally profitable relationship (*un établissement assé lucrative*) may certainly present itself in the next few years, the matter is settled.[63] Two years later, the next candidate brings with him "great wealth, a pleasant family," and "good moral character," although "(as they say) limited spiritual and intellectual gifts." Once again, the courted daughter's judgment remains decisive, and she states that she is on the whole "very unhappy" with this man, since he does not share her "sensibility" or her "way of thinking."[64] This could be understood as a reference to her religious beliefs. At the age of 29, the daughter Henriette finally marries her younger brother Frizli's tutor of many years, Sigmund Ludwig Langhans, who would later become a pastor. The diary makes it clear that the parents are both the suitor's addressees and their daughter's advisors.

In matters of marriage politics, Henriette Stettler-Herport conducts herself more as a Bernese patrician than as a godly Pietist. The suitors come from among the city-state's elite. When her husband is shortlisted for a seat on the Council (*Kleiner Rat*), she finds the prospect attractive not only because of the "great advantage" this appointment would offer "the whole Stettler family," but also because 23-year-old Henriette would then become a so-called "baretli daughter," whose marriage would open up the prospect of the bridegroom becoming a councilor one day.[65] So the mother still had hope that the eldest daughter would make a good match. Moreover, as we have seen, it is clear that affection was considered a prerequisite for a good marriage. More still, marriage was supposed to

---

62 *Journal*, vol. 4, July 5, 1776.
63 Ibid., August 26, 1776. See also March 2, 1777.
64 *Journal*, vol. 5, August 16, 1778 (all citations).
65 *Journal*, vol. 5, December 2, 1781. On the Bernese 'Barettlitöchter', see Wittwer Hesse, *Die Familie von Fellenberg*, 33, and "Die Bedeutung der Verwandtschaft."

offer the couple not only spiritual, but also worldly happiness; as the diary puts it, marriage should bring "temporal and eternal happiness to this young engaged couple."⁶⁶

Nevertheless, it was precisely in this respect that the Stettler-Herports' matchmaking efforts led to disaster. At the end of 1787, 21-year-old Carl Gottlieb Dachselhofer, the son of a grand councilor, proposes to 15-year-old Anna Maria Stettler. The proposal is not made directly; instead, the young man's mother calls on the Stettler-Herport parents to convey his willingness to marry their daughter. Carl Gottlieb and Anna Maria (Marianne) are distantly related, but they have never met. Anna Maria is initially kept in the dark with regard to these matrimonial intentions.⁶⁷ Instead, the two mothers, who are on friendly terms, meet to discuss the matter. The parents want this marriage. The catch is that, even after the first meeting between the intendeds, "my dear good Marianne [...] is still quite undecided"⁶⁸ and, at only 15 years old, has to be more or less persuaded to agree to the marriage. Thus, after only about six weeks of shyly getting to know each other, the marriage contract is signed. We can certainly call this an arranged marriage. Henriette Stettler-Herport is euphoric about this prospect. She notes: "Mr. Daxelhofer is certainly a good, well-behaved, and amiable man; I hope they will indeed make each other happy; they do love each other."⁶⁹ This hope for earthly happiness is framed in prayer. The wedding follows in July 1788, but then the diary falls into a long silence. Only in December does the mother resume the thread of her entries, confessing that her daughter's marriage to Dachselhofer is a disaster. Even the wedding day was dreary. Marianne has not developed a growing "inclination" or "love" for her husband, as expected, but in fact the exact opposite. She finally reveals her misfortune in a conversation with her mother, "in confidence, accompanied by many tears and the utmost anguish."⁷⁰ Henriette now describes her son-in-law with a cascade of negative adjectives. His character contains "nothing yielding, nothing sympathetic"; he is "completely taken in by his own opinions"; he is "stubborn, overly sensitive, very sensual," and has "a tendency to excessive frugality" as well as "something quarrelsome and contradictory" about him.⁷¹ Here the mother

---

66 *Journal*, vol. 5, January 28, 1788, especially with reference to her relationship with her daughter Anna Maria ('Marianne', or sometimes 'Mariannli').
67 Ibid., December 2, 6, and 16, 1787. Anna Maria Stettler was Dachselhofer's fourth cousin twice removed.
68 Ibid., December 31, 1787.
69 Ibid., January 28, 1788. On endogamy and arranged marriages among the Bernese patriciate, see Wittwer Hesse, *Die Familie von Fellenberg*, 30–40.
70 Ibid., December 5, 1788 (all citations).
71 Ibid., December 31, 1788.

is not primarily concerned with a pious lifestyle, but rather with marital companionship and her daughter's well-being, as Anna Maria is also pregnant. At the end of this entry she reproaches herself, since "I, yes *I*, have contributed a great deal to bringing about this marriage."[72] In contrast, the bride's father takes a very detached attitude. The problem, which was already smoldering even before the wedding, is kept between mother and daughter: "and for a long time we said nothing to her father, so as not to worry him."[73] Rudolf Stettler holds his daughter's emotional problems at bay by pointing out that no other man "would suit Marianne as well as Mr. D." In the end, all his wife can do is to pray to God: "Make this marriage a happy one."[74]

The parameters for matchmaking in the patrician milieu can be summarized as follows: evident social endogamy, a sometimes very short phase of getting to know one another, the bride's and the groom's consensus and inclination, and the parents' influence and participation in the process, with the end goal of a happy marriage. However, when it came to individual inclination, we should note the presumption that one's 'affectionate' feelings for a partner of commensurate status were not necessarily present from the beginning, but could develop over time, as the relationship progressed.

Marriage as Hierarchy and Companionship

Any attempt to answer the question of whether Henriette and Rudolf Stettler's marriage was a happy one would yield no valid insights beyond a vague 'more or less.' It is more interesting to trace the practices and the distribution of roles in everyday life within the marriage. Yet this is no easy task – even with reference to a diary that was kept daily, at times. Henriette does indeed take an interest in her husband's professional career, and often refers to him as 'my husband' or 'my dear husband,' or even as 'Mr. Stettler.' For long stretches of her diary, however, his personality remains remarkably vague. Although the two of them spend more time together than most married couples do today, when husband and wife are often both employed outside the home, reading her diary gives the impression that these are two people with different ideas about life who nevertheless live side by side.

---

[72] Ibid., emphasis in the original. On Pietist marriage as companionship, see Gleixner, *Pietismus und Bürgertum*, 209–36.
[73] Ibid., December 5, 1788.
[74] Ibid., December 31, 1788 (both citations).

Where and how was this marriage lived out? Their ideal day begins and ends with prayer and edifying reading. For Henriette, spending time with Rudolf is directly connected to prayer and edification; he prays with her after she gets up in the morning and is supposed to read aloud an edifying text early in the morning as well as in the evening, before dinner.[75] In addition to her rules for the perfectly pious daily routine, many of Henriette's entries prove that Mr. Stettler regularly fulfills his domestic and fatherly duties, reading sermons or even contemporary fiction to his wife, his children, and their relatives. Such readings often take place on Sunday afternoons or evenings. On Sunday mornings, the housefather goes to church with his family and their servants, while the housemother may well stay home. Moreover, we should not overlook the fact that the couple produces eight children. Responsibility for their upbringing and education falls mainly to their mother. The couple takes numerous walks in the vicinity of the bailiwick. A more distinctive practice is their joint water cure.[76] Their everyday life also includes joint appearances at visits, dinners, and other forms of visiting culture. However, the two have different opinions about the meaning and necessity of such visits, and this requires a closer look. Do Rudolf Stettler and his wife live in 'separate spheres'? We cannot make such a statement in general terms with regard to life at the bailiwick. According to the diary, the housefather is not very present in the family sphere for most of the day. He holds court and audience days for the bailiwick's peasant subjects; conducts discussions with other officials, such as bailiffs and priests; and travels. Official activities and family life take place in the same structural complex, but mostly in separate spheres.[77] However, if one considers the politically and socially important, semi-public and semi-private gatherings in the family's living quarters, then the husband's and wife's spheres are not actually separate. Henriette, as head of the household and lady of the house, is responsible for hosting guests in a manner befitting her station and for seeing to it that they are well entertained. The salon culture which proliferated in Bern over the course of the eighteenth century, following the French model, emphasized women's role as hosts.[78] Compared to the country bailiwick, the couple's later life in the city opened up more opportunities for gender-specific sociability both inside and outside the home. In addition to their representative role in the salon, women were also typically engaged in the practice of paying visits, which was part of vis-

---

75 *Journal*, vol. 3, "Régles Générales," items 2, 3, and 14.
76 Ibid., August 21, 1772.
77 On the households of public officials in Sweden, see Ågren, "Lower State Servants."
78 See Schnegg, "Soireen, Salons, Sozietäten," 169; De Capitani and Schnegg, "Die Oberschicht der Hauptstadt," 144.

iting culture and enabled togetherness among friends and close relatives, while the men also met at the inn.[79]

Marital power relations become conspicuous when conflicts arise. In the tradition of the Protestant doctrine of marriage, Pietist tracts emphasized the idea of mutual support and spiritual amity between a man and a woman, with a simultaneous hierarchy of the sexes. At the same time, as Ulrike Gleixner has shown in her study of self-narratives written by women from the Württemberg Pietist tradition, it was precisely the new claim to female autonomy in spiritual matters that could lead to disputes between spouses.[80] This also applies to Henriette Stettler-Herport, who values the rituals of religious edification she enacts with her husband. Rudolf Stettler fulfills his pious duties by means of joint prayers, readings, and attendance at church services. *Prima facie* there is little doubt that a patriarchal hierarchy obtains between Henriette and Rudolf in religious as well as in other matters. Henriette's desire for closeness and partnership with her husband, while simultaneously acknowledging his dominion, is succinctly expressed in a critical conversation following their reading together on a Sunday evening in late January 1774, coincidentally at the end of the exhausting week in which the pigs were slaughtered. Henriette relates the content of this conversation at length. She and her husband had talked about their ways of doing things (*façons de faire*), and Rudolf had begun to speak about her personal mistakes. This conversation apparently signifies a resolution after a period in which the two did not speak. At the end of the conversation, when Henriette offers gratitude for her husband's correction, we must consider the fact that her addressee is God the Father in heaven. At the same time, however, she makes it clear that a good husband takes an interest in his wife's spiritual well-being and is also a true, tender friend:

> With joy I have found that my husband urges me to recognize my faults; for quite some time I have noted with sorrow that he does not seem to take much interest in me; indeed I felt that he was often dissatisfied with me, and I took his silence about this as a sign of indifference; he appears to me [now] as a tender spouse and true friend.[81]

At the same time, Henriette Stettler-Herport, who constantly grapples with herself and her environment, cannot be accused of lacking individuality and obstinacy. The power the bailiff's wife has is party formal and partly informal. She rules over a large household. Aware of her limited right to a say in other matters, how-

---

[79] *Journal*, vol. 5, July 26, 1778. On gender-specific communication among siblings and on women's prominent role in the 'relational arena', see Lanzinger, "Schwestern-Beziehungen," 264.
[80] See Gleixner, *Pietismus und Bürgertum*, esp. 222, 251, and 510.
[81] *Journal*, vol. 4, January 30, 1774 (both citations).

ever, in one of the first entries she writes after she takes up diary writing once again, she complains about her husband having sold of a plot of land in Kirchberg without consulting her about it.[82] Usually, however, she does not interfere in her husband's official business; instead, housekeeping, child-rearing, communicating with relatives, and dealing with the politics of marriage are among her *métiers*. The division of duties between the spouses is evident, and on the whole unchallenged.

House vs. Family: Two Models of Living Together

The significance of the latent conflicts between Stettler, the bailiff and councilman, and his pious wife goes beyond the patriarchal framework or the religious sphere. They are also an indicator of the incompatibility of two different models of domestic and familial cohabitation. In the Stettler-Herports' case, there is a fundamental disagreement concerning the distinctive semi-public visiting culture in the domestic sphere. In the 1772 preface to her diary, Henriette explicitly identifies the problem. In terms of maintaining social relationships, their disagreement is "a real grief to her husband, whose preference is quite different, and who enjoys having visitors often." She considers her primary duties to be maintaining order in the household, educating her children, and supervising the servants. The guests and visitors who arrive almost daily are a horror to her, and according to the tally sheets of her transgressions, they strain her patience to the breaking point. For Rudolf Stettler, on the other hand, visits and dinners are an essential aspect of his professional duties. Anyone who wanted to have a career in the official hierarchy of the Bernese city-state had to cultivate social relationships. He explains to his wife that she cannot change the world, but she asks him "not to extend his invitations and acquaintances any further."[83] Despite this, the couple's disagreement about visiting practices remains a theme in her diary over the years, even after the family moves to the city. In January 1779, for example, she comments at length on the unavoidable social obligations in Bern:

---

82 *Journal*, vol. 3, January 3, 1772.
83 In the original French: "un chagrin réel a mon Mari, dont le gout tout oposé est portés a avoir souvent du Monde"; "je dois tenir mon Ménage en ordre, élevér mes Enfants, les préservér des mauvais Exemples,veillér sur mes domèstiques"; "mon Mari me dit que je ne changerai pas le Monde"; "je prierai mon Mari de ne pas étendre encor plus ses invitations, et ses Connoissances"; ibid., 1772, Introductory Resolutions, item 14 (all citations).

> The world today is vain; this way of life doesn't suit me at all, the constant socializing, showing off, dances, comedies; I withdraw from everything as much as I can, but since I have to pay nearly 80 calls – I can only rarely be alone at home – if I went to each place only once – and every week to my mother's, and then the days when I receive visitors at home, the winter would be almost over [...] I seldom have time to read, I have almost no time for my children, and all this makes me unwilling – I am discouraged, sad – moody.

Her husband's advice, which she records, is succinct: "Mr. Stettler tells me that one must acquiesce to the world."[84]

Henriette Stettler-Herport's tally sheets document the 'open house' culture of the patrician elite, which was based on different principles than our modern ideas of undisturbed privacy.[85] We can also identify striking differences between visiting practices at the country bailiwick and those in the city. What is remarkable about the family's time in Frienisberg is the large number of visitors who stay overnight or for several days. In contrast, at the Stettler-Herports' residence in Bern from 1778 onward, the number of calls and short visits – often involving small meals – increase significantly, as do the number of evenings spent outside the home. It is easier to grasp the types of visitors they receive in the bailiwick than the later visitors to the townhouse. Essentially there are three intertwined groups: Reformed clergy, secular officials and military officers, and relatives and friends. Among the people Henriette Stettler-Herport notes in her diary are many well-known names among the Bernese patriciate, such as Wattenwil, Bonstetten, and Tscharner. In contrast, neighbors as such do not play a significant role in the household or the family's social network. In addition, people who are paid to work in the household are also present: women who do the laundry and the ironing, dressmakers, a tutor, and a harpsicord teacher for one of the daughters. On a few occasions, the couple also take in poor people and beggars off the street.[86] Visits to the official residence alternate between short visits and stays of several weeks. Such visits are often unannounced, and the housemother finds this particularly disturbing. She does not seem to prefer visitors from among their relatives

---

84 In the original German: "Eitel ist doch die heutige Welt; die lebensart gefällt mir gar nicht, beständige gesellschafften, puz, tanz, comedie ich enziehe mich so viel möglich von allem, doch da ich nahe bei 80. Visiten zu machen habe – kann ich wenig bei Hause alein sein – ginge ich an jedes ort nur ein mahl – und jede woche zu meiner Mamma, und dann die tage da ich bei hause Visiten habe so ist der winter fast gar vorbei, [...] selten kan ich lesen, meinen kindern kan ich fast keine Zeit geben, dieses alles macht mich unwillig – da bin ich muthloos, traurig – mürrisch"; "herr Stettler sagt mir mann müße sich in die welt schiken"; *Journal*, vol. 5, January 10, 1779 (both citations).
85 On this topic, see Eibach, "Das offene Haus"; on changes to the 'open house' model around 1800, see Eibach, "Das Haus," 31–34; Eibach, "From Open House to Privacy?", 354–59.
86 *Journal*, vol. 3, August 21, 1772; December 10, 1782.

to her husband's colleagues.[87] Henriette's duties include planning the meals and entertaining the guests. Sometimes there are tours of the bailiwick's various buildings, and sometimes the visitors' children have to be entertained. The typical procedure is as follows: "I arranged everything for the midday meal, starting after breakfast, and laid out all the necessary items. The company arrived at 11 o'clock. It was composed of Mr. Vogt Grouber from Buchsee and Mrs. Major Fischer [...] we chatted, looked over the accommodation, dined, drank coffee, and at 4 o'clock the tea, and a 5 o'clock they went away again."[88]

The move to Bern seems to have aggravated this problem for Henriette Stettler-Herport. While it is true that visits from bailiffs and clergyman ceased, from this point on she was expected to participate in the socially differentiated visiting culture of the patrician milieu. A few weeks after the move, she sums up her daily routine with frustration. She rarely goes out in the mornings, but in the

> afternoon there is occasional business to be done and one or another short visit to receive, [though] I make as few of these [visits] as possible, preferring to work until 4 o'clock when I can, then I dress to spend the evening in company, since I have almost 70 houses, and relatives and acquaintances with whom I spend the evenings at their place, and they in turn at my place, so I have few evenings to spend at home alone [...] If I could live according to my taste, I would go into large companies only rarely.[89]

Thus the urban visiting culture began in the afternoon. During the summer season, the social network extended to the family's country estate in Kirchberg, several hours away by carriage. Under stress, she notes that "we had a lot of socializing – daily arrivals and departures – for several days I was quite ill."[90] A look at these 'petites visites' clarifies the connections between visiting culture, career, and politics. Contrary to the trend in other types of visits noted in the diary, in 1786 the number of such short visits was very high; this was also the year in which Rudolf Stettler was finally elected to the Council (*Kleiner Rat*) as a so-called *Heimlicher*, after several unsuccessful attempts. His investiture takes place in May 1786. For the first half of 1786, his wife records 112 short visits to their home, and for the six months after he takes office, she notes 145. This was clearly a hectic time, when visitors were constantly ringing the bell at the new councilor's

---

87 *Journal*, vol. 5, February 20, 1778.
88 *Journal*, vol. 3, May 4, 1772.
89 *Journal*, vol. 5, January 18, 1778.
90 Ibid., August 6, 1780.

house.[91] The subsequent decline in the number of visits at which food and drink were offered may also have been due to the housemother's failing health.

Henriette Stettler-Herport was by no means an entirely antisocial person. She welcomes some visits, such as those of her beloved "Bäsi Wyttenbach."[92] She is very fond of visiting some of her female relatives, among whom she explicitly refers to some as friends. Her social context is and remains Bern's elite, those families close to the council. Pietist gatherings and prayer meetings play no role in her social life. But the social round that befits her status is a constant burden to her. The needs of this well-read, Pietist patrician woman cannot simply be attributed to a fragile constitution. As a contrast to the daily practice of the 'open house,' her idea of domestic life is a harbinger of the future family model in which domestic space is understood as private. The place where she can live out her "preference for solitude [...] in contrast to the passion for a large company"[93] is her own room (*ma chambre*). This privacy is primarily intended to serve her children's religious edification and education, but it does not stop there. She desires a more domestic lifestyle (*häusliche Lebensart*) and more time for family. After about a year in Frienisberg, she outlines her program for an intimate family life:

> I am impatiently awaiting my husband's return; I would like to have my husband and children always in the house, to live quietly with the family in this way, to have visits only from my close relatives or most intimate friends, and that only once a week; the rest of the time I would devote to my household, to my children's education, to walking, to reading, to work; that would be my greatest happiness.[94]

For this actor, a fulfilling family life means conversations and reading together, time for amusement with the young children and for education with the older ones, walks with her husband, and sometimes music at home. The eldest daughter

---

[91] On the council election on May 11, 1786, see *Journal*, vol. 5, May 24, 1786. According to the tally sheets in vol. 5, the number of visitors making 'petites visites' broke down to: 92 in the first half of 1785, 99 in the second half of 1785, 112 in the first half of 1786, and 145 in the second half of 1786. On the following, see ibid., May 26, 1786; and vol. 5, *passim*.
[92] *Journal*, vol. 5, August 13, 1780; August 5, 1781. On the following, see ibid., August 16, 1778; January 18, 1778; August 22, 1779.
[93] *Journal*, vol. 3, 1772, Introductory Resolutions, item 14.
[94] In the original French: "j'atande avec impatiance le retour de mon Mari, je voudrois avoir toujours mon Mari et mes Enfants a la maison, vivre ainsi tranquilement en fammille, n'avoir des visites que de mes proches parants, ou amis, les plus intimmes, et cela une fois par semaine seulement, le réste du tems je voudrois le donér a mon mènage, a l'education de mes Enfants, a la promenade, la lecture, l'ouvrage, ce seroit là mon plus grand bonheur"; *Journal*, vol. 3, October 11, 1772. On the following, see May 10, 1772; see also vol. 5, January 18, 1778; December 5, 1779.

receives harpsicord and singing lessons.[95] Reading within the family circle consists not only of sermons and edifying texts, but also the works of Samuel Richardson, Johann Jakob Scheuchzer, Sophie von La Roche, and Friedrich Gottlieb Klopstock. The couple tries to keep at least Sunday afternoons and evenings free for this kind of family togetherness.

The children's character development as well as their relationships to each other and to their mother take up a lot of space in the diary entries. Henriette Stettler-Herport attaches much importance to their upbringing and education, for which she and the tutor are essentially responsible, with fixed hours for these activities in the morning and the afternoon. Eventually she also begins to keep tally sheets of other children's visits to her children, because she is concerned that her children might become overly involved in the vain pleasures of the sophisticated world.[96] Today some might call her a helicopter mother. This busy housemother undoubtedly has close, emotional relationships with her children. The eldest daughter, who is much older than her younger siblings, grows into the role of an important caregiver for the other children and a partner to her mother. She receives almost as much attention in the diary as Stettler-Herport's husband. The mother's high educational ideals, emotions, and need for control repeatedly lead to conflicts. The educational goals are summed up at the end of 1789, when the mother proudly reports on her 19-year-old son ('Frizli') Albert Friedrich's departure to study at the University of Göttingen: "God be praised, we have the most well-grounded hope for this dear son; his principles are noble and good, he studies diligently, with zeal, with joy – every duty is sacred to him, that of the Christian, of the man, of the citizen; he flees debauchery of every kind, weakness, pomp, idleness – also the superficiality of an addiction to fashion."[97] In what is an unusual style for the diary, this entry is a success story. As the children grow up, Henriette Stettler-Herport increasingly records her own misconduct toward her children in her tally sheets, and in this way she reflects on her behavior as a mother and an educator.

The occasions for her oft-noted 'anger' and 'impatience' are not clear from the tally sheets. If we take the narrative entries into account, however, we see that the intimate family relationships observed *in nuce* in these entries prove to be extremely fragile. Already here *in statu nascendi*, the bourgeois family shows a face that is clearly distinct from the harmonious family ideal. On the one hand,

---

95 *Journal*, vol. 3, June 28, 1772; vol. 5, January 18, 1778. On music in the house, see also January 1, 1772; January 22, 1775.
96 *Journal*, vol. 5, January 18, 1778. On the history of education, see Opitz-Belakhal and Guzzi-Heeb, "Family, Community and Sociability"; on the role of emotion, Jarzebowski, *Kindheit und Emotion*.
97 *Journal*, vol. 5, December 10, 1789.

we have the mother's permanent state of stress and feelings of failure, and on the other, we see an everyday life in which many disputes arise. She desires to be a "teacher of virtue and godliness" for her children, but she fears that they will not go to heaven, and that this will be her fault.[98] A few years prior to Albert Friedrich's departure for Göttingen (he would go on to become a judge and a history professor in Bern), the diarist confesses to her God that there have been massive disturbances in the children's coexistence. It is a report from the midst of a real-life family muddle, and it is worth quoting:

> I have an oppressive weight on my heart that plagues me more and more – my younger children are constantly quarreling and fighting with one another, and for such a long time – I had hoped things would get better as they got older, attributed it to their great vivacity, belittled them, rebuked them, suggested all kinds of things, and alas! Everything is in vain. My God, you know it all.

She follows this with a prayer asking God to improve her children's character: "Friz [Albert Friedrich], who is so tall, who is already 15 years old, even he does no better than the younger ones, oh! By your grace, you have given them so many good and useful gifts; they are promising children, and everything, everything is spoiled by the fact that they live together in such a way." Apparently conflicts often erupt during the family ritual of sharing a meal. At the table, people cannot avoid one another:

> none of them can suffer or tolerate the slightest thing from the other; it happens every day [...] they also often hit each other; when we come to the table, instead of pleasant conversation or otherwise pleasant, even amusing entertainment, one cries and complains about the other – then we have to rebuke them; we ourselves become recalcitrant, peevish, as our meals become increasingly bitter [...] this has already cost me many bitter tears.[99]

This example shows that intra-familial emotions involve more than just harmony or love. In well-off families – in which the offspring were not sent out of the house as apprentices or maids at around 14 years of age, as they were in peasant's or craftsman's families – the fact that growing children spent a longer time at home opened up new areas of conflict.

In contrast to the intimacy of the bourgeois nuclear family, scholarly research views the premodern household as a place of work – not least of female work. We can distinguish different types of work: household management, care for children

---

98 Ibid., August 30, 1778.
99 Ibid., January 9, 1785 (all citations). See also ibid., December 24, 1789. On the importance of conversation at the table, see Keppler, *Tischgespräche*.

and the elderly, services provided to ensure subsistence, and also paid work.[100] The example of the Stettler-Herports suggests we add a fifth type of work to this list: representational work, in which the wife and housemother played an important role. Representing the home and the family as well as hosting and entertaining guests in the house translates into work for the Bernese officeholder's wife, namely effort and commitment, which are linked to her displeasure and low motivation. Yet this kind of work generates substantial social capital, which can then be converted into financial capital in the form of professional contacts and her husband's career.[101]

In the patrician Pietist context of the Stettler-Herport house, we can identify clear signs of a new era emerging. It is no coincidence that when the eldest son leaves for Göttingen – in the same year as the revolution – his mother emphasizes his moral virtues as a Christian, a human being, and a citizen. Henriette's resolve to live a self-disciplined life, with a strong orientation toward standards and performance, as well as the goal of optimizing her demanding everyday life, could easily be translated into the emerging bourgeois milieu. Following this thread, we can also note her devotion to writing and reading, her health consciousness, and the inner life for which she strives. Above all, her domestic family ideal, with its strong emphasis on the intimate sphere, points ahead to middle-class society's understanding of the family. She reluctantly accepts her role as the house's representative to the outside world, with no conviction and no fervor. Her criticism of vanity and intemperance, of invitations and festivities in the patrician milieu, corresponds to the emerging bourgeois criticism of the aristocracy – with parallels to the old republican discourse on virtue as well.[102] The domestic world should be closed off from the outside, accessible only to close relatives and friends. The aim is a privatized family space, supported by a few servants with whom one has no personal relationship. While the councilor Rudolf Stettler represents an older model of the 'open house' with representative, manorial, and political functions, his wife desires a life *en famille*.

---

[100] For clarification on these terms, see Whittle, "A Critique of Approaches to 'Domestic Work'"; Zucca Micheletto, "Husbands," and "Paid and Unpaid Work."
[101] For further details on Bourdieu's theory of different types of capital, see the summary in Bourdieu, "Ökonomisches Kapital."
[102] See Schnegg, "Tagebuchschreiben als Technik," 126; Schnegg, "Soireen, Salons, Sozietäten,"; on the bourgeois intimate sphere, see Reckwitz, *Das hybride Subjekt*, 145–50; on bourgeois morality and criticism of the aristocracy, see Maurer, *Die Biographie des Bürgers*, 236–38. and 588–90.

Chapter 5
Bourgeois Marriage and Open Domesticity: Ferdinand and Caroline Beneke

Hamburg, Germany (1805–1816)

General opinions on the modern middle class or bourgeoisie (*Bürgertum*) have been many and varied since its emergence in the mid-eighteenth century. For some, *Bürgertum* constitutes the social foundation for all democratic aspirations and for a liberal culture that overcame traditional class divisions and paved the way for enlightened education, economic advancement, and individual autonomy. Others are critical of *Bürgertum*'s political compromises in the struggle with authoritarian states; its insistence on distinguishing itself from the lower classes; its stern habitus, perceived as hostile to pleasure; and its hierarchical gender relations.[1] Regardless of one's opinion on these matters, one certainly cannot ignore *Bürgertum* in any study of marriage and domestic relations in the century of the bourgeoisie. An elective affinity between the bourgeoisie (*Bürgerlichkeit*) and domesticity (*Häuslichkeit*) certainly existed, and not only in Germany.[2] Around 1800, *belles lettres* also postulated the love marriage.[3] As I have outlined in the first chapter, the intellectual leaders of middle-class society had developed a model of marriage as an "ethical relationship" (Hegel) and the basis of all "human and civic happiness" (Rotteck). Thus the family could not be omitted from the 'horizon of bourgeois values.' It is true that the 'educated classes' (*gebildete Stände*) or the 'bourgeoisie' comprised numerically small groups in all the

---

[1] Among the wealth of literature available on this topic, see esp. Hausen, "Die Polarisierung der Geschlechtscharaktere"; Kocka, "Das europäische Muster"; Hein and Schulz, *Bürgerkultur im 19. Jahrhundert*; Hettling and Hoffmann, *Der bürgerliche Wertehimmel*; Studer, "Familialisierung und Individualisierung"; Budde, *Blütezeit des Bürgertums*; Fahrmeir, "Das Bürgertum"; Reckwitz, "Wie bürgerlich ist die Moderne?"; on the bourgeoisie around 1800, see Maurer *Die Biographie des Bürgers*; Bödeker "Die 'gebildeten Stände'"; with reference to Beneke, see most recently Hatje, "Die private Öffentlichkeit," and "Domestic Sociability."

[2] Tosh (*A Man's Place*, 4) understands 'domesticity' as "not just a pattern of residence or a web of obligations, but a profound attachment: a state of mind as well as a physical orientation."

[3] Trepp, "Emotion und bürgerliche Sinnstiftung." On the practice, see also R. Habermas, *Frauen und Männer*, chap. 5; on the scholarly debate over the emergence of love marriage, see Gestrich, *Geschichte der Familie im 19. und 20. Jahrhundert*, 30–32 and 80–81; Gestrich et al., *Geschichte der Familie*, 484–86; Saurer, *Liebe und Arbeit*, 47–49.

countries of Europe and beyond,[4] but their habitus and lifestyle radiated out to other milieus. This bourgeois, early liberal model of culture in its purest form – which focused on progress through the extension of education and property rights to a broader swathe of society, as well as the positive effects of industriousness and enlightenment values – was already on the defensive prior to the revolution of 1848/1849. With the advent of modern mass and consumer societies, counter-movements had begun by 1900 at the latest. These also found expression in processes of subject formation in self-narratives.[5] In order to have a meaningful discussion of these topics, it is important not to mutilate 'bourgeois' into a term denoting a particular political camp or a colloquial platitude, but rather to differentiate between historical phases of the bourgeoisie. As an example, the everyday disorder of bourgeois family life during the *Sattelzeit* in the 1800s may have been more open and innovative than the orderly family life that characterized later phases of middle-class modernity.

The Bourgeois Romantic Subject

In many respects, Ferdinand Beneke embodies a bourgeois prototype. He sees himself expressly as "a citizen, housefather, and husband," and also as the "head of the household" and a *Bürger.*[6] Born into a merchant family in Bremen on August 1, 1774, the third of seven children, he was part of the social group that provided the upwardly mobile *homines novi* in many German cities during the transition from estate-based to bourgeois society.[7] He studied law and public administration (*Kameralwissenschaften*), which gave him the option to pursue a career in the civil service, and received his doctorate from the University of Göttingen, then the leading German university, in 1795. He was a member of the 'educated classes' and maintained good contacts with the elite circles that were close to the senates of the northern German Hanseatic cities. As a student, he sympathized with the ideas behind the French Revolution and even considered emigrating to the 'Land of the Revolution' or to North America. However, marked by Napoleon's bid for power and the French occupation, he later became a Napoleon-hater

---

4 Kocka, "Das europäische Muster," 10; Osterhammel, *Die Verwandlung der Welt*, 1079–81; Dejung et al., "Worlds of the Bourgeoisie," 1–3.
5 Reckwitz, *Das hybride Subjekt*, 282–95; see also recently Bänziger, *Die Moderne als Erlebnis*.
6 In the original German: "Bürger, Hausvater, und Gatte"; "FamilienVater"; "Bürger"; Beneke, *Tagebücher*, January 30, 1811, vol. 3.1, p. 27; August 13, 1813, vol. 3.1, p. 524.
7 Gall, *Vom alten zum neuen Bürgertum*, and *Stadt und Bürgertum*.

who turned toward Prussia instead. Rather than emigrating or becoming a Prussian civil servant, he settled in Hamburg in 1796 and began to work as a lawyer.

Beneke has his finger on the pulse of his time. His work combines the patriotism of the Enlightenment era with the philanthropic liberalism of the nineteenth century: he wants to do good, but he still calls members of the lower classes "rabble" when there is a riot.[8] He writes memoranda on Hamburg's future political constitution, statutes for the citizens' militia, and a municipal constitution for the Portuguese-Jewish community. In the context of his patriotic commitment to the common good, he holds several voluntary posts – he works in poor relief (as an *Armenpfleger*) and serves as a superintendent in the school system, among other roles. In the Hamburg courts, Beneke has a reputation as a lawyer who is able to negotiate fair settlements between the parties to a dispute. After Hamburg is annexed to the French Empire, Beneke refuses several offices that the new authorities offer him and has to flee the city for fear of imprisonment. He hopes that political change will come "not by dint of states, but by dint of ~~men~~ peoples, as soon as it is ripe."[9] At the end of May 1814, the day before his return to Hamburg, he writes down a prayer: "Grant that I may return to my home a better person and a more salutary citizen!"[10] In 1816 – not without the help of his father-in-law, Otto von Axen – he obtains a dream post: he is elected legal secretary (*Syndikus*) of the influential Council of Elders (*Oberaltenkollegium*). Although Beneke never becomes a senator, he is a well-known man in Hamburg and is well connected beyond the city as well.

So far, this reads as a success story. But Ferdinand Beneke also learns about the shadow side of bourgeois existence early in his life; he lives with strong inner tensions and embodies the ambivalence of the modern subject. Although he comes from a wealthy family and attends the Bremen Cathedral High School (*Bremer Domgymnasium*), as a child he witnesses the economic decline of his parents' trading house. As an adolescent, he has to withstand the deaths of three of his siblings. The fact that his parents and his uncle, the Hamburg merchant Johann Friedrich Frederking, get into a dispute and eventually a lawsuit over an inheritance – whereupon his uncle, who is victorious in court but also addicted to gam-

---

[8] Beneke, *Tagebücher*, February 24, 1813, vol. 3.1, p. 369: "PöbelAufruhr"; March 1, 1813, vol. 3.1, p. 375. On Beneke himself, see the very informative analysis in Hatje, "Aus dem Leben eines Diaristen," and "Tagebücher und Korrespondenzen."
[9] In the original German: "nicht durch Staaten, – sondern durch ~~Männer~~ Völker, sobald's reif ist"; Beneke, *Tagebücher*, November 16, 1812, vol. 3.1, p. 325 (strikethrough and underlining in the original).
[10] In the original German: "Gieb, daß ich als ein beßrer Mensch, u. als ein heilbringender Bürger zurückkehre in meine Heimath!"; Beneke, *Tagebücher*, May 30, 1814, vol. 3.1, p. 113.

bling, goes bankrupt nevertheless[11] – anticipates the circumstances in Thomas Mann's *Buddenbrooks*. Beneke himself never becomes wealthy, but is always in debt to varying degrees and depends on loans from his friends.[12] Perhaps for this reason, he maintains a critically distanced view of the self-staging of Hamburg's upper class (*Großbürgertum*). His constant striving for personal and political 'improvement' corresponds to his tendency toward skepticism and his frequent crises: "The whole day my temper was gloomily melancholic."[13] He dislikes opulent banquets, drinks water, and smokes a pipe. His "dietary habits" include daily walks through Hamburg in all weathers, hikes in the surrounding countryside, and visits to the bathing ship on the Alster river in the summer.[14] This highly motivated hypochondriac – who became ill and was in poor health for months in the second half of 1814, after his triumphant return to Hamburg with the citizens' militia (*Bürgergarde*) – is interested in everything. He studies and writes almost manically, combining scientific work on the geography and cartography of his native Northern Germany and precise observations of the weather in Hamburg with Romantic inclinations.[15] Not only does he read Goethe, Jean Paul, Kleist, and de la Motte Fouqué, but this active Romantic's long walks also take him through the Hamburg cemeteries during the day or by moonlight, which holds "a great charm for me, especially in winter, when everything is so solitary, so ethereally melancholy, so intimately serene."[16]

Beneke writes about himself and his social environment daily. As a modern subject, he functions self-reflexively. The diary he kept over more than five decades, until his death in 1848, and the other documentation of his own life – which he ultimately handed over to his son, Otto Adalbert – took on almost Goethean proportions.[17] In the bourgeois mindset, a diary is a cultural resource to be safeguarded for future generations. Unlike Goethe's *Dichtung und Wahrheit*, however, Beneke's diary is not artfully composed from A to Z, nor is it dedicated to the stylization of his own greatness – but it does fulfill several purposes. It performs

---

11 Hatje, "Aus dem Leben eines Diaristen," 61–62.
12 Beneke, *Tagebücher*, August 30, 1811, vol. 3.1, p. 131; June 22, 1813, vol. 3.1, p. 470; June 12, 1814, vol. 3.2, p. 122.
13 Beneke, *Tagebücher*, September 9, 1812, vol. 3.1, p. 291.
14 Beneke, *Tagebücher*, overview for the year 1814, vol. 3.2, p. 195.
15 On Beneke's notes about the weather and his state of health, see Bischoff, "Der Himmel über Hamburg."
16 Beneke, *Tagebücher*, December 30, 1812, vol. 3.1, p. 345.
17 For an introductory overview, see Hatje, "Tagebücher und Korrespondenzen"; on securing resources as a bourgeois strategy, see Reckwitz, *Das hybride Subjekt*, 161.

the role of an "absent friend."[18] Unlike the pietistic diary, it is not a matter of a sinful man's confession to God, but rather very much a technique or 'technology of the self' (Foucault). The textualization of the subject's experiences primarily enables him, a man so susceptible to crises, to reassure himself. The subject strives for orientation, both to himself and to the world. If the goal is "to know yourself,"[19] then no medium is better suited to this than the diary. Additionally, there is also the motive of documentation, which both the eventful course of history – Beneke begins his daily entries three years after the storming of the Bastille – and the author's own eventful life invite. Beneke's subject combines a bourgeois striving for order with a Romantic creativity; both find expression in his diary. For this reason it makes little sense to see the bourgeois subject and the Romantic subject as opposing models.[20] From the beginning, bourgeois and Romantic subjectivity are conflated.

Although Beneke uses a code in some places to protect his remarks from being read by an unwanted audience, his diary is less private than one might assume. The free-flowing text not only addresses Beneke's alter ego, but also contains messages to his circle of confidants. It sometimes happens that Ferdinand and his wife, Caroline ('Karoline' or 'Line'), read aloud to each other from their diaries at their morning coffee hour.[21] His closest friends are also among his chosen readers, and sometimes he even directly addresses his "dear descendants! who will one day read this."[22] Significantly, Beneke's son, Otto Adalbert, eventually becomes an archivist and the director of the Hamburg State Archives. The fact that this busy lawyer, office holder, husband, father, and friend takes the time to keep daily accounts of the course of events over decades, often for pages at a time, makes it clear how important this activity was to him. In addition, there are also annual overviews at the turn of the year – comparable to the "final account of a financial year in a tradesman's journal"[23] – in which he and his wife take stock of the past year and also of their relations in the circles of their family, household, relatives, friends, and acquaintances. The author also collects letters, drafts, and even arti-

---

18 Cited in Hatje, "Tagebücher und Korrespondenzen," 23. On the functions of Beneke's diary and his motivations for keeping it, see ibid., 18–20.
19 Foucault, "Technologies of the Self," 20.
20 Cf. Reckwitz, *Das hybride Subjekt*, 120–21.
21 Beneke, *Tagebücher*, July 19, 1811, vol. 3.1, p. 114; see also Hatje, "Tagebücher und Korrespondenzen," 12–13; spelling the name of Caroline Beneke, née von Axen, with 'C' follows the convention in the critical edition of Beneke's diaries.
22 Beneke, *Tagebücher*, August 31, 1811, vol. 3.1, p. 132.
23 As aptly put in Hatje, "Tagebücher und Korrespondenzen," 17. On Caroline Beneke's participation, see *Tagebücher*, January 3, 1813, vol. 3.1, p. 349: "Reading morning with Line; the overview of the year 1812 kept us busy for quite some time".

facts such as locks of hair from his wife and daughters, and includes them as supplements.

Bürger Beneke is not unknown in contemporary research. Based on the critical edition of his diaries, which has been in progress since 2012, Frank Hatje has analyzed this actor from various perspectives.[24] Taking a gender-historical approach, Anne-Charlott Trepp depicts Beneke as a representative of a new kind of 'gentle masculinity' that emerged around 1800.[25] By no means all the volumes of his diaries are currently available in print, but the colossal extent of what is available makes selecting from the whole inevitable. The following observations – apart from the period during which Ferdinand and Caroline Beneke became acquainted in 1805/1806 – refer primarily to the particularly densely documented years from 1811 to 1816, a period in which Caroline Beneke is to be understood as an implicit reader. This period combines years of normal family life with years of crisis. At this point, Hamburg has been occupied by French troops since 1806 and has been part of the French Empire since January 1811. The city is suffering economically under the Continental Blockade.[26] Nevertheless, Beneke continues to practice law and is admitted to the bar despite his anti-Napoleonic stance. The family moves to a house on Holländischer Brook at the end of March 1812, and their social interactions are not restricted. Two daughters, Emma and Minna, are born in 1808 and 1810, respectively, and their brother, Otto Adalbert, joins them in 1812.

After the French troops retreat in the face of the advancing Russian military forces in March 1813, Beneke works on a draft of a new constitution for the Hanseatic city. However, the French soon reconquer Hamburg, and Beneke – as a major in the citizens' militia – is forced to flee the city at the end of May 1813. His family also flees to a different location – to Klein Flottbek. Caroline Beneke is not employed in the modern sense. Over the following year, Caroline and Ferdinand Beneke see each other only rarely; they communicate by letter. The children stay with Caroline, who finds accommodation in various places while her husband acts on behalf of the Hanseatic Citizens' Militia (*Hanseatische Bürgergarde*) and the Russian General Bennigsen, hoping that Hamburg will be liberated. The family is reunited in May 1814 and returns to their home in early June. Beneke is plagued by "oppressive worries about nourishment"[27] after his exile ends, but as I have already mentioned, he nevertheless succeeds in putting his professional life on a firm foot-

---

24 See most recently Hatje, "Domestic Sociability," which includes further references.
25 Trepp, "Anders als sein 'Geschlechtscharakter'"; "Männerwelten privat"; and *Sanfte Männlichkeit*.
26 See Hatje, "Aus dem Leben eines Diaristen"; see also the timeline in Beneke, *Tagebücher*, supplementary vol. 2.1, pp. 5–8.
27 Beneke, *Tagebücher*, overview for the year 1814, vol. 3.2, p. 191.

Fig. 8: The Beneke Family, daguerreotype dated 1844. Source: Museum für Hamburgische Geschichte, Hamburg, Germany

ing in February 1816 by taking up a position as secretary of the Council of Elders. The years 1811 to 1816 also lend themselves to analysis because, alongside Beneke's diary, the couple's correspondence has also been preserved, and thus we can hear Caroline Beneke's voice as well. In the crises brought on by external events, their marriage is put to the test, and topics which would otherwise hardly feature in everyday family life are addressed.

The House and Household

The Benekes' household consists of more than just the nuclear family. In addition to the married couple and their children, the household at 67 Holländischer Brook also includes Beneke's mother, Justine Dorothea, and his unmarried older sister, Regine.[28] When Beneke wants to ascribe a higher dignity to family life together, he likes to use the term 'house' (*Haus*) in different variations. Thus in the annual

---

[28] On kinship relations, see the genealogies in Beneke, *Tagebücher*, supplementary vol. 1, pp. 224–30; on cohabitation with siblings, see B. Kuhn, "Mitwohnen im 19. und frühen 20. Jahrhundert"; on bourgeois habitation, see von Saldern, "Im Hause," 151–53.

overview for 1812, he refers to "the history of our house," "our small home state," and the "members of our household federation."[29] In addition to the extended family living in the house – that is, Ferdinand's mother and sister – the household also includes "non-resident members" (*Genossen*), namely his younger brother, Johann Friedrich ('Fritz'), and Minna, a friend from Bremen, as well as the "domestics" or servants. He also refers to other families who are related to the Benekes by blood or by friendship as "houses," as if they were dynasties.[30]

Despite their ongoing financial problems, the Benekes maintain two maids or servant girls and a manservant. While the cook, the nanny, and the servants do not play a major role in the daily diary entries, they are repeatedly mentioned in passing and are also characterized in the annual reports. Thus in the column labelled 'members of the household,' Beneke mentions "our grumpy but faithful Anna" and a recently employed "girl" named Friederike. The couple also employs a "hired man" (*LohnBedienten*), the former citizen guardsman Scheiffler, who is described as "a very well-behaved and attentive man."[31] Ferdinand Beneke also lists "our old dog Werda" as a *Hausgenosse*.[32] The dog's role as a domestic actor is made clear in Beneke's comments on the animal's relationship with the children, Minna and Otto. One year later, the maid Anna has moved to another household "but is still attached to us, and also has the right to return at any time." In the meantime, Scheiffler has turned out to be an "honest but not very useful person" to Beneke.[33] Mrs. Beneke, on the other hand, is satisfied with her two new maids, Catherine and Anna II. The 'houseparents' have a personal relationship with their servants. The cook, Marie, accompanies Caroline Beneke and the children when they flee Hamburg, foregoing half a year's wages in exchange.[34] In April 1811, the housefather is best man at the wedding when his long-time servant, Joseph Gutensohn (Scheiffler's predecessor), marries the Beneke's former maid, Marie Weseloh. Gutensohn leaves the Benekes' house after the wedding and moves in with his bride, "but will probably remain my servant."[35] Their relationship with the servants no longer nec-

---

29 In the original German: "Die Geschichte unsres Hauses"; "unsren kleinen Hausstaat"; "Genoßen unsres Haus-Bundes"; Beneke, *Tagebücher*, overview for the year 1812, vol. 3.3, pp. 368–69.
30 In the original German: "auswärtigen Genoßen"; "Domestica"; "Häuser"; ibid., pp. 369–71.
31 Beneke, *Tagebücher*, overview for the year 1814, vol. 3.2, p. 192. On female servants, see Budde, "Das Dienstmädchen."
32 Beneke, *Tagebücher*, ibid., p. 192. Beneke also mentions "the good house cat" (des guten Hauskaters); see *Tagebücher*, April 1, 1812, vol. 3.1, p. 240.
33 Beneke, *Tagebücher*, overview for the year 1815, vol. 3.2, p. 336.
34 Beneke, *Tagebücher*, Caroline to Ferdinand Beneke, July 1, 1813, vol. 3.4, p. 285; July 3, 1813, vol. 3.1, p. 481.
35 Beneke, *Tagebücher*, April 21, 1811, vol. 3.1, p. 60. On the following, see June 6, 1811, vol. 3.1, p. 86.

essarily implies living under the same roof. Gutensohn opens a shop selling coffee, tea, and tobacco, but he still drops in on the Benekes in the mornings and the evenings to see whether there is any work for him to do. Less than six months after their wedding, Joseph and Marie Gutensohn are already the parents of a daughter. Beneke mentions this without any moral misgivings. Instead, Mr. Beneke notes that Mrs. Beneke is named the child's godmother at her baptism. The old patron–client relationship is still in effect, as we see when Mr. Beneke sums up his feelings on the subject: "I will always take heartfelt pleasure in these people's advancement."[36]

In the context of estate-based society, home ownership in the city was linked to burgher status and was thus only available to a privileged minority of the population. Not only were real estate laws liberalized around 1800, but the demolition of the city fortifications also opened up opportunities for new residential quarters to be constructed outside the area of the old city and facilitated the separation of professional and family life. The best residential locations were no longer found in the center, around the church and the marketplace, but rather outside the city gates, where neighborhoods consisting of villas sprang up around the country houses. As was the case for both the nobility and the peasants, owning a stately home was a sign of symbolic capital: the self-confident, free *Bürger* lived in a detached house. Beneke's diary reflects this development:

> Mr. B., a rich merchant, has only his office in the city; incidentally, he lives entirely on his immensely comfortable country estate in Horn; an elegant, beautifully situated house [and] a tasteful garden [...] complete the amenities of his life, which he enjoys in possession of an interesting wife, handsome children, and a large fortune.[37]

Beneke had grown up in a spacious, old-fashioned mansion in the center of Bremen, which – in addition to living rooms and halls – also included the *comptoir* and a packing house.[38] He would never again live in such generous surroundings. In Hamburg, he rents comparatively cheap rooms. Before moving to the house on Holländischer Brook, the family spends years living in cramped quarters with the customs officer Johann Christian Sandberg, whose low level of education offends Beneke.[39] The diary contains descriptions of the house at 67 Holländischer

---

36 Beneke, *Tagebücher*, October 17, 1811, vol. 3.1, p. 159. Gutensohn died in 1814, probably of typhus; Beneke notes with distress: "The honest soul had always clung to me so faithfully!"; see *Tagebücher*, May 17, 1814, vol. 3.2, p. 104.
37 Beneke, *Tagebücher*, January 27, 1813, vol. 3.1, p. 358.
38 Beneke, *Tagebücher*, Beneke's drawings from 1792, vol. 1.4, pp. 45–48.
39 Beneke, *Tagebücher*, November 14, 1811, vol. 3.1, p. 170; January 9, 1812, vol 3.1, p. 207; March 24, 1812, vol. 3.1, p. 235. See also Hatje, "Leben und Ansichten," 43; on the 'invention' of the rented apartment and the flat, see Wischermann, "Mythen, Macht und Mängel," 347 and 353–55.

Brook, which the Benekes move into in March 1812 and for which they pay an annual rent of 900 marks; this remains the family's home for the next several decades. The diary also includes a drawing of the house's front façade. In addition, there are photographs of the street line along the Brook before the area was razed to make way for the warehouse district (*Speicherstadt*) beginning in the 1880s.

Fig. 9: The Beneke Family Home (right-hand side), 67 Holländischer Brook, Hamburg. Source: Otto Beneke, Liederkranz zum Andenken an das alte Beneke'sche Haus, Hamburg 1849

In the context of research on the impact buildings and spaces have on social relations,[40] it is worth taking a look at the side-effects this move has on Beneke's state of mind. The new domicile – which is rented out by "Dame Herrmann," a merchant's wife – has many advantages for Beneke: "It is actually a small palace with two wings, which partly enclose a small courtyard and garden."[41] The Beneke family occupies one of the two wings, which has two floors of residential rooms and offers much more space than the old house did, not least for the children. The house on Holländischer Brook is situated on a quiet lane near the old ramparts, with a view of the Elbe valley, and it allows the family to entertain a larger number of guests. Moreover, the wealthy family of the half-English merchant William Burrowes, who occupy the other wing of the house, brings "much pleasure in

---

40 See Gieryn, "What Buildings Do". On the sociology of space generally, see Löw, *Raumsoziologie*; Conrad et al., *Wohnen*.
41 Beneke, *Tagebücher*, December 18, 1811, vol. 3.1, p. 182.

Fig. 10: The view down Holländischer Brook to the west; Beneke's house was on the left-hand side. Source: Bernd Nasner

good neighborliness."[42] The south-facing garden offers recreation. Beneke had been speculating about precisely this house for some time, but immediately prior to the move, his mood darkens. During his final "housefather round" (*Hausvatergang*) through the old residence on Bei den Mühren, he becomes "more and more melancholic." In his now "barren chamber," he sinks to his knees with a sigh and thanks God. He then bids farewell to his landlord and his erstwhile neighbors, and is driven through the city "in a heavy snowstorm" for several hours before he reaches the new house on Holländischer Brook.[43] After the first night in his new home, he is still "very disgruntled," noting: "The house almost disgusts me, and I have to fight my fearful forebodings with manly strength, and trust in God in order to remain upright."[44] Even setting up his beloved home library and arrang-

---

42 Ibid., p. 183.
43 All citations taken from Beneke, *Tagebücher*, March 24, 1812, vol. 3.1, p. 235.
44 Beneke, *Tagebücher*, March 25, 1812, vol. 3.1, pp. 236–37. Two days later, Beneke writes: "When I went home, those same anxious forebodings against the new house arose again, with which I have been suffused in these first days"; *Tagebücher*, March 27, 1812, vol. 3.1, p. 238; and again on April 3, 1812, vol. 3.1, p. 241: "I'm very disgruntled – as I generally am, since I've been in the new house".

ing his already furnished study do not immediately assuage the feeling of mistrust that overcomes Beneke in his new domicile.

Moving into the new house constitutes a minor social event. On the first day, close friends appear, and the Benekes introduce themselves to their new neighbors and to acquaintances who live nearby. On the second day, the "ladies" from the neighborhood pay a "return visit" to Caroline Beneke, her sister-in-law, and her mother-in-law, who continue to be members of the household.[45] In the days that follow, other visitors from the Benekes' wider circle of friends and relatives ring the bell. The climax of all this is a celebration on a Sunday afternoon, barely three weeks after the family had moved in. Beneke's description of this event shows that he is slowly adjusting to his new home: "From midday (until late in the evening) we finally had the greater part of my wife's family with us, which we could not do in the previous small house, the entire houses of von Axen, Westphalen, Rists, Schuchmacher." In addition to these related dynasties (*Häuser*), upper middle-class friends are also present as guests: the "Wehners, Dr. Chaufepié, and Senator Hudtwalker."[46] Beneke, a self-confessed water drinker who does not dance, emphasizes that the entertainment was offered "with an economy befitting us," namely sparingly, but still in such a way "that everyone was quite merry. The large, beautiful premises pleased everyone, and the young people even danced to the piano."[47] In the spring, the small garden behind the house makes an enthusiastic gardener out of Beneke. But at the end of May 1812, he once again notes: "Still no reconciliation with the new household gods!"[48] A good two years later, after his return from exile, Beneke would happily return to his "dear house on Holländischer Brook again," where, as he emphatically declares, "my pleasant, faithful, joyful wife received me, and where [...] a legion of joys great and small surged over me."[49]

The layout of the rooms in the new house is both personally and functionally differentiated. Not all the rooms can be heated in the winter. In order to save money, the family only lights a fire in the large hall on Christmas Eve; this room is otherwise mainly reserved for festivities. In addition to the hall, the living

---

45 Beneke, *Tagebücher*, March 26, 1812, vol. 3.1, p. 237.
46 Beneke, *Tagebücher*, April 12, 1812, vol. 3.1, p. 244. Christoph Johann Wehner was a judge in Hamburg; his wife, Sophie Dorothea, was a chief magistrate's daughter (see supplementary vol. 3, p. 247); Jean Henri de Chaufepié was a physician in Hamburg (ibid., p. 151); Johann Michael Hudtwalcker had been a senator in Hamburg since 1788 (ibid., p. 188).
47 Beneke, *Tagebücher*, April 12, 1812, vol. 3.1, p. 244.
48 In the original German: "Noch keine Versöhnung mit den neuen HausGöttern!"; Beneke, *Tagebücher*, May 20, 1812, vol. 3.1, p. 254.
49 Beneke, *Tagebücher*, June 9, 1814, vol. 3.2, pp. 119–20.

room, and the children's room, the lawyer has a study on the middle floor of residential rooms. His mother has her own room on the upper floor, and Caroline Beneke also has a room to herself. The couple's sacrosanct morning "coffee hour" usually takes place "in Line's room."[50] The function of the various rooms and parlors changes often, according to the season and the temperature. The servants probably have their chambers in the cellar, where the kitchen is also located. Furnishing the house – both when the family moves in and after they return from exile – is Caroline's task. The curtains are also important to the couple; with her sister Ida's help, Caroline puts up curtains to protect the private domestic sphere from the intrusive gaze of outsiders.[51] In actual fact, the Benekes' house is open in many respects. I will return to this point below. Nevertheless, constant visibility and its corollary, a continuous respectable staging of family life – as demonstrated in the well-known seventeenth-century paintings of Dutch bourgeois homes – is not something the Benekes desire.[52]

Why Caroline? The Complications of Finding a Partner

The central axis of the Benekes' domestic and family life is undoubtedly the marriage of Ferdinand and Caroline Beneke, née von Axen. By the time the two marry on June 8, 1807, Ferdinand is 32 years old and has already undergone a long, highly varied, mostly unhappy period of searching for a partner. One circumstance in particular complicated these matters: the years-long love triangle between Beneke, his close friend Johann Jakob Rambach – a physician who, like Beneke, does voluntary work in poor relief – and Charlotte de Chaufepié, the sister of another of Beneke's friends, the physician Jean Henri de Chaufepié.[53] In 1803, at the age of 31, Rambach married 26-year-old Charlotte. Beneke – for whom the news of his Charlotte's engagement to Rambach had already triggered a personal crisis accompanied by an alcohol-induced collapse – is invited to the wedding celebration but declines to attend. Nevertheless, the friendship between the three of them – which later extends to include Caroline as well – outlasts Beneke's disappointment. Not only his crises, but also his capacity for resilience are characteristic of Beneke as an actor – and in

---

50 Beneke, *Tagebücher*, September 18, 1812, vol. 3.1, p. 301. On the hall, see the entry for December 24, 1812, vol. 3.1, p. 340; on his mother's room, see the entry for November 3, 1812, vol. 3.1, p. 319.
51 Beneke, *Tagebücher*, March 23, 1812, vol. 3.1, p. 234; September 17, 1812, vol. 3.1, p. 300. Thanks to Frank Hatje for information on the layout of the rooms in the house.
52 On domesticity in Dutch paintings, see recently Hammer-Tugendhat, "Dutch Paintings."
53 For further details, see Trepp, *Sanfte Männlichkeit*, 117–22; see also the overview in Hatje, "Aus dem Leben eines Diaristen," 86–89.

this he virtually embodies the modern bourgeoisie.[54] As a lawyer, Beneke gets around quite a bit in Hamburg, for both professional and personal reasons. Although he is chronically short of money, he has made a name for himself. He possesses the necessary social and cultural capital to make him an object of interest for the daughters of the merchant class and the liberal professions. Over the years, his diary bears witness to several female acquaintances with whom the relationship oscillates between fleeting flirtation and hopeless adoration. In the end, what counts most for Beneke is the woman's suitability for marriage – or more precisely, the question of whether he can imagine marrying her. For him, women from lower-class backgrounds are out of the question. At this point, it is worth taking a closer look at the perspectives of both the male and the female actors as they engage in the practice of getting to know one another in the bourgeois milieu, using Ferdinand and Caroline as an example. In this sense, it is no doubt problematic that the sources we have come solely from his hand. However, the diary's daily-log style also reflects his conversations with her in a fairly straightforward manner, without reworking or revision. Moreover, we can assume that Beneke would have recited these passages to his wife later, so it seems they would have met with her approval.

What does Maria Magdalena Caroline – known as Caroline – von Axen have that her competitors – such as the merchant's daughter "Hannchen E." (Johanna Charlotte Eimbcke, born in 1788), whom Beneke mentions in parallel as "one of the best and handsomest girls" in the city[55] – do not have? From the very first mention of his future wife in the diary on June 17, 1805, Caroline's habitat and habitus play a key role. Beneke reports on an evening visit to the home of Otto von Axen – the son of a Hamburg merchant, himself also a merchant, married to a Hamburg senator's daughter. Von Axen has been active in approximately 30 public offices since 1788 and will be elected *Oberalter* in 1814. Also present that evening are the theater director Herzfeld and his wife, and Senator Jänisch's family. As Beneke briefly notes: "O. v. Axen's eldest daughter is a pretty girl. His house and garden are unique in Hamburg. I'd like to see it once during the day. Arrived home late and tired."[56] Beneke's residence on the outskirts of the city – at that time still on Bei den Mühren, east of the harbor, and later on Holländischer

---

54 Trepp (*Sanfte Männlichkeit*, 138–44) overlooks this. My interpretation differs from Trepp's view of Beneke's marriage to Caroline von Axen in important particulars; Trepp emphasizes the issue of Caroline's childishness and presumes that a consensus on the marriage existed between the von Axen parents from the beginning.
55 Beneke, *Tagebücher*, January 16, 1806, vol. 2.2, p. 205.
56 Beneke, *Tagebücher*, June 17, 1805, vol. 2.2, p. 84. On Otto von Axen, see Hatje, "Aus dem Leben eines Diaristen," 88, n. 85.

Brook am Wall – was not the best location in Hamburg. In the premodern city, poor people's quarters were often far from the center, close to the city wall. In contrast, von Axen's splendid house was in a prime residential location, on Jungfernstieg. Beneke was impressed not only by the pretty daughter, but also by the von Axens' habitat.

When they meet, Ferdinand is 30 years old, and Caroline is 16. While this constitutes a large age difference from our contemporary perspective, it was not unusual in the bourgeois milieu both before and after 1800, and it was also legally unproblematic. The Prussian General State Law stipulated that men could marry from the age of 18, and women from the age of 14.[57] Bridegrooms in the bourgeois milieu were expected to be professionally independent. They were often over 30 years old, and their brides were often 10 to 20 years younger. Nevertheless, this is indeed an asymmetrical relationship. Beneke's age is about halfway between that of Otto von Axen and that of the daughter Beneke is courting. He acts as her father's counsel (legal advisor) and maintains friendly contact with him. Beneke is educated, has lived in various places, and is established as a lawyer. In contrast, the nonstandard grammar of Caroline von Axen's letters suggests that her formal education was merely rudimentary. She is a girl from a family of means, whose path in life should lead to marriage at some point. The fact that Beneke will become her husband is not immediately apparent at their first meeting, but he soon begins to mention her in his diary more frequently, and the entries become longer and – typically for Beneke – more brooding.[58]

Here we are concerned with both the matchmaking process and Beneke's motives, which finally lead him to risk making a formal proposal of marriage. The city of Hamburg had a population of approximately 100,000 inhabitants around 1800. If we take into account that communication among the city's elite took place primarily face to face, between actors who were present in person, and not by means of media,[59] then what first becomes apparent is that the parents – especially those of the woman being courted – are involved from the beginning and are usually also

---

57 See opinioiuris.de/quelle/1623: Allgemeines Landrecht für die Preußischen Staaten, June 1, 1794, part 2, first title, "Von der Ehe" § 37. On the age difference, with further references, see Gestrich et al., *Geschichte der Familie*, 501; Wienfort, *Verliebt, Verlobt, Verheiratet*, 74–78; on professional independence, see Hettling, "Die persönliche Selbständigkeit."
58 In terms of complexity and the tendency toward self-doubt, Beneke's son Otto – whether coincidentally or not – repeated his father's matchmaking experience some 35 years later in his own premarital relationship with Marietta Banks, a daughter of the Hamburg bourgeoisie, which dragged on for years. For a psychoanalytic analysis of this situation, see Gay, *Die zarte Leidenschaft*, 11–21 and 28–36; see also Trepp, *Sanfte Männlichkeit*, 148–60.
59 On the idea of the 'Anwesenheitsgesellschaft,' see Schlögl, "Vergesellschaftung unter Anwesenden."

present. Second, the ritualized process of getting to know each other takes place in the context of semi-private or semi-public home visits (*Hausbesuche*). In this respect, the spacious garden of the von Axen house on Jungfernstieg, which Beneke noticed right from the beginning, becomes a particularly important place. These visits are public insofar as other visitors beyond the circle of immediate family members are often present. Thus, beginning in the summer of 1805, Ferdinand Beneke repeatedly turns up at the von Axen house or partakes in a "Thée parlant" in the garden.[60] Thus the matchmaking foreshadows *Buddenbrooks* in a sense. In Thomas Mann's novel, the Hamburg merchant Bendix Grünlich appears out of nowhere in the Lübeck merchant family's garden, with the clear goal of marrying Tony Buddenbrook. But apart from the locus, the milieu, and the circumstances – namely Grünlich's indebtedness, which mirrors Beneke's – there are also clear differences between the two stories. Such divergences must be considered in our history of the bourgeois family.

Otto von Axen's plans for a summer pleasure trip, on which his eldest daughter and Beneke are to accompany him, mark the beginning of the matchmaking process. These travel plans fall through, and Beneke emphasizes that this is fine with him, since he has no desire to become the object of a girl's "infatuation."[61] Nevertheless, a mutual sympathy does develop over the subsequent period. Only six weeks later, after a visit to the von Axens, the diarist confesses his "vain pleasure" that "Mademoiselle Karoline [...] took the liberty of telling me today that the intuition she had this morning, that I would come in the evening, had come true after all."[62] A mere week later, there is already talk of love or "Cupid" (*Amor*), which Beneke nevertheless cannot take seriously quite yet, due to the age of this "really quite lovely girl."[63] For this reason, at the end of October he turns down an invitation to a party at the von Axens' to celebrate the renovation of the house and Caroline's birthday. The fact that the now 31-year-old lawyer regularly goes to Jungfernstieg and begins a liaison with a 17-year-old is not a scandal in Hamburg society. Nevertheless, acquaintances approach Beneke about his relationship with Caroline, and he fears for her good reputation, the loss of which could "harm the girl [...] with others."[64] But perhaps our hesitant moralist is primarily addressing his alter ego here. Reading the diary, one gets the impression that all those involved – the von Axen parents, Beneke's mother, and Caroline herself – are always already one step ahead of Beneke. Is it a coincidence that Caro-

---

60 Beneke, *Tagebücher*, July 13, 1805, vol. 2.2, p. 96.
61 In the original German: "Schwärmereyen"; Beneke, *Tagebücher*, August 15, 1805, vol. 2.2, p. 114.
62 Beneke, *Tagebücher*, October 2, 1805, vol. 2.2, p. 155 (underlining in the original).
63 Beneke, *Tagebücher*, October 8, 1805, vol. 2.2, p. 157.
64 Beneke, *Tagebücher*, October 29, 1805, vol. 2.2, p. 167.

line's father proposes a trip for himself, his marriageable daughter, and a bachelor friend (although his wife, Luise von Axen, intervenes to forbid Caroline's participation)? When Beneke finally confides to his mother about the advanced stage of the relationship, she too has long been in the know.[65]

We need not review the matchmaking stages here *in extenso*. One important step is that unannounced visits and return visits sometimes occur between the von Axen house and the Beneke house. Beneke's straitened circumstances do not seem to be a sufficient reason for the von Axens to break of the connection with the educated gentleman and his mother and sister. Ferdinand, for his part, looks "ever deeper into pretty Karoline's eyes"[66] and asks himself more and more frequently whether he loves this young woman and wants to marry her. Until the very end, he is not sure whether she loves him. This mutually contingent interaction builds up over months – he does not know whether he is interpreting her behavior correctly, or whether she understands him correctly, and vice versa – and is complicated by the conventions that delay open declarations of love and unambiguous physical contact as long as possible. Just a few days before making his decision, Beneke notes: "Without objective cause, I am already doubting Karolinen's affection again. And reminding myself of all the happy signs over and over again doesn't help."[67] In contrast to the case of the intimate – though probably unconsummated – 'bed courtship' that took place between the peasant's son Ulrich Bräker and the innkeeper's daughter Anna Lüthold 50 years earlier, the bourgeois variant of matchmaking is almost completely incorporeal. The ideal of chastity applied not only to unmarried women, but also to unmarried men around 1800, and both were expected to postpone sexual intercourse until they were married. Beneke's diary confirms that this norm was relevant in practice as well.[68] Thus he makes a relatively explicit gesture when he clasps and holds her hand, and she allows him to do so. Things become unambiguously clear in the extended form of this interaction, when the couple retreats or is permitted to retreat "to the more remote part of the garden," where she offers him "her hand, with her face averted"; "I pressed it fervently to my breast."[69] Two days after this scene, an embrace finally takes place: Ferdinand Beneke, who loves Caroline von Axen and asks her to marry him, spontaneously and briefly – as he puts it,

---

[65] Beneke, *Tagebücher*, May 22, 1806, vol. 2.2, p. 262.
[66] Beneke, *Tagebücher*, December 6, 1805, vol. 2.2, p. 185.
[67] Beneke, *Tagebücher*, May 16, 1806, vol. 2.2, pp. 255–56. From January 1806 onward, Beneke reflects on his relationship with Caroline von Axen in detail either in a separate diary or on extra sheets of paper; see ibid., 201 and 258–62.
[68] See Trepp, "Männerwelten privat," 79–82.
[69] Beneke, *Tagebücher*, May 21, 1806, vol. 2.2, pp. 217, 258, and 260.

"hastily" – embraces her father! He exclaims, "I love your Karoline!" and leaves the house in a hurry.[70] This surprising turn of events corresponds to the logic of the matchmaking process. For in the end, everything will depend – not only legally – on her father's approval. In Foucault's terms, it is a matter of linking the older dispositive of alliance to the new dispositive of sexuality that emerged around 1800.[71]

The fact of his marriage proposal – which must still be delivered in the form of a letter, by his own hand, not by means of a messenger or an intermediary – and the expectation of Caroline's assent already make Beneke euphoric. He must break the news to his closest confidants: his mother, his sister, and Charlotte Rambach, whom he still adores. But a decision on the proposal has not yet been made. Caroline's parents hold the reins. Otto von Axen has been devoted to Beneke from the beginning. Luise von Axen is skeptical of Beneke based on her first impression of him, but later becomes his advocate. The mother presides over the matchmaking proceedings in the merchant's house. When Beneke appears with his written proposal – once again in the garden – Caroline's mother and sister, who are present, leave the couple alone as if by chance. But to Beneke's horror, 17-year-old Caroline refuses to accept his letter, with its anticipated contents. Instead she replies, "'Give the note to my mother.' 'What, your mother?' I cried in amazement. 'Yes, she knows everything.'"[72] There follows an attempt at a clarifying conversation between the suitor and the bride's mother. She tells him that her daughter is "certainly not averse" to him, but at the same time "surprised, and in great anguish of heart." When asked why he had not first informed her and her husband – that is, the bride's parents – before proposing, Beneke parries laconically with a reference to his honor. His fear that Caroline von Axen is "already promised to someone else," however, proves to be unfounded. Taken together, this conversation shows that around 1800, there were indeed several different ways to propose marriage, and various practices involved in the process. No clarifying conversation takes place between Ferdinand and Caroline beforehand. Beneke is certainly encouraged by Mrs. von Axen's ambiguous response, but she does address one matter unambiguously: "She must raise an honest concern with me: whether I would be able to carry them both – Caroline, and my mother and sister – through the world re-

---

70 Beneke, *Tagebücher*, May 23, 1806, vol. 2.2, p. 264.
71 Foucault, *Sexualität und Wahrheit 1*, 105–8.
72 Beneke, *Tagebücher*, May 23, 1806, vol. 2.2, p. 263. On the wife's role as hostess, see Tolkemitt, "Knotenpunkte."

spectably?"[73] Mr. von Axen would also like to speak to him about the question of respectable maintenance. Beneke immediately agrees. Coincidentally, at that moment Mr. von Axen enters the house, and the aforementioned manly embrace takes place.

At this decisive stage of the marriage negotiations, the bride plays the role of a supporting actress. However, it is clear that her parents make their consent contingent upon their daughter's agreement. Therefore we cannot speak of an arranged marriage in this case. Whether they will give their consent, however, remains uncertain at this point. A few days later, Mr. von Axen and Mr. Beneke meet. It is up to the bride's father to address the financial issues over a pipe, which he offers to the nervous suitor. Mrs. von Axen leaves the scene, and Caroline is not present. According to Beneke's account, Otto von Axen wastes no time coming to the essential point. As Beneke puts it, he says:

> I was dear to him – only he wished to know my financial circumstances. I related them en deux phrases: increasing income, enough already to feed a whole family decently and to save a remainder annually, a completely furnished house, but on the other hand still debts, the gradual amortization of which would depend solely upon me and had already begun 2 years ago.[74]

Beneke explains that he "would wish to have Karoline without any further gift" – that is, that he (unlike Thomas Mann's character Grünlich) is not seeking a dowry from the bride's parents. They come closer to an understanding. Unlike his wife, von Axen finds a cohabitation with Beneke's esteemed mother and sister desirable "for the sake of Karoline's happiness." The material circumstances and the potential bride's young age, however, remain problematic. According to Beneke, the merchant would like "us to wait a few more years, so that I could first discharge my debts, and then Karoline would be 20 years old." Beneke also remains uncertain about the opinion of the young woman herself, who is not involved, but who is actually at issue: "But then I pressed to know Karoline's inclination." Her father insists that she will follow his direction, and he "said she would explain to me [Beneke] what he said to her, that she was permitted to explain it; therefore he [von Axen] would first have to speak with her." Beneke is welcome to stay until the evening. The father quits the scene and leaves the suitor in the garden, where he has to converse with a lady who happens to be present. Mrs. von Axen then manages to situate the couple alone in the garden. Here Caroline von Axen and Ferdinand Ben-

---

73 All citations taken from Beneke, *Tagebücher*, ibid., 263–64. (underlining in the original). On Beneke's completely different approach in the case of Meta von Elking, see Trepp, *Sanfte Männlichkeit*, 111–15.
74 Beneke, *Tagebücher*, May 28, 1806, vol. 2.2, p. 268.

eke finally confess their love to each other, unequivocally and very emotionally – with a "handshake."[75]

But it is not over yet. Since the father's approval is still pending, the von Axen family shares a tense evening meal with Caroline's suitor. Afterwards they again go out into the garden, where it emerges that Mrs. von Axen has had enough of the spectacle: "What is the point of this tension? Is this how you pass the most beautiful moments of your life?" Relieved, the couple then retreats "into the garden's dark corridors," where the two finally arrive at a sustained "wordless embrace." When they return to the family circle, everyone involved embraces. For Beneke, the matter has now reached its happy conclusion, but it is not yet fully settled. Once again, Mrs. von Axen intervenes. Turning to her husband, she exclaims: "'I hear this tension is to endure for years,' and then she harangued her husband for his concerns, finding it unjust that, in view of my acknowledged ability to support a woman, further consideration should be given to my debts, etc. Mr. v. A. was quite embarrassed." The bride's father, whose consent is required by law, then gives up his resistance, but still wants to "conceal" his daughter's engagement.[76] But in the face-to-face society of the Hanseatic elite, where it is customary for single people to seek advice from friends on matters of love and marriage, the news is unstoppable. One year later, the wedding takes place.

If we view this matchmaking procedure in the elite bourgeois milieu not simply as a love story, but as a negotiation, then three aspects of this process are noteworthy: first, the intensive involvement of the families, especially the bride's parents, without whose consent nothing will happen; second, the expectation that the potential husband will be able to provide for his wife and future children in a manner befitting his class; third, the prominent role played by the bride's mother, who – as an initiate into the ritual and a sometime confidant of her daughter – holds the reins in her hand and prevails over the hesitant father. The suitor – like Ulrich Bräker 50 years earlier – can also count on his own mother's approving collusion.

Yet the question remains: What makes Caroline von Axen not only attractive, but also a serious marriage candidate in Ferdinand Beneke's eyes? Why is she the one among all the Hamburg merchants' daughters who ultimately becomes the object of his suit? The case of the von Axens and the Benekes underscores the fact that it is not plausible to draw a clear line between love marriages and marriages

---

75 All citations taken from ibid., pp. 268–69. On dowries, see the brief overview in Wienfort, *Verliebt, Verlobt, Verheiratet*, 84–87.
76 All citations taken from pp. 269–71. On the legal situation, see opinioiuris.de/quelle/1623: Allgemeines Landrecht für die Preußischen Staaten, June 1, 1794, part 2, first title, "Von der Ehe," § 45. On the following, see Trepp, *Sanfte Männlichkeit*, 110.

of convenience, nor to understand the generally increasing endogamy in matters of marriage around 1800 as the opposite of love.[77] Caroline von Axen's person is necessarily linked to her habitat, her social context, but Ferdinand Beneke is by no means primarily concerned with securing his place among Hamburg's elite, or with rehabilitating his finances by means of a dowry. The fact that it is all about the emotion understood as love in Ferdinand's case – an emotion which ranks so highly in the 'horizon of bourgeois values' due to sensibility, *Sturm und Drang*, and Romanticism – is demonstrated not only by his various remarks on the subject, but also by the fact that he "had a dream about Caroline, just as I used to have about Charlotte."[78] In addition, in January 1806 he begins to keep an extra diary about his relationship with Caroline, alongside his regular diary. These private remarks are thus privatized to a greater extent and – as is characteristic of that communication known as love – self-referentially sealed off from external observers.[79] The path to marriage is not mapped out from the beginning, but for both of them a perspective on life together develops out of their initial playfulness. This game, which lasts for months, is actually quite serious, and young Caroline proves to be an equal partner, one who also offers resistance: "she is mischievous, witty, and enjoys a dispute, like a young scholar, and whoever marries her will get eternal war in the house."[80] Above all, it is this challenging "disputatiousness," coupled with her penchant for ironic "paradoxes,"[81] that appeals to Beneke. In addition, the unavoidable moral standard, the genuinely bourgeois pattern of thought according to which physical satisfaction must be deferred,[82] opens up more possibilities for the woman being courted than for the proactive man. The 17-year-old deliberately takes advantage of this leeway. A month before the engagement – half fascinated, half despairing – Beneke notes the following interaction: "I held out my hand to her as I walked away. Teasingly, I held her hand for a while."

---

77 Cf. Borscheid, "Geld und Liebe"; similarly, with regard to Beneke, see Böth, "'Ich handele,'" 267–68. On "social endogamy" among the bourgeoisie in the process of selecting a partner, see Gestrich et al., *Geschichte der Familie*, 502; Wienfort, *Verliebt, Verlobt, Verheiratet*, 49–52; on the topic in general, see Johnson and Sabean, *Sibling Relations*.
78 Beneke, *Tagebücher*, February 10, 1806, vol. 2.2, p. 214. On the concept of the love marriage around 1800, see Trepp, "Männerwelten privat," 39–41; Trepp, "Emotion und bürgerliche Sinnstiftung"; but cf. R. Habermas, "Spielerische Liebe."
79 Beneke, *Tagebücher*, see the indented entries beginning on January 1, 1806, vol. 2.2, p. 201. On the specifics of love as a form of communication, see Luhmann, *Liebe als Passion*, 177–78; Reckwitz, *Das hybride Subjekt*, 118 and 224–30.
80 Beneke, *Tagebücher*, January 12, 1806, vol. 2.2, p. 204. On play as an aspect of courtship behavior, see R. Habermas, "Spielerische Liebe."
81 Beneke, *Tagebücher*, April 15, 1806, vol. 2.2, p. 240.
82 Cf. Bänziger, *Die Moderne als Erlebnis*, 17.

She asks: "What's the point?" He replies: "Why don't you squeeze my hand once, Karoline?" She responds: "Nevermore." He replies: "What? Do friends not shake hands?" She answers: "When your birthday comes around."[83] Despite their differences in age and experience, Caroline von Axen is not simply an object condemned to passivity right from the start.

Beneke the good *Bürger* does not simply fall for the young woman's looks, but also for her thoroughly self-confident habitus: "much grace in her whole attitude, that's her, as she lives and breathes."[84] The 'social made body' (Bourdieu) that transcends class is what distinguishes her from other desirable women. Ferdinand desires a companion and a friend. The concept of friendship is typical of bourgeois marriage, as Reckwitz also recognizes; moreover, it connects to premodern notions of companionship. This implies certain qualities, which Beneke searches for and finds in Caroline's self-presentation. For the educated man, these include her spirit and her knowledge of literature. Thus it is explicitly "Karolinen's spirit" that impresses him, in comparison to the "pure cheerfulness" of her competitor, Hannchen E. She reads Jean Paul, whom he admires, although her parents do not appreciate this particular author. She can draw like him and takes an interest in history as well.[85] They clearly emerge not only as lovers, but also as an educated couple over the course of their acquaintance. Beneke also recognizes a future mother and hostess in this young woman. He observes how she plays with her younger siblings and notes enthusiastically: "On her mother's birthday, she played the hostess. And how! So attentive, so joyfully pleasing, so thoroughly, heartily happy."[86] At 17 years old, Caroline promises to become a good *Bürgerin*.

Marriage Beyond Stereotypes

The Benekes' marriage offers a wellspring from which to challenge stereotypical ideas about the bourgeois nineteenth century. In what follows, we will pay partic-

---

83 Beneke, *Tagebücher*, April 29, 1806, vol. 2.2, p. 246. In this context, Beneke refers to his beloved as "the little witch" (die kleine Hexe); ibid. Yet he has long been "deucedly devoted" to her; see the entry for March 12, 1806, vol. 2.2, p. 227.
84 In the original German: "viel Grazie in der Haltung des Ganzen, das ist sie, wie sie leibt und lebt"; Beneke, *Tagebücher*, April 29, 1806, vol. 2.2, p. 246.
85 Beneke, *Tagebücher*, January 16, 1806, vol. 2.2, p. 206 (underlining in the original). See also the entries for January 12, 1806, p. 204; March 28, 1806, p. 232; February 19, 1806, pp. 216–217. On bourgeois marriage as a "friendship relationship," see Reckwitz, *Das hybride Subjekt*, 118.
86 Beneke, *Tagebücher*, January 8, 1806, vol. 2.2, p. 202; see also the entry for January 12, 1806, p. 204.

ular attention to the normal years of the marriage – between January 1811 and May 1813, and then between June and December 1814 – as well as the year in which the couple was separated due to the war and communicated regularly by letter, from late May 1813 to late May 1814. Our focus is on practices within and ideas about marriage. Overall, both the diary and the letters show that in this case, we cannot speak of separate spheres or of fixed 'gender characters.'[87] As a lawyer, Beneke receives his clients at home, while his wife and children are in the adjoining rooms. He is undoubtedly a professional man, but this adjective describes only one aspect of his complex personality. In the same way, he is a husband and a family man for whom being at home with his family is of great importance. As a prototype, Beneke the actor fits the pattern of both 'male domesticity' common among the English middle class and the so-called 'men at home.'[88]

What does everyday domesticity look like for the Benekes in concrete terms? After the family returns to the house on Holländischer Brook in Hamburg, Beneke – who strives for structure in life – assigns himself an ideal "daily schedule": get up a 7 o'clock, "coffee and family hour" until 9 o'clock, "business hours" from 9 to 3 o'clock (this includes receiving clients and keeping appointments at court, the stock exchange, and various offices), a walk or visits from 3 to 4 o'clock (either alone or with his wife), lunch and "family time together" from 4 to 6 o'clock, more "walks" or visits from 6 to 7 o'clock, evening work at the lectern until 10 o'clock, "with Karoline" from 10 to 11 o'clock, and "then to bed."[89] Of course reality intrudes, and deviations from this norm occur. Yet the basic structure of his days is quite consistent. Throughout the day, there are three fixed family meeting times, each of which is associated with drinks or meals. Of particular importance for the couple are the leisure hours spent reading: the 'reading morning' together with coffee, and the 'reading evening' with tea. Also worth noting are those aspects of domestic life that Beneke does not mention because they do not play a role for him. This bourgeois actor has nothing to do with household chores in the narrow sense of the term – shopping, food preparation, washing, and so on. Moreover, this ideal schedule does not reveal how often visitors come to the house. Nevertheless, on Monday, February 24, 1812, for example, the lawyer notes "20 to 30 client visits."[90] Often the (late) evening time together is not a private hour with his wife, but

---

[87] See Vickery, "Golden Age of Separate Spheres?" for a critique of these two classic theses in research on gender; see also Shoemaker, *Gender in English Society*; on the many facets of everyday bourgeois married life, see Trepp, *Sanfte Männlichkeit*; R. Habermas, *Frauen und Männer.*
[88] Tosh, *A Man's Place*; Sarti, "Men at Home."
[89] Beneke, *Tagebücher,* June 27, 1814, vol. 3.2, pp. 131–32. See also Hatje, "Aus dem Leben eines Diaristen," 98–99.
[90] Beneke, *Tagebücher,* February 24, 1812, vol. 3.2, p. 227.

rather a 'tea time' at which friends may drop in. Contrary to the assumptions often made in sociological research on the family, this middle-class couple's home and family life are not simply a private space for relaxation and retreat from the stress of public life.[91] Indeed, what is striking is the multifunctionality of the domestic sphere, which includes various types of activities. In addition to the lawyer's 'home office' and his wife's housekeeping duties, we should again mention the couple's representational work at social events as well as the invitations they give and receive. However, as in the case of the Bernese patrician Henriette Stettler-Herport, Beneke also articulates a desire for leisure and privacy as a couple: namely the longing "for domestic norms and peace, for a quiet morning hour with Line, for that sweet dual solitude that adheres in such togetherness!"[92]

We learn relatively little about Mrs. Beneke's daily work from her husband's diary. Prior to his return in June 1814, he notes: "Karoline prevails creatively in our house at Holl[ändischer] Brook." In other words, "Karoline manages" the house and household.[93] When visitors are formally invited, as the "housewife" it falls to her to entertain the guests.[94] Furnishing the house and daily housekeeping duties are her *métier*. Beneke reports hardly anything about the division of labor between Caroline Beneke, her mother-in-law, her sister-in-law, and the maids. The repudiation of the concept of 'separate spheres' in general should not obscure the fact that there were indeed gender-specific functions and divisions of labor in the bourgeois household. Beneke does not perceive his wife as his work partner, nor as the head of a household of ten or more people, but rather as a friend, a soulmate, and the "faithful comrade of my very being!"[95]

Where and how is this marriage lived out in practice? In addition to raising children and appearing together at social events, morning and evening reading are centrally important to this educated couple. There is something sacred about this ritualized time spent reading together at the beginning and the end of the day. In this respect, 17-year-old Caroline's penchant for Jean Paul can be understood as a signpost along the path to an educated bourgeois marriage. This domes-

---

91 On the "tension-balancing function" of the modern family, see Nave-Herz, "Unkenrufe," 994, and "Der Wandel der Familie," 17.
92 Beneke, *Tagebücher*, May 25, 1814, vol. 3.2, p. 110.
93 Beneke, *Tagebücher*, June 2 and 3, 1814, vol. 3.2, p. 117. On the distinction between different categories of domestic work, see Whittle, "A Critique of Approaches to 'Domestic Work,'" 38; Zucca Micheletto, "Paid and Unpaid Work"; see also Sarti et al., *What is Work?*.
94 Beneke, *Tagebücher*, September 30, 1811, vol. 3.1, p. 150; see also the entry for February 5, 1811, p. 31.
95 In the original German: "treue Genoßin meines Wesens!"; Beneke, *Tagebücher*, June 6, 1813, vol. 3.1, p. 454.

tic exchange over literature, history, and political events is definitely more important than attending the theater or concerts together.[96] German-language fiction dominates the agenda during these leisure hours, though not exclusively: Beneke also notes a "reading evening with Caroline – Shakespeare."[97] When the family moves into the house on Holländischer Brook, their home library numbers 400–500 volumes. This collection, which had been growing since Beneke's student days, includes not only fiction, but also books on administration and accounting, the Prussian General State Law, historical works, geographical texts, and maps. With gender in view, it is interesting that "my wife's still small but rather neat library" has a different orientation. According to Beneke, it contains "belles lettres, educational and economic" works.[98] The large house certainly offers Beneke the opportunity to withdraw from the family, even on Sundays and holidays: "With the family until 11 o'clock. Then in my study until 3:30 – [I did] not go out, but [was] in the small garden behind the house, where I sometimes go to escape the machine of civic life and eavesdrop on nature's course."[99] The room dedicated to work and study is the typical abode of the educated bourgeois father, who is simultaneously physically present in and attentively absent from the house. Friedrich Schiller had an entire floor of his house in Jena to himself, which was physically separated from the floor his family occupied and from the servants' rooms on the ground floor.[100]

Yet that which is essential to our everyday life often comes into focus only once we can no longer take it for granted. This happens to the Benekes in May 1813, when Hamburg is bombarded and subsequently captured by French military forces, and the family is separated for approximately one year. After a cannonball hits the neighboring house, Caroline Beneke moves to Nienstedten an der Elbe to live with her children, who had already been sent there for their own safety. Her husband remains at the house on Holländischer Brook for the time being, and she visits him. Ultimately, few days after one of these visits, he also leaves the city. At that time, he reflects on his relationship with his wife: "These serious moments are of great value for our eternal love. Karoline often thinks differently than I do; no matter how much her ideas contradict mine, I still hear her out, and consider how

---

[96] Beneke is often dissatisfied after visits to the theater: "silly, actually even bad stuff"; see *Tagebücher*, October 26, 1812, vol. 3.1, p. 315.
[97] Beneke, *Tagebücher*, August 17, 1811, vol. 3.1, p. 123.
[98] Beneke, *Tagebücher*, March 27, 1812, vol. 3.2, p. 238; 'economic' is probably used in the older sense of the word here, meaning: housekeeping.
[99] Beneke, *Tagebücher*, May 31, 1812, vol. 3.1, p. 258.
[100] See www.klassik-stiftung.de/schillers-wohnhaus/.

the old Germans heeded the words of wise and noble women."[101] The nationalism which was on the rise during the Napoleonic Wars, which also grips Beneke and provokes his reference to "the old Germans" here, is of no further interest to us. Once again, this passage illuminates his esteem for his wife as an intellectually independent partner capable of contradicting him.

The year of separation and exile turns out to pose many challenges for the Benekes – some foreseeable, and some unexpected. While in Mecklenburg, Beneke seeks to make friends with other Hamburg citizens who had fled, plans the re-establishment of the Hanseatic Citizens' Militia, and ultimately becomes adjutant to the Russian general Bennigsen, who lays siege to Hamburg. For our citizen of Hamburg and his comrades in arms, this is certainly a war of liberation. Caroline Beneke and her children initially find accommodation in the country house belonging to their Hamburg neighbors the Burrowes, which is located in Nienstedten, near Klein Flottbek. In January 1814, she and the children move to Lübeck, where Beneke is also staying at the time. In March, however, he moves to Benningsen's headquarters in Pinneberg. The family would not be reunited until May 1814, shortly before the French troops leave Hamburg. For most of this period the couple corresponds by mail, at times exchanging letters every other day or even daily.

The circumstances of their separation and the medium of letters once again open up new perspectives on bourgeois marriage and family. Despite their somewhat idiosyncratic syntax, Caroline Beneke's letters bespeak an eloquent partner. She informs, advises, reassures, challenges, makes suggestions, and contradicts. Both the man and the woman like to complain once in a while; both need consolation, and both also offer it. The couple's 'sayings' also include confessions of love, longing, and fidelity. In view of the complete uncertainty of their situation as far as the future is concerned – after all, there is a war going on – the letters also serve to exchange news about the military situation in Hamburg and in Europe more generally during the final phase of the Napoleonic Wars. Not only he, but also she comments on politics: "In my opinion the armistice is not good, and probably not good for us at all, but I think it will be useful on the whole."[102] She doubts whether "Bonaparte would be able to subjugate the whole of Germany," in which case men and women would once again be "slaves with free spirits."[103] The children's well-being is also a recurring theme. In 1813, Caroline has with her 5-year-old Emma, 3-year-old Minna, and Otto Adalbert, who is just under 1

---

101 Beneke, *Tagebücher*, May 26, 1813, vol. 3.1, p. 440.
102 Beneke, *Tagebücher*, Caroline to Ferdinand Beneke, June 11, 1813, vol. 3.4, p. 207.
103 *Tagebücher*, Caroline to Ferdinand Beneke, June 12, 1813, vol. 3.4, p. 214.

year old. The maid Anna had accompanied them when they fled; nevertheless, the immense amount of care work required of the mother is evident in her letters.

The correspondence makes it clear that while the spouses define themselves and their relationship by the time they spend reading together, the children represent the family's center of gravity. The children's illnesses are a constant topic: the father asks worried questions, and the mother offers reassuring answers. These exchanges read something like this: the father writes to the mother: "The dear children's illness worries me very much. If only you would soon put me at ease! But do tell the truth [...]. I press you with a fervent heart, which longs, oh! how fiercely for you. Kiss my dear, dear children!" The mother responds: "On my honor, be assured that Minna and the children are most certainly, truly quite well."[104] The children's development is meticulously noted, character traits are listed, and prognoses are made. This applies, for example, to their youngest child and first son, who is teething and learning to walk. As Caroline Beneke reports, somewhat ambivalently:

> Now our Otto will probably not conform to any of my ideals, but you shall see that he will become a capable human being, you shall see that he will annoy some people with his defiant, even bold behavior; he will become quite reasonable; strangely his <u>temperament</u> does not yet express itself; with the girls it was much earlier. I think he will truly become quite similar to you inwardly, only I think he will not be as calm, as gentle, as you are in essence.[105]

The father's diary contains regular observations on the children's mental and physical development.[106] When it comes to children, the bourgeois family is both an emotional community and a developmental project. Caroline promises Ferdinand that she will "awaken this slumbering seed" – that is, the children's capacity for love – and that "nurturing this heavenly plant shall be my most cherished concern."[107] Thus the Benekes' distribution of roles does not really correspond to the stereotype of the strict father, who insists on reason and discipline, and the sensitive, emotional mother. Beneke's children spend more time with their mother than with their father, even in normal years. Nevertheless, both father

---

104 Beneke, *Tagebücher*, Ferdinand to Caroline Beneke, March 25, 1814, vol. 3.5, p. 323; Caroline to Ferdinand Beneke, March 31, 1814, vol. 3.5, p. 408.
105 Beneke, *Tagebücher*, Caroline to Ferdinand Beneke, March 18, 1814, vol. 3.5, p. 251 (underlining in the original).
106 See, for example, Beneke, *Tagebücher*, June 20, 1811, vol. 3.1, p. 94; June 30, 1811, p. 102; July 7–11, 1811, pp. 108–10.
107 Beneke, *Tagebücher*, Caroline to Ferdinand Beneke, July 28, 1813, vol. 3.4, p. 362.

and mother play with the children in a meadow full of haystacks in the summer.[108] When Beneke is "a little bored" at a winter party with "Count Westphalen at the Burrowes' house," he prefers "to mingle with the children after the meal, playing Blind Man's Bluff etc.," rather than conversing with the adults.[109] Before the children return to the house on Holländischer Brook in 1814, it is their father who sets up their table and arranges their toys, full of memories and "melancholy tears."[110]

The family's fragile financial situation is also an important issue in the year in which they flee Hamburg. The Benekes have no secure income at this time. Apparently accounting and financial management are not among Ferdinand's strengths. Thus his wife – with the support of their friend, the merchant Johann Andreas Schlingemann – repeatedly urges him to list his outstanding invoices and send them to his clients in order to collect money.[111] One of the issues here is that Hamburg's citizens are hard up in monetary terms due to both the Continental Blockade and the so-called contribution imposed by the French administration. In consultation with her father, Caroline Beneke suggests renting out the house on Holländischer Brook.[112] Since it is unclear when or whether the family will be able to return to Hamburg, she also advises her husband to reorient himself professionally and consider a career in the Prussian civil service or at a university.[113] Their financial situation improves when some of Beneke's clients – after receiving invoices – actually pay their debts to him, which only encourages his wife, who is 14 years younger, to urge him again: "Just don't forget to get your invoices in order right away!"[114] On Schlingemann's advice, it is Caroline who signs the invoices. In this way, she also receives the money, which she uses to pay off their debts, build up a reserve, and contribute toward her mother-in-law's living expenses. Unfortu-

---

108 Beneke, *Tagebücher*, July 4, 1811, vol. 3.1, p. 106. See also Hausen, "Die Polarisierung der Geschlechtscharaktere," 368; on the division of roles in bringing up children, see Budde, *Auf dem Weg ins Bürgerleben*, 151–92.
109 Beneke, *Tagebücher*, February 21, 1813, vol. 3.1, p. 368.
110 Beneke, *Tagebücher*, June 11, 1814, vol. 3.2, pp. 120–21.
111 Beneke, *Tagebücher*, Caroline to Ferdinand Beneke, June 11, 1813, vol. 3.4, p. 206; June 16, 1813, p. 215; Johann Andreas Schlingemann to Beneke, June 17, 1813, vol. 3.4, p. 232.
112 Beneke, *Tagebücher*, Caroline to Ferdinand Beneke, June 3 and 4, 1813, vol. 3.4, pp. 171–72 and 177.
113 Beneke, *Tagebücher*, Caroline to Ferdinand Beneke June 3 and 4, 1813, vol. 3.4, p. 179; June 14, 1813, p. 219.
114 Beneke, *Tagebücher*, Caroline to Ferdinand Beneke, July 5 and 6, 1813, vol. 3.4, p. 294; see also Schlingemann to Beneke, July 6, 1813, vol. 3.4, p. 295; Otto von Axen to Beneke, July 6, 1813, vol. 3.4, p. 297.

nately his reaction to her management and his answer to her brief question: "Is it alright?" have not been preserved.[115]

The final throes of the crisis facing estate-based society around 1800, brought on by the Enlightenment and the French Revolution, and the war-induced crisis facing the Beneke family from 1813 onward offer the opportunity to rethink a few things and to try out some new approaches. Caroline dislikes the way in which the rich refugees from Hamburg present themselves in Lübeck, which contrasts with the great need in which many other people find themselves. She initially avoids balls because, as she argues, "as long as [...] there is still so much misery in the city, I don't like to see the luxury of the rich."[116] For this reason Ferdinand describes the daughter of the House of Axen as stuck up. Even more sensitive is the fact that exile also entails new social encounters for the children. Caroline Beneke reports on her quarters in Klein Flottbek, writing that they constitute a sort of "Cossack inn"(*Cosacken Wirthschaft*) in that every day "approximately 20 peasants from the Landwehr" come to the house, bringing noise and dirt with them. She explains to her husband: "Your children, especially Emma, make themselves so familiar with the children of these peasants; she has no concept at all of the difference between the estates, and I truly do not know whether it would be right for me to teach her anything about it."[117] Such particular considerations correspond to the early liberal utopian vision of a 'classless civil society,' which would transcend the boundaries between the old estates.

Vulnerable Love and Volatile 'Gender Characters'

Despite her criticism of balls and luxury, Caroline Beneke eventually accepts an invitation to a dance in Lübeck, which subsequently puts her marriage to the test and also sheds light on relationships between the sexes after 1800. At the same time, this situation uncovers a problem inherent in the love marriage, the fragility of which increases due to the constant invocation of love, regardless of the authenticity of the feeling, which is difficult to assess. Caroline Beneke's dance partner in

---

115 Beneke, *Tagebücher*, Caroline to Ferdinand Beneke, July 20, 1813, vol. 3.4, p. 354.
116 Beneke, *Tagebücher*, Caroline to Ferdinand Beneke, March 5, 1814, vol. 3.5, p. 215. On the following, see Ferdinand to Caroline Beneke, March 12, 1814, p. 221. Caroline had already reported from Lübeck on an event with merchants and officers on March 1, 1814: "The company this evening was outrageously boring[;] you cannot imagine the nature of such a company[; they] always speak Low German and what!?"; ibid., March 1, 1814, vol. 3.5, p. 184.
117 Beneke, *Tagebücher*, Caroline to Ferdinand Beneke, June 17, 1813, vol. 3.4, p. 235. On the following, see Gall, *Stadt und Bürgertum*, 27.

Lübeck is 23-year-old Carl Ludwig Roeck, a lawyer and volunteer guardsman, who in the same year will become secretary to the Senate and later mayor of Lübeck. Beneke, who – unlike his rival – dislikes dancing, had casually mentioned Roeck in his diary a year before as a "handsome young man."[118] After they get to know each other at the dance, an enduring attachment develops between Mrs. Beneke and "young Roeck."[119] They meet regularly – as Caroline candidly reports to Ferdinand in her letters – for walks or at social gatherings at Roeck's home. He recites his own poems to the accompaniment of a guitar, and this moves Caroline – a good year-and-a-half older than he is – to tears. He escorts her home in the evening, and in a particularly striking turn, they read to each other from literary works. As it happens, Roeck, like Caroline and her husband, appreciates the works of Jean Paul and de la Motte Fouqué. Caroline's husband reacts calmly at first, but becomes irritable after only two weeks. He accuses his wife of trying to make him "jealous" by spending time with Roeck and other men in Lübeck.[120] A week later, he refers to Roeck as "your lover."[121] Caroline makes repeated attempts to explain her relationship with Roeck to her beloved Ferdinand, but she does not mince words. She refers to Roeck as "a sweet man" whom "I am quite fond of," a "quite dear friend" for whom she feels a "truly motherly love" and whose "guardian angel" she desires to be.[122] Ferdinand vacillates between accepting this relationship and objecting to it in aggrieved terms. Another factor also plays a role in the couple's communication on this subject: as Caroline knows, Ferdinand himself often casts an admiring eye over "pretty girls" in exile in Mecklenburg, or pours out his heart to someone he adores, as his diary also documents.[123] Thus she can easily counter his jealousy with reference to "your polygamy,"[124] and she makes no effort to end the relationship with Roeck.

This episode concerns not only a flirtation, but also a testing of gender norms – specifically the male attempt at paternalization and the purposeful deployment

---

118 Beneke, *Tagebücher*, April 10, 1813, vol. 3.1, p. 402; see also November 4, 1813, vol. 3.1, p. 621. As Beneke notes regarding a ball at the Hamburg stock exchange: "My Linchen amused herself with a few dances"; ibid., April 6, 1813, vol. 3.1, p. 399.
119 Beneke, *Tagebücher*, Caroline to Ferdinand Beneke, March 5, 1814, vol. 3.5, p. 216.
120 Beneke,*Tagebücher*, Ferdinand to Caroline Beneke, March 16, 1814, vol. 3.5, p. 243; see also ibid., March 14, 1814, pp. 241–42.
121 Beneke, *Tagebücher*, Ferdinand to Caroline Beneke, March 22, 1814, vol. 3.5, p. 273.
122 Beneke, *Tagebücher*, Caroline to Ferdinand Beneke, March 8, 1814, vol. 3.5, p. 219; March 13, 1814, p. 228; March 18, 1814, p. 251; March 26, 1814, p. 366; April 13, 1814, p. 470.
123 Beneke, *Tagebücher*, July 2, 1813, vol. 3.1, p. 480; see also the entries for August 9, 1813, p. 521; August 25, 1813, p. 532.
124 In the original German: "deine Vielweiberei"; Beneke, *Tagebücher*, Caroline to Ferdinand Beneke, March 8, 1814, vol. 3.5, p. 219.

of female obstinacy (*Eigensinn*). For example, Mr. Beneke repeatedly urges his wife to adhere to a regular daily routine and go to bed early. She simply refuses to take this advice to heart and prefers to write her letters – a conspicuously large number of which mention her new friend – late in the evening, always marking them with the time.[125] She also reacts irritably, and sometimes pointedly, to his jealousy of a man 16 years his junior. In the elaborate letter-writing culture of the time, it constitutes an affront when she addresses him as "My good old man" or closes with a simple "Adieu, old man," after mentioning Roeck.[126] She lets Roeck read texts and letters from Ferdinand. It must have been particularly hurtful for the husband and father to learn, in a letter from his wife shortly before the family returned to Hamburg, that his 4-year-old daughter Minna has written a letter to his rival and "instructed him to take care of me, to rent a pleasant apartment for me outside the gate, at her expense [...] and in general, R[oeck] should attend to my circumstances. Isn't she a true angel?"[127] For Ferdinand Beneke, who in the meantime has come to terms with the young man's presence in his wife's life, this crosses a line. Shortly before returning to family life in Hamburg, he insists upon male dominance and female obedience. While he believes that her "independent existence" in exile in Lübeck has done her good, "of course I will have to do something about it once I get my wife, who has been spoiled by having things her own way, back under my control, where she must obediently submit and bend her will to that of her lord and husband."[128] He flanks this announcement with the remark that he has just reencountered his old flame, Sophia Emilia von Ehrenstein – who, by the way, has invited his wife to visit as well – and sends his smug greetings to Roeck. Two days later, however, he follows up with a contrite declaration of love to Caroline, his "beloved!"[129] And how does Caroline Beneke react? She flatly rejects the invitation from the aristocratic lady, the wife of a landowner – alluding to bourgeois criticism of the aristocracy – because "I don't like her; she's a bad mother." In all other respects, however, she gives in, thus accepting the gender

---

125 Beneke, *Tagebücher*, Ferdinand to Caroline Beneke, March 14, 1814, vol. 3.5, p. 241: "In your letter, dear beloved, I still find that you go to bed so late. Since you cannot do the opposite out of love for me, at least do not let me read about it in the future".
126 Beneke, *Tagebücher*, Caroline to Ferdinand Beneke, March 21, 1814, vol. 3.5, p. 315; March 18, 1814, p. 252.
127 Beneke, *Tagebücher*, Caroline to Ferdinand Beneke, April 18, 1814 ("Abends spädt"), vol. 3.5, pp. 489–90.
128 In the original German: "selbstständige Seyn"; "freilich werde ich zu thun bekommen, wenn ich nun die durch eignes Wollen verwöhnte Gemalin erst wieder unter meine Zucht bekomme, wo sie ihren Willen gehorsamlich unter den ihres Herrn, und Gemahls fügen, u. beugen muß"; Beneke, *Tagebücher*, Ferdinand to Caroline Beneke, April 24, 1814, vol. 3.5, p. 493.
129 Beneke, *Tagebücher*, Ferdinand to Caroline Beneke, April 27, 1814, vol. 3.5, p. 503.

hierarchy in her marriage. She has indeed "enjoyed" her "freedom," but her life in Lübeck has not corresponded to "a woman's nature": "No no, my Ferdinand, it will do me good, especially as it will calm me to return to my narrower domestic boundaries."[130] The escalation of their dispute over Caroline's freedom reads like an echo of the hierarchical gender ideas among liberals at the time, for whom demands for women's legal equality represented a threat to the natural foundations of civic existence.[131] The Benekes' everyday marital life, however, is less hierarchical than the housefather's angry insistence on the duty to obey might suggest; instead, their relationship is characterized by partnership and mutual respect.

Is Caroline Beneke naïve or sophisticated? This self-confident woman takes liberties, and at the same time knows her limits. In many respects, she becomes more independent as she ages and is also equipped with clear reasoning, provocative obstinacy, and assertiveness – much more so than her bourgeois 'gender character' would lead one to expect. In contrast, Ferdinand Beneke is characterized by the supposedly feminine qualities of high emotionality and a certain "fickleness," as Karin Hausen would have it.[132] The couple consolidates the bourgeois identity project of the time: the joint task of raising children and the fragile emotion of love, which still has to be rendered sustainable in everyday life. Passionate love triangles of the kind outlined here were not uncommon around 1800. The history with Roeck reaches its provisional conclusion in Caroline's telling messages to Ferdinand: "I will read of Werther's suffering!" she writes, referring to Goethe's famous novel; and again three days later: I "read *Werthers Leiden*"; yet she adds: "and what is worse, write letters to Roeck."[133] Caroline and Ferdinand's relationship endures this test, and the Benekes remain in contact with Roeck.

---

130 In the original German: "der Natur des Weibes"; "Nein nein mein Ferdinand, es wird mir wohl thun, zumal mich ruhiger machen, komme ich wieder in meine engern häußlichen Grenzen"; all citations taken from Beneke, *Tagebücher*, Caroline to Ferdinand Beneke, April 27, 1814, vol. 3.5, p. 509.
131 See the article written by the leading early liberal Carl Theodor Welcker on "Geschlechterverhältnisse" in the 1838 *Staatslexikon*, cited in Hausen, "Die Polarisierung der Geschlechtscharaktere," 375–76.
132 See the comparison in Hausen, "Die Polarisierung der Geschlechtscharaktere," 368; cf. the critique of Hausen in Trepp, "Anders als sein 'Geschlechtscharakter.'"
133 Beneke, *Tagebücher*, Caroline to Ferdinand Beneke, May 17, 1814, vol. 3.5, p. 533; May 20, 1814, pp. 539–40.

The Domestic Sphere as a Social Relay

To focus solely on the classic themes of the history of the family, of the kind outlined thus far, would be to provide only a partial reflection of the Benekes' domestic microcosm. At certain points, we have already seen that domesticity at the house on Holländischer Brook is not to be confused with the privacy of a modern home. From a social-historical point of view, there is no nuclear family (*Kleinfamilie*), but rather an 'extended family' that includes other relatives. In addition, there are also the servants, with whom the Benekes develop personal relationships. Furthermore, a certain culture of sociability is centrally important to the bourgeois context. In his classic work on the structural transformation of the public sphere, Jürgen Habermas pointed out that the bourgeois public first emerges as a literary public sphere in the private space of the home.[134] The history of the family is also social and political. As David Sabean emphasizes, the milieus of bourgeois society are formed via sociable communication,[135] and it is essential to note that this takes place in private homes. Alongside associations and voluntary societies, practices of domestic sociability constitute the second pillar of the new society. Thus it is striking to note the enormous contrast between the idea of privacy as self-contained 'domestic bliss' and the openness of the house in actual practice. This discrepancy – and the tensions arising from it – constituted a leitmotif in Henriette Stettler-Herport's diary, as we saw in the previous chapter. A look at recent research on self-narratives from Switzerland as well as northern and southern Germany confirms this finding.[136]

The example of the Benekes underscores the "compatibility of *familiarity and sociability*."[137] One outstanding feature of Beneke's diary is his documentation of meetings and contacts. Over the years, he notes thousands of names of people to whom he relates in various ways. The house very often functions as the space in which he interacts directly with these people. The innumerable visits and return visits make the house a social hub. Thus in 1811, the lawyer feels that his cramped rented apartment is "like an inn."[138] The Benekes' domestic life is not a special

---

[134] J. Habermas, *Strukturwandel der Öffentlichkeit*, 107–16; see also, as mentioned above, Clark, *Preußen*, 295–99 and 309.
[135] Sabean, "Kinship and Class Dynamics," 304–5; see also Mettele, "Der private Raum"; on the bourgeoisie in Hamburg, see Tolkemitt, "Knotenpunkte"; Trepp, *Sanfte Männlichkeit*.
[136] See esp. Trepp *Sanfte Männlichkeit*, 174–80; R. Habermas, *Frauen und Männer*, 182–84; and recently Hatje, "Domestic Sociability"; Eibach, "Das Haus," and "From Open House to Privacy?"; on the English research, see esp. Vickery, *The Gentleman's Daughter*, and *Behind Closed Doors*.
[137] Trepp, *Sanfte Männlichkeit*, 174 (italics in the original).
[138] In the original German: "wie ein GastHof"; Beneke, *Tagebücher*, May 7, 1811, vol. 3.1, p. 65.

case. As we have seen, there are continual comings and goings at the von Axen house on Jungfernstieg, and the situation is probably quite similar at the Chaufepié house, the Schlingemann house, and other houses in Hamburg that Beneke regularly visits. Beneke receives clients every day, and those who came from out of town sometimes stay overnight with him.[139] As early as 1805, he establishes office hours so as not to be continually disturbed. Additionally there are return visits from family friends, female friends, and acquaintances, even late in the evening. It is impossible to draw a clear line between professional or public occasions and purely personal meetings between friends. The "society of gentlemen at our place" might bring together – notably as a result of "chance, or politics" – close friends and high-ranking officeholders in the Hanseatic city.[140] We should also remember that his relationship with the woman who would become his wife arises during the visits he pays to Otto von Axen as a legal advisor. It is easier to distinguish between large celebrations, such as balls and formal dinners, and standard, often spontaneous gatherings. A comment Beneke makes in retrospect when looking back on 1816, the year he was appointed secretary of the Council of Elders, reveals this intertwining of public and private spheres. Beneke states that, due to new business and illness, given everything that is happening "with my private life, I have almost completely disappeared from the public."[141] Thus the connection between private and public life was expected. He notes that in the past year, he had "persistently declined all invitations" to the "body-, heart-, and spirit-destroying [...] gala feasts," which "are now more prevalent than ever." He would rather devote his scarce time to "me and mine."[142] This circle of 'mine' – or, as he formulaically puts it, 'among ourselves' or 'entre nous' – includes not only the members of the nuclear family, but also close relatives and intimate friends. A phrase such as: "Midday entre nous at the Schuchmachers'" is significant.[143] Nor are Sundays purely family days for the Benekes; they are devoted to meetings with their closest friends, relatives, and kindred spirits.

---

139 Beneke, *Tagebücher*, February 13, 1813, vol. 3.1, p. 365. On the following, see Hatje, "Die private Öffentlichkeit," 515 and *passim*.
140 Beneke, *Tagebücher*, September 30, 1811, vol. 3.1, p. 150.
141 In the original German: "bin ich mit meinem Privatleben fast ganz aus dem öffentlichen verschwunden"; Beneke, *Tagebücher*, overview for the year 1816, vol. 3.2, p. 480.
142 Both citations ibid. On the following, with reference to the example of the Roth family in Munich, see R. Habermas, *Frauen und Männer*, 223–24.
143 Beneke, *Tagebücher*, January 21, 1807, vol. 2.2, p. 422. Johann Diedrich Schuchmacher was a merchant in Hamburg; see supplementary vol. 2.1, p. 264. Thanks to my student Sibylle Kappeler (Bern) for this reference!

Beneke's diary reveals the house less as a private space than as a space of pronounced co-presence. This co-presence is anything but random. Beyond the permanent cohabitation of servants and often close relatives as well,[144] we can also distinguish specific functions and occasions. First, we must mention professional contacts. Not only in craft work and agriculture, but also in the bourgeois liberal professions, paid work was regularly performed at home in the nineteenth century. Second, we can observe the multifaceted spectrum of visiting culture, which included everyday sociability and formal events, birthday visits and get-togethers with relatives, reading societies and political meetings, spontaneous drop-in visits and a permanent social round reminiscent of a club. Third, we must not forget that in times of war, such as the years 1813/1814, co-presence also arose as a result of accommodating refugees. In addition to this, we can distinguish among types of visitors: the friend, the neighbor, the suitor, the condoler, the friend of the household (*Hausfreund*) who appears weekly for a meal ("Midday among ourselves, including our Tuesday Habitué"),[145] the dear friend, the favorite cousin, the distinguished lady, women who came to visit after a birth, and more. Some of this visiting culture is segregated according to gender: a "company of gentlemen at noon" and "tea visits [...] with the ladies" in the afternoon.[146] However, the greater and, to the Benekes, probably more important part of the socializing permits both men and women to participate. Caroline and Ferdinand Beneke act as a couple in the context of a wide-ranging social network, the nodes of which are private homes.

The actual openness of the house in the bourgeois milieu as we have observed it stands in stark contrast to ingrained notions of the nineteenth century as the "golden age of private life."[147] With regard to the history of the bourgeoisie (*Bürgertum*), amid the sweeping references to the family ideal as a central pillar of the bourgeois lifestyle, one must ask whether we might also consider that marriage and domesticity were lived out much more openly in the formative phases of both the bourgeoisie and the modern family than has previously been thought. In this respect, the open domesticity of the bourgeois elite differs in essential aspects from the 'open house' in both town and country during the early modern pe-

---

144 On this topic, see B. Kuhn, *Familienstand*, 293–95, and "Mitwohnen im 19. und frühen 20. Jahrhundert."
145 Beneke, *Tagebücher*, February 5, 1811, vol. 3.1, p. 31. This is a reference to the lawyer Georg Friedrich Nolte, who regularly appeared at the Benekes' table on Tuesdays.
146 Beneke, *Tagebücher*, October 9, 1811, vol. 3.1, p. 155; October 28, 1811, p. 162.
147 Perrot, "Introduction," 2.

riod.[148] Although William Burrowes was the Benekes' immediate neighbor, and Caroline Beneke and her children found refuge at his country house when they fled Hamburg in 1813, the neighborhood nevertheless no longer serves the same function as it had in estate-based society. This applies to the provision of support services as well as to the exercise of social control.[149] The merchant Burrowes acts as a friend, not as a neighbor. Beneke's friends are not drawn from the social proximity of the neighborhood, but rather live scattered across the city. In this respect, his social network is a rather modern, horizontal one. It is striking that this network, which in turn comes together in private houses, is not 'classless' but rather bound to certain cultural norms and emotional prerequisites. Beneke's friendships, which are based on an affinity of mind and soul, on reciprocity and trust, are particularly relevant to both. As chosen relatives, friends provide the link between family and social milieu. In this sense, after his close friend Rambach dies and other friends leave the city, Beneke reflects on what actually constitutes friendship. His criteria include "a confluence of many external circumstances and internal characteristics." He goes on:

> For not only in religious, moral, and intellectual education, not only in temper, and sensibility, and natural inclination, but also in the way of life, and opinion, in all kinds of outward inclinations, and in civil relations, there must be a certain proportionality between friendly families consisting of many persons, if an intimate social intercourse is to arise from friendly dispositions.[150]

---

148 For further details, see Eibach, "Das offene Haus"; "Das Haus"; and "From Open House to Privacy?"; on the early modern period, see Jancke, *Gastfreundschaft*.
149 On the history of the neighborhood, with different emphases, see Capp, *When Gossips Meet*; Wrightson, . "The 'Decline of Neighbourliness' Revisited"; Eibach, "The Open House: Communication Practices in and around the Domestic Sphere during the Early Modern Period" (forthcoming).
150 Beneke, *Tagebücher*, overview for the year 1815, vol. 3.2, p. 337. On concepts of friendship around 1800, see van Dülmen, "Freundschaftskult"; Wydler, "'Wie könnte ich euch vergessen'"; and in general Kühner, "Geschichte der Freundschaft."

Chapter 6
The Parsonage as Labyrinth: Ursula and Abraham Bruckner-Eglinger

Basel, Switzerland (1819–1833)

Parsonages were meant to set an example.[1] Particularly in rural areas, the Protestant pastor and his wife stood out from the rest of the village sphere by virtue of their status and education, and also as guardians of morality and lifestyle. As clergymen, pastors in the early modern period were members of an elite class. In research on the period, Protestant clergymen are not considered prototypes of the new bourgeoisie in the way that merchants, entrepreneurs, doctors, and judges are; nevertheless, they are usually included among the educated bourgeoisie, despite reservations regarding their status under the estate-based system.[2] The parsonage was usually quite visibly located in the center of the village. The members of the household were expected to exemplify family morality. The pressures of these expectations, which stemmed not only from the church as an institution, but also from the church members, created a unique situation – all the more so when the pastor and his wife internalized the moral performance mandate in which the wife served the function of 'companion' and 'co-ruler' (Schorn-Schütte). The intended and often accepted goal was an exemplary household and an ideal family. This constellation already suggests discrepancies between norm and practice – between a pious utopia and earthly, everyday life.

Ursula Eglinger, the protagonist of this chapter, was born into a pastor's family on October 21, 1797 in Liestal, near Basel, as the tenth child. In 1819, at the age of 22, she married Abraham Bruckner, who was officiating as pastor in the parish of Binningen, just outside Basel.[3] Abraham and Ursula Bruckner-Eglinger were closely intertwined with the Basel bourgeoisie through relatives and acquaintances,

---

[1] Greiffenhagen, *Das evangelische Pfarrhaus*; Schorn-Schütte, "'Gefährtin'"; on the parsonage as a building, see Spohn, *Pfarrhäuser*; and the brief overview in Ricker, "Evangelische Pfarrhäuser."
[2] See Gall *Von der ständischen zur bürgerlichen Gesellschaft*, 34; but cf. also Kocka ("Das europäische Muster," 9–10), who excludes Catholic clergymen.
[3] For biographical details, see the introduction to Hagenbuch, *"Heute war ich bey Lisette in der Visite"*, 10.

Chapter 6 The Parsonage as Labyrinth: Ursula and Abraham Bruckner-Eglinger — **105**

such as the Brenner, Bernoulli, Burckhardt, Sarasin, and Stähelin families.[4] The Moravian Brethren were also closely interwoven with this urban elite. Both the Bruckners and the Eglingers were members of this Pietist community, which was no longer a sect or a reform movement in opposition to church orthodoxy, as it had been in the mid-eighteenth century. By the beginning of the nineteenth century, Pietism of this variety had arrived at the center of both church and society. In no place in Switzerland can this development be better traced than in the prosperous city at the bend of the Rhine, which was sometimes disparagingly, sometimes admiringly referred to as 'pious Basel.'[5] The influence exercised by Pietism and other Christian creeds was not a remnant of the *ancien régime*, as one might suppose from the perspective of modernization theory. Rather, specific religious beliefs shaped the emerging liberal–conservative milieus well into the nineteenth century, both in Switzerland and beyond.

From the age of 19 (in July 1816), Ursula Eglinger wrote in her diary regularly. Most of the entries were written in the period of political calm during the 1820s, when Ursula presided over the Binningen parish household and gave birth to five sons, the first of whom was stillborn. Ursula's own parents had lost five of their eleven children in early childhood. No entries have survived for the years 1821–1823. The pastor's wife's diary ends abruptly at the end of March 1833, in the period of revolutionary unrest that eventually led to Basel's separation into two half-cantons. The Basel Turmoil (*Basler Wirren*) forced the country parsons, the majority of whom were conservative – among them numerous Moravian Brethren, such as Abraham Bruckner – to flee to the city of Basel, as people in the Basel countryside (*Landschaft*) were demanding political participation and equality.[6] The flare-up of proto-revolutionary protests in Switzerland as well as in Germany in the wake of the 1830 July Revolution in Paris showed that the post-1815 'restoration' had been such in name only. The transformation from an estate-based to a bourgeois society could no longer be held in check by decisions made in the Privy Cabinet. This raises the question of how this macro-level transformation was shaped and lived out in the domestic sphere. As we have already seen in the case of Henriette Stettler-Herport, Pietism constituted an important context for the formation of new ideas

---

4 See the names listed in the family register in Hagenbuch, *"Heute war ich bey Lisette in der Visite"*, 549–51. More generally, see also Heer et al., *Vom Weissgerber zum Bundesrat*; Hebeisen, *Leidenschaftlich fromm*.
5 See T. Kuhn, "Basel," and "Basel – ein 'Liebling Gottes'"; Hebeisen, *Leidenschaftlich fromm*. On the Moravian Brethren generally, see Mettele, *Weltbürgertum oder Gottesreich*.
6 On the riots in Binningen and local history more generally, see von Scarpatetti et al., *Binningen*, 125–32; the parish assembly had voted for Bruckner to stay: ibid., 312.

regarding familial inwardness (*Innerlichkeit*).[7] Where should the reformative project of *praxis pietatis* begin, if not in the home: alone with oneself, in one's private chamber, in the relationship with one's spouse, in everyday life with one's children and servants?

Sociability and Self-Accusation

The religious point of departure in this case is thus comparable to that of Henriette Stettler-Herport's diary fifty years earlier. Ursula Bruckner-Eglinger uses her diary – which usually consists of several lines per day, although she does not keep it daily, but rather completes entries in retrospect following breaks and interruptions – as a form of confession and a record of her transgressions. The subject wants to better herself. As the years go by, the pastor's wife from Basel becomes increasingly distressed about her state of mind and therefore appeals to her Lord and Savior. In several respects, however, this text – which formed part of the Ursula Bruckner-Eglinger's estate after she died in 1876, and was edited for publication by Bernadette Hagenbuch – should not be understood simply as an expression of pietistic rhetoric or the standard self-accusations.[8] The diary also serves first the single pastor's daughter, and then the married pastor's wife as an account of her many visits and meetings with friends and relatives. In a cheerful style, particularly in the early years, she records dozens of 'visits' and walks in company. She also notes prayer and singing sessions, household chores, and social events – not least weddings – among relatives and acquaintances. The pillars of the sociability she describes are the walk, which is not subject to pietistic suspicion – and which she mentions as an excursion, '*Partie,*' '*Promenade,*' or '*Lustwandeln*' – and the convivial meal.

The character of the diary as a report on the state of its author's soul, with an emphasis on subjective experience, only intensifies with the passage of time, as the protagonist's everyday burdens and unrealized ideals begin to overshadow her. Even then, however, her descriptions of her own state of mind appear less as procedural steps in a formulaic discourse than as attempts to put her inner life and personal experiences into words in a variety of ways. Thus we read in an entry from August 16, 1830:

---

[7] With regard to Basel, Hebeisen (*Leidenschaftlich fromm*, 205) notes that "emotional Moravian piety was especially attractive to women"; see also ibid., 208–10; Gleixner, *Pietismus und Bürgertum*, 209–11.

[8] Although this is precisely what Hagenbuch argues: see Hagenbuch, "*Heute war ich bey Lisette in der Visite*", 20 and 34.

> I woke up at 3 in the morning, and unfortunately I could not go back to sleep, because the agonizing thoughts came to such a degree that I no longer knew where to turn. Nor could I pray, because such thoughts were immediately displaced again. O dearest Lord! Do you really wish to lead me through this hard lesson in patience too, even if I become mentally ill [Gemüths krank] [?] Oh, in your mercy, only spare me from this.[9]

Neither prayer nor church attendance in Binningen – where her husband is the one who presides over the service – offers any reliable relief in such situations. As she writes on May 12, 1831: "My nerves are under attack to such an extent that I can hardly bear to go to church in the morning." By contrast, on the same day, Ascension Day, a change in the weather has a liberating effect on her. The entry continues: "Today we have had the first beautiful day in a long time. Oh, how good it feels after all that rain."[10] In addition, with regard to her internal struggles, the 33-year-old pastor's wife not only hangs her hopes on dialogue with God or edifying reading, but also goes to see a doctor the following day. He recommends that she "drink Baldrian and snail broth" to calm her down.[11] Keeping a diary, especially in the pietistic context, can be described as a ritualized practice: an ongoing dialogue with God the Father. But the possibilities of the medium may overpower the writing self. In Ursula Bruckner-Eglinger's case, this applies to two different aspects. First, the ritual can become an obligation. Thus after a long break, the pastor's wife notes that she needs to "catch up on" her diary entries because continuity is a priority, but confesses that this is something she has "been dreading for so long."[12] Second, the text may contain more information than the author actually intends to convey. It is here that the diary becomes interesting as a source of domestic and family history.

An Unexpected Yet Predictable Proposal of Marriage

Our 21-year-old actor's marriage comes out of nowhere, and yet it is a more or less predictable affair. At the beginning of March 1819, Abraham Bruckner sends a written marriage proposal to Ursula Eglinger, who is seven years his junior, via inter-

---

[9] The following citations from Ursula Bruckner-Eglinger's diary are based on Bernadette Hagenbuch's edition: here the citation is from the entry for August 16, 1830, p. 423. On Pietism's emotional culture and subjective experience, see Gleixner, *Pietismus und Bürgertum*; Hebeisen, *Leidenschaftlich fromm*; Mettele, *Weltbürgertum oder Gottesreich*, 205.

[10] Hagenbuch, May 12, 1831, p. 466. Unless otherwise indicated, and with the exception of ellipses, all of the insertions in square brackets are Hagenbuch's.

[11] Ibid., May 13, 1831, p. 466.

[12] Ibid., June 14, 1829, p. 375.

mediaries – a pastor and his wife from the Basel countryside. Ursula and Abraham know each other only casually. Ten months earlier, she had briefly noted the visit of a Reverend Bruckner.[13] In contrast to Caroline von Axen and Ferdinand Beneke, there is no period of getting to know one another, no interaction by means of public promenades or secret rendezvous. Thus she remarks that she had "as little inkling as a child" that the proposal was imminent.[14] Yet after it takes place, things move quickly. Presumably in retrospect, with some temporal distance, she provides daily summaries of the events she found significant. On Thursday, March 4, a Reverend Meyer appears at the Eglinger home and delivers the letter on Bruckner's behalf. On Friday, she is already leaning toward saying yes. On Saturday, she reaffirms her consent, whereupon her father replies to her suitor by letter. To support the agreement, Ursula's older sister and one of her cousins arrive at the Eglingers' home. On Sunday, "the first visit of my beloved bridegroom" takes place.[15] This is followed by the first congratulations from third parties. On Monday, the bridegroom appears with the engagement ring. The couple visits the Binningen parsonage, the bride's future home, and the bridegroom's relatives in Basel. Over the following days and weeks, the bride and groom meet repeatedly and visit relatives.[16] Three months later, on June 8, 1819, her father performs the wedding ceremony. "The church was full to the rafters with spectators," but the banquet that follows is simple and intimate, with only 22 guests. At half-past nine in the evening, people leave the tables and go to bed. At the post-wedding ceremony the next day, where gifts are presented, 46 guests appear: "friends and relatives" as well as "officials from the local parish."[17]

Ursula Eglinger understands her duties and knows what she wants on the day she makes her decision to marry: "only to fulfill the will of the one [...] to whom I owe life and limb."[18] Nevertheless, the match is not a foregone conclusion, and she certainly has the option to reject the proposal, especially since her parents give her a free hand in the decision. A few years later, her younger brother, Emanuel Eglinger, also a pastor, is likewise permitted to choose for himself and is initially reject-

---

13 Ibid., May 25, 1818, p. 125. The first mention, which was quite incidental, was six months earlier: November 24, 1817, p. 119. On the following, see Hagenbuch 2014, pp. 46–50.
14 Ibid., March 4, 1819, p. 137.
15 Ibid., March 7, 1819, p. 138.
16 Ibid., March 17, 1819, p. 138.
17 All citations taken from ibid., June 8–9, 1819, p. 143.
18 Ibid., March 5, 1819, p. 137.

ed when he proposes marriage, which disappoints him greatly.[19] Ursula Eglinger makes the decision to say yes remarkably quickly, but it costs her many tears and quite a number of prayers. On the night before the wedding, she is seized by "a great uneasiness."[20] Eventually she vomits, whereupon they fetch the doctor. This information does not necessarily fit the standard pietistic matchmaking model. For those involved, the marriage is enormously important and transcendentally charged, but this does not mean that social contexts are therefore irrelevant. The fact that Bruckner, a Moravian Brethren pastor, directs his proposal of marriage to the home of this Moravian Brethren pastor's daughter doubly corresponds – socially as well as religiously – to the pattern of endogamy.[21] It is a typical connection within the milieu. Through conversations, visits, and social engagements, the immediate social environment is usually involved even before a marriage takes place. Such a marriage is not about love in today's sense, but it is very much about emotion – namely, a necessary sympathy and affection. In this case, as a woman being courted, Ursula Eglinger finally dresses her decision-making process in words as sober and succinct as she can find: she has "neither reason nor inclination to say no."[22]

The Perfect Household as Chronic Overload

Ursula Eglinger's experiences in her parental home, in the church community, and the several years she spent at Montmirail, a Pietist boarding school for girls near Neuchâtel, have prepared her for her future as a mother, mistress of a household, conjugal 'helper,' and companion. Marrying a Moravian Brethren pastor constituted the realization of the desired ideal. What are the concrete features of the house and the parsonage household in the village of Binningen, near Basel, with a population of approximately 800 souls?[23] The parsonage, built in 1705 in the style of a

---

[19] Ibid., April 29, 1832, p. 510; May 13, 1832, p. 512; June 3, 1832, p. 512. The entry in which Ursula reports that her friend Rosine Gessler has declined a proposal (August 19, 1832, p. 518) may also refer to a marriage proposal.
[20] Ibid., June 8, 1819, p. 142.
[21] On pietistic-bourgeois matchmaking in Basel, see Hebeisen, *Leidenschaftlich fromm*, 254–57.
[22] In the original German: "weder Ursache noch Neigung zum Nein sagen"; Hagenbuch, March 4, 1819, p. 137.
[23] On the history of Binningen, see von Scarpatetti et al., *Binningen*; on the number of inhabitants, see 125 and 158–59.

Fig. 11: Castle and Parsonage (No. 3), Binningen 1738, by Emanuel Büchel. Source: Staatsarchiv Basel-Stadt, Bild_Falk._Fb_2.7

baroque manor house, just below Binningen Castle, is a spacious two-story building, with high ceilings, large windows, and half-paneled rooms.[24]

At the time when the Bruckner-Eglingers lived there, this grand complex also included farm buildings and a stately parish garden. From the outside, the house presents a brilliant scene. It is enclosed by a wall, and anyone who wants to enter has to ring a bell at the entrance gate. Curtains also protect the house from prying eyes. In addition to the kitchen and the bathroom, the spacious interior includes several parlors and bedchambers. The kitchen has a stove and an oven for baking bread and pastries. The mistress of the house finds the fact that a visitor wishes to use "our bathing chamber" inappropriate and "very unpleasant" with regard to her privacy.[25] The parsonage includes a large living room on the lower level, as well as an upstairs study and additional nurseries and bedchambers. The maids most likely have their own chambers, and the nanny shares a room with the youngest child. The fact that the house is the pastor's place of work is indicated

---

24 Here and below, see Steiner, "Das 'alte' Binninger Pfarrhaus"; my comments on the premises also refer to remarks made in passing in the diary.
25 Hagenbuch, August 4, 1829, p. 379.

Fig. 12: Binningen Parsonage 1842 (artist unknown). Source: Kantonsmuseum Baselland, Liestal, Switzerland

by his large study and the "little classroom."[26] Both the pastor and his wife have their own chambers – "my dear little room" – as places of retreat within the house.[27] Twice a year, when the seasons change from warm to cold and vice versa, the inhabitants of the house change their sleeping quarters. Although Ursula develops an affinity for her chamber, the function of the various parlors and chambers also changes often – regardless of the season – for the sake of childcare requirements, or when visitors come, or when they are required to provide lodging for soldiers. Fixed, personalized, individualized rooms do not seem to have been features of the house. Some of the diary entries even seem to indicate that the couple did not share a bedchamber – at least not all the time. Ursula's notes on her moves within the house concern only herself; an entry dated March 1828 provides an example: "In the morning I made the change with the beds and moved back

---

26 Ibid., October 31, 1831, p. 488.
27 In the original German: "mein liebes Stübchen"; ibid., April 19, 1830, p. 410 (citation); May 13, 1830, p. 413.

into the small bedchamber." Then in November 1829, she writes: "I moved into my winter quarters, which filled me with my own private thoughts this year."[28]

The fact that there is a parish garden attached to the house is not incidental. This area serves two different purposes: it supplies the household with agricultural products and offers a bourgeois form of recreation. Like Martin Luther and his wife Katharina's household in Wittenberg in the sixteenth century, or indeed the bailiwick in Frienisberg in Bern toward the end of the *ancien régime*, the parish household had not yet been completely separated from the agricultural context by the middle of the nineteenth century. The parsonage was nowhere near achieving self-sufficiency; rather, cultivating a small piece of land should be seen as an aspect of pious housekeeping. With the help of the maids, the pastor's wife plants and harvests potatoes and vegetables, lettuce and fruit. The property includes a chicken coop as well. Supplies are stored in the attic. The diary entries also mention drying fruit, pressing juice, and churning butter.[29] The other part of the estate, which professional gardeners cultivate, displays the garden's bourgeois face. Here the pastor's wife reads and knits with a pleasant view of well-tended flowerbeds. In the evenings, the couple walks along the paths and has "quite a lovely, intimate heart-to-heart."[30]

Ursula Bruckner-Eglinger's diary relates conspicuously little about her formal duties as a pastor's wife. She does mention church services, communion, prayer meetings, teaching the children in Sunday school, weddings and funerals, visiting the sick, meetings with other pastor's wives, and pastoral elections in the parishes around Basel. All of this is important to her. Yet it does not seem that she was obligated to be present at most of these events. At one time the Moravian Brethren Society had offered meetings specifically for families, but these probably no longer played an important role in the 1820s.[31] Ursula's occupations include writing the 'poor roll' – that is, listing the poor people in the parish who are in need of care – and the so-called Ply, a handwritten circular letter that is passed consecutively from parsonage to parsonage. Although she enjoys reading this newsletter, with the onset of her psychological problems, writing in it becomes a burden.[32] As in the early modern period, the pastor's wife is given authority over her domestic subordinates in the house. Thus when a snowstorm hits on a Sunday, she as-

---

28 Ibid., March 21, 1828, p. 346; November 6, 1829, p. 388. See also November 27, 1826, p. 297.
29 On making butter, see ibid., February 2, 1828, p. 341; on horticulture and agriculture in Martin Luther's household, see Heling, *Zu Haus bei Martin Luther*, 33–45.
30 Hagenbuch, August 12, 1824, p. 200; August 2, 1828, p. 354 (citation).
31 With a view to the eighteenth century, cf. Hebeisen, *Leidenschaftlich fromm*, 56 and 205–8.
32 Hagenbuch, October 8, 1827, p. 327. On poor rolls more generally, see von Scarpatetti et al., *Binningen*, 312.

sumes the role of head of the household as a matter of course: "I read a sermon to the entire household during church."[33] The importance of this domestic practice is underlined by recourse to the notion of the 'house' or 'members of the household' (*Hausgenossenschaft*).[34] As a rule, Ursula prefers to use the term 'family.' But if she wishes to confer a higher dignity upon them – including the servants – she may well use the term 'house.' Thus at the beginning of 1831, in response to news of an impending revolutionary siege on the city of Basel, she writes: "I did not much fear for the city, but above all for my dear husband and our house."[35]

Mrs. Bruckner-Eglinger puts a lot of effort – both actively and discursively – into the success of her household in the broader sense. In keeping with the pietistic approach, her ambition (which is comparable to Henriette Stettler-Herport's) is to combine perfect order in the house with her own spirituality – specifically a sense of drawing near to God. Her diary documents the fact that this set of ambitions and expectations would eventually overwhelm the mistress of a nine-person household under the strains of a grueling daily routine. What was everyday housekeeping like in a parsonage in the 1820s? The time at which Ursula rises in the morning varies, from 4 a.m. on baking days to 7:30 a.m. when festivities have taken place the night before. She goes to bed at 10 p.m. during the summer, which is relatively late for her. Depending on the work that needs to be done, however, her day can last until midnight.[36] The pastor's wife tries to get up early to have some time to herself for prayer and edification, but on many days she has no time for either. More than anything, she dreads the extremely laborious washing days. In spite of the help provided by her close female relatives and the maids, and later also by women who are hired to do the laundry and ironing, the whole procedure – from soaking to drying in the garden, from bleaching and darning to smoothing and ironing, from folding the items to putting them away in the cupboards – takes well over a week. From the beginning, her notes on her own housekeeping indicate that she hates this business,[37] which is a matter not only of the arduous physical labor, but also of the need for members of the parsonage household to appear publicly in clean, neat clothing: "Today I started a wash; it isn't really necessary yet, but I'm glad when everything is clean again." When she spots her

---

[33] Hagenbuch, January 10, 1830, p. 396. See also March 6, 1831, p. 457: "In the evenings I sang verses with the entire household."
[34] On the history of these terms, see Mathieu, "Domestic Terminologies."
[35] Hagenbuch, January 11, 1831, p. 444. On the course of the turmoil surrounding the cantonal separation in Binningen, see von Scarpatetti et al., *Binningen*, 125–30.
[36] Hagenbuch, January 10, 1827, p. 302; January 27, 1827, p. 304; August 13, 1829, p. 380; February 13, 1830, p. 401.
[37] Ibid., October 9–28, 1819, pp. 150–51. On the history of laundry, see Orland, *Wäsche waschen*.

husband and four children on their way back from town, she is proud and "so glad that they are now also sensibly dressed and can be let out of the house."[38]

Certain activities, such as the daily task of heating the house or hiring day laborers to chop wood, are so self-evident that she notes them only rarely or in passing.[39] The household work is divided among the domestic staff. One maid is responsible for cooking and baking, another for cleaning, and another for looking after the children. The cleaning must be particularly thorough before feast days and important visits – such as gatherings of fellow pastors. The 'ruler' of the household is often unsatisfied with her maids' work and lends a hand herself. The diary contains no evidence of the kind of convivial, communal village labor that we find in the early modern period, when women gathered to do laundry near running water, to bake at the bakehouse, or to spin wool in the evenings. Instead, housekeeping in this context is highly domesticized, though not necessarily privatized. As the number of children increases, so do doctors' and dentists' visits, and tailors and shoemakers come to the house regularly to take measurements and mend shoes. Ursula Bruckner-Eglinger keeps track of all these expenses in a book of household accounts.[40]

This type of household domestication is not to be confused with the everyday isolation of the housewife as we know it in the late bourgeois era, after the Second World War. The parsonage in the 1820s offers support and many helping hands. Nevertheless, Ursula Bruckner-Eglinger's diary unintentionally records the housemother's sense of chronic strain as well as the family's 'functional overload,' according to which fulfilling every expectation is impossible. The household and domestic relationships – which are inextricably linked – are an almost constant source of stress for her, as she documents at length. She uses the terms 'turbulence' (*Strubel*), 'turbulent day' (*Strubeltag*), and 'labyrinth' over and over again. She is "horribly displeased" with "the work done" and "so tired all evening." After a day of "tidying up," she writes: "Nothing displeases me <u>more</u> than such a muddle." One Saturday, she notes that she has not had time for a single prayer in the past week, and instead "always had work on my mind. I felt like a beast of burden." Elsewhere she characterizes herself as "a complete slave" to her work.[41]

As in the case of the bailiff's wife, Henriette Stettler-Herport, the pastor's wife is weighed down by enormous burdens. Some of her formulations suggest a kind of depression or – in the diarist's own terms – a "severely depressed mind." In August

---

[38] Hagenbuch, May 3, 1832, p. 511; October 30, 1829, p. 387.
[39] Ibid., April 24, 1826, p. 274; November 23, 1827, p. 332.
[40] Ibid., December 29, 1830, p. 440; see also November 26, 1824, p. 217.
[41] Citations (in order): ibid., December 13, 1828, p. 367; July 15, 1831, p. 473; October 23, 1829, p. 387 (underlining in the original); February 13, 1830, p. 401; March 11, 1831, p. 457.

1830, she confesses that she has not experienced "even a single joyful moment" for some time.[42] But as we shall see, Ursula Bruckner-Eglinger is not consistently melancholy. Her self-diagnosis must also be understood against the background of her religious disposition. She is predestined to experience fear as well as feelings of guilt, fear, and extreme frustration, especially on Saturdays or days before she takes communion, on the basis of which she hopes for "peace in my heart and forgiveness of sins."[43] She expects nothing less than to "become a completely new creature" through her participation in Holy Communion.[44] But on Easter Sunday 1832, for example, the pastor's wife is "not at all in an Easter-like mood"; instead she describes herself as "ill-tempered, distracted, and without love. What a state of mind."[45] The fact that she falls asleep repeatedly during the church service should not be interpreted as intentional obstinacy, but simply as an expression of her exhaustion.[46]

The high expectations concerning inner peace and pious community in the context of an orderly household at the Binningen parsonage were dashed against the rocks of the family's everyday reality, in which the wife and mother was assigned a litany of tasks that we would refer to today, in completely secular terms, as 'multi-tasking.' Here a look at the central marital and household relations is illuminating. Ursula Bruckner-Eglinger describes her relationship with her husband, Abraham Bruckner, in a relatively formulaic, literally abbreviated way: she refers to him as 'm. l. Mann' (my dear husband), 'm. l. AB' (my dear AB), or simply as 'AB.'[47] She considers marriage a sacred connection, one that is not easy to chat about in her diary. Nevertheless, the text does provide insights into a complex relationship that combines hierarchy and companionship, practical arrangements and emotion. All things considered, the pastor's wife is by no means simply a 'helper' (*Gehilfin*) in this relationship, nor is her husband a 'master.' The Bruckner-Eglingers' gender roles are distinct, but Ursula has room to maneuver, and her everyday radius is certainly not limited to her home and her marriage. Indeed, she acts as a housemother endowed with power and rights, and also as a sister and a friend. Abraham is first and foremost a professional man and head of the house-

---

42 In the original German: "schwer gedrücktes Gemüth"; "auch nicht einen einzigen freudigen Augenblick"; ibid., August 18, 1830, p. 424.
43 Ibid., September 6, 1828, p. 358.
44 Ibid., September 1, 1827, p. 325.
45 Ibid., April 22, 1832, p. 510. See also May 21, 1831, p. 467: "It doesn't really feel like Pentecost to me."
46 Ibid., June 17, 1832, p. 514; September 9, 1832, p. 520.
47 The editor of the original diary supplies the remainder of the words in square brackets: 'm[ein] l[ieber] Mann'; 'm[ein] l[ieber] AB.'

hold, but he also demonstrates the characteristics of 'gentle masculinity.'[48] In this respect, small details are significant. For her 35th birthday, Mrs. Bruckner-Eglinger receives "money and a bonnet from my husband" as well as "honey and a sheep-cheese bowl from my children" – things which she "had long desired."[49] She gives her husband a silk hat and a pair of gloves for his 39th birthday. In addition to the gender-specific symbolism of gifts such as the hat, the bonnet, and the kitchen utensil, the gift of money should be understood as an indication that the wife has no direct access to the family assets. At that time, when a couple married, the bride's dowry usually passed into the husband's keeping.[50] Thus when Ursula's father, Simon Eglinger, dies in 1826, and it comes time for the inheritance to be divided, it is her husband who steps in when the distribution of capital is at stake.[51]

The fact that Ursula Bruckner-Eglinger describes her marriage predominantly as a happy one, but also lets her frustration rise to the surface time and again, is not particularly unique. Her husband certainly offers a sympathetic ear into which she can pour her fears and her needs. Despite the extremely short period in which they got to know each other prior to marriage, the spouses build a relationship based on trust. Ursula records no major marital crises in her diary. As far as we can see, the marriage relationship is practiced in small, everyday rituals: in walks and conversations together, on 'family days' and at other social gatherings, and not least through their mutual faith. At a "home communion" for two "in my quiet little room" following the Pentecost service, she reports that "both of us dissolved into tears."[52] In other respects as well, Mr. Bruckner shows his emotions more openly than his bourgeois 'gender character' would lead us to expect. This applies to their 'heated' political discussions during the so-called Basel Turmoil after the 1830 July Revolution as well as to his performance of his domestic duties. While engaging in a kind of punitive prayer for the household after the housemother suffers certain insubordinate behavior, not only the maids, but also the housefather cry at the end.[53]

The pious couple shares basic convictions about strict housekeeping norms. As we have seen, however, implementing such norms in everyday earthly life is diffi-

---

48 See Trepp, *Sanfte Männlichkeit*. On the tension between hierarchy and companionship in pietistic concepts of marriage, see Gleixner, *Pietismus und Bürgertum*, 271–73.
49 Hagenbuch, October 21, 1832, p. 524. see December 1, 1829, p. 391.
50 On this phenomenon in the nineteenth century, see the brief overview in Wienfort, *Verliebt, Verlobt, Verheiratet*, 85; on the early modern period, see Lanzinger, "Spouses and the Competition for Wealth."
51 Hagenbuch, August 23, 1826, pp. 287–88.
52 Ibid., June 7, 1829, p. 375. On intimate communication, see Frevert, *Vertrauensfragen*.
53 Hagenbuch, January 5, 1831, p. 442; September 3, 1828, p. 357.

cult, and in some respects downright precarious. As a pastor, 'AB' spends a lot of time in the house. In this respect, we cannot speak of separate gender-differentiated spheres. Yet there are clear assignments and allocations. Ursula is and remains the mistress of the household. Abraham only appears before the maids when there is something serious to say. Moreover, he is not as involved in the children's upbringing as their mother would like. She complains that he "always has a lot to do and is usually busy with his studies."[54] He does not always take part in family walks, which also displeases her. Abraham Bruckner has all the traits of a typical bourgeois figure: the physically present but attentively absent father, the man who takes up a position in the background when it comes to the family. He is certainly present in the house – more precisely, in his study on the upper floor – and at meals, but he is not always present for important moments of domestic life together. This applies to matters of housekeeping as well as to child-rearing. Even at an evening get-together with Ursula's brother Emanuel and the vicar Balthasar Stähelin, who have come to the Binningen parsonage for an overnight visit, the housefather prefers to slip away to his chamber.[55] Characteristically she often finds herself waiting for him. While she tends to the house, he goes to parish association or friends' association meetings in the evening, which take place in turn at the homes of Basel's middle-class families.[56] On the other hand, the father does go for walks around the village with his children, or to Basel to meet his wife. Ursula likes to see her husband in the pulpit, but she insists on having her own opinions in matters of faith, and also during the political turmoil in the context of Basel's separation into two half-cantons – even to the point of open conflict, which she then confesses to God the Father in writing.[57]

Emotional Care Relationships

The relationships Ursula Bruckner-Eglinger has with her children are centrally important, very emotional, and thus also fragile. On October 20, 1820, sixteen months

---

54 Ibid., January 6, 1827, p. 302. On what Ursula considers the inadequate religious education of her eldest son, Theophil, see November 5, 1830, p. 433: "What do you want to become of this boy?" On pietistic child-rearing practices, see Gestrich, "Ehe, Familie, Kinder im Pietismus." On the following, see Hagenbuch, May 29, 1831, p. 468.
55 Ibid., June 13, 1827, p. 317.
56 Ibid., September 1, 1828, p. 356; October 27, 1825, p. 251; March 11, 1828, p. 345; October 22, 1829, p. 386.
57 Ibid., March 18, 1830, p. 405; February 16, 1831, p. 453.

after the wedding, she suffers a stillbirth.[58] Four healthy boys follow: Theophil (b. 1821), Carl Gustav (b. 1824), Wilhelm Eduard (b. 1825), and Emil Albert (b. 1829). After the second birth, she would have preferred to have a girl. Each birth is a dramatic event – a home birth in which the mother is supported by a midwife, her sister-in-law, or a maid, and in case of emergency, by a doctor – which brings anxieties and burdens in its wake.[59] Bringing up the children and ensuring their welfare constitute two major causes of Ursula's feelings of guilt and dissatisfaction with herself. She feels that she is "a negligent mother" who has too little time for her children and is "disheartened and impatient" with them.[60] Even the final entries in her diary, written in March 1833, are devoted to the precarious imbalance between her high standards with regard to the children and her irritable, bad temper, which she ultimately attributes to her own lack of ability.[61] At least until the two older boys start school in 1830, the children's upbringing is a task for their mother and their nanny. The housemother keeps a close eye on the nannies and frequently hires new ones in quick succession. Tense competition for the children's affection develops. Thus Ursula notes with a certain jealousy that 5-year-old Theophil cries silently on the day the nanny Henriette is dismissed, and some months later she is quite pleased to observe that Henriette's successor, the coarse Salome, "is not the type to win their [the children's] trust, so their hearts are not divided; they love me tenderly."[62]

Ursula's eldest son, Theophil, holds a special place in her heart; he is her favorite, and later her problem child. This is a key relationship in the Bruckner family's community of emotion and care, as we can see from the number of times he is mentioned in the diary. Theophil's 5th birthday is an occasion for his mother "to give heartfelt thanks" to her Savior, who gives her "so many motherly joys." When Theophil is 8 years old, she prays with him on her lap both morning and evening. But to her sorrow, he and his younger brothers know "many bad words and expressions." When Theophil is 9 years old, his poor "religious education" leads her to reproach her husband and to ask God the Father for mercy. The eldest son's poor performance at school is also cause for concern. Theophil receives no present for his 10th birthday because he gives his parents "little pleasure through

---

58 Ibid., October 20, 1820, p. 165.
59 On female perceptions of childbirth, see Labouvie, *Andere Umstände*, 137–39.
60 In the original German: "eine liederliche Mutter"; "muthlos u. ungeduldig"; Hagenbuch, May 1, 1827, p. 313 (first citation); November 26, 1831, pp. 490–91; March 24, 1832, p. 506 (second citation).
61 Ibid., March 24 and 28, 1833, p. 531.
62 Ibid., December 26, 1826, p. 300; May 17, 1827, p. 315 (citation); see also December 26, 1827, p. 335. On the "emotional parent–child relationship" in pietist Basel, see Hebeisen, *Leidenschaftlich fromm*, 216; on maids in the nineteenth century, see Budde, "Das Dienstmädchen."

his learning." When he fails to show his parents another bad report he receives at school, he is given "a serious talking-to and a spanking." Other domestic punishments for the children include being locked up, sent to bed early, and "not dining at the table with us."[63] Theophil will go on to study medicine – not theology – at universities in Germany and in Basel, where he will earn a doctorate in medicine in 1846. In 1847 he will emigrate to North America, whence he will return in 1856 to open a homeopathic practice in Basel.[64] His son Wilhelm will become a professor of German linguistics at the University of Basel in 1905.

For all its distance from worldly things, the Pietist parsonage does not constitute a world apart from society. In addition to imparting bourgeois ideals such as self-discipline, order, and cleanliness, the family has a mission – one which is reinforced in the liberal era after 1830, when schooling is emphasized. Thus, combining several cultural codes, the Bruckner family is not only concerned with religious education by means of children's Sunday-school lessons, prayer, singing, and Sunday recitations – which Theophil, who would rather go out with the maid, hates "terribly"[65] – but also with secular education and the principle of achievement. Education begins with language and rote memorization. It also includes physical education: in keeping with the times, 10-year-old Theophil is sent to gymnastics lessons.[66] Success at school is important to the Bruckner-Eglingers, and bad report cards are accordingly an expression of family failure. In 1832, the need to choose the right school for 7-year-old Wilhelm Eduard leads to a days-long sequence of arguments and discussions between his parents, as we saw in the introduction.[67]

Thus the Bruckners are not only a family of faith, but also of education. Ursula and Abraham have already discovered the bourgeois educational canon for themselves. She plays the piano as a hobby and also attends art exhibitions and a Haydn concert in the Leonhardskirche in Basel, given by the 'Swiss Music Lovers Society.'[68] The couple has their portrait professionally painted. They read to the children and sing songs together. In the evening, exuberant socializing is enriched

---

63 Hagenbuch, November 5, 1826, p. 294 (first citation); November 25, 1826, p. 296 (second citation); October 11, 1829, p. 385; October 30, 1829, p. 387 (third citation); November 5, 1830, p. 433 (fourth citation); September 2, 1831, p. 481; November 5, 1831, p. 489; February 11, 1832, p. 499 (fifth citation); November 8 and 10, 1829, p. 389 (sixth citation).
64 Schroers, *Lexikon deutschsprachiger Homöopathen*, 18.
65 Hagenbuch, April 18, 1830, p.410. On the tensions between Pietism and the bourgeoisie, see Hebeisen, *Leidenschaftlich fromm*, 220–21.
66 Hagenbuch, May 10, 1832, p. 511. On the relationship between the bourgeois family and school, see Budde, *Auf dem Weg ins Bürgerleben*, 362–68.
67 Hagenbuch, May 1, 1832, p. 511.
68 Ibid., June 14, 1820, p. 159 (citation); June 18 and 19, 1826, pp. 281–82. On the following, see June 11, 1824, p. 191.

by making music together. The parents and close family members also read to each other – not only edifying literature, but also Schiller's *Intrigue and Love* (*Kabale und Liebe*).[69] The stress of everyday domestic life overshadows these practices, but perhaps for this reason, these moments seem all the more precious and also worth recording in the diary. Last but not least, the practice of keeping a diary bridges the gap between pietistic and bourgeois self-reflection. It is true that the Bruckner-Eglinger family's success in terms of education is not immediate, nor does it proceed as desired. But this is a question of perspective. None of the four sons study theology or follow in the footsteps of their father, who prays with them and teaches them the catechism. As mentioned above, Theophil becomes a doctor, Carl Gustav a lawyer, Wilhelm Eduard a master builder, and the youngest, Emil Albert, a customs official.[70] Not only their professions, but also the names of the wives they choose from among their social milieu in Basel – Ursula's daughters-in-law – point to the new nineteenth-century bourgeoisie. In this respect, the Bruckner sons remain true to their milieu.[71]

Despite the intensity of these emotional relationships, it would be wrong to understand the Bruckner-Eglingers simply as a typical case of the nuclear family model. Rather, the Binningen parsonage turns out to be an 'open house' in important ways. First, there is the permanent co-presence of the three maids, without whom the household would not function. Unfortunately it remains unclear whether they dine at the same table with the family. In a manner that seems obsessive, the housemother pores over the maids' actual or perceived deficiencies. However, she also develops a close relationship with the nanny Henriette, who looks after the children for more than two and a half years. Henriette's departure at the end of 1826 is not only difficult for Theophil, but also for his mother. As Ursula notes on the day of her dismissal, Henriette's "indolence and disorder were unbearable" to her. Yet less than two weeks later, she remarks that she is "depressed and dejected" over "what I have lost in H[enriette] with regard to the children." Years later, she still remembers "the vigilant Henriette" wistfully.[72] A woman named Barbel – to whose daughter, baptized Anna Ursula, the pastor's wife rather unwillingly becomes godmother in 1832 – is presumably also one of the Bruckner-Eglingers' former maids.[73]

---

[69] Ibid., February 14, 1824, p. 174; July 26, 1826, p. 285; February 9, 1832, p. 499. On music in the home, see Claudon, "Hausmusik"; Eibach, "Die Schubertiade."
[70] These details are based on the research in Hagenbuch, "*Heute war ich bey Lisette in der Visite*", 172, n. 496; p. 234, n. 825; p. 372, n. 1419.
[71] On continuities in Basel's elite milieu in the nineteenth century, see Sarasin, *Stadt der Bürger*.
[72] Hagenbuch, December 26, 1826, p. 300; January 6, 1827, p. 301; April 3, 1830, p. 407.
[73] Ibid., February 5, 1832, p. 499.

In addition to familial-domestic relationships, Ursula's diary documents the importance of kinship in both the narrower and the broader sense. Emotional care relationships are not limited to the spouses or to parent–child relationships. Around 1800, sibling relationships also take on a new quality in terms of affinity and emotion.[74] In this respect, certain patterns and roles can be identified. Ursula's sister Susanna ('Susette'), who is 13 years older, is an important caregiver who repeatedly offers assistance in the course of everyday domestic life. Ursula also has a very close relationship with her brother Emanuel, who is six years younger. When 26-year-old Emanuel returns from a stay in Herrnhut, Germany in 1829, Ursula feels "the indescribable joy of embracing my dear Emanuel again. I cried tears of joy at the sight of him."[75] Emanuel often comes to spend the night at his sister's house. It is not her husband, but rather Emanuel who reads to her from Schiller's *Kabale und Liebe*. Brother and sister have intense exchanges about their problems ('pouring out their hearts'), although her diary entries usually only hint at the content of these conversations. Last but not least, the older sister is made party to her brother's marriage plans early on. We can read Ursula's entries about this event as betraying a hint of jealousy: "These days E[manuel] is completely preoccupied with his marriage saga; one hears of nothing else from him."[76]

Ursula also has an intense but mercurial relationship with her brother Christoph, who is seven years older than she is. Christoph has taken on the role of the black sheep or "the prodigal son" in the Eglinger family.[77] The reasons for this are not entirely clear, but it is evident that there are strong tensions between "our poor wayward brother" Christoph and the rest of the Eglinger family concerning his plans to marry "that girl."[78] In notes about their frequent family meetings, Christoph's name is often missing. Several times Ursula mentions incriminating rumors about him, but she does not elaborate on them. She protects potentially explosive entries from undesired discovery by using laconic wording, transposing them into French, or even using symbols instead of names. She mentions the name of Christoph Eglinger's wife – Maria, née Weber – only once, four and a half years after the first entry on Christoph's marriage plans, when Ursula finally meets her sis-

---

74 Sabean, "Kinship and Issues of the Self," 223; see also the contributions in Johnson and Sabean, *Sibling Relations*; Lanzinger, "Schwestern-Beziehungen"; Davidoff, *Thicker than Water*.
75 Hagenbuch, May 23, 1829, p. 374.
76 Ibid., February 14, 1824, p. 174; August 27, 1826, p. 288; May 28, 1829, p. 374; March 10, 1832, p. 504; April 29, 1832, p. 510 (citation); May 13, 1832, p. 512; June 3, 1832, p. 512.
77 Ibid., January 19, 1826, p. 262.
78 Ibid., December 29, 1819, p. 153.

ter-in-law for the first time.[79] She never mentions the wedding. In addition to this perceived misalliance, the relationship between Christoph Eglinger and his father is permanently shattered. As a daughter and a sister, Ursula is eager to see whether her brother and her beloved father manage to reconcile when the latter is on his deathbed. Christoph remains silent for a long while before he finally "utters a few words asking for forgiveness." Her father, on the other hand, has more than "words of love" to say. As Ursula notes with horror (and with appropriately disturbed grammar in the German), he announces to his assembled children: "My sons have always had certain characteristics. Emanuel was always a good friend to the house. Ch[ristoph], on the other hand, was always a more peculiar person whom it was best not to trust."[80] When the inheritance is divided after the paterfamilias dies, Christoph's wife also appears, much to Ursula's surprise and displeasure, and the two women have a dispute over the toys.[81] Apart from this event, material interests play no discernible role in the conflict. While the older brother is and remains a problem from his sister's point of view, family ties ultimately prove stronger, and the rift is never permanent. A year and a half after their father's passing, both brothers come for the evening and stay overnight at the Binningen parsonage. Their sister notes: "We were very merry and happy together."[82] A year after this event, Christoph Eglinger even becomes godfather to Ursula's youngest son, Emil Albert, while her closest friend, the teacher Rosine Gessler, is named godmother.[83] Thus the family – understood here as the nuclear family – proves to be remarkably resilient. Mutual bonds and the importance the actors attribute to the family clearly make it possible to endure conflicts and tensions.

Domestication or 'Open House'?

The extreme effort Ursula Bruckner-Eglinger puts into being a mother, housemother, wife, and housekeeper suggests that she is – in the sense of the concept of 'separate spheres' – a passive women confined to the domestic space. The repeated entries about everyday domestic stress and exhausting conflicts with the maids, as well as her insistence on 'trifles' and her continuous self-accusations with regard to the children's behavior, suggest what we today might call a kind of domestic neu-

---

79 Ibid., July 29–31, 1824, p. 198; see also Hagenbuch, "*Heute war ich bey Lisette in der Visite*", 257, n. 936.
80 Ibid., January 20, 1826, p. 262. See also July 17, 1826, p. 284.
81 Ibid., August 18, 1826, p. 287.
82 Ibid., February 7, 1828, p. 341. See also November 10 and 11, 1824, p. 215.
83 Ibid., February 8, 1829, p. 372.

rosis (*Haushaltsneurose*). But this is only one side of her personality. On the other side is a woman who repeatedly reports with great amusement on meetings with friends, hundreds of visits, various excursions, and walks. This pastor's wife is by no means 'domesticated' or socially isolated; she has an extensive network in the Basel area, which she also works to maintain. Thus her diary – in a similar way to Beneke's – provides us not least with a record of a specific visiting culture, which is distinct from the communal work and neighborhood sociability of the early modern period. It is no coincidence that the manorial parsonage complex is walled off from the neighborhood, and that the part of the house that faces the street has no windows on the ground floor. The manor-house style is supposed to provide privacy in both house and garden. However, the most relevant feature proves to be the familial and kinship relations. Social gatherings fall into various categories: from frequent, unannounced visits, to written invitations, to clubbish meetings for the men who participate in parish or friends' associations. Invitations as such do not necessarily indicate a high degree of formality. Ursula also receives "a billet" from her dear friend Rosine with a last-minute invitation for the evening.[84] In a relatively unpietistic manner, Ursula – who is barely 19 years old at the time – stops at an inn in Baden, in Aargau, with her sister and some other women, where they enjoy "delightfully tasty wine and ham."[85] Friendship – especially with other women – is extremely important to her. The circle of friends and acquaintances with whom she socializes is largely made up of relatives. She regularly meets with her sister, her cousins and second cousins, her mother's cousin, and her sisters-in-law for a meal or a chat. One exception to this is Rosine Gessler, to whom she is not related, but who is one of her closest confidants from beginning to end. Long after she is married, Ursula still needs to have an "intimate" or a "true female friend." Even shortly before her death, she still mentions her "dear female friends" in her handwritten life story.[86] The new concept of friendship that emerged around 1800 is based on a mutual, voluntary, no longer corporately bound kinship of the soul.[87] However, in this case friendship as well as kinship is linked not only to the Pietist families in the parish, but also to Basel's elite bourgeois milieu. A corresponding habitus formation takes place not only by means of pietistic-bourgeois educational principles, but also with regard to the parental or-

---

84 Ibid., June 2, 1826, p. 280.
85 Ibid., September 10, 1816, p. 101.
86 Ibid., May 26, 1826, p. 278; October 23, 1826, p. 293. On her "beloved Rosine," see also September 4, 1832, p. 519; on her "life story," see Bruckner-Eglinger Lebenslauf & Leichenrede, p. 8; on pietistic autobiographies, see Mettele, *Weltbürgertum oder Gottesreich*, 198–208.
87 See Reckwitz, *Das hybride Subjekt*, 145–51; van Dülmen, "Freundschaftskult"; Kühner, "Geschichte der Freundschaft"; Wydler, "'Wie könnte ich euch vergessen.'"

ganization of the children's social contacts. Not once does Ursula's diary mention her children playing with other children from the village or simply being sent out onto the street to amuse themselves. Instead, from an early age, they are "invited" to socialize with Basel's bourgeois families.[88]

The Bruckner-Eglingers' 'open house' has many facets. People may – and commonly do – visit or drop in on any given day. Sunday is a popular day for a visit – especially for the women, who at that time are not yet participating in the new culture around voluntary associations. After the church service and lunch are over, Ursula has the opportunity to "go into Sunday" – that is, to take part in women's meetings organized in turn at specific houses in and around Basel.[89] Compared to the strict Moravian Brethren rules that structure Sundays around the sermon and liturgy in the morning and assembly, Bible reading, and the 'common hour' in the evening, the actual organization of the day proves to be more open and liberal in this case. In general, "a Sunday at home on which we are all alone" proves to be the exception rather than the rule.[90] One ritual of interaction that combines family practice, kinship connections, and domestic openness is the 'family day.' This form of entertaining takes place sporadically – at times every two weeks – on Sundays after the church service, often in the Binningen parsonage. Ursula also mentions family gatherings in smaller groups on Thursdays, at the home of relatives in Basel. Her repeated mention of family gatherings at the Bruckner-Eglinger house on Sundays could be an indication of the parsonage's central role in this kinship network. The members of the nuclear family, siblings, in-laws, and cousins all come for the family day, although she does not spell this out in detail. The maids, who either help out or have Sundays off, do not sit at the table with the family. Significantly, after the family quarrel about his unwelcome bride, Ursula's brother Christoph comes on a Sunday in June 1820 and attends church in Binningen, but the diarist notes that he "did not have lunch with us because it was family day."[91] The core of this ritual is the common midday meal, which the family shares "in corpore."[92] Characteristically the procedure on family day combines the formal and the informal, custom and staging, the public and the private – all in the domestic context. Although the participants are related and are all familiar with each other, Ursula mentions them a few times as "gentle-

---

[88] Hagenbuch, Noveember 18, 1832, p. 526.
[89] In the original German: "in den Sonntag zu gehen"; ibid., March 21, 1824, p. 178. See also May 2, 1824, p. 185; August 22, 1824, p. 202.
[90] Ibid., February 3, 1828, p. 341. On the normative configuration of Sundays, see Mettele, *Weltbürgertum oder Gottesreich*, 60.
[91] Hagenbuch, June 1, 1820, p. 159.
[92] Ibid., June 13, 1824, p. 191.

men" and "ladies."[93] Family days are a true joy for Ursula Bruckner-Eglinger. When she is acting as hostess and something goes wrong, however, the day becomes a "labyrinth" – one such day is Sunday, October 19, 1828. Because she has a fever, she becomes "very anxious about the family day, set for next Sunday," on the Thursday before. On Friday she begins to prepare the meal, with homemade pastries for dessert. As a result of the time-consuming preparations that "are common on such occasions," she does not leave the house at all on Saturday. But then disaster threatens: her husband did not mention in the written invitation that the meal was to begin at 1 o'clock in the afternoon. So at 12 o'clock, the guests are already at the door. And then, "because of the roasting, it [the meal] is later than 1 o'clock"; "but after this, praise God, everything else went well." She sums up the day as follows: "How happy and grateful I was in the evening."[94] Despite the familial trust and intimacy among the participants, the family day is also a social event at which the Bruckner-Eglinger household presents itself. Here we already find the concurrence of a private meeting and a formalized appearance as 'gentlemen' and 'ladies,' which is typical of later bourgeois familial festive culture.

As in the case of the patrician Henriette Stettler-Herport in Bern and the lawyer Ferdinand Beneke in Hamburg, this pastor's wife in Basel places enormous importance on family, and this is notable in her diary. Yet there are also differences, especially when we compare the two women's perspectives. The bailiff's and later councilor's wife abhors obligatory social intercourse and would rather concentrate on her family in the narrow sense, and on keeping house. Fifty years later, Ursula Bruckner-Eglinger fully accepts the tasks associated with the 'pious house,' but she clearly suffers under this burden. Visits from friends, socializing over lunch, making the social rounds, and going for walks are all forms of recreation for her, which she does not perceive to be in conflict with her duties as a mother and a housemother. The pastor's wife's everyday radius is not domesticated, and she makes decisions independently. Nevertheless, the beautiful parsonage repeatedly becomes a psychological 'labyrinth.' In her "life story," which she writes by hand in her old age, the pastor's widow looks back with gratitude on her "happy family life" in Binningen.[95] In contrast, the reality documented in her diary depicts a domestic muddle and the bourgeoisification of a woman's everyday suffering. In its central as-

---

93 Ibid., December 24, 1820, p. 168; see also December 12, 1819, p. 152.
94 Ibid., October 16–19, 1828, p. 362. On bourgeois festive culture, see Baumert, *Bürgerliche Familienfeste*.
95 Bruckner-Eglinger, Lebenslauf & Leichenrede, p. 9.

pects, the Bruckner-Eglinger family is in line with the trend of the time, which concerns social and religious endogamy in matchmaking and marriage, exclusively kinship-based sociability, gender roles in the home, and the formation of a bourgeois habitus.

Chapter 7
A Traveling Journeyman's Home: Friedrich Anton Püschmann

Stollberg, Germany, and on the Road (1848 – 1856)

The reader might be surprised to find a chapter on an itinerant journeyman's 'home' in a book on family history. However, as we have already seen, the domestic microcosm encompasses more than the members of the immediate family. To achieve a broader understanding of the home and the family in the age of bourgeois modernity, we must also explore the social spaces on the border as well as beyond the boundaries of the bourgeoisie. On the one hand, this chapter focuses on the journeyman Püschmann's family of origin, to whom he returns several times over the course of his travels; on the other hand, it is about the various forms of domesticity that he passively experiences or actively practices, both during his apprenticeship and on his travels as a journeyman. How do the experiences of a journeyman on the road relate to the concept of the privatized bourgeois nuclear family?

Friedrich Anton Püschmann, born on July 25, 1829 in Mitteldorf, in the Erz Mountains near Stollberg, was not necessarily born into his craft. He grew up as the second of eight children, the son of a schoolteacher in Saxony, but only three of these eight siblings lived to adulthood: Friedrich Anton, his elder brother Ernst, and his younger brother Wilhelm.[1] From today's perspective, his father's profession might lead the reader to expect that the family enjoyed financial security and middle-class social status. But as a schoolteacher in a village with a population of around 600 people, Johann Gottfried Püschmann received a meager annual salary of no more than 120 talers, which was barely enough to feed his family. During the transition from church to state control of the school system in the nineteenth century, the struggle for civil-servant status, the establishment of minimum salaries, and the regulation of training for elementary schoolteachers were decades-long processes. At that time, rural schoolteachers were paid less than their colleagues in urban contexts. At least the Püschmanns were able to move into a rent-free apartment on the upper floor of the school building, which

---

[1] Püschmann, "Vorerinnerung" to his diary, vol. 1, no date (probably January 1848), p. 3. In the following references, dates and page numbers refer to the critical edition of the diary edited by Matthias John.

stood in the middle of the village.² The government did not approve of teachers earning money on the side. Nevertheless, to make ends meet, the Püschmanns were dependent on subsistence farming. Their household included a potato field as well as a cow and her calves. In the winter months and in preparation for large family celebrations, they slaughtered livestock. To save money, the family also baked bread and *Stollen* (fruitcake) at home.³ A maidservant, whom Püschmann visited after his apprenticeship, rounded out the household.⁴ The material and spiritual limitations that life as a village schoolteacher entailed were both idealized and ridiculed in the literary fiction of the time, such as in Jean Paul's *The Life of the Merry Little Schoolmaster Maria Wutz in Auenthal* (*Leben des vergnügten Schulmeisterlein Maria Wutz im Auenthal*). Any attempt to pinpoint Friedrich Anton Püschmann's place in the social hierarchy provides a telling example of the problems inherent in applying social-historical categories to specific individual circumstances. As the son of a schoolteacher, who in turn came from a family of schoolteachers, Friedrich Anton was raised in modest circumstances, but he had access to pedagogical techniques. From an early age, he assisted his father in teaching the village children. Yet pursuing higher education – in her biography of his life, his daughter mentions that he had wanted to become a pastor⁵ – was out of the question for financial reasons. His uncle, a village blacksmith, wanted to train him in that profession, but Püschmann was not physically strong enough for the work. If we examine the visiting culture and practices that obtained in the Püschmanns' social context in the villages and small towns of the Erz Mountains, we see that the family's network of relatives and neighbors included members of the professional class (schoolteachers and pastors), village craftsmen (blacksmiths and bricklayers), and lower-class laborers (hosiers, soldiers, miners, and maidservants).

---

2 On Johann Gottfried Püschmann's salary, see the biography written by Friedrich Anton Püschmann's daughter: Görnandt, *Die von der Tochter verfasste Lebensskizze*, 844. On the number of inhabitants in Mitteldorf, see Digitales Historisches Ortsverzeichnis von Sachsen: hov.isgv.de/Mitteldorf. On the schoolteachers' struggle for social standing and fair wages in the nineteenth century, with reference to Baden as an example, see B. Wunder, *Vom Dorfschulmeister zum Staatsbeamten*, 17–79.
3 John, March 20, 1848, p. 84; June 20, 1848, p. 204; June 28, 1848, p. 211; December 21–22, 1849, p. 378; January 1, 1855, p. 682; May 26, 1855, p. 708.
4 Ibid., June 24, 1848, p. 208; see also the entry for June 18, 1848, p. 203.
5 See Görnandt, *Die von der Tochter verfasste Lebensskizze*, 843.

The Craftsman's Honor, Bourgeois Values (*Bürgerlichkeit*), and Leisure Time

In 1843, when he was not yet 14 years old, the boy called Anton was sent to the printworks in Grimma, about 100 kilometers from his home village, to become a typesetter's apprentice. This came about more by chance than by design, as news of a vacant apprenticeship reached the Püschmann family. Thus Friedrich Anton became a journeyman letterpress printer. Later in life, however, he repeatedly identifies his profession simply as "worker."[6] Pro forma, Püschmann's social status during this phase of his life would be classified as falling somewhere between the petite bourgeoisie and the proletariat.[7] After five years working as an apprentice in Grimma, at just 19 years old, Püschmann began his journeyman's tour in July 1848. His travels took him from Saxony via the Rhineland to Rostock, through Switzerland to Lake Geneva, and via Bavaria through Austria to Vienna. Yet by the time he returned home for a visit in January 1855, Püschmann had become resigned to the fact that the printing trade offered no prospect of a secure livelihood. At the age of 25, with the encouragement of his father and family friends, he decided to retrain as a teacher at the Saxon teacher training college, which was also located in Grimma, and thus to carry on his father's profession.[8] Püschmann began keeping a diary toward the end of his first apprenticeship, in January 1848, and his diary ends during his teacher training.

In order to understand the statements in the diary on which this chapter is based, its author must first be introduced in more detail. Püschmann the journeyman printer's personality integrates various aspects that reveal him to be a complex 'hybrid subject' (Reckwitz). His thoughts and actions combine the old corporate codes of the craftsman's honor with the virtues of the bourgeoisie, which in some respects cannot be clearly distinguished. For example, Püschmann's thrift and modesty are not only attested in the retrospective account given by his daughter, but can also be deduced in numerous entries written by the diarist himself. Despite long periods of unemployment, he managed to set aside the sum of 100 talers – approximately two-thirds of a Saxon schoolteacher's annual salary – between the time he began his journeyman's travels and his return to Mitteldorf at the beginning of 1855. He intended to use this money to outfit himself with "sufficient clothing," and these savings then serve as start-up capital and provision for

---

6 In the original German: "Arbeiter"; John, August 27, 1851, p. 511; July 24, 1853, pp. 585–86; September 10, 1853, p. 590; April 29, 1855, p. 704.
7 See F. Lenger, *Zwischen Kleinbürgertum und Proletariat*; see also F. Lenger, *Sozialgeschichte*, 70–71 and 90.
8 John, esp. the entries beginning on January 16, 1855, pp. 684–87.

Fig. 13: Friedrich Anton Püschmann in his old age. Source: Matthias John

his teacher training.[9] Many of the entries testify to the author's sense of propriety with regard to proper, clean clothing, but he also participates in the common practice by which the apprentices in the Grimma printworks lend each other items of clothing as well as money, when necessary.[10] Püschmann's love of order sometimes leads to conflicts with his work colleagues. Although the honor of his guild is no longer an issue for him, and the expected corporate support extends merely to a snack ('Viaticum') that he receives at the various printworks on his travels, he places a high value on collegiality. His comrades repeatedly elect him to office or appoint him to perform particular tasks, such as in April 1848, when he writes a petition on behalf of the apprentices at the Grimma printworks to the publisher,

---

9 Ibid., January 16, 1855, p. 685.
10 Ibid., May 14, 1848, p. 144; May 6, 1848, p. 138; May 9–16, 1848, pp. 141–46.

the privy councilor Ferdinand Carl Philippi, and also presents it on their behalf.[11] In Basel, he is elected president and then secretary of the German Singing Society in 1851.[12]

Püschmann is a political man. He vigorously supports the demand for press freedom and sympathizes with the National Assembly in Frankfurt as well as the revolution in Vienna. He makes fun of the kings of Prussia and Austria, and attends meetings of the workers' (educational) associations in Hamburg.[13] His diary documents the ways in which the politicization that occurred in the context of the Revolutions of 1848 pervaded everyday conversation among the lower classes. For example, he reports on a "lively political debate" at the Grimma printworks in March 1848, "in which unfortunately I had to fight alone as the sole moderate liberal against a chorus of radicals, republicans, and communists."[14] While he classifies himself as a liberal, his habitus is nevertheless that of someone who supports the revolution. When he arrives in Hamburg in January 1849, at the age of 19, to take up a job in the Rauhes Haus printworks, his appearance immediately attracts the attention of a police officer: "By virtue of his office as one who sniffs out demagogues, a police officer (who probably thought I looked too democratic, with my shirt untucked, my German watchband, and the cockade on my partisan's hat) stopped me and asked for my passport."[15] Püschmann is also a religious man, and at times regularly attends church services and – although he is a Lutheran – sometimes a Catholic mass.[16] While he distances himself from "Hamburg philistinism,"[17] he embodies educational aspirations that we can perhaps identify as genuinely bourgeois, but that – by the mid-nineteenth century – have long since extended beyond the social boundaries of the bourgeoisie, narrowly defined. In their rare free time, the apprentices at the Grimma printworks read aloud to each other from various books, go for walks, recite poems, and play cards and chess.[18] At each place he stops, Püschmann likes to go to the theater – about which he makes meticulous notes and comments in his diary – much more often than Beneke did in Hamburg, as well as to concerts, churches, and museums.

---

11 Ibid., April 13, 1848, pp. 113–15; April 15, 1848, pp. 119–21. Conflicts also arose later in the teacher training seminar, for which Püschmann acted as an "Ordnungsaufseher" (supervisor): November 30–December 21, 1855, pp. 742–48.
12 Ibid., July 23, 1851, p. 504.
13 Ibid., May 28, 1849, p. 344; August 12, 1855, pp. 355–56.
14 Ibid., March 16, 1848, p. 77.
15 Ibid., January 18, 1849, p. 324.
16 Ibid., July 16, 1848, p. 226; February 18, 1849, p. 327.
17 Ibid., May 28, 1849, p. 344.
18 Ibid., January 8, 1848, p. 16; March 12, 1848, p. 67; April 30, 1848, p. 134.

Püschmann reads, writes, draws, sings in the choir, and learns to play the piano. In Hamburg, he obtains a copy of Goethe's *Wilhelm Meister's Apprenticeship* from a lending library, which he reads in the botanical garden.[19] In Stuttgart, he attends advanced training courses for master craftsmen and journeymen, including physics and chemistry lessons.[20]

His 'gender character' is constructed along bourgeois lines. He paints a picture of himself as a morally conscientious young man, sensible and curious. But this is only one facet of our subject. In another of his facets, compared to the other diarists we have encountered thus far, a new tone comes into play. Even as an apprentice, and also later as a journeyman, Püschmann is an enthusiastic dancer, noting: "I danced a lot today."[21] Joint ventures with other apprentices or journeymen regularly end in the pub over beer. During his journey through German-speaking Central Europe, the diary increasingly becomes a record of his leisure activities, which take place primarily on Sundays. In the process, as Peter-Paul Bänziger notes of other diarists writing around 1900, we see a novel orientation toward experience already unfolding. Regardless of whether Püschmann goes dancing or ice skating, visits a fair or attends a soiree, amusement is important to him: "I still had a very good time," he writes, and again: "We had a good time."[22] Amusement means shared fun and entertainment with male companions, and often also with single women. Püschmann's diary makes a much clearer distinction between work and leisure than the other diaries we have considered thus far. Here pleasant, substantial leisure time becomes a value in itself.

Püschmann's diary brings together various purposes, some of which no longer have much to do with the Foucaultian concept of self-conditioning. Nor is it about giving an account of the author's soul, his psychological problems, or his perpetual introspection, as was the case in the pietistic milieu. As an apprentice, a journeyman, and later as a trainee teacher, he prefers a concise, sober writing style. He sometimes refers to his diary as a "chronicle," sometimes as a "notebook," and toward the end he also calls it "my self-biography."[23] Autobiographical texts written by traveling journeymen were not uncommon in the nineteenth century. Typically they were intended to document the author's competence as a craftsman as well as the topoi of an educational journey.[24] Both of these aspects are evident in Püsch-

---

19 Ibid., June 3 and 10, 1849, pp. 346–47.
20 Ibid., "Ende Januar" 1854, p. 619.
21 Ibid., May 21, 1848, p. 158.
22 Ibid., March 13, 1851, p. 490; May 4, 1851, p. 495. On this topic more generally, see Bänziger, *Die Moderne als Erlebnis*, 17.
23 John (in order of citation), July 31, 1848, p. 248; August 15, 1848, p. 269; June 1, 1855, p. 681.
24 See Wadauer, *Die Tour der Gesellen*, esp. 18, 80–83, and 194–96.

mann's diary, although craftsmanship is a particularly important topic during his apprenticeship and becomes less important later. In addition, as mentioned above, the diary includes numerous entries on the leisure activities its author finds worth remembering. Last but not least, the diary contains – as Beneke's diary did – an extremely large number of names, which is an indication of the significance the actor attributes to everyday interactions and social relationships. Every now and then, Püschmann's entries display a flash of his sense of irony and his literary talent. On December 12, 1955, which was King John of Saxony's 54th birthday, a lady who lives in the house invites the teacher trainees in Grimma to dinner. As Püschmann notes: "In the evening, Madame Zschau (perhaps less in honor of the king's birthday, and more to celebrate the death anniversary of a pig) treated us to sausage broth."[25]

Collective Domesticity Among Young Men

Where and how do home and family come into play in a traveling journeyman's diary? On the one hand, Püschmann gives relatively detailed reports on stays with his family in Mitteldorf, Saxony after the end of his apprenticeship, on stopovers during his travels, and after he returns to his home village, when he makes the decision to change his profession. He is in constant contact with his parents and brothers during his journey, sending and receiving letters and parcels. On the other hand, in this case we benefit from extending our question beyond the nuclear family to the domestic sphere more broadly.[26] Püschmann himself repeatedly refers to his various lodgings as 'home' during his apprenticeship in Grimma, when he lives with the other apprentices in the same building that houses the printworks, and later, when he stays in various accommodation as he travels for work: he goes "home," spends evenings "at home," or recounts how he "warmed up completely and enjoyed a simple supper at home."[27] Even when he changes quarters daily during his travels, this way of life can be compared to the bourgeois family's relatively stable form of accommodation under the rubric of the 'domestic sphere.'

---

25 John, December 12, 1855, p. 747.
26 For more on this approach, see Eibach and Lanzinger, *The Routledge History of the Domestic Sphere*.
27 In the original German: "nach Hause"; "zu Hause"; "zu Hause vollkommen erwärmt und ein einfaches Abendbrot genossen"; John, January 3, 1848, p. 15; March 2, 1848, p. 57; January 2, 1848, p. 14; and many other similar formulations, *passim*.

Püschmann's account of how the apprentices lived together at the printworks in Grimma, Saxony in 1848 is reminiscent of a groundbreaking text in new cultural history, which is also based on a journeyman worker's self-narrative: Robert Darnton's article on the great cat massacre at a Paris print workshop in the 1730s. According to the account provided by a certain Nicolas Contat, the apprentices in the Paris printworks lived in precarious circumstances. Their dormitory was dirty and cold, and they had to endure the journeymen's harassment and the master's mistreatment. Above all, they were not allowed to sit at the master's family table and were served inedible leftovers from the family meal. One day, the journeymen and the apprentices decide to kill the cats that had been depriving them of sleep at night, both the stray cats and their hated master's wife's favorite cat.[28] Püschmann's diary entries from his time as an apprentice in Grimma do not offer such dramatic accounts, but certain parallels do exist. The apprentices refer to their filthy quarters in the printworks as "our tough-luck tar village" (*Pechdorf*) or a "miserable bedbug's nest," where they are forced to live together as a "*Pechdorf* fraternity."[29] Thanks to Matthias John's research on the subject, we have photographic evidence of how the former printworks looks today.

Fig. 14: The former printworks building on Frauenstraße in Grimma, as it appears today. Source: Wikimedia Commons

The relationship between the apprentices and the journeymen seems to have been relatively unproblematic. Yet Püschmann does mention that the foreman, Mr. Krüger, employs violence against the apprentices, which is one reason for their pe-

---

28 See Darnton, *Das große Katzenmassaker*, esp. 91.
29 John, March 12, 1848, p. 74; June 2, 1855, p. 714; July 25, 1848, p. 242; *passim*.

tition demanding his suspension in April 1848.[30] The living and working conditions in the Grimma printworks are nothing like a 'whole house' (*ganzes Haus*). Rather, this is a small factory in which more than 20 'workers' – meaning apprentices – also eat together and sleep in a dormitory together.[31] In addition, a roughly equal number of journeymen work in the building. Working hours are not regulated and often extend late into the night and include Sunday mornings. As Püschmann notes, the printers in Leipzig demand a 10-hour workday in April 1848.[32] The 'principal' of the publishing house, Privy Councilor Philippi, does not fulfil the role of the housefather, but is rather an aloof entrepreneur who enforces his authority in the printworks by means of a manager and a foreman. The food served by the cook in the canteen is sometimes so bad that it causes nausea and vomiting. Unlike their Parisian counterparts more than a century earlier, the Saxon apprentices send the food back to the kitchen and receive a few pennies as compensation.[33] When Püschmann is finally allowed to move out of the *Pechdorf* at the end of his five-year apprenticeship and into lodgings with a Mrs. Stockmann in Grimma, he enthusiastically notes the quality of the meals: breakfast consists of "coffee and rolls," and also "(on request) zwieback, sugar, and fresh water." Lunch on Whitsunday is "more and better than it has been for a long time" and consists of soup, a veal roast, and salad.[34] The entries he makes during his journey concerning overnight stays in simple inns also indicate that a good breakfast in the mid-nineteenth century usually consists of coffee and a roll, and in Bavaria a beer as well.[35] On Sundays and holidays, Püschmann's wish list includes meals with meat.

While the journeymen live in private lodgings rather than on the premises of the printworks in Grimma, the apprentices' cohabitation can be understood as a non-hierarchical domestic model consisting solely of young men, in contrast to the bourgeois nuclear family. The premises serve many purposes and are used collectively. To the extent that a private sphere exists, it is merely situational. In the typesetting room, the main workroom where Püschmann typesets the *Saxon Church Newspaper* (*Sächsische Kirchenzeitung*) during the day, he also writes letters, diary entries, and occasionally poems in the evenings or on Sundays. The ma-

---

30 Ibid., April 9, 1848, pp. 106–7; April 12, 1848, p. 110; April 13, 1848, p. 113; see also the entry that mentions the manager Förk slapping an apprentice in the face for insubordination: April 18, 1848, p. 124.
31 Ibid., May 4, 1848, p. 137 (citation); see also April 14, 1848, p. 119.
32 Ibid., April 5, 1848, pp. 102–3. On the number of journeymen ("Gehilfen") at the Grimma printworks, see June 7, 1848, p. 176.
33 Ibid., March 7, 1848, pp. 63–64; April 1, 1848, p. 99.
34 Ibid., June 11–13, 1848, pp. 181–86.
35 Ibid., August 14, 1848, p. 268.

chine room – which, like the typesetting room, can be heated with a stove – serves as a living room for the apprentices, where they play cards at night. The dining room also has a stove and is used on Sunday afternoons for communal singing, dancing, and birthday parties. The clothes closet provides bathing facilities, which Püschmann monopolizes once a week, on Sunday mornings.[36] The apprentices cut their own hair in the book room. The communal dormitory and the kitchen complete this picture.

Although a cook is engaged to provide hot food, the 'boys' are also involved in certain household activities and have to take care of their personal needs on their own. Püschmann makes coffee with one of his comrades in the morning and "roasts a pan of apples on the side." The apprentices clean together and make their own beds with fresh bedlinen. Mrs. Beilig, a widow from Grimma, regularly takes in the apprentices' clothes to wash for a fee, but Püschmann also often does the "big laundry" himself – in the typesetting room, on weekends – and also mends his own clothes.[37] The 18-year-old apprentice notes these activities as evidence of his independence. His diary documents a different concept of masculinity than the bourgeois 'gender character' or the concept of 'gentle masculinity' in the period around 1800. In this regard, we should also take note of the collective leisure activities in which he participates, as these perpetuate a premodern, corporate understanding of honor.[38] The apprentices regularly attend "dancing lessons" at dance halls in the vicinity of Grimma, sometimes accompanied by the journeymen, and even take lessons from a dance master.[39] This activity is associated with the hope that female dancers will also attend. Nevertheless, when the young women fail to show up, the men, "in the absence of female dancers, dance among themselves without music."[40] On the one hand, this is a matter of amusing themselves and enjoying recreation in their scarce leisure time; on the other, it is also a collective performance of masculinity. Thus after their dance lessons, the boys from the printworks parade through the streets with the girls, or even "with comrades."

---

36 Ibid., Sunday, January 23, 1848, p. 28: "I prepared warm water for myself and washed myself in the cold clothes closet". On the following, see January 21, 1848, p. 26; February 2–6, 1848, pp. 35–37; February 13, 1848, pp. 41–45; February 19–20, 1848, pp. 47–49; February 26–27, 1848, pp. 53–54.
37 Ibid., esp. January 16–22, 1848, pp. 24–26 (citations); January 1, 1848, p. 11; February 27, 1848, p. 54; March 18, 1848, p. 77; April 16, 1848, p. 121; June 3, 1848, p. 172. On the following, see Hausen, "Die Polarisierung der Geschlechtscharaktere," esp. 368; Trepp, "Anders als sein 'Geschlechtscharakter'"; "Männerwelten privat"; and *Sanfte Männlichkeit*.
38 See Grießinger's groundbreaking study on the 'symbolic capital' of the craftsman's honor: Grießinger, *Das symbolische Kapital der Ehre*; on the history of apprentices, see Grießinger and Reith, "Lehrlinge."
39 John, January 3, 1848, p. 15; January 10, 1848, p. 19; January 31, 1848, p. 34.
40 Ibid., April 2, 1848, p. 100.

They sing their "press freedom song" loudly in public and engage in verbal duels with soldiers, who also roam the city in groups when they are off duty.[41] Whether matchmaking and starting a family are also a motive for these dance lessons with single women is a question we will consider below.

The Journeyman's Travels: Variable Accommodation and No Privacy

Contrary to his hopes, Püschmann's completion of his apprenticeship on June 10, 1848, which he celebrates with his fellow journeymen by consuming copious amounts of alcohol, does not lead to a job at the Grimma publishing house – which is rumored to be on the verge of bankruptcy.[42] After a few weeks' rest at home in Mitteldorf, Püschmann has to undertake a journeyman's tour in search of employment ('condition') and wages. Even more so than the community of young men in the factory-like printworks, Püschmann's itinerant existence on the road stands in stark contrast to the ideal concept of the bourgeois family, which is associated with stability and a fixed location. From this point of view, we would do well to examine Püschmann's six-and-a-half-year journey (*Walz*), which was repeatedly interrupted by periods of steady employment. Our journeyman traveled primarily, but by no means exclusively, on foot. Over the course of his journey, he travels more and more often by train or even by steamboat on the Rhine, the Elbe, the Danube, and several Swiss lakes. He usually stays in simple inns or taverns, the price and quality of which the journeymen discuss among themselves. In these locales he meets other journeymen, as well as soldiers and traveling salesmen. One aspect of this uncertain life on the road is that he cannot plan where he will stay next. Time and again Püschmann ends up in "a miserable pub," a shed, a barn, or – as in Brno – sleeping "in straw with a bunch of strangers."[43] From a bourgeois point of view, sharing a bed with an itinerant companion was unthinkable – both hygienically and morally – yet this was a necessary aspect of life on the road.[44] One typical feature of this transient lifestyle was that the traveler developed short-term traveling companies with two or three other journeymen, and also with women of very different origins who were looking for work.

---

41 Ibid., March 12, 1848, p. 74 (first citation); March 19, 1848 p. 79 (second citation); April 11, 1848, p. 109; see also February 23, 1848, p. 51; February 27, 1848, p. 55.
42 Ibid., June 7, 1848, p. 176; June 10, 1848, pp. 178–81.
43 Ibid., August 25, 1848; p. 277; October 18, 1854, p. 660.
44 Ibid., September 5, 1850, p. 431; see also November 12, 1854, p. 674, in which Püschmann reports staying overnight with his cousin and sharing a bed.

Püschmann's entries show that making new acquaintances was easy in this mobile society. He never mentions problems with the language, either in Germany or in Switzerland.[45] It seems that everyone speaks their own dialect. He is never robbed, nor does he complain about the everyday uncertainties of life on the road. When he receives his first 'condition' at a printworks in Rostock in October 1848, after three months of traveling, he is more than happy and gives thanks for "the Lord's goodness," despite working 12 hours a day.[46]

During his travels, which last several years, Püschmann finds employment with printers or publishers in the following cities: Rostock (October 1848 – January 1849), Hamburg (January–November 1849), Dresden (February–June 1850), Sulzbach (July–August 1850), Zug (November 1850), Basel (December 1850 – May 1852), Zurich (May 1852 – April 1853), Lausanne (April–September 1853), and Stuttgart (September 1853 – September 1854). These posts could be terminated by either party at any time. Thus Püschmann works and earns wages in Rostock for only three months, in Sulzbach for six weeks, and in Zug for two weeks. He works for the longest periods in Basel, Zurich, and Stuttgart. His living conditions are also often temporary, as Püschmann frequently changes his lodgings during longer stays. At this time, journeymen have long since ceased to live in the master's household. As a rule, they can rent a simple room cheaply on the local housing market, sometimes including meals. However, it is not uncommon for Püschmann to take his meals at an inn, at a butcher's, or at the home of a widow, who earns extra money in this way.

Püschmann's domestic relations range from a distant, solely financial landlord–tenant relationship that seems distinctly modern to a family connection that may even extend to calling his landlords 'father' and 'mother,' as he does in Hamburg. He pays 6 marks per month in rent for his "small, decent room" with the Brust family in Hamburg, and 1 thaler per week "for the midday meal with the Schultzens at the 'Schinkenkrug.'"[47] The 19-year-old journeyman, who is not the only tenant in the Brust household, becomes a temporary member of the family. When he falls ill with scabies, he is not sent to the hospital, but is cared for by his landlords at home. Püschmann accompanies Mr. Brust to the oratory and Mrs. Brust to church and on walks; he also takes a trip with the whole family at Pentecost. He exchanges birthday gifts with the family's young son.[48] After ten months

---

45 One exception to this occurs at an inn in Bonn, where Püschmann was more than a little amused by the recruits' peculiar dialects: ibid., September 7, 1848, p. 291.
46 Ibid., October 11, 1848, p. 310.
47 Ibid., January 18, 1849, p. 325.
48 Ibid., February 4, 1849, p. 326; February 18, 1849, p. 327; May 27, 1849, p. 343; July 26, 1849, p. 354.

together, their farewell is tearful, and Püschmann maintains a correspondence with Mrs. Brust after he leaves.

The conditions of open domesticity in which tenants and landlords had everyday contact were definitely not an exception in the first half of the nineteenth century. In Hamburg, 22-year-old Ferdinand Beneke is regularly invited to dinners or parties by his landlord, a broker, and is also on good terms with his maid.[49] However, Püschmann's diary reveals that his close personal relationship with his landlords, the Brusts, also has its downsides. Due to his "dear landlady's curiosity," he writes his diary entries in code for a time.[50] And after a week of recovering from an illness at the Brust family home, he notes that "the constrained behavior I was obliged to adopt toward my foster parents and my brother Alex was most annoying to me."[51] His refusal to eat lunch with the family, which he explicitly notes more than once, indicates that he perceives this co-presence and personal closeness as problematic. The end of the traditional table fellowship shared with other journeymen and apprentices, which Wilhelm Heinrich Riehl laments in another context during the same period as an indicator of the decline of patriarchal mores and the 'whole house' model,[52] is not something Püschmann experiences as a loss. He finds himself in the same situation six years later, as a trainee teacher who lives in his trainer Mr. Kohl's house in Thalheim, Saxony. Püschmann appreciates this church-school teacher as an educator, but just before the Easter holidays, the housefather informs him that he and his wife "would prefer it if I bought bread and butter for myself on my return and took lunch at the inn, which suggestion was very welcome to me, since I always felt a bit embarrassed in the house and at Mr. Kohl's table."[53] Püschmann's experience corresponds to the results of English research on the social history of relations between neighbors, according to which the idea of what constituted being a good neighbor changed in the modern era from a relationship of mutual support to one in which certain rules of social distance were observed.[54] Püschmann appreciates his connections with his landlords and enjoys spending time with them on certain occasions. In Zurich, his relationship with his landlords, Mr. and Mrs. Brunner, is so good that they invite the journeyman from Saxony and his colleague, Mr. Lamm, to a garden party given by the owner of the house – the mayor of Zurich, Alfred Escher – in the Enge district

---

49 Beneke, *Tagebücher*, October 17, 1796, vol. 2.2, p. 128; November 25, 1796, pp. 147–48; May 28, 1797, p. 238; June 11, 1797, pp. 244–45; with thanks to Frank Hatje for bringing this to my attention.
50 John, February 25, 1849, p. 329.
51 Ibid., February 4, 1849, p. 326. On the following, see July 31, 1849, p. 354.
52 See Riehl, *Die Naturgeschichte*, 153.
53 John, April 1855 (no exact date), p. 698; see also May 2, 1855, p. 706.
54 See Wrightson, "The 'Decline of Neighbourliness' Revisited"; Cockayne, *Cheek by Jowl*.

of the city. Five months after leaving Zurich, as Püschmann travels through the city once again on his way from Lausanne to Stuttgart, he does not neglect to pay a visit to his former landlords.[55] In Stuttgart he does not develop a close personal relationship with his landlords, although the couple "are friendly and obliging"; but he does become close to Mrs. Pfeifer, a widow who makes lunch for Püschmann and Lamm.[56] The two journeymen spend Christmas, New Year's Eve, Shrove Tuesday, and some Sundays with the elderly Mrs. Pfeifer and some young women with whom they are acquainted. Overall, good relationships with his landlords are quite gratifying to Püschmann, but he finds the obligation to be present for regular convivial meals and to maintain a close connection with the family ambivalent and problematic. Despite his frequent use of the term 'home,' his relationship with his landlords – which is temporary and expedient for both parties – remains distant in most cases.

Yet Püschmann's temporary living conditions give no indication that privacy – understood as a socially demarcated sphere for his own, individual use – would have been important to him. In fact, the opposite is true: he often uncomplainingly shares his room with a 'fellow lodger.' In Rostock, he is relieved at the prospect of "hopefully moving into and occupying a pleasant little room for a longer period of time" at the home of a widow. The fact that another typesetter named Miers from Prenzlau arrives a few days later and "will lodge with me" does not bother him. Moreover, Püschmann spends his limited free time going for walks, scouring the city for young women, and visiting a dance hall with his "roommate," Miers.[57] They remain in contact even after their time together in Rostock comes to an end. Although Püschmann is quite happy to spend time alone in his room reading or writing, two people sharing a room is very much the norm. He never mentions this living situation as a problem, and even looks for a room along with a 'colleague' a few times. In Rostock, Püschmann shares a room with Miers. With the Brust family in Hamburg, he has a room to himself, but he is happy when two Prussian (actually Polish) soldiers also take up lodgings in the house, because he "has a lot of fun" with them.[58] In Dresden he shares a room with a man named Dotzauer; in Sulzbach, with his Saxon compatriot, Lamm; in Basel, first with a Mr. Ott, and then again with Lamm; in Zurich, also with Lamm; in Lausanne, with the Norwegian printer Nielsen; and finally, back in Stuttgart, "with my old roommate" Lamm

---

55 John, September 12, 1852, p. 556; September 19–20, 1853, p. 608.
56 Ibid., December 30, 1853 until the end of February (no exact date) 1854, pp. 617–19; July 2, 1854, p. 627 (citation).
57 Ibid., October 11, 1848, p. 311; October 17, 1848, p. 312; April 21, 1849, p. 334.
58 Ibid., August 31, 1849, p. 360.

again.⁵⁹ On the question of co-presence versus privacy, it is remarkable that Püschmann and Ott, whom he has known only briefly, have two rooms at their disposal in Basel, but instead of each taking one room, they divide their domestic sphere into a "living room" and a shared "bedchamber."⁶⁰ Apparently it was normal and common to sleep two to a room. In this respect, one cannot detect a 'passion for privacy';⁶¹ Püschmann does not desire a private, personal retreat.

One of the basic tenets of this journeyman's diary is his appreciation of social interaction on an equal footing. Püschmann spends an enormous amount of time with 'comrades,' 'colleagues,' and 'fellow lodgers.' Two bachelors cohabiting in a confined space – a situation which, in contrast to the nuclear family model, could be described *cum grano salis* as the Bert and Ernie domestic model – was not an exception to the norm in this mobile society, but in this case the arrangement was temporary in nature. Two men living together in this way were also more likely to be suspected of homosexuality than two single women cohabiting.⁶² While our two Sesame Street roommates are known to be quite different characters, one cannot say much about the character traits of many of Püschmann's roommates. In addition, this also raises the question of whether one can speak of friendship beyond camaraderie and collegiality, as one can with Bert and Ernie. The issue of friendship primarily concerns Püschmann's compatriot Lamm, with whom he spends months on the road, sharing lodgings in Sulzbach, Basel, Zurich, and Stuttgart. Püschmann and Lamm leave coveted job vacancies to each other, give notice jointly, and inform each other by letter when a journeyman is wanted at their respective printworks. If the other then moves to the city, they rent a room together at the next opportunity.⁶³

Püschmann first meets the journeyman printer "Herr Lamm" in July 1848, while he is looking for work, and then encounters him again two years later, when he is 20 years old and employed at the Teubner publishing house in Dresden.⁶⁴ The index of the critical edition of Püschmann's text shows that Lamm's name is the most frequently mentioned over the eight years in which Püschmann kept the diary. Püschmann never mentions his colleague's first name, but this is probably not a good indication of the closeness of their relationship. Even Ferdinand Beneke, who pondered the nature of friendship, usually notes the names

---

59 Ibid., October 7, 1853, p. 615.
60 Ibid., March 23, 1851, p. 491.
61 See the title of Heyl's book on the subject: *A Passion for Privacy.*
62 See B. Kuhn, *Familienstand*, 303–7.
63 John, November 3, 1850, p. 467; May 10, 1851, pp. 495–96; May 15, 1852, p. 535; September 10, 1853, p. 590; October 7, 1853, p. 615.
64 Ibid., July 17, 1848, p. 228; February 1, 1850, p. 387 (citation).

of his closest friends briefly and succinctly, as 'Rambach' or 'Schlingemann.' Püschmann alternately refers to Lamm as his 'fellow lodger,' his 'roommate,' his 'faithful companion,' and increasingly as his 'friend': "my good friend," "my dear friend and colleague," and also "my friend Lamm's fiancée."[65] Their relationship is voluntary, reciprocal, and goes beyond corporate camaraderie. Püschmann and Lamm trust each other, a fact which becomes particularly clear when they exchange information about available jobs or visit each other's sickbeds, such as when Lamm is in the hospital with scabies.[66] They share formative interests, such as a penchant for the theater, which they regularly visit together, as well as poetry and time spent in nature. Here and there, the entries also suggest Romantic intimacy. As Püschmann reports on the end of a Sunday excursion from Basel to Binningen: "I lingered with Lamm at St. Margarethen" – coincidentally the very church at which Abraham Bruckner had been a pastor 20 years earlier – "until after sunset."[67] The friendly relationship between these two journeymen printers also has an emotional aspect. When Püschmann receives a 'condition' in Basel and Lamm does not, but Lamm then receives one in Zurich a week later, Püschmann notes "that a weight has been lifted from my heart."[68] After enduring a frustratingly lonely Christmas in Basel, Püschmann thinks longingly of his "friend Lamm in Zurich." And years later, when Lamm decides to leave Stuttgart for his native Saxony, "I escorted the perennial companion of all my experiences to the train. He was very moved when we said goodbye."[69] All things considered, Lamm and Püschmann had much more in common than a practical living arrangement or a boozy camaraderie. The affinity of spirit and soul between these two journeymen corresponds to the style of friendship that was common at the time, and their friendship indicates that this was not solely the domain of the educated bourgeoisie (*Bildungsbürgertum*).[70] Püschmann's entries offer no indication of homosexuality.

---

[65] Ibid., November 28, 1850, p. 474; June 13, 1854, p. 626; April 27, 1855, p. 701; April 29, 1855, p. 704.
[66] Ibid., March 14 and 21, 1852, p. 529. On the history of friendship more generally, see Kühner, "Geschichte der Freundschaft"; on friendship in the nineteenth century, see van Dülmen, *Entdeckung des Ich*.
[67] John, July 6, 1851, p. 504.
[68] Ibid., December 4, 1850, p. 477. On the following, see December 31, 1850, p. 481.
[69] Ibid., June 13, 1854, p. 626.
[70] On friendship around 1800, including a comprehensive bibliography, see Wydler, "'Wie könnte ich euch vergessen,'" 23–25.

Limited Marriage Prospects: The Barmaids and the Young Lady

Püschmann's diary mentions numerous encounters and acquaintances with single women. But both the apprentice typesetter and the journeyman remain discreet in this regard. The diarist only rarely gives his implicit readers insight into his emotional state. He never explicitly mentions love, nor any intention to marry – with one important exception. When 25-year-old Püschmann decides to change professions following several months of unemployment, the main reason he gives is his "disinclination" to "remain unmarried."[71] Friedrich Anton Püschmann reaches a marriageable age in the mid-1850s, but he gives no thought to marriage. As a rule, journeymen were not allowed to marry, and given the developments in the crisis-ridden printing trade at that time, master craftsman status was not an option for Püschmann. In addition, until the 1860s discriminatory restrictions on marriage applied to members of the lower classes who did not have an income. While the principle of freedom in marriage was promulgated in the reform era after 1800, the period of pauperism between 1830 and 1860 constituted a heyday for state bans on marriage.[72] This is illustrated by the example of Püschmann's brother Ernst, who is two years older. Ernst Püschmann works as a law clerk. Waiting in vain for his employer to grant him permission to marry, he fathers a daughter with his bride-to-be, Pauline. His daughter is born in 1847 and named Antonie, after his younger brother. Ernst only confesses this illegitimate birth to Anton in a letter four months after the event, in January 1848. In the same letter, he expresses the hope that they will soon "achieve the realization of our desires, our marriage [...], which would necessarily have to be preceded by my finding permanent employment in an office somewhere."[73] Thus Friedrich Anton Püschmann is certainly aware of the legally defined connection between marriage and the ability to support a family. His marriage to Auguste Kuniß from Stollberg takes place in 1860, only after he has obtained a position with the school district as a salaried teacher.[74] There are no further diary entries relating to this period. The 'dishonorable' birth of his brother Ernst's daughter does not seem to have led to any discord within the Püschmann family. The relationship between the brothers remains close and is characterized by mutual trust.

---

71 John, January 16, 1855, p. 684.
72 See Ehmer, "Ehekonsens"; on this topic in general, see Matz, *Pauperismus*; on 'wild marriages,' see Gröwer, *Wilde Ehen*.
73 Püschmann found this letter so important that he transcribed it: see John, January 15, 1848, pp. 21–24 (citation pp. 22–23).
74 On this subject, see his daughter's account: Görnandt, *Die von der Tochter verfasste Lebensskizze*, 850.

Püschmann repeatedly writes about his contacts with single women. He notes affection and advances on the part of such women – not without pride – as minor successes. At the same time, he emphasizes his honor and morality. From his perspective, the initiative seems to come primarily from her side, and at most we find vague hints at intimacy.[75] In his early twenties, while he is still on the road, he cannot even consider marriage. Nevertheless, the diary definitely indicates his tendency to flirt, as well as attraction at first sight. Thus the 18-year-old apprentice finds that his evening conversations and amusing dances with Therese – the Grimma privy councilor's chambermaid, whom he refers to as the "chamber kitten" – merit several entries.[76] In Altdorf on Lake Lucerne, the journeyman notes: "It's been a long time since I have seen such a perfectly beautiful female figure as that of the waitress at this establishment."[77] At the end of 1854, when he once again inquires – in vain – about a vacancy with a publisher in Waldenburg, Saxony, he concludes with the remark: "I would have liked to look into her handsome daughter Marie's clear blue eyes even longer."[78]

So then, which woman enters the picture as a potential spouse? The women with whom Püschmann dances and flirts all come from lower-class backgrounds: they are maids, daughters of innkeepers, 'barmaids,' a plumber's daughter, and a 'manual laborer.' After a few encounters at most, each relationship ends, and Püschmann never expresses regret over this. But it is a different story when he meets "the amiable young lady (*Fräulein*) Emilie Jacobi from Hartenstein" after a concert in Wildenfels on January 14, 1855.[79] Admittedly, love or a desire to marry are never explicitly addressed in this case either. Yet Püschmann's diary also contains more information than its author wishes or realizes. His attribution and the fact that he underlines her name the first time he writes it down are already striking. And his aforementioned disillusionment over the prospect of ever being able to marry as a wandering journeyman or laborer is first formulated two days later, on January 16, 1855 – precisely the day when Mrs. Jacobi and her daughters, Emilie and Bertha, pay a visit to the Püschmanns in Mitteldorf.[80] Püschmann's

---

75 See the following, remarkably opaque formulations: John, June 8, 1851, p. 500: "Then in the evening I was at home. 'Nice dirndel, nice dirndel,'" an allusion to an unnamed woman and her dress; an identical formulation occurs on May 2, 1852, p. 535; see also the account of his meeting with a cook in "my little parlor" one evening, which lasted "for a long time": October 8, 1853, p. 615.
76 In the original German: "Kammerkätzchen"; ibid., April 2–3, 1848, pp. 101–2; May 2, 1848, p. 136; June 12, 1848, pp. 184–85.
77 Ibid., September 17, 1853, p. 605.
78 Ibid., November 8, 1854, p. 673.
79 Ibid., January 14, 1855, p. 684, underlining in the original.
80 Ibid., January 16, 1855, pp. 684–85.

interactions with Emilie and the Jacobi family differ from those with all the other women he mentions in his diary. Visits and return visits take place. The small town of Hartenstein is approximately eight kilometers from Mitteldorf. Püschmann actively tries to maintain and intensify this contact. In addition, the parents on both sides are involved in the exchange by means of visits to one another's homes. The fact that Emilie's mother appears at the Püschmann home just two days after their first meeting is remarkable in this respect; Emilie's father visits four weeks later. Moreover, compared to his experiences with 'barmaids,' Püschmann's discourse in his diary is quite different in this case: "In the evenings, Mrs. Jacobi honored us with her visit, together with her dear daughters, Emilie and Bertha."[81] These contacts become more frequent and familiar. The Jacobi daughters are invited to a masquerade party at Püschmann's brother Ernst's house on Shrove Tuesday, and also to the baptism of Ernst and Pauline's youngest son, Anton, who is Püschmann's godson. One is sometimes in a "cheerful mood" at these entertainments, but sometimes "rather subdued," as Püschmann notes with disappointment.[82] During unannounced visits to the Jacobi house, accompanied by one of his brothers, Püschmann either does not encounter the Jacobi daughters or else partakes in a "large company" "with several young ladies," among them "a teacher and a pastor's daughter."[83] Yet all this eventually comes to nothing. As early as March 1855, when 25-year-old Friedrich Anton moves to Thalheim to train as a teacher, he does not say goodbye to 22-year-old Emilie in person, but instead gives his brother Ernst "a little letter for her."[84] He writes more letters to Emilie from the teacher training college in Grimma. The end of this contact between them comes abruptly in January 1856, when Püschmann notes briefly and succinctly in his diary the "engagement of Emilie J."[85] He never mentions Emilie Jacobi again; instead, he remarks on another series of fleeting encounters with other women.

We can only speculate about Püschmann's emotional state. As a diarist, he does not confide in his diary or in his potential readers. Yet the diary does dem-

---

[81] Ibid., p. 684. On further invitations and visits from the Jacobis, see January 16–February 20, 1855, pp. 684–88; February 18, 1855, p. 688.
[82] Ibid., February 2, 1855, p. 687. On the baptism, which took place in Hartenstein, see May 27, 1855, p. 709.
[83] Ibid., August 6, 1855, p. 727.
[84] Ibid., March 7, 1855, p. 696. According to the Hartenstein church register for the year 1832 (no. 35, p. 427–28), Wilhelmine Emilie Jacobi was born on June 30, 1832. Many thanks to Erhard Franke, the former cantor in Hartenstein, for his research into the Hartenstein parish church records in Saxony.
[85] In the original German: "Verlobung der Emilie J."; John, January 5, 1856, p. 757, underlining in the original.

onstrate that the journeyman, who was on the verge of changing his profession, made an effort with Emilie Jacobi in a way he did with no other woman. According to the index of the critical edition, no woman is mentioned more often than Emilie. If we take the diarist at his word, then habitus and milieu once again come into play. The magic of their first encounter unfolds at a concert – Haydn's *The Creation*, performed in the village by "the combined singing and musical powers of Hartenstein and Wildenfels" – and at the ball that follows. Püschmann the well-traveled concert-goer finds the orchestra unremarkable, but he notes that the Earl of Wildenfels, who is present in the audience, applauds.[86] Emilie's first appearance is not as a sweaty 'barmaid,' but as a demure *Fräulein* at an elite bourgeois stage production. Her father owns a shop in Hartenstein, where Püschmann buys canvas cloth and chocolate as a pretense for seeing Emilie. She is the daughter of Friedrich August Jacobi, a "gifted burgher, weaver, and merchant," according to the church register.[87] Her father's profession is more properly described as grocer than merchant, but he is one of the local dignitaries who attend concerts and the Agricultural Society banquet. Thus an evening invitation to the Jacobi house also figures in Püschmann's diary as a "soirée."[88] Regardless of his emotions, for Püschmann the journeyman and schoolteacher's son, a connection with this 'lovely young lady,' a shopkeeper's daughter from the neighboring village, presents itself as desirable. Emilie Jacobi would be a good match, and she seems within reach in terms of social status. Yet a few months after their last contact, she marries a merchant from Schneeberg.[89] Thus she decides to marry a man who comes from the same immediate social milieu as she does.

The Family as an Emotional and Supportive Community

Friedrich Anton Püschmann's home consists not least of his immediate family and his relatives in the Erz Mountains region of Saxony. His record of visits and correspondence shows that the journeyman has a strong sense of family. These family

---

[86] Ibid., January 14, 1855, pp. 683–84. Hartenstein had a population of approximately 2,200: see hov.isgv.de/Hartenstein.
[87] In the original German: "begüth[erten] Bürgers, Webers und Handelsmanns"; Hartenstein church register, "Marriages" for the year 1856, no. 20, pp. 507–8.
[88] John, February 2, 1855, p. 687; August 6, 1855, p. 726; February 2, 1855, p. 687 (citation).
[89] Hartenstein church register, "Marriages" for the year 1856, no. 20, pp. 507–8. Traugott Heinrich Baumann, Emilie's bridegroom, who lived in the neighboring village of Schneeberg, is not mentioned in Püschmann's diary. Emilie's sister Bertha married an architect and "master mason" in 1859: ibid., 1859, no. 14, pp. 543–44.

ties can be described both as an emotional relationship and in terms of concrete support. The emotional aspect primarily concerns his relationships with his parents and his two brothers. On New Year's Day 1848, the apprentice in Grimma sends his "beloved parents" a long poem dedicated to and written especially for them. He also prefaces his diary with a copy of this poem.[90] After a visit to Mitteldorf in July 1850, he bids – in an interesting formulation – "goodbye to my dear mother, and to my paternal home."[91] During his travels, he keeps up a correspondence with his parents and his brother Ernst. If the journeyman sends no letters for several months, as is the case during his time in Hamburg, then the result is that "everyone" in the family "is very worried about me."[92] The letter in which his older brother confesses the "indiscretion" of his daughter's illegitimate birth corresponds to the emphatic, emotional letter-writing style of the time. The letter is centrally concerned with forgiveness and the assurance of mutual "love," and the signature reads: "Your loving brother, Ernst."[93] Püschmann maintains regular, close contact with Ernst and his wife, Pauline. His relationship with his other brother, who is 10 years younger, is less intense, but Anton nevertheless accompanies 15-year-old Wilhelm on his way to school in Waldenburg, about five hours' walk from Mitteldorf.[94] In a pedestrian society, the ritualized practice of escort and accompaniment is an indicator of close social ties. When he sets out on his journey in July 1848, Püschmann's father and his little brother Wilhelm provide him with "an escort" to the next town but one. Ernst and Pauline Püschmann accompany their brother to the neighboring village of Beutha after his visit. His work colleagues escort the journeyman to the town gate when he leaves. Püschmann escorts Lamm to the train station, as already noted, and finally he also "accompanies" the Jacobi family "home" in the evening after a family celebration.[95] Even considering the emotional importance of sibling relationships after 1800 – an importance emphasized by research on the subject – it is nevertheless remarkable that the diarist several times remembers his two sisters, Agnes and Wilhelmine, who died in childhood (at 1 and 5 years old, respectively). He misses "a dear little sister" waiting for him at home and finds a substitute for this relationship in his 6-year-old niece.[96] Although Friedrich Anton Püschmann's writing style, as men-

---

90 John, January 1, 1848, p. 7.
91 Ibid., July 2, 1850, p. 419.
92 Ibid., July 29, 1849, p. 354; and similarly December 5, 1849, p. 374.
93 Ibid., January 15, 1848, pp. 21–24 (citation pp. 23–24).
94 Ibid., November 8, 1854, p. 673.
95 Ibid., July 13, 1848, p. 223; June 18, 1848, p. 202; January 18, 1849, p. 324; May 27, 1855, p. 709.
96 Ibid., October 26, 1854, p. 672; see also January 26, 1848, p. 30; April 17, 1848, p. 123. On sibling relationships more generally, see the contributions in Johnson and Sabean, *Sibling Relations*.

tioned above, is more sober than that of other diarists at the time, intense emotional relationships within the nuclear family can nevertheless be detected in the lower-class and petit bourgeois milieus. He and other members of his family also frequently visit other relatives in the region.

The importance Püschmann attributes to his family of origin is evident not only in terms of emotional ties, but also in terms of financial support, the latter more clearly than in any of the examples we have considered thus far. In his diary Püschmann reports on financial transfers not only in passing, but also sometimes meticulously – particularly after his apprenticeship ends, when he draws up tables recording his current income and expenses, including various types of assistance and significant monetary payments. As an apprentice in Grimma, he receives parcels from his parents with new clothes, sausages, and weekly newspapers from Stollberg, as well as several letters containing money. When he starts his journeyman's tour after his apprenticeship ends, his parents send him a start-up allowance of 20 talers, which is equivalent to two months of his father's salary.[97] Some of Püschmann's other relatives also contribute smaller sums to this fund, including his uncle and his aunt, his grandmother, his godfather, and two of his cousins.[98] The ham his mother gives him for his journey lasts him five days. While he is on the road, Püschmann sends home parcels containing his dirty laundry, which is then freshly washed and returned to an agreed-upon location.[99] Laundry is certainly one of Püschmann's key expenses. Yet the Christmas parcels the Püschmanns send to their son indicate that they are not rolling in money. On December 24, 1850, Friedrich Anton is in Basel for the Christmas holiday and notes: "My parents have sent me a new shirt as a Christmas present, and a Saxon sausage from the pig slaughter also found a place in the box."[100]

Undoubtedly Püschmann's travels as a journeyman also offer him the opportunity to break away from his parents. He seems to enjoy a particularly close relationship with his father, who is always involved in his professional decisions.[101] He accompanies his father on visits as well as to church services and concerts. He also supports him as a teaching assistant. His 'dear mother' also pays visits to rel-

---

97 John, January 5, 1848, p. 16; April 3, 1848, p. 101; May 5, 1848, p. 137; May 19, 1848, p. 156.
98 Ibid., table with information on income, June/July 1848, p. 821. On the following, see July 18, 1848, p. 230.
99 Ibid., July 29, 1848, p. 246.
100 Ibid., December 24, 1850, p. 479, underlining in the original. On the construction of identity with recourse to foods from one's homeland, see the letters Liselotte von der Pfalz sent from the French court: Böth, "'Ich handele,'" 259–63.
101 According to his daughter's account, Friedrich Anton was "his father's favorite" and enjoyed a special relationship with him: Görnandt, *Die von der Tochter verfasste Lebensskizze*, 843.

atives, but is mentioned far less often in this regard. Püschmann provides no information about the relationship between his parents, but at the end of his diary he mentions conflicts between his brother Ernst and his sister-in-law Pauline, which "once again disturbed the conjugal peace."[102] Over the course of the five and a half years in which Püschmann's travels do not permit him to visit Mitteldorf, he mentions his family members less and less frequently. When he returns home in October 1854, however, there is no indication of any break in the familial relationship or family problems of any kind. The Püschmann family functions as a community of mutual emotional and financial support through many challenges, including the illegitimate birth of Püschmann's niece; the death of his godson, Ernst and Pauline's youngest child, who is buried "early one still morning" when he is only a few months old;[103] and Püschmann's own professional crisis.

Open Domesticity in a Small-Town Context

This case study, situated as it is in the context of small towns and villages in Saxony, provides new insights into the question of the family as a closed private sphere. As we have seen, the previous examples – drawn from the Bernese patriciate, the Hamburg bourgeoisie, and a parsonage in the Basel countryside – do not support the conventional view of the bourgeois era as the prototypical era of privacy. However, these families obviously moved in elite social circles. The same cannot be said for the social context of the village schoolteacher's family. Yet our analysis of Püschmann's diary entries about his immediate family, the neighborhood, and his relatives in the Stollberg area shows that an intensive, sustained, and multifaceted visiting culture obtained in this context as well. The Püschmanns' network, which can be reconstructed on the basis of their contacts, includes the members of the nuclear family who have moved out of the family home – such as Püschmann's brother Ernst, his sister-in-law Pauline, and their children, as well as Wilhelm and Friedrich Anton himself, who left home to go to school or were apprenticed when they were still young – as well as numerous other relatives, such as uncles, aunts, cousins, and in-laws who live scattered throughout the area between Zwickau and Chemnitz, in places such as Niederdorf, Gablenz, and Dorfchemnitz. In addition, Püschmann mentions people from the neighborhood, either immediate neighbors whom he explicitly identifies as such or other actors from the mid-sized village of around 600 inhabitants. Neighborliness plays a more

---

102 John, July 30, 1856, p. 785.
103 Ibid., August 2, 1755, p. 726.

frequent and explicit role in Püschmann's diary than in the other sources we have examined thus far; examples include visiting the sick at a neighbor's house, bidding his neighbors farewell before he leaves on his journeyman's tour, and social gatherings of various kinds at the homes of neighbors who are mentioned by name in his diary.[104]

Visiting practices in Mitteldorf and the surrounding area do not differ significantly from those of the bourgeoisie (*Bürgertum*) in larger cities: this is another type of open domesticity. One distinctive feature, however, is that in the rural context a visit often requires several hours of walking, sometimes in the dark, and sometimes on bad roads. The aforementioned ritual of accompanying a traveler on their way should also be seen against this backdrop. Similarly to the Benekes in Hamburg, informal, everyday visits that do not require an invitation are distinguished from more formal meetings that do. As it was for the Bruckners in Basel, Sunday is frequently a day for paying visits, but dropping in on an acquaintance is also possible on any other day. It is not unusual to pay a series of visits after church services on Sundays: "Now I first stopped at Ruther's, then went with my father to see Herr Diaconus, to the post office, and then up the Herrngasse, where I wanted to visit the plumber Bochmann, my brother Ernst's former landlord. There I had to stay for a meal."[105] Playing games and staging masquerades on Shrove Tuesday, baking fruitcake, and slaughtering livestock in the winter also provide particular occasions for paying visits. After visiting his cousin in Niederdorf between Christmas and the new year, Püschmann notes: "Our visit today was well timed; we arrived just in time for the pig slaughter. There was a little music and singing. At the tenth hour, we took our leave."[106] Family celebrations such as weddings and birthdays do not play a significant role, while baptisms (as previously mentioned) do. Püschmann refers to gatherings with a higher degree of formality as "small circles" (*Kränzchen*), "soirées," or "grand visits," and he characteristically uses the latter two terms, as well as "return visits," for visits to the Jacobi family.[107]

---

104 Ibid., June 30, 1848, p. 213; July 3, 1848, p. 215; July 11, 1848, p. 222; December 6, 1848, p. 375; December 14, 1848, p. 377. On "Mitteldorfer visits," see November 24, 1854, p. 675; *passim*.
105 Ibid., July 2, 1848, p. 214. Unfortunately the name Ruther, as well as certain other names, are missing from the index in the critical edition of the diary, which is otherwise very useful in analyzing the Püschmann family's network. Presumably this Ruther was a baker in Stollberg: see the entry for June 23, 1848, p. 207.
106 Ibid., December 28, 1854, p. 679. On baking fruitcake with his sister-in-law and his niece, see the entry for December 21, 1849, p. 378.
107 Ibid. (in order of citation), February 18, 1855, p. 688; February 2, 1855, p. 687; August 6, 1855, p. 727; January 16, 1855, p. 684.

Rural visiting culture was not only or even primarily about lavish weddings, funerals, and feasts when livestock were slaughtered – this fact cannot be overemphasized. Rather, in reading the diary entries on Püschmann's visits in Stollberg and the surrounding area, we repeatedly encounter domestic practices that have bourgeois connotations. In the summer of 1848, for example, Püschmann and his father repeatedly attend their immediate neighbor Kunze's "reading circle" in Mitteldorf, where they "read aloud" and discuss the Saxon Parliament's newsletter.[108] Püschmann's diary demonstrates that music at home was by no means solely a high-culture, urban bourgeois phenomenon. In small towns and villages as well, spontaneously singing together after dinner – to piano accompaniment, if possible – was a common form of sociability: "In the evening, we sang for a while."[109] Stollberg also boasts a singing club, in which Püschmann's father and sometimes Püschmann himself participate.

Upon closer examination, Friedrich Anton Püschmann's diary proves to be a rich source in our analysis of the history of the family in the narrower sense, as well as the domestic sphere more broadly. As an apprentice and a journeyman, he experiences various forms of domestic co-presence that can be understood as counter-models to that of the bourgeois nuclear family. In this context, the relationships and ways of life Püschmann experiences on his travels seem very modern in certain respects: itinerant and temporary, with a strict separation between work and private spheres, oriented toward leisure and entertainment, with a series of shifting acquaintances and fleeting interactions. His relationships with his 'landlords' are usually distant; he perceives the expectation to participate in convivial meals and excessively close personal relationships as problematic. However, a private sphere in one's own 'chamber' is not something to pursue; instead, cohabiting in pairs is a common model. The family of origin offers emotional and financial support, as does the wider network of kin and neighbors in this small-town context. In this world, the Püschmann family's strength lies not least in ensuring continuity despite their limited financial resources. On the one hand, this means overcoming setbacks, such as the deaths of multiple children and illegitimate births; on the other hand, it means providing a haven for the children, who may have to

---

108 In the original German: "in den Leseverein"; "die Landtagsblätter vorgelesen"; ibid., July 11, 1848, p. 222; see also the entries for June 29–July 6, 1848, pp. 212–17. Kunze's profession is not mentioned.
109 Ibid., June 27, 1848, p. 211; see also the entries for June 19, 1848, p. 203; July 3, 1848, pp. 215–16; December 28, 1854, p. 679. For comparison, see an example from his time in Zurich: January 23, 1853, p. 571; see also an example from Lausanne, where the journeymen printers meet in the evening: May 8, 1853, p. 583. On music in the home more generally, see Claudon, "Hausmusik"; Eibach, "Die Schubertiade."

leave home at the age of 14 but are still welcome to return as adults in times of crisis. Even when they have not seen one another for more than five years, family is always family.

Chapter 8
Marital Crisis and Social Decline Among the Petite Bourgeoisie: Barbara and Johann Baumgartner

Krems and Vienna, Austria (1870–1885)

The cyclical nature of high industrialization and the rapid growth of metropolitan areas had an impact on domestic relations as well. Beginning in the mid-nineteenth century, a new economic dynamic developed in the German-speaking world, and this was coupled with migration, social mobility, and the urbanization of Europe.[1] Population growth and periodic economic crises were not entirely new phenomena in and of themselves. In contrast to the early modern period, however, these crises were no longer the result of crop failures, and the old corporate guild arrangements had dissolved before state social security systems were established to replace them. As a result, the family – designed as an enduring community of support – took on new importance. At the same time, case studies of life in small-town contexts (such as the example from the Erz Mountains in Saxony analyzed in the previous chapter) demonstrate that, alongside the expanding metropolises, living conditions in rural settings – and the traditional forms of social integration still prevalent in such contexts – persisted into the second half of the nineteenth century.

The diary kept by Wetti Teuschl – whose full name was Barbara Teuschl, the daughter of a country coachman, later also known as Betti – provides parallel insights into everyday life in the small town of Krems, situated on the Danube river in Austria, and the capital city of Vienna, which was riven by economic crises at the time. Her entries – which begin in April 1870, when she was 18 years old and living in Krems – reflect on the matchmaking process that led to her marriage, followed by periods of marital crisis that are closely linked to the economic decline after the 'big crash' of May 9, 1873 and the resulting recession, which was harsh and lasted for several years.[2] In addition, her diary sheds light on different facets of honor and the social control exercised over marital life in a small town. Finally,

---

[1] F. Lenger, *Metropolen der Moderne*, 50. On urbanization in Austria, see Sandgruber, *Die Anfänge der Konsumgesellschaft*, 34–35; on Vienna, see Eigner, "Mechanismen urbaner Expansion," 643–45.
[2] For more details on the effects of the economic crisis, which ended the *Gründerzeit* boom following the French–German War of 1870–1871, see Chaloupek, "Industriestadt Wien," 360–62.

this chapter addresses not only a marital crisis that comes to a head several times, but also the continuation and consolidation of that same marriage as an economic household. In the process, Barbara and Johann Baumgartner's marriage is dependent on outside support for quite some time. My analysis benefits from Nikola Langreiter's exemplary critical edition of Wetti Teuschl's diary, as well as her accompanying research on the author and her family environment.[3]

From Naïve Girl to Sought-After Marriage Partner

After two of her younger siblings died early, Barbara – who was born on December 3, 1851 – grew up as an only child. In a letter to one of her admirers, 19-year-old Barbara describes herself as "the simple *Bürgersmädchen* from Krems."[4] The milieu from which she originates – in comparison with the tone-setting, educated bourgeoisie – is best characterized as petite bourgeoisie (*kleinbürgerlich*) or lower middle class.[5] In this respect, her parents – both of whom came from agricultural backgrounds – had certainly achieved something. After starting his career as a postillion rider and courier, Anton Teuschl founds a carriage business in Krems. With his horse-drawn carriages, which could carry up to 16 passengers, this small businessman offers a kind of omnibus to neighboring towns, such as St. Pölten and Stockerau. In addition, he carries the mail and offers 'private transport.' In official documents, Teuschl identifies himself as a "burgher and homeowner."[6] He is a well-known man in Krems. At his funeral on December 29, 1878, his daughter proudly notes that "countless people line up" to pay their respects.[7] Barbara does not mention her mother's professional activities. As she later recollects, her mother is the "soulful wife, the best support for her husband, the best loving mother for her child." "Our beloved little dog" completes the family.[8] From this perspective, the gendered role distribution in the Teuschl household

---

[3] Langreiter, *Tagebuch von Wetti Teuschl*. In this chapter, all the quotations and information taken from Barbara Baumgartner's (née Wetti Teuschl's) diary refer to Langreiter's edition; see her 'Nachbemerkungen' (follow-up comments) throughout: pp. 151–94.
[4] Entry for December 8, 1870, p. 32.
[5] See Kocka, "Das europäische Muster," 10; on the history of the petite bourgeoisie and small businesses, see Haupt and Crossick, *Die Kleinbürger*.
[6] In the original German: "Bürger und Hauseigenthümer"; testimonial, January 14, 1877, p. 89 (citation); obituary, p. 111; memorial page, pp. 136–37. See also Langreiter, *Tagebuch*, 19, n. 5.
[7] Entry for December 28, 1878 (this date is probably incorrect), p. 110.
[8] Memorial page (Gedenkblatt), p. 140 (both citations). On the history of family pets, see Möhring, "Das Haustier"; Steinbrecher, "Dogs."

corresponds to that of a bourgeois or indeed a modern nuclear family. With this in mind, the maid does not appear in the diary. The members of the family maintain close emotional ties.

The young Wetti is sometimes permitted to drive her father's carriages and sleighs, but at the age of 18 she attends a culinary course at a Piarist monastery (the Piarists had taken over the Krems grammar school from the Jesuits at the end of the eighteenth century) in order to prepare for her future role as a housewife.[9] She mentions no further education. On June 3, 1872, 20-year-old Barbara marries Johann Baumgartner, who owns a general store in Vienna's Josefstadt district. They set up house together in Vienna. Here we can briefly note the subsequent stages of her life:[10] On July 7, 1873, their son Johann Anton, known as Hans or Hansi, is born. Like his mother, he remains an only child. After countless, mostly unsuccessful attempts to gain a professional foothold in Vienna, as well as several moves, illnesses, and ever more problems, the family moves into Barbara's parents' house at 7 Herzogstraße in Krems in February 1878, where Barbara and Johann open a shop on the ground floor. At the end of December 1878, Anton Teuschl dies as a result of an accident. Hans attends elementary school in Krems from 1879 and high school from 1883. Barbara's mother, Anna Maria Teuschl, whom Barbara cares for over a period of months during her final illness, passes away on April 5, 1885. Barbara's husband, Johann Baumgartner, dies of 'dropsy' (edema) in 1892, at the age of 47. His wife does not mention his death in her diary; although she keeps the diary regularly at first, and subsequently with increasingly longer breaks between entries, it ends after her mother's death. The widow Barbara rents out the business premises in Krems and gets to know her tenant, the student Karl Gerstl. Although Gerstl is almost 20 years her junior, they become close, and Barbara eventually marries him and moves to Vienna again in 1898, once he has obtained secure employment with the railroad. Hans Baumgartner, her son from her first marriage, becomes a postal and telegraph inspector in Vienna. In the 1920s, Barbara – then known as Betti Gerstl – writes articles for the magazine of the Reich Organization for Austrian Housewives (*Reichsorganisation der Hausfrauen Österreichs*). In the 1930s she sells her childhood home, the house at 7 Herzogstraße in Krems, thus breaking her ties to her hometown. She dies of old age on January 10, 1944.

---

9 Entry for June 1, 1870, p. 25; see also p. 142. On carriage driving, see the entry for July 31, 1871, p. 47; memorial page, p. 139.
10 See the chronology Langreiter compiled in the appendix to the critical edition, pp. 141–49.

While the few testimonies we have from Barbara's later years suggest a secure income and a happy second marriage,[11] our focus in this chapter is on Barbara and Johann Baumgartner's extremely volatile fortunes – in both emotional and financial terms – between 1870 and 1885. This is precisely the period covered in the diary, in which its author's relationship with Johann Baumgartner occupies – or rather requires – a great deal of space from the very beginning. It is the story of Barbara's journey from a somewhat naïve girl to a coveted marriage partner, to a coachman's sole heiress, and finally to a desperate wife and mother. The young Wetti Teuschl likes to be amused. She takes trips in her father's carriage and goes to the Krems town ball. She spends a lot of time on her appearance and dances late into the night with "Messrs. Baumgartner, Haselgruber, Meier, and Steiner," whom she mentions by name as if they were trophies.[12] In the early years, she often mentions Mary, "the sorrowful Mother of God," and how "I laid my broken heart at her feet,"[13] particularly in the context of prayers for her parents or for Johann Baumgartner. But as the years go by, religion loses its status as a guiding force in her life. Even before her marriage and the first marital crisis, the young woman suffers from various moods: "melancholy," which does not lift, and "desolation." Terms such as "exhaustion" and "resignation" are reminiscent of neurasthenia, the typical clinical framework of the time.[14] The various types of malaise she mentions later – such as abdominal cramps and loss of appetite, peritonitis, and "nervous fever"[15] – correspond to her experiences of various crises and can be interpreted as psychosomatic.

While the diary's beginning and end are abrupt and enigmatic, as is often the case, it nevertheless serves several functions for the writing subject. The author's mutable intentions – and relatedly, the variable discourse – are typical of diary writing in the modern period. According to Foucault's concept of 'technologies of the self,' this narrative flexibility is not deliberate. The youthful Wetti Teuschl primarily renders the experiences one typically finds in a young girl's diary, including a love story.[16] For the married woman Barbara Baumgartner, the diary

---

11 See, for example, the salutation in her will (undated), p. 199: "My beloved husband, I thank you for many of the most beautiful years of my life"; see also Langreiter, "Nachbemerkungen," 153.
12 Entry for February 19, 1871, p. 37.
13 Entry for July 3, 1871, p. 42.
14 Entries for April 23, 1871, p. 38; September 5, 1871, p. 47. On the 'age of nervousness', see Radkau, *Das Zeitalter der Nervosität*; from a psychoanalytic perspective, see Gay, *Die zarte Leidenschaft*, 331, where he speaks of nervousness as the "illness of the age."
15 After her mother's death, Barbara Baumgartner spends four weeks in the hospital with a "Nervenfieber"; entry for May (without an exact date) 1885, p. 126.
16 On the diary as a record of experience (Erlebnis-Journal), see Bänziger, "Jenseits der Bürgerlichkeit," and *Die Moderne als Erlebnis*; see also Foucault, "Technologies of the Self."

then becomes a 'wailing wall' (as Langreiter puts it). Disillusioned at a personal low point in 1877, she takes stock as follows: "I am 25 years old, and my future stretches before me, black as a raven; no point of light beckons me; everything is bleak and desolate; truly a destroyed, ruined life."[17] Nevertheless, one of this woman's characteristics – and indeed also a characteristic of the Baumgartners as a couple – is a refusal to give up, a hard-earned resilience, at least inasmuch as their story continues. In some of its later passages, the diary evinces features consistent with a chronicle of family events (although the entries are irregular), such as her son's birth and enrollment in school, household moves, the commencement of new business ventures, and the deaths of her parents. The author's awareness of sensitive passages and potential readers is demonstrated by the fact that she cuts certain half-pages out of her diary in the period before her marriage – when some of the entries are put down on paper with anger and verve – and in this way censors herself.[18]

Matchmaking and Marriage in a Small Town

The first part of the diary provides information about matchmaking practices in a small town in Lower Austria. Around 1870 Krems has a population of just under 20,000 people. The mercantile town offers advanced schooling, and the town council has liberal tendencies.[19] In 1872 the town is connected to the railroad network, which facilities transport to Vienna. In 1868, when she is 16 years old, Wetti Teuschl meets Johann Baumgartner, a shop assistant seven and a half years her senior.[20] According to her diary, the time leading up to their marriage, which takes place four years later, is a time of confusion – a rollercoaster of emotions comparable to the complicated courtship of Ferdinand and Caroline Beneke.[21] In

---

17 Entry for April 6, 1877, p. 97.
18 See, for example, pp. 24, 32, and 41. We cannot know with any certainty whether one of Barbara's descendants or a later owner of the diary may be responsible for these mutilations of the text. However, when it comes to awkward entries, the author herself also resorts to code: see the entry for January 10, 1880, p. 115.
19 Langreiter, p. 19, n. 2. On the population of Krems, see https://bevoelkerung.at/bezirk/krems-an-der-donaustadt; on Krems and other towns and cities in Lower Austria, see Gutkas, "Die Städte Niederösterreichs"; Frühwirth, *Die Doppelstadt Krems-Stein*.
20 See the retrospective entries for May 13, 1870, p. 24; July 17, 1870, p. 28.
21 Even in the first entry (April 2, 1870, p. 19), she mentions "the beloved" from whom she has just been "separated," "reconciliation" with him, and "her father's opinion" of her romantic relationship. On the following, see the first part of the diary: from the first entry until the wedding on June 2, 1872, p. 55. On the bourgeois semantics of love, see Trepp, "Emotion und bürgerliche Sinnstif-

addition to emphatic declarations of love, the young woman also notes interference and intrigue on the part of third parties. Baumgartner has rivals – whether from his own circle of friends or in the form of a high-school teacher in Krems or a well-off merchant – who unexpectedly ask for 18-year-old Wetti's hand by letter or via intermediaries.[22] The small town is a stage that cannot be avoided, and the audience observes every courtship. These matchmaking practices are multifaceted and can be divided into the following categories: first, the couple communicates in private, away from prying eyes; second, they visit each other's homes (*Hausbesuch*); and third, they make appearances in public. For Wetti and Johann, the first step includes letters declaring the sender's love, making accusations, or bidding farewell; meetings that result in quarrels and subsequent reconciliations; an exchange of portraits and rings, as well as other gifts, such as fruit, a dress for her birthday, and song sheets with lyrics. As the relationship becomes more concrete, the potential bridegroom appears daily at the Teuschl home for seemingly innocuous chats or to play card games, although it is worth noting that "my father also plays with us quite often."[23] They then make their courtship public, taking walks and promenades through the town streets, where they meet sometimes by chance, and sometimes intentionally. Finally, as a clear message to observers, the couple hold hands, and she leans her head against his shoulder in her mother's presence; they take joint trips with her parents in the carriage; and they attend church, eat, or go bowling at the inn together.

Who has a say in the matter of matchmaking? In this case, as we have seen in previous chapters, it is certainly not simply the couple's decision. The potential bride complains about "gossip," which poses a threat to her "whole love life," and about "lies and incitement" spread by "wicked people."[24] Competing interests on the local marriage market in this small town clearly play a role here. Yet despite her complaints, the young author does not refrain from making her own bitter, nasty comments about other couples: "Today Mr. Schober celebrated his wedding – he married Lori Vogl from Weinzirl – this man is truly pitiful, and as much as we were enemies, I have now forgiven him everything. I have too much sympathy for his miserable situation to think of revenge or hatred. This woman – and these debts."[25]

---

tung"; Saurer, *Liebe und Arbeit*, 21–24; on the town as a public sphere in matchmaking processes, see R. Habermas, "Spielerische Liebe," 164–67.
22 Entries for April 21, 1870, p. 22; August 22, 1870, pp. 29–30.
23 Entry for November 22, 1870, p. 32.
24 All citations taken from the entry for April 8, 1870, p. 20.
25 Entry for November 22, 1870, p. 31. According to Nikola Langreiter's research, Eleonora (Lori) Vogl was an innkeeper's daughter from a village near Krems.

From a legal perspective, what is more important for the couple than public opinion among the residents of Krems is their parents' consent – both her parents and his. More precisely, their fathers' consent is key. It takes some time for the couple to get Mr. Teuschl to agree to the marriage. Wetti's mother is willing to accompany the couple on their evening walks through Krems even before a final decision on the marriage has been made. Yet more time passes before the daughter, who is in love, can report: "we even managed to bring about a rapprochement with my father."[26] The main reason for Anton Teuschl's lengthy intransigence is the fact that his daughter's suitor is not self-employed. According to the bourgeois self-conception, economic independence was a central requirement for a man who wished to marry. In urban society, the ideal of self-employment was embodied in the merchant, whether he was a small trader, a shopkeeper, or a traveling salesman.[27] In the case we are considering here, as soon as the couple's relationship is consolidated – when Wetti speaks increasingly often of "our love" and the "bond of love"[28] – the shop assistant Johann Baumgartner begins to look for a business he can take over. Wetti Teuschl's entries comment on his attempts to build up a bourgeois livelihood: "Mr. Baumgartner is already looking for a livelihood; he wants to become independent," namely by acquiring a general store or, better yet, a shop selling fine cloth.[29] She records his plans and his purchase considerations in detail, sometimes including specific amounts of money. Each failed negotiation is a blow to her. After some time, Baumgartner at last succeeds in finding employment in a women's clothing shop in the prosperous Viennese business district of Mariahilf. However, this is not sufficient to win them the necessary paternal approval: "God grant that he will soon find his own and not have to be a salesman much longer."[30] They do not reach the finish line until six months later, when the bridegroom-to-be is about to buy a shop with an apartment in the middle-class Josefstadt district: "If he succeeds, then the time to ask for my hand will be very near."[31] The connection between success in business – or more precisely, economic independence – and marriage could not be more explicitly expressed. In the end, not only her father, but also his must give their consent. When Baumgartner's father also agrees, the wedding is immediately scheduled and takes place only three weeks later.[32]

---

26 Entry for May 31, 1870, p. 25. On the problems between Baumgartner and her parents, see also the entries for April 2, 1870, p. 19; April 17, 1870, p. 21; July 17, 1870, p. 28.
27 See Hettling, "Die persönliche Selbständigkeit," 60–66.
28 Entries for April 27, 1870, p. 23; July 17, 1870, p. 28; May 17, 1870, p. 25.
29 Entry for April 23, 1871, p. 37.
30 Entry for August 5, 1871, p. 47.
31 Entry for January 9, 1872, p. 52. On the following, see the entry for May 10, 1872, p. 54.
32 Entries for May 10, 1872, p. 54; June 3, 1872, p. 55.

This relationship between a small-town burger's daughter and a shopkeeper's assistant was not entirely in keeping with her status. Leaving aside the peasant milieu from which they came, the Teuschls had worked hard to achieve burgher status in Krems. In contrast, Johann Baumgartner came from the lower peasant class of the Weinviertel. His parents, Sebastian and Elisabeth Baumgartner, were winegrowers and cottage farmers in the village of Fallbach, north of Vienna.[33] As the sixth of twelve children – four of his siblings died in infancy – the suitor could not hope for financial support from his family. Thus it is all the more remarkable that he not only wins over the girl, who is seven and a half years younger than he is, but also her parents, whom he sees as wealthy. As we have already seen, this is a love match – at least to the extent that we can rely on the testimony of her diary entries. Once again, habitus also plays a particular role – in this case, his appearance: "his earnestness and particularly his masculine, handsome *character*" impress her.[34] In the small-town milieu in which they find themselves, the couple certainly cannot barricade their emotional relationship from the outside world – as would be consistent with the Luhmannian view of love as a self-referential code – but must rather periodically, purposefully stage the relationship in public. This is why, when a ball takes place in Krems, it is particularly important to her that, "in the presence of many of our peers, he proved to me that he loves me."[35] For her part, however, the young bourgeois woman also has criteria for an advantageous marriage that go beyond mere infatuation. The bride-to-be does not romantically rebel against the social norm of economic independence, and even speculates that her suitor will purchase a fine cloth store rather than a simple general store.[36] Indeed, as we have already seen, her tirade against the marriage of Lori Vogl, the innkeeper's daughter, culminates in the noteworthy exclamation: "This woman – and these debts"![37] At the age of 32, eleven years after her wedding, Barbara Baumgartner lays out further criteria for a good marriage when her friend Henriette (Betti) Beer marries for the second time: "Betti married again this year and did very well, considering her circumstances; he is an educated, kind man; a good, attentive husband; and a dutiful father." She also mentions her friend's partner's professional background: "trained as a goldsmith, until recently he held the position of secretary at the *Tagblatt*, and now he is unemployed." What is striking here is Barbara's assessment of this union as a very good match, despite the fact that her friend's bridegroom is currently unemployed.

---

33 This is according to Langreiter's research: see Langreiter, *Tagebuch*, 33–34, n. 47 and n. 49.
34 Entry for May 13, 1870, p. 24, italics in the original.
35 Entry for February 19, 1871, p. 37. See also Luhmann, *Liebe als Passion*, pp. 177–78.
36 Entry for April 23, 1871, p. 38.
37 Entry for November 22, 1870, p. 31.

This praise for her friend's husband can certainly be read as a reckoning with Barbara's own husband, to whom the qualities she mentions have long since ceased to apply. Thus the wife, who is deeply frustrated at this point, sums up her friend's marriage as follows: "she is very happy."[38]

According to the marriage contract, Wetti Teuschl brings a 3,000-florin "cash dowry" into her marriage with the shopkeeper Baumgartner. The bridegroom must confirm in writing that he has received this sum from her – or more accurately, from her parents – and that he himself holds assets in the same amount, in the form of stock and merchandise. Apart from this dowry, which is declared in writing by both parties and confirmed by a notary, the soon-to-be-married couple also constitutes "a general community of goods."[39] The coachman's daughter's dowry thus offers the couple a financially solid jumping-off point from which to enter into married life; not by chance, this coincides with the beginning of Johann Baumgartner's life as an independent businessman. To give an idea of how considerable the sum of this dowry was: Johann Baumgartner had purchased his new business, which was situated in a good location in Vienna's Josefstadt district, a few months previously for the price of 2,000 florins.[40]

On June 3, 1872, the couple celebrates their wedding in two stages: as a public event in church, and as a family celebration. Compulsory civil marriage was still a long way from being introduced in Catholic Austria-Hungary at this time. Therefore the priest in charge of the ceremony investigates possible obstacles to the marriage and checks that the couple who wishes to marry has all their papers in order.[41] Wetti notes her conscious decision to celebrate her wedding in Krems. The 20-year-old wants to show off once again, in front of all her rivals and also her hometown in general. The wedding party rides in her father's carriages through the streets to the church, both of which are "lined with a multitude of curious people"; the scene Wetti describes recalls Lyndal Roper's description of weddings in the

---

[38] All citations taken from the entry for December 4, 1883, p. 121. On the following, see the timeline, p. 149.

[39] In the original German: "allgemeine Gütergemeinschaft"; see the transcript of the marriage contract, October 30, 1872 (originally dated June 3, 1872), in Langreiter 2010, pp. 195–98. See also Wienfort, *Verliebt, Verlobt, Verheiratet*, 84–87; Lanzinger, "Spouses and the Competition for Wealth."

[40] Entry for February 9, 1872, p. 53.

[41] On this and the following, see the entries for May 10 – June 3, 1872, pp. 54–57. Compulsory civil marriage was not introduced until 1938; for an overview of this subject, see Griesebner, "Marriage Jurisdiction"; for a case study from the eighteenth century, see Griesebner, "Property, Power, Gender."

Reformation era in her article "Going to Church Street."[42] In the sixteenth century, however, the public practice of going to church was still an integral aspect of a legal act, whereas here it is a ritual without legal implications. The bride is extremely emotional – so much so that, in her own words, "they feared I would faint" in the church.[43] Wetti Teuschl's fragile state of mind both before and during the wedding is reminiscent of the agitation experienced by Ursula Eglinger, the pastor's daughter, and the crises faced by Ferdinand Beneke, the romantic ladies' man, in similar situations. The importance of this irreversible decision to marry is also reflected in a page-long documentation of the wedding in Wetti's diary, in which she lists the guests by name and provides a detailed menu of the wedding feast at the Gasthof zum Goldenen Stern. A smaller circle of family and close friends takes part in the festivities after the church ceremony, namely the dinner at the inn. In this respect, it is not comparable to an early modern wedding in the village or at the guildhall. Wetti's bridesmaids are her friends 'Dini' and 'Milli.' Dini's husband, the Krems book printer Max Pammer, and Johann's sister Maria's husband, the Viennese hairdresser Wenzel Stawinoha, serve as witnesses at the wedding.[44] This privatization of the festivities by means of social restrictions around the ritual underscores the increased importance of family as well as friendship in this milieu.

Logbook of a Married Couple in Crisis

Two days after the wedding, Barbara Baumgartner says goodbye to her parental home and, accompanied by her mother, leaves to begin her new life in Vienna. Coupled with professional business success and the prestige of the district in which she lives,[45] this the happiest phase of her relationship with Johann Baumgartner. The specialty food shop, which opens in February 1872 in a new building in the bourgeois Josefstadt district, earns good money, so that Johann Baumgartner is able to hire a 'commis' and an assistant.[46] The couple moves into an apartment near the store, presumably on the floor above. This apartment includes a salon, a

---

42 See Roper, "Going to Church and Street"; see also van Dülmen, "Fest der Liebe"; for further details, see Lischka, *Liebe als Ritual*; for a general overview, see Seidel Menchi, *Marriage in Europe*.
43 Entry for June 3, 1872, p. 56.
44 On the groomsmen, see the marriage contract, Langreiter, *Tagebuch*, p. 197.
45 For further information on the Viennese districts, see Eigner, "Mechanismen urbaner Expansion," pp. 630–35; Langreiter, *Tagebuch*, pp. 57–58, n. 137.
46 See the entry for February 9, 1872, p. 53. On the building, see ibid., n. 116; on the following, see the entry for November 20, 1872, pp. 59–60.

Fig. 15: Johann and Barbara Baumgartner's wedding photo, 1872. Source: Private collection

dining room, a bedroom, and a large kitchen, plus a room for the servants. The separation of the salon and the dining room in particular suggests a certain spaciousness to the living arrangements in this neo-classical building. Later they also hire a maid.[47] Barbara Baumgartner works in her husband's shop. When there is time, the couple enjoys the leisure activities the metropolis offers: parks, pubs, the theater, and the opera. There is no record of quarrels during this period. When Barbara gives birth to a healthy son on July 7, 1873, the family's happiness seems com-

---

[47] This is suggested by a remark in the entry for August 6, 1874, p. 65.

plete. But by then a catastrophe on a larger scale – the May 9 Vienna stock market crash – had already occurred. Looking back on the year 1873, for the first time the diarist has to report a "generally poor run of business, price increases, and illness as gifts."[48] Over the next few years, the Baumgartners fall deeper and deeper into a downward spiral. One failed business follows another, and they move from place to place in Vienna; with each move, the neighborhoods get worse and the apartments shabbier. Rapid economic fluctuation is characteristic of small trade. Johann Baumgartner is forced to go into debt, and soon he has to sell his store for less than the purchase price. And so the shop in Josefstadt closes after just over two years, in April 1874. They sell the shop and the apartment at a huge loss. The family moves into an apartment on an arterial road in Vienna for a few months.[49] In order to generate income, Johann Baumgartner rents a shop for smaller businesses. Their next hope arrives when they open a specialty food shop and delicatessen in the Leopoldstadt district in September 1874, with an apartment on the third floor of the building. Leopoldstadt, Vienna's second municipal district, is located on an island in the middle of the Danube river and is still a middle-class neighborhood, but with the onset of industrialization it begins to experience social decline. The business runs reasonably well for a while, but the Baumgartners are ultimately forced to capitulate in the face of competition from a new co-operative. Initially they successfully resist the landlord's termination notice by soliciting financial support from a couple with whom they are friends, Christof and Henriette Beer. However, to avoid bankruptcy, the Baumgartners ultimately have to sell the business at the end of 1875 for "the ridiculous price of 900 florins," "just to get rid of it."[50]

The male breadwinner's periods of employment subsequently become shorter and bring in less money. As a result, the family moves from house to house in rapid succession within the city of Vienna. This new mobility is typical of urban society at the time, especially when it comes to living arrangements among the lower classes. After the couple sells the business, they rent a small shop with an apartment in Leopoldstadt in February 1876.[51] This apartment consists of a single

---

48 Entry for January 7, 1874, p. 63.
49 See the entry for August 6, 1874, p. 64. On fluctuation in the retail trade, see Chaloupek, "Industriestadt Wien," 381; on the developments in the Vienna housing market, see Sandgruber, *Die Anfänge der Konsumgesellschaft*, 347–59.
50 Entry for January 1, 1876, p. 71. The diarist comments on the owner's attempt at eviction with the words: "our landlord, a miserable dog without a conscience (Jew)"; see the entry for August 17, 1875, p. 68. On Leopoldstadt's "social depreciation," see Eigner, "Mechanismen urbaner Expansion," 634.
51 Entry for March 9, 1876, p. 72. On the following, see ibid., pp. 72–73; on residential mobility as a "new nomadism," see Wischermann, "Mythen, Macht und Mängel," 448.

room, plus a *Kabinett* (a small adjoining room) and a kitchen, the latter two of which are rented out. The maid, who appears in the diary neither as a person nor as a laborer, is dismissed. With financial support from her parents, Barbara Baumgartner opens a wool shop that also offers laundry services on site. She succeeds in building up a regular clientele and just about manages to feed her family. Johann Baumgartner is earning no income at this time. After several months of searching, he finally finds a job as a book salesman. In conjunction with these events, the couple's marital relations also deteriorate. She confides in her diary that "my husband surrendered completely to tavern life and games, and toward me he became repulsive and almost crude. I suffered in silence for a long time, and finally I wrote to my parents to [ask them to] remind him of his duties."[52] Her parents' intervention leads to a serious, strident marital dispute, which clears the air as far as she is concerned. But the couple has not yet reached their lowest point, and her parents subsequently play an important role in some respects. She has no more money to buy goods for her shop, and she and her son temporarily move back in with her parents in Krems. In August the Baumgartners can no longer afford the rent on their apartment and small shop. They move out and rent new accommodation on the same street, which consists of only a small, simple room. Their decline is typical of many formerly well-off Viennese who could no longer afford their expensive apartments after the recession set in. At least Johann Baumgartner manages to earn a little money as a "book retailer."[53]

The family reaches the deepest point of this depression – in professional and financial terms – at the end of 1876 and the beginning of 1877. Following a complaint from one of his creditors, the indebted Johann Baumgartner is remanded in custody for three months on suspicion of selling seized goods, embezzlement, and fraud. The case is even covered in the newspaper, the *Neues Wiener Tagblatt*, which reports the total amount of Baumgartner's debts as 2,300 florins. His classification as a 'Fallit' (fraudster) is tantamount to death in terms of his bourgeois status. Upon hearing the news of her husband's imprisonment, Barbara Baumgartner is completely distraught: "So I came [...] home and threw myself on the bed, my whole body in a fever, every nerve raging."[54] During this period, she shuttles back and forth between her parental home in Krems and the dank, one-room apartment on Vienna's Springergasse, until the landlady cancels her contract with only a

---

52 Ibid., p. 73.
53 Entry for October 23, 1876, p. 73. For further details on the following, see ibid., pp. 73–79; on the housing market, see Sandgruber, *Die Anfänge der Konsumgesellschaft*, 354.
54 Entry for October 23, 1876, p. 74. For the newspaper report on the proceedings, see ibid., pp. 74–75; on 'bourgeois death' due to insolvency, see Suter 2016, p. 15; on bankruptcy proceedings, see Häusler, *Ökonomisches Scheitern*.

week's notice. Her son stays with her parents permanently. Yet her husband's imprisonment does not provoke thoughts of separation; indeed, the Baumgartners' marriage proves to be enormously resilient under these stressful conditions. Her visits to the prison are emotional and tearful for them both. They write letters to each other, and she confides in him. In the end, the Vienna Regional Court dismisses the case, and Baumgartner is declared innocent. Before he can be released, however, his father-in-law must sign a declaration stating that his daughter "lives on the best of terms with her spouse, and that I will administer and support my son-in-law, Johann Baumgartner, with the necessary subsistence at any time he requires it."[55] In this way, the court seeks to ensure that the debtor will not be a burden on the welfare system after his release. Barbara reports on the reunion with Johann after his release from prison as follows: "Johann, my sweet little man, was here, and I spent happy hours at his side, because he loves me truly and dearly, and I love him no less."[56]

Nevertheless, the Baumgartners' severe economic problems are not resolved with his release from prison. It takes him three months to find work as a streetcar conductor, but he is fired after only ten weeks, when he is once again remanded in custody for three days due to the same legal dispute. Against his will, Barbara plans to train as a midwife. Yet when he contracts smallpox, which claims 3,300 lives in Vienna in 1872 alone, she has to abandon her plan in order to nurse him.[57] At this point, their marriage enters a new, critical phase. She spends a lot of time with her parents and son in Krems. He continues to try to build up a professional livelihood in Vienna, and he wants her to join him there. Initially she decides to return to him in Vienna, although she finds it difficult "to be apart from my dear child," who in the meantime has begun attending kindergarten in Krems, and to give up her "structured domestic life" with her parents.[58] Despite his debts and his unemployment, Johann Baumgartner manages to rent a small apartment on Rueppgasse in Leopoldstadt after he is released from prison. But the couple has only a single room to themselves. They rent out the small adjoining room to a railroad worker and the kitchen as a bedroom for nightly lodgers (*Bettgeher*) at a per diem rate in order to be able to pay the rent.[59] The discrepancy between the bour-

---

[55] See the testimony, January 14, 1877, p. 89.
[56] Entry for February 5, 1877, p. 91.
[57] See the entries for October 23, 1876, p. 78; April 6, 1877, p. 96. On the number of victims, see ibid., n. 256.
[58] Entry for February 25, 1877, p. 93.
[59] Ibid. On housing arrangements involving nightly lodgers and subtenants, which were widespread among the lower classes, see B. Kuhn, "Mitwohnen im 19. und frühen 20. Jahrhundert,"

geois domesticity she enjoys with her family in Krems and the reality of the couple's living situation in Vienna is difficult for Barbara to bear. Mrs. Baumgartner reports: "The apartment Johann took disgusted me as soon as I moved in, so much so that I would have preferred to go back right away."[60] Her parents finance the termination of their rental contract by paying a few months' worth of their outstanding rent.

The couple's situation is striking, not only in terms of their progressive decline in social status against the backdrop of the economic crisis that began in 1873, but also in their capacity for resilience. In the midst of these crises, the Baumgartners seize every conceivable opportunity to resist impoverishment. After Johann is dismissed from his job as a conductor, the next opportunity for him to cultivate a professional existence comes in the form of an offer from his family. The Baumgartners take over the hairdressing salon, along with two assistants, from his sister Maria and brother-in-law Wenzel Stawinoha for the price of 350 florins. The store's location on 80 Rennweg, an arterial road in the southeastern part of the Landstraße district, is not particularly good.[61] Their move to the suburbs – Rennweg leads to the working-class district of Simmering – can be understood as an indicator of decline. A room and a kitchen are connected to the shop. Johann wants his wife to move in with him permanently and help out in the shop, but Barbara Baumgartner hesitates and has reservations. In the meantime, she has bought a sewing machine, and while living with her parents and her son in Krems, she earns some money by sewing. She fears that her husband has "too much free time" as a hairdresser, "which can lead to other evils." Moreover, she is concerned about the influence of his sister, Maria, who is still present in the shop as one of the hairdressers; her relationship with Maria has been strained since their time in Josefstadt.[62] During a three-day visit to Krems, Johann succeeds in convincing his wife – "Oh, how lovely he was to me" – to move back to Vienna with his son, Hans, and to let Maria teach her how to cut and dress women's hair. The two hairdressers' assistants also live in the building on Rennweg – initially a Hungarian and a Serb, and then two Serbs, "decent young people" who, in addition to their wages, are provided with breakfast, lunch, "a Sunday roast, and beer money."[63] Thus pro-

---

373–78; on Vienna as an example, see Ehmer, "Wohnen ohne eigene Wohnung"; Brüggemeier and Niethammer, "Schlafgänger."
60 Entry for March 8, 1877, p. 94.
61 Entry for July 31, 1877, pp. 99–100; August 8, 1877, p. 100. On the shop's location, see Langreiter, p. 99, n. 263; on the suburbs as 'the other' to bourgeois Vienna, see Maderthaner and Musner, *Die Anarchie der Vorstadt*; Eigner, "Mechanismen urbaner Expansion," 633–35.
62 Entry for August 8, 1877, p. 100.
63 Entries for August 18, 1877, p. 101; November 5, 1877, pp. 101–2 (citations p. 102).

fessional and domestic relationships are not clearly distinguished. In this way, the family ventures a new beginning – and succeeds, to some extent. Their introduction to the hairdressing business takes place in 1877, when the severe recession in Vienna is coming to an end and a slow recovery is beginning. After two months, Barbara Baumgartner sums it all up: the hairdressing salon will not earn them a fortune, "but it will provide a quiet livelihood free from worry."[64] Thus she formulates an important norm and a goal of family life.

Fig. 16: The Baumgartners' (formerly the Teuschls') house on 7 Herzogstraße in Krems, with the store on the ground floor, 1901. Source: Private collection

In the end, however, the hairdressing salon in the Viennese suburbs remains just one more episode in the fast-moving personal history of the Teuschl-Baumgartners. This time the reason for the change is not a termination notice, bankruptcy, or suspicion of fraud, but an offer from Anton Teuschl. The street-side business premises in her "father's house" at 7 Herzogstraße in Krems has been vacated.[65] Her father wants to buy the furnishings from the specialty food shop that had previously occupied the premises and sell them to his daughter and son-in-law at a low price, offering low monthly rent and no risk of rent increases. From a purely

---

[64] Entry for November 5, 1877, p. 101. On the stages of the economic crisis in Vienna, see Chaloupek, "Industriestadt Wien," 360–67.
[65] Ibid., p. 101.

financial perspective, the prospect of guaranteed subsistence is an important aspect of this matter. Barbara Baumgartner's further reflections, however, shed light on relationships within the family as a community of emotion and conflict. Her relationship with her sister-in-law has not exactly improved as a result of their daily contact in the hairdressing salon. Barbara must "bear her [Maria's] whims patiently," which is clearly difficult for her. In Krems, her husband would once again be the "boss" and work as a "merchant," but she fears "whether misunderstandings would arise between Johann and Father, which would drain life of its pleasantness." In a resigned tone, the diarist continues: "I'll just have to wait and see. There's nothing I can do about it." Their departure from the Viennese metropolis and their definitive return to the social confines of her hometown are not easy for her – all the more so because her return home can be construed as a failure: "I'm already afraid of what the people in Krems will say," and "in the end, they say we're already finished once again."[66]

In economic terms, the family's move to Krems proves to be a turning point. The general store opens in February 1878 at 7 Herzogstraße and generates a profit overall; despite some setbacks, the business is successful enough to provide the family with a long-term livelihood. After 15 months, Barbara records increasing sales and believes "good times are still ahead." In addition, "our life is more peaceful than ever, and Johann behaves well."[67] The family's modest (from today's perspective) prosperity enables them to hire a maid and to eat lunch at the inn, rather than at her mother's house. They also take in the child of one of Anton Teuschl's friends who has died, offering room and board. Nevertheless, it still takes years for them to pay off their debts. As mentioned above, Anton Teuschl dies at the end of December 1879. After Barbara's mother, Anna Maria Teuschl, also passes away on April 5, 1885, the Baumgartners inherit the family home on Herzogstraße, and they buy another house in Krems in the same year. According to the land register, half of each house is signed over to Barbara Baumgartner, and half to Johann Baumgartner.[68]

In contrast to the consolidation of the household, the couple's relationship deteriorates drastically. From the perspective presented in the diary, happy periods have alternated with unhappy periods since the beginning of their relationship. Johann Baumgartner's perspective has survived only in his wife's words. It is impossible to determine whether his repeatedly unsuccessful attempts to start a business were

---

66 All citations taken from ibid., p. 102.
67 Entry for May 1879 (without a specific date), p. 113. On repaying their debts, see the entry for December 4, 1883, p. 122.
68 See the entries in the Krems land register, pp. 148–49, n. 5–6.

solely due to the general economic crisis, to bad luck, or to incompetence. She does not reproach him in this regard. All things considered, during this crisis the marriage proves to be a community of care. Yet Barbara Baumgartner's entries often reveal a severe disappointment in her husband. When his business ventures begin to fail, she describes him as depressed, coarse, moody, and "alienated from his family."[69] The latter statement reflects her feelings about his frequent visits to pubs, which are accompanied by drunkenness, which in turn makes him "grumpy and sullen at home."[70] Having overcome the nadir of their relationship while he was in prison, her previous grievances nevertheless extend to include their time in Krems, after they establish their business and after her father dies. She remarks: "home does not suit him at all, and yet he drinks diligently."[71] As a result of his voluntary absence, the house becomes a space for women and child-rearing. In addition, he commits another serious faux pas. The text is not entirely explicit on this point, but nevertheless leaves little doubt that Johann Baumgartner is persistently cheating on his wife. In a long entry on April 20, 1881, she laments "a woman's deepest mortification" and "deepest pain," as well as "my deeply offended honor." She notes that he gives in to "his base desires" and questions whether she "still owes him love and loyalty" at all, since he deserves neither. She considers leaving her husband. However, from her point of view, the argument against taking this step is that she would then also be leaving her son and her elderly mother. In addition, people's "gossip" would reflect badly on the whole family.[72] Following this entry, almost two years and eight months pass before she writes again. On December 4, 1883, she sums up the waning year. Barbara Baumgartner has not left her marriage, but she did have to leave home to pursue treatment for peritonitis over the summer. Thanks in part to the general economic recovery after the financial crash, business is going well. Her husband is "once again kinder and better," but she "still suffers greatly as a result of his whims and his jealousy."[73] By the time her mother passes away in early April 1885, she has written only a few more entries. In contrast to what we might expect of a family chronicle, she makes no comment on her husband's death, which takes place on March 7, 1892.

---

[69] Entry for June 23, 1875, p. 68.
[70] Entry for September 29, 1875, p. 71.
[71] Entry for March 1, 1880, p. 118.
[72] All citations taken from the entry for April 20, 1881, p. 120. On adultery as a theme in literary fiction at the time, see Saurer, *Liebe und Arbeit*, 139–41; on gender-specific honor, see Arni, *Entzweiungen*, chap. 4.3, 204–06; for an overview of the subject, see Frevert, *Mann und Weib*; on divorce more specifically, see below.
[73] Entry for December 4, 1883, p. 122.

Fig. 17: The Baumgartner Family, c. 1885. Source: Private collection

Female Labor and Precarious Familial Support

When we analyze the case of the Teuschl-Baumgartners against the background of the current state of research on the family, several aspects stand out. If we disregard Johann Baumgartner's affinity for the pub, for which his wife has no equivalent, then we cannot speak of separate gender-specific spheres here. Instead, their situation is characterized by the daily co-presence of husband and wife in the shop – whether a general store or a hairdressing salon – in order to earn money together. In most of the Baumgartners' domiciles in Vienna, and also in Krems, their place of work and their home are under the same roof. The Baumgartners constitute a working couple, a concept we know from the early modern period, albeit differently conceived: they embody the 'two-supporter' model, in which both spouses directly contribute to the family's upkeep.[74] Johann Baumgartner takes his wife's participation in the shop as a given. Yet the fact that she brings in money becomes a matter of dispute when she wants to work independently and on her own account, thus challenging the bourgeois principle of the male breadwinner. This proves to be the case when she wants to begin training as a midwife after her husband is imprisoned. He is "jealous" and believes that her training would constitute – as she puts it – a threat to "our love and our happy domesticity." To justify her career plans, Barbara Baumgartner combines arguments that conform to the patriarchal concept of marriage with emancipatory arguments: "I want to support him, and I want to be in a position to care for my child, to create a structured, happy domestic life, and to protect myself from any kind of dependence. These are the aims that I want to and will achieve, with God's help."[75] Although her husband's illness and the care he requires ultimately stand in the way of her training, it is clear that only Barbara's continued participation and labor saves the household and the family from ruin. As we have already seen, she opens her own successful wool shop and laundry service, earns extra money with her sewing machine, and learns how to cut and dress hair. Back in Krems, she works part-time as a reporter for a local Catholic newspaper – which, as she notes, brings in 6 florins per month. In order to free the family from debt, she opens a fabric printing and dyeing shop next to the main shop on Herzogstraße.[76] As long as her activities do not cast doubt on her husband's role as the independent 'head of the household,' Johann Baumgartner – who is struggling professionally – has no objections.

The Baumgartners are also saved from complete ruin by repeated support from their parents. During the crisis, their immediate families and more distant relatives prove themselves to be a community of support based on reciprocity. This is true not only of Barbara's parents, but also – albeit to a much lesser extent – of Johann Baumgartner's family of origin, which is comparatively worse off financially. The norm of intra-family support is reinforced after the wedding, when Johann's sister Maria receives her new sister-in-law at the apartment in Vienna's Josefstadt district and does her "the honors."[77] However, the Baumgart-

---

74 On the working couple, see H. Wunder, "*Er ist die Sonn'*," chap. 4; see also Ågren, *Making a Living*; Whittle, "A Critique of Approaches to 'Domestic Work,'"; Zucca Micheletto, "Paid and Unpaid Work."
75 All citations taken from the entry for February 5, 1877, p. 92.
76 Entries for January 1, 1880, p. 114; December 4, 1883, p. 122.
77 Entry for June 3, 1872, p. 57.

ners also exemplify the fragility of this community of support, especially when it comes to money. With extremely bad timing, while Johann is in prison, his older brother Sebastian writes to demand the return of 700 florins which Johann had previously borrowed from him, employing "threats and imprecations" in the process.[78] In another case, Johann and Barbara loan a sum to Johann's younger sister, Leni, and their efforts to recover this money also lead to disagreements.[79] During the crisis, Barbara Baumgartner is bitterly disappointed by the lack of support from her husband's family. However, while Maria is certainly not a beloved sister-in-law, her surprising offer for Johann and Barbara to take over the hairdressing salon does help the family get back on their feet after Johann is released from prison. After the Baumgartners divest from the hairdressing salon and move to Krems, their relationship with Maria is completely shattered. Antipathies are expressed in insulting letters and quarrels over payments due, with Anton Teuschl also getting involved in these disputes.[80] Thus the harsh financial crisis and high unemployment after the 1873 stock market crash directly impacts people on the level of their familial relationships. In this precarious general situation, we cannot imagine that the morally conscious and highly stressed author of this diary is an innocent angel. At the end of 1883, nine months after her mother-in-law's death, she writes: "Johann's mother died on March 1, and I still don't know how much his portion of the inheritance will be; I am also very distressed and fear that another falsehood may enter in here."[81]

We have already noted in passing the support Barbara's parents provide. They repeatedly pay subsidies for new business ventures, take over rent payments on which their daughter's family has defaulted, and make security deposits on their son-in-law's behalf. In keeping with the criterion of self-sufficiency, which was already a concern regarding their daughter's potential husband's fitness for marriage, the parents do expect their son-in-law's family to stand on its own feet financially. The financial support they provide is neither guaranteed nor a matter of course. Despite their ongoing misery, the Baumgartners pay back the sum of 200 florins to Barbara's parents after they sell the shop in Leopoldstadt.[82] Subsequently a dramatic scene takes place between Anton Teuschl and his daughter over financial matters: a payment of 1,500 florins must be made, but the father becomes

---

[78] Entry for October 23, 1876, p. 78. This sum was later repaid: see the entry for February 26, 1878, p. 110.
[79] See the entries for March 8, 1877, p. 95; August 8, 1877, p. 100.
[80] See the entry for January 25, 1878, p. 105: "Deadly enmity now reigns between me and Mrs. Stawinoha." See also the entry for February 26, 1878, p. 106.
[81] See the entry for December 4, 1883, p. 122.
[82] See the entry for January 1, 1876, p. 72.

hot-tempered and abusive, and Barbara, in tears, throws down the pen with which she had been ready to sign the agreement. Her mother and Johann, who has just returned from prison, try to mediate.[83] Yet the Baumgartners have no choice but to keep accepting payments from their parents, despite the dependence this entails. The decisive turning point in this story comes when Mr. Teuschl essentially purchases the general store on the ground floor of his home in order to hand it over to his daughter and son-in-law cheaply, in return for interest payments.[84]

In the end, the Teuschl family functions not only as a financial, but also as an emotional support community. The parents' house in Krems provides a retreat for their daughter when she can no longer stand the miserable accommodation in Vienna or, for that matter, her husband. She practically commutes between Vienna and Krems, which does not always please her husband. When the first business fails after just two years of marriage, reading between the lines, it is clear that her personal balance sheet is also sobering. She spends the summer months of 1874 with her son at her parents' home in Krems, and afterwards remarks that this period has been "my happiest time in two years."[85] Despite her "fun-loving," quarrelsome father – who repeatedly provokes emotional altercations within the family, which Barbara's mother smoothes out – the house in Krems serves as a "temporary home," a refuge for the married daughter in crisis.[86]

In the emotional community of the family, children play a central role as meaning-makers. 'Hansi' is his mother's comforter, and increasingly also the most important purpose in her life. When her son is only one year old, she notes: "All our joy, our comfort in every sorrow, is our beloved child." Many entries use this or similar language: "My sweet child is [...] my only support."[87] The child is clearly more closely associated with his mother than his father, which is why he accompanies her on her moves between Vienna and Krems. The 3-year-old boy can then also be left with her parents for a while in the 'structured domesticity' of their home, while the Baumgartners desperately try to build up the means to earn a livelihood in Vienna. At the same time, the father–child relationship is not a secondary issue, and emotions such as love and happiness are apparently not exclusive to the child's mother. In an optimistic tone, Barbara Baumgartner reports on the encounter between father and son after the former's imprisonment ends: "Hansi gives Johann great joy; [the boy's] cleverness surprised him quite a bit; he adores his child, and Hansi also shows [Johann] his love in a touching

---

[83] See the entry for February 5, 1877, p. 92.
[84] See the entry for November 5, 1877, p. 101.
[85] Entry for August 6, 1874, p. 65.
[86] Entries for December 28, 1878, p. 110 (first citation); New Year's Eve 1876, p. 86 (second citation).
[87] Entries for August 6, 1874, p. 65 (first citation); April 6, 1877, p. 97 (second citation).

way."[88] As the boy grows up, another layer is added to this picture. It is no longer simply a matter of love or the child's role in providing comfort, but also of developmental progress and pride in his academic achievements. Various entries in the diary document important stages in this respect, including the 4-year-old boy's enrolment in a reformed pedagogical-style kindergarten in Krems, his first day of school, his admission to the high school run by the Piarist monastery at age 10, his exemplary scholastic achievements, and last but not least, the piano lessons he takes for 50 kreuzers per hour.[89] Thus the young Hans Baumgartner from the small Catholic town of Krems is already unmistakably in the process of completing the bourgeois *parcours*, which combines certain familial expectations with educational and performance aspirations.

The Absence of Visiting Culture and the Presence of Gossip

While we can certainly see parallels between the family history in this chapter and those we have analyzed in previous chapters, the Baumgartners' case also points to clear differences. On the one hand, this concerns the question of open domesticity, and on the other, it relates to the small-town public sphere, which constrains behaviors under certain circumstances. In stark contrast to the examples of Stettler, Beneke, Bruckner-Eglinger, and Püschmann, Wetti Teuschl's (and later Barbara Baumgartner's) diary provides hardly any evidence of a domestic visiting culture. The exceptions to this assertion can easily be enumerated: the bridegroom-to-be appears daily at his future bride's parental home for informal visits, during which they get to know each other playfully, by means of chit-chat and card games.[90] The fact that he is granted permission to enter the house is already a statement, because other suitors merely walk up and down Herzogstraße under their beloved's window. Otherwise it appears that no social rounds, salons, or similar gatherings took place at the Teuschls' house – at least, Wetti does not consider them worth mentioning. Instead, her father regularly goes to the local pub in the late afternoon.[91] Social events in which the whole family participates include Sunday outings and trips to the countryside in Anton Teuschl's carriage.

---

88 Entry for February 5, 1877, p. 93. See also the entry for April 20, 1881, p. 120.
89 See the entries for January 25, 1877, p. 90; January 1, 1880, p. 113; July 15, 1880, p. 119; December 4, 1883, p. 122.
90 See the entry for November 22, 1870, p. 32. On the following, see the entry for April 9, 1870, pp. 20–21.
91 See the entry for December 28, 1878, pp. 106–7.

The young Baumgartner couple also apparently receive few, if any visitors in their various Viennese apartments. In their rare free time, they prefer to go to the theater or for a walk. Johann frequents the tavern "across from us" and comes home late.[92] This example shows that urban bourgeois visiting culture has certain spatial and material prerequisites. In addition to the costs an invitation entails for the hosts, one also needs a salon or a separate living room.[93] The housework that arises as a result should be done by a maid, if possible. The Baumgartners' first apartment in Josefstadt offers such comforts, but their subsequent, progressively smaller apartments – with a room, a *Kabinett*, and a kitchen, some of which they sublet as sleeping quarters for other people – make the option of receiving visitors unthinkable. Instead, the family's private sphere is disturbed by subtenants and nightly lodgers. Furthermore, the diary never mentions a spontaneous, informal drop-in visit or any sort of neighborly support. The Baumgartners' continued professional failure in Vienna clearly correlates to the lack of a social network and corresponding practices of ritualized domesticity.

Yet the Baumgartners do have a few important friendships that constitute exceptions to this rule. Maintaining these relationships is primarily Barbara's responsibility. When she moves to Vienna, Barbara loses the close contact she had enjoyed with her childhood friends Milli and Dini, who were her bridesmaids. In place of these friendships, she develops a lasting relationship with the married couple Henriette (Betti) and Christof Beer, with whom Barbara and Johann use the informal 'you' in German.[94] The Beers support the Baumgartners financially – he is a magistrate, and she owns a laundry business – as well as with advice and spiritual counsel. The latter is especially true for Barbara, who is glad to find in Henriette Beer – a Jewish woman 13 years her senior, who will later convert to Catholicism – "at least one friend in Vienna who takes up our cause in some matters."[95] In the midst of a deep depression, she simply takes the streetcar to her friend's house in the Rudolfsheim district and "stayed there for a long time because I felt at home with them." Later she again stays with the Beers for a few days, taking her diary with her and writing in it while she is there.[96] This co-presence in the house by means of prolonged overnight stays is a clear indication of a close relationship. Even after the Baumgartners return to Krems, the friendship between the

---

[92] Entry for October 23, 1876, p. 74.
[93] On the bourgeois apartment, see Wischermann, "Mythen, Macht und Mängel," 353–55.; on bourgeois housing in general, see von Saldern, "Im Hause, zu Hause," 151–53.
[94] Entry for August 17, 1875, p. 69. On the following, see p. 118, n. 329.
[95] Entry for November 20, 1876, p. 85.
[96] Entry for November 14, 1876, p. 79. See also the entry for April 6, 1877, pp. 96–97; on the following, see the entries for January 1, 1880, p. 115; August 8, 1880, p. 118.

couples continues. In the summer of 1879, the Beers spend a week with the Baumgartners in Krems. A year later, Barbara becomes godmother to Henriette's fourth child and is thus inducted into the Beer family, in a manner of speaking. After Christof Beer dies suddenly of a stroke, Barbara – "as her best friend" – wants to offer financial help to the widow and her four children, but to her dismay, Johann Baumgartner refuses to convert social and emotional capital into pecuniary capital.[97]

One recurring theme in the diary is gossip among the people of Krems and the associated fear of dishonor. The social control exercised over matchmaking, everyday marital life, and family problems in a small town around 1870 is clearly a match for the proverbial 'village eye' as we know it from the early modern period.[98] With this in mind, the functional decline of the neighborhood as a sphere of social control and support, which we identified in previous chapters, needs to be relativized. Even as a young woman, Wetti Teuschl is already explicitly afraid of "rumor" and "people's laughter."[99] In 1876 Barbara Baumgartner and her son spend Christmas at her parents' home in Krems, while her husband is in prison at the Vienna Regional Court. She comments on the situation in her parents' house as follows: "It is also more than a little embarrassing to have to tell the neighbors, who were eagerly waiting to see whether my husband might still come at some point during the three-day holiday, a white lie."[100] After he is released from prison, the couple takes a few demonstrative walks in Krems, "so at least people [...] saw us."[101] Conversely, during the happy period she spends in Josefstadt, she finds that "the greatest triumph I can achieve" is to go to Krems on a visit as a married woman, which causes a "great stir" every time.[102] In contrast to the early modern period, conflicts over the symbolic capital of honor in the modern period are not only settled by means of informal communication, but also via the mass medium of the newspaper, or rather reporting in general. Thus an anonymous person sends the *Wiener Tagblatt*'s report on the fraud case involving Johann Baumgartner by post to Anton Teuschl, enclosing a note with the remark: "Surely the terrible person we read about here cannot possibly be your son-in-law?" For his part, after the tenant who rents the shop on the ground floor of

---

97 Entry for April 20, 1881, p. 121.
98 For more on social control in the early modern period, see Eibach, "Das offene Haus"; Capp, *When Gossips Meet*, chap. 5; on the precarious relationship between marital conflict and the public sphere in the context of bourgeois marriage, see Arni, *Entzweiungen*, 105–10.
99 Entry for June 17, 1871, p. 38.
100 Entry for December 25, 1876, p. 86.
101 Entry for February 5, 1877, p. 93.
102 Entry for November 20, 1872, p. 59.

Teuschl's house (prior to the Baumgartners) has loud disputes with his family, gossip about Teuschl's relationship to his son-in-law begin to circulate, and Teuschl feels compelled to publish a notice in the *Kremser Wochenblatt* to counter "malicious rumors" that he has "violently mistreated" his son-in-law.[103]

Barbara Baumgartner also feels that her honor has been violated by her husband's adultery. However, the added dishonor that a marital separation would bring to her, her son, and her mother constitutes an important reason not to get divorced. Moreover, the right to divorce in Austria was not introduced nationwide until 1938. In the diary entries in which she mulls over the possibility of moving away from Krems and explicitly refers to "a divorce," she is referring to the 'separation from bed and board' which had been possible under ecclesiastical marriage law since the early modern period, and which was primarily sought by women. Despite the fact that marriage was a sacrament, Catholic marriage courts could grant this version of marriage dissolution, especially in cases of adultery, but in contrast to Protestant marriage law, this solution excluded the possibility of remarriage.[104] In the second half of the nineteenth century, social norms ensured the permanence of marriage even more effectively than legal statutes. Nevertheless, the general acceptance of marriage as a way of life did not protect it from increasingly becoming the target of criticism toward the end of the century. Thus bourgeois marriage – both as an institution and as a gender hierarchy – entered a period of crisis, which was reflected first discursively, in treatises and novels, and then in increasing numbers of divorces as well.[105]

A Modern Couple

In many respects, Barbara and Johann Baumgartner are a very modern couple. Unlike the Stettlers, the Bruckners, and the Benekes, they do not associate their entry into marriage and the concept of family with a mission in life. It is not a matter of setting up a 'pious house,' nor of establishing a 'moral relationship' which is intended to be refined through shared formative experiences and to become the nu-

---

[103] Entry for October 23, 1876, p. 77 (first citation); November 5, 1877, wording of the declaration, p. 103 (second citation).
[104] See the entry for April 20, 1881, p. 120. On the dissolution of marriage under Catholic law, see Scholz-Löhnig, "Eheauflösung," esp. 53–54; on the practice of 'separation from bed and board' before the Vienna Civil Court, see Dober et al., "Strittige Scheidungen"; on the history of divorce in general, see Blasius, *Ehescheidung in Deutschland*.
[105] On the crisis of marriage around 1900, see Arni, *Entzweiungen*; on divorce rates in the last quarter of the nineteenth century, see ibid., 24; Saurer, *Liebe und Arbeit*, chap. 3, 134–36.

cleus of a new society. Instead, it is simply a matter of personal happiness and of the family's well-being in everyday terms: a "structured, happy domesticity" and a "livelihood free from worry."[106] In addition to mutual affection, the husband should be a reliable, faithful, and devoted partner. Moreover, Barbara Baumgartner's diary is the first in this book to mention sexual pleasure, albeit in a somewhat obscure manner. A few months after the wedding, Barbara reports on her new life in Vienna. She is happily married, and on Sundays they go to parks or to the Volksgarten, to the coffeehouse or the theater. Her apartment is presentable. And as she writes all this, her "little man" is looking over her shoulder "and saying I should also write down how we spend our evenings, and that we are often both very bad."[107]

Undoubtedly numerous families in the early modern period as well as in the nineteenth century faced financial ruin or were forced to give up. Ulrich Bräker and Ferdinand Beneke also struggled with debt. What is striking in Barbara Baumgartner's diary, however, is that the discourse on personal and family well-being is actually monetized. The diarist repeatedly –although not regularly or in tabular format, as one would in a household budget – underpins her entries with concrete figures: the purchase and sale prices of various shops, rental expenses and income, the assistants' wages at the hairdressing salon, the price of the new sewing machine, the cost of piano lessons for her son Hansi, and so on. When the family moves into her parents' home in February 1878, she provides an account not only of the official business relationship they agree on with her parents, as concerns the shop, but also of the bill for breakfast and lunch at her mother's table: "17 florins and 10 kreuzers" altogether.[108] Precise agreements of this sort were not uncommon in the early modern period when it came to property transfers or marriage contracts, but the author of this diary even assesses her premarital love affair in financial terms. As the 18-year-old Wetti reports on a conversation with her suitor, Johann: he "offered up all his kindness," and she "paid him back in kind, with double the interest." A few months later, after she remarks on the debts incurred by Mr. Schober and his bride, Lori Vogl, in Krems, she writes:

---

[106] In the original German: "geregelte glükliche Häuslichkeit"; "sorgenfreie Existenz"; entries for February 5, 1877, p. 92; November 5, 1877, p. 101.
[107] Entry for November 20, 1872, p. 60. On the "orientation toward happiness, fun, and pleasure" in diaries around 1900, see Bänziger, *Die Moderne als Erlebnis*, 17. A few years later, sexual matters were discussed more openly before the court: see Arni, *Entzweiungen*, 235. On repressed sexuality in the bourgeois era in general, see Gay, *Die zarte Leidenschaft*, and *Erziehung der Sinne*.
[108] See the entry for February 26, 1878, p. 106, strikethrough in the original. See also the entry for May 1879, p. 113. On the following, see Lanzinger, "Spouses and the Competition for Wealth."

"the shares of my love are in good standing."[109] Even fluctuations in marital affection can be influenced by money: "my husband has been good and kind ever since I managed to get him 300 florins from my parents."[110] This bald account of numbers in times of economic crisis has nothing to do with pietism, romanticism, or aesthetics.

---

109 Entries for April 17, 1870, p. 21; November 22, 1870, p. 32.
110 Entry for June 23, 1875, p. 68. On the following, see the analysis of the bourgeois subject in Reckwitz, *Das hybride Subjekt*, chap. 2.

Chapter 9
Growing Up Among the Proletariat: Friedrich Engels' Report and Adelheid Popp

Manchester, England (1845); Inzersdorf and Vienna, Austria (1869 – 1902)

Taking up Enlightenment ideas, early liberalism's optimistic expectation of progress had relied on the effects of education and economic development. From this perspective, reform – as opposed to revolution – would bring about increasing knowledge and prosperity, which would then eventually transform the old estate-based society into a "bourgeois, 'classless civil society.'"[1] This expectation of expansion – that is, a social extension of economic opportunities, a better standard of living, and the political participation of all citizens – was a decisive factor. The free, independent (male) citizen would not only have the right to vote, but would ideally also possess a detached house, a dwelling where he would raise his respectable family in orderly circumstances. Yet these well-intentioned utopias, dreamt up by leading bourgeois intellectuals during the period of transition from estate-based to bourgeois society, were manifestly shattered by the social realities of the mid-nineteenth century. The two decades between the July Revolution in 1830 and the March Revolution in 1848 constituted the heyday of 'pauperism,' rampant mass poverty and unemployment, and social protest.[2] After the 1848 Revolution, high industrialization began in the German-speaking lands of Central Europe, creating new modes of employment, but also displacing the old trades. Population growth and industrialization did not give rise to a homogenous middle-class society, as expected, but rather to a 'bourgeois class society.'[3] This development was evident in the construction of entirely new city districts outside the old city walls. In such contexts, neighborhoods full of splendid villas sprang up next to the overpopulated, dirty, unhealthy quarters that housed the industrial proletariat.[4]

---

[1] Gall, *Von der ständischen zur bürgerlichen Gesellschaft*, 27.
[2] See Gailus, *Straße und Brot*, which is representative of many other studies.
[3] See the classic texts by Hobsbawm, *The Age of Revolution*; and Wehler, *Deutsche Gesellschaftsgeschichte*, vol. 2, chap. 3.1; on the 1850s, see F. Lenger, *Industrielle Revolution*, 139 – 41.
[4] On the emergence of new residential neighborhoods, see Wischermann, "Mythen, Macht und Mängel," 455 – 57; on pauperism as a challenge for social-reformist housing and family policy, see Zimmermann, "Wohnen als sozialpolitische Herausforderung," 524 – 26.

Engels' Report on the Slums in English Cities

Friedrich Engels' early treatise *The Condition of the Working Class in England*, first published in German in 1845 under the title *Die Lage der arbeitenden Klasse in England*, offers a concise impression of the proletariat's living conditions. In the subtitle, the author declares that the book was written based on "personal observations and authentic sources."[5] Long sections of the text read like a trailblazing social report. For this reason it does not qualify as a self-narrative, although Engels certainly addresses his own origins and implicitly writes about himself in this early work. Engels was born in 1820, the son of a cotton manufacturer from Barmen. His pietistic father sent him to Manchester in 1842 to complete his commercial apprenticeship in the family business there, the Engels & Ermen cotton mill.[6] His education, including this vocational training abroad, was typical of the bourgeois entrepreneurial milieu in Barmen, in the Rhineland, and beyond. Engels was a member of the bourgeoisie and was already familiar with the miserable living conditions of the working class in his hometown prior to his stay in the booming industrial city of Manchester. His 'anti-bourgeois emancipation treatise' on the heart of European industrialization was a reckoning with both his parental home and the milieu from which he originated. This classic text is included here because we can identify some parallels between the content of Engel's *Condition of the Working Class in England* and the main text we are considering in this chapter, Adelheid Popp's autobiographical account, *The Autobiography of a Working Woman* (*Die Jugend einer Arbeiterin*), which was written more than 60 years later. Popp was an Austrian social democrat and women's rights activist who met Engels in person several times, read his reportage from the English workers' districts, and was impressed by it.[7]

Here we will first focus on the precarious living conditions and family circumstances facing the English industrial workforce, as told from Engels' perspective. During his 21-month stay in England, he traveled from Manchester to other major cities, such as London. He also gathered information about other British industrial centers. His sources were not only statistical documents and expert treatises on working-class grievances, but also his 'personal observations.' Engels sought direct contact with the people about whom he was writing. He walked through the slums in Manchester and London, went into the houses, and initiated conversations with both male and female actors. In a preface addressed to the

---

5 Engels, *The Condition of the Working Class.*
6 On this and the following, see Przyrembel, "Friedrich Engels."
7 Popp, *Jugend einer Arbeiterin*, 105 and 124–25; see also Hauch, *Frauen bewegen Politik*, 210.

working class in Britain, he explained his social-anthropological approach in a nutshell: "I wanted to see you in your own homes, to observe you in your every-day life, to chat with you on your condition and grievances, to witness your struggles against the social and political power of your oppressors."[8] Thus the young Engels made no secret of the fact that he was taking sides. His conclusions may be debatable and open to question, but there is little doubt about the grim reality of what he saw. Three aspects are of particular interest to us here: the material living conditions, the migration factor, and the repercussions of factory work on gender relations in the home and the family. Engels describes different types of housing for factory workers' families and the lower classes in general, all of which are precarious: separate residential districts with new-built 'cottages,' back courtyards and basement apartments in dilapidated buildings, and 'lodging houses' for the homeless. The problems are always similar: in addition to damp, dirty, and smelly conditions due to the lack of sewage systems, these living arrangements were primarily characterized by massive overcrowding, with people crammed in from basement to attic. According to Engels' sources, between two-thirds and three-quarters of English working-class families in the 1840s, with their many children, occupied a single small room.[9] Even newly constructed buildings become dilapidated or stood empty after only a few decades. The residents changed often, necessary repairs were not carried out, windowpanes were broken or missing, and wooden features such as doors and doorframes were ripped out and burned.[10] In the places where the "poorest of the poor" resided, we can observe a very different form of the 'open house': "in this thieves' quarter [St. Giles in London] [...] no doors are needed, there being nothing to steal." Out of the basement apartments, "puny children and half-starved, ragged women emerge into the light of day."[11] Summarizing his forays through the working-class districts of Manchester, Engels uses bourgeois discourse to describe what he saw: "no cleanliness, no convenience, and consequently no comfortable family life is possible." The dwelling becomes an actor, as it were – reciprocal interaction takes place between the domestic sphere and its inhabitants. As Engels verbosely declares: "in such dwellings only a physically degenerate race, robbed of all humanity, degraded, reduced morally and physically to bestiality, could feel comfortable and at home."[12]

---

8 Engels, *The Condition of the Working Class*, 11. On Engels' authenticity discourse, see also Przyrembel, "Friedrich Engels."
9 Engels, *The Condition of the Working Class*, 28.
10 Ibid., 28 and 60–1.
11 Ibid., 61 and 28.
12 All citations taken from Engels, *The Condition of the Working Class*, 63. On the house as an actor, see Gieryn, "What Buildings Do"; on the domestic sphere more generally, see Eibach and Lanzing-

Friedrich Engels' social topography of English industrial cities also offers the reader a "moral topography."[13] In this vein, migration from Ireland is one of the primary subjects he has in mind. The large number of workers of Irish origin constituted a labor pool and thus a basic prerequisite for England's early, rapid industrialization.[14] Tens of thousands of Irish people and their descendants inhabited the worst districts of the industrial cities. Engels – who meets the Irish worker Mary Burns in Manchester and lives with her for much of the time he is in England, maintaining a relationship with her until her death in 1863 – sees migrant women from rural, preindustrial Ireland as victims of radial exploitation on the one hand, and on the other hand he essentializes them by comparing them to 'savages' from other continents. According to him, the Irish would not sleep in beds, but rather on straw; they walked around dressed in rags and immediately drank away their wages in the form of brandy. He is particularly repulsed by the fact that many Irish families keep a pig, which sometimes lives and sleeps with them under the same roof and serves as a playmate for the children. "The southern, facile character of the Irishman, his crudity, which places him but little above the savage, his contempt for all humane enjoyments, in which his very crudeness makes him incapable of sharing, his filth and poverty, all favour drunkenness."[15] Thus Engels emphasizes not the necessity of domestic self-sufficiency or the inevitability of alcohol as a means of escape from a merciless daily routine, but rather the moral aspect of these issues.

Engels also sees gender relations in the home and the family, which factory work has altered, through the lens of morality. Certainly the monotony of a 12-hour workday 6 days a week, for men as well as for women and even underage children, means that any family life worthy of the name is a rarity. As a bourgeois subject, Friedrich Engels does not see women's employment as an opportunity for emancipation, but rather as a threat to established gender roles. With reference to his statistical source material, he shows that well over half of the English factory workforce is female, and just under half of the total workforce is younger than 18 years old.[16] Engels notes that this fact has several fatal consequences for the family. Mothers can no longer take care of their children, but have to leave even their infants in the care of another woman or girl in return for a small fee. The mother's

---

er, *The Routledge History of the Domestic Sphere*; on cleanliness in bourgeois discourse, see Frey, *Der reinliche Bürger.*
13 Przyrembel, "Friedrich Engels," n. p.
14 Engels, *The Condition of the Working Class*, 45, 74, and esp. 111–15, also on the following.
15 Ibid., 93. On pig keeping, see 92. See also Marx and Engels' criticism of the 'Lumpenproletariat' in the Communist Manifesto a few years later: Engels and Marx, *The Communist Manifesto*, 20.
16 Engels, *The Condition of the Working Class*, 142; see also 147; and on the following, see 142–50.

absence is also one reason for the high infant mortality rate; moreover, "a mother who has no time to trouble herself about her child, to perform the most ordinary loving services for it during its first year, who scarcely indeed sees it, can be no real mother to the child, must inevitably grow indifferent to it, [and] treat it unlovingly like a stranger." Many small children grow up completely unsupervised. The fact that 14- and 15-year-old adolescent children performing wage labor in the factories are soon earning more than they need to hand over to their parents for room and board then leads to the complete "dissolution of the family," because the result is that "the children emancipate themselves, and regard the parental dwelling as a lodging-house."[17] Engels the social theorist finds the "total reversal of the position of the sexes" even more problematic. He explicitly rejects "the pristine rule of the husband over the wife" as "inhuman" because it is based not on "family affection," but on notions of property and "private interest." However, he does not see women's employment in the factories as a step toward a solution. "Women's work" has disastrous consequences in that it turns the family upside down: "The wife supports the family, the husband sits at home, tends the children, sweeps the rooms, and cooks." In Manchester he observes hundreds of men who are "condemned to domestic occupations" and thus effectively "unsexed," which accordingly leads to protests.[18] On the other hand, young, single, female factory workers receive no training in domestic activities, such as cooking, cleaning, sewing, and raising children. For this reason they are "wholly inexperienced and unfit as housekeepers."[19] These passages from Friedrich Engels' early work involuntarily demonstrate the normative power of the bourgeois family model in the mid-nineteenth century, with its characteristic gender roles. While he mentions family love in passing, as the basis of familial relationships and therefore as desirable, the Communist Manifesto – written a few years later – contains a general attack on the family as an institution, which is understood in this later text as a "mere monetary relation" hidden behind a "sentimental veil." In their epoch-defining, programmatic 1848 text, Engels and Karl Marx whip up their attack on bourgeois society with the rallying cry: "Abolish the family!"[20]

---

17 All citations taken from ibid., 144. See also 142.
18 All citations taken from ibid., 144–46.
19 Ibid., 146.
20 Engels and Marx, *The Communist Manifesto*, 11 and 26.

The Female Subject's Emancipation from the Precariat

The Autobiography of a Working Woman, written by Adelheid Popp around 1908 and first published anonymously in 1909, attests to an individual story of emancipation. According to Marx and Engels' terminology, the author of this text, born Adelheid Dwořak on February 11, 1869, was born into the 'Lumpenproletariat' in the suburbs of Vienna.[21] Her mother, Anna Dwořak, and her mother's first husband, Joseph Kubeschka, had migrated to Vienna sometime before 1850 – like many thousands of other people from the rural Bohemian milieu – to find a means of making a living in the textile or another industry. Despite meticulous research in the relevant church records and other sources, biographical data on the members of this family is not easy to come by[22] – the spelling of the Bohemian names varies too much, the official records are too inconsistent, and perhaps the family, which moved often, was simply too insignificant. Adelheid's mother was orphaned at an early age and worked as a maid from the age of six; she never attended school and remained illiterate throughout her life. In 1843, at the age of 19, she married Kubeschka, a farmer's son and master weaver who was almost twenty years her senior, and they lived in a suburb of Vienna. Together they had five children before he died of tuberculosis in 1854. At least four of these five children died before they reached the age of 5. In 1857 Anna Kubeschka married Adalbert Dwořak, a journeyman weaver who was also from Bohemia, with whom she had seven more children. One of these children died at birth, one at the age of 3, and another at the age of 11. The youngest of these children was Adelheid, who would grow up to write her autobiography, and whom her mother brings into the world when she is 45. Only five of Anna Dwořak's twelve children live to reach adulthood. The others die of tuberculosis, measles, or fever. Yet even when it comes to these details, we cannot be entirely certain; in her book, Adelheid Popp will later state that she was her mother's fifteenth child.[23]

In contrast, we do know that the author comes from the weaving milieu to which Engels, in the section of his treatise depicting England before machine production took over, ascribes a quasi-idyllic life – one in which mentally limited people languished in an "unthinking quiet." However, it was out of this class of "farming wea-

---

21 Ibid., 20: "the Lumpenproletariat, that passively rotting mass thrown off by the lowest layers of old society." On the "misery of suburban life" in Vienna, see Maderthaner and Musner, *Die Anarchie der Vorstadt*, 68.

22 For further biographical details on Adelheid Popp and her family, see Prager, "Adelheid Popps (fest-)geschriebenes Leben," 18–21; on the following, see 16; on 'Bohemian Vienna,' see Csáky, *Das Gedächtnis der Städte*, 137–45.

23 Popp, *Jugend einer Arbeiterin*, 67.

Fig. 18: Adelheid Popp, née Dwořak. Source: Wikimedia Commons

vers" that the landless "industrial proletariat" then emerged.²⁴ The Dwořak children's godparents are also weavers. Adelheid's godmother is a weaver with Bohemian or Slovakian roots who cannot write her own name.²⁵ We also know for certain that Adelheid Dwořak grows up in circumstances one would not wish on anyone. The Viennese textile industry has been in rapid decline since the mid-1850s, while brick production is booming as a result of the city's structural expansion. The brick factory in the suburb of Inzersdorf (Vösendorf) am Wienerberg is by far the largest in the vicinity of Vienna.²⁶ Several thousand workers are employed there. Perhaps the Dwořak couple hoped to find work in the brick factory, and that is why they moved to Inzersdorf. In this small village, two worlds collide: on the one hand, the village is a rural idyll and a popular destination for excursions among Vienna's high society; on the other hand, it provides living quarters for migrant workers of ill repute. The brick factory's rapid expansion went hand in hand with the construction of cheap housing for the workers. Long-established 'villagers' (*Dörfler*) and newcomers known as 'brick Bohemians' (*Ziegel-*

---

24 Engels, *The Condition of the Working Class*, 4–6.
25 Prager, "Adelheid Popps (fest-)geschriebenes Leben," 19. On the following, see 19–21.
26 On the decline of the textile industry, see Chaloupek, "Industriestadt Wien," 336; on brick making, see ibid., 334.

böhm) live in immediate proximity and yet pay hardly any attention to one another.²⁷ Adelheid Dwořak's family lives in the housing development on Triester Straße, a major thoroughfare, in the midst of the brickmaking proletariat. It is worth noting that the Dwořak family of weavers, unlike their neighbors, subsists on work done at home. Thus the everyday life of the proletarians and Bohemian immigrants who live on this street (and are referred to as *Straßler* or 'street people') is comparable to the conditions Friedrich Engels describes.

Fig. 19: A brickmaking family in Vösendorf, barefoot at work. Source: Historical archive of the Wienerberger company

Our next task here is to outline the writing subject's biography and her motives for writing. The life of Adelheid Popp, née Dwořak, is truly remarkable.²⁸ Born into

---

27 For an account of this situation, written by a elementary school teacher, see Freund, *Inzersdorf am Wienerberge*, 121–23, although the author speaks of a "massive, unemployed working population" only in passing (122). See also Iglauer, *Ziegel*; Streissler, "Die Inzersdorfer Ziegelarbeiter."
28 On Adelheid Popp's biography, see the outlines in Prager, "Adelheid Popps (fest-)geschriebenes Leben"; Hamann, "Adelheid Popp und wir," and "Eine muss immer die Erste"; and with particular attention to her political activities, Hauch, *Frauen bewegen Politik*, 205–23; more generally, see Re-

abject poverty, illiteracy, and domestic violence, she not only succeeds in making a living wage, with which she feeds herself and other members of her family. She can also be seen as an example of Kant's Enlightenment formula – as 'humanity's emergence from its self-inflicted nonage' – although neither her situation, nor those of all the women and men whom mass poverty and industrialization cast headlong into new ways of life and whose stories have not been preserved, can be described as self-inflicted. Adelheid Dwořak's formal education consists of three years attending the elementary school in Inzersdorf. She no longer understands Czech, which is her parents' native language. She will have to learn correct German spelling and written German grammar later, as part of her journalistic work. The young Adelheid has no concept of childhood as an idyllic period, as the early nineteenth-century pedagogical discourse had conceptualized this phase of life: "In later years, I was often overcome by a feeling of boundless bitterness [over the fact] that I had enjoyed nothing at all, truly nothing at all of the pleasures of childhood and the happiness of youth."[29] Instead, after her father's death, at the age of 6 she has to earn money to help support the family. Not only in the factories, but also in traditional rural society, it was taken for granted that children would work as part of the family economy. Adelheid knits stockings and sews on buttons, looks after children even younger than herself, and runs errands. More than 30 years later, she can still remember that she received the tiny amount of one and a half kreuzer for sewing on 144 buttons, and that her maximum earnings per week amounted to 27 kreuzer.[30]

Changing jobs in quick succession, enduring humiliating conditions, hunger, and poor nutrition are all basic tenets of her biography, even after 10-year-old Adelheid moves to Vienna with her mother in 1879. We will explore this in more detail below. The first change for the better comes when Adelheid secures permanent employment and a fixed wage in a Viennese cork factory, when she is 15 years old. A second professional improvement comes in 1892, at the age of 23, when she is hired as the editor of the new *Working Women's Newspaper* (*Arbeiterinnen-Zeitung*).[31] In the time between these two events, she makes her first

---

iter, *Adelheid Popp*; and on childhood among the Austrian working class from a socio-historical perspective, see Hanisch, "Arbeiterkindheit."

29 Popp, *Jugend einer Arbeiterin*, 56. All subsequent citations of Adelheid Popp's work refer to the 2019 edition of the *Jugend einer Arbeiterin*, edited by Sibylle Hamann. On childhood among the bourgeoisie, see Budde, *Auf dem Weg ins Bürgerleben*; on the premodern period, see Jarzebowski, "Kindheit"; Papathanassiou, "Kinderarbeit."

30 Popp, *Jugend einer Arbeiterin*, 48–49; see also Prager, "Adelheid Popps (fest-)geschriebenes Leben," 30–31.

31 Popp, *Jugend einer Arbeiterin*, 82–84 and 122.

contacts with supporters of the Austrian workers' movement and awakens to socialist ideas, which Adelheid Popp later describes as an experience akin to a revival. She refers to herself synonymously with the terms "socialist" and "social democrat."[32] Promoted by Victor Adler, the founder of the Austrian Social Democratic Workers' Party, and his wife, Emma, Adelheid Dwořak – who marries the social democrat Julius Popp in 1893 – becomes one of the first women in the party to make public appearances and to get involved in 'the woman question.' In 1919 she is elected as one of the first female members of the Austrian Parliament. The fact that she is also the first woman to make a speech to the National Council elevates her to an icon of the Austrian women's movement. Her political activities closely correspond with her own life experience. Popp demands not only women's suffrage, but also an eight-hour workday and effective monitoring of factory conditions – not least to combat child labor – as well as better protection for pregnant women and mothers.[33] As a subject, Adelheid Popp, née Dwořak, weaves together several cultural strands: she is the daughter of migrants from the subproletariat, a factory worker, a moralist, and a politician in the workers' and women's movements. As the author of an autobiography, Popp also makes use of a genre with a bourgeois heritage.

The autobiographical text about her childhood and youth, which ends with her husband's early death in 1902 – which resulted in her assuming sole responsibility for her two sons, born in 1887 and 1901 – must be seen in the context of Adelheid Popp's political convictions. Thus she describes her personal conversion from childlike religiosity and infatuation with the Habsburg monarchs to a new kind of faith. Unlike many diaries, this text is underpinned by a coherent narrative – a red thread – which in the end transforms her into a social democrat who wants to "convert" others.[34] Popp's book, the first edition of which is published in 1909 by a press based in Munich, combines two goals: first, to raise awareness of the concrete grievances and precarious conditions summarized in the phrase "oppression and exploitation";[35] second, to appeal primarily to working-class women to emancipate themselves by means of education and political engagement. In his preface to the first edition, August Bebel calls the anonymous author a "champion of her sex." In the preface to the third edition, published only a year

---

[32] Ibid., 88 and 133. On women in Austrian politics after the 1848 Revolution, see Hauch, *Frauen bewegen Politik.*
[33] For a brief discussion, see Hamann, "Eine muss immer die Erste sein," 12; for further details, see Hauch, *Frauen bewegen Politik*, 205–07.
[34] Popp, *Jugend einer Arbeiterin*, 109.
[35] Ibid., 99.

later, Adelheid Popp thanks Bebel in turn, and under her own name, as a champion of "women's liberation."[36]

This coming-of-age story of a working-class woman is not merely a flat piece of propaganda, but also a textual processing of traumatic experiences. Adelheid Popp's self-narrative reveals much about herself. She gives the reader a glimpse into her childhood in Inzersdorf, describes her brother's infirmity and her husband's illness. Moreover, the text bears witness to a problematic mother–daughter relationship. Comparably to the diary of Wetti Teuschl, later Barbara Baumgartner, Adelheid Popp broaches the topic of exhaustion, which leads to anxiety and fainting spells.[37] Her psychological crises do not come to an end simply because she begins a new life as a social democrat – especially since the double burden of factory and party work hits her like a firehose. Only at the very end does the text sometimes tip its hand and employ confessional discourse to describe how the author finds meaning and purpose in socialism, or what she calls: "My faith in socialism."[38]

In contrast to Friedrich Engels, Adelheid Popp refrains from analyzing society as a whole. It is noteworthy, for example, that she writes not a single word about the severe economic crisis that began in 1873 and constituted the framework of her childhood. Nor do the brickworks in Inzersdorf – about which Victor Adler had written a stirring study of the workers' catastrophic living conditions – in which she herself never worked, fit into Popp's subject-oriented narrative.[39] Moreover, she scrupulously refrains from mentioning concrete names of places, factories, and people, presumably in order to avoid exposing anyone, and perhaps also to preclude legal action. The author is concerned with the illustrative and emblematic nature of her experiences. Some passages can be read as a direct link to Engels' book on the condition of the working class in England, especially when it comes to the effects of factory work, which she illustrates with the example of her years working in the cork factory in Vienna. Thus Adelheid Popp scrutinizes the issue of wages paid to the women who look after the children during the day and mentions the relationships between working wives and their unemployed husbands, the double burden of gainful employment and household work that falls on female factory workers, and not least the children under 14 years of age who work

---

[36] In the original German: "Vorkämpferin ihres Geschlechts"; "Befreiung der Frau"; ibid., 35 and 38.
[37] This even led to suicidal ideation; see ibid., 68–69 and 81. On the following, see 121 and 124.
[38] Ibid., 132–33.
[39] For more on Adler's writings, see Iglauer, *Ziegel*, 160–62; Prager, "Adelheid Popps (fest-)geschriebenes Leben," 21–22.

in the factories illegally.⁴⁰ Yet in terms of content as well as style, we can identify differences between Engels' work and this self-narrative, written two generations later. Popp does not plead for radical, systemic change, nor does she endlessly pillory the bourgeoisie. Instead, she seems to believe in the possibility of reform: "The working woman is still exploited, and the lot of the married proletarian woman is still a doubly oppressed one, but nevertheless the path to a better social order is already revealing itself."⁴¹

Migrant Families and One-Room Domesticity

What does domesticity mean in the proletarian district of Inzersdorf am Wienerberg around 1875? Adelheid Popp answers as follows: "I only knew the large room where people worked, slept, ate, and quarreled."⁴² At that time, the Dwořak family of seven lives in a single room in a housing complex on Triester Straße. Seven or eight people do the cooking in the communal kitchen. The privy for all the residents is located in a wooden shed with a cesspit in front of the house. New lavatories and laundry rooms would not be installed until 1892. The Bohemian migrants' living conditions resemble those of the 'Irish people' in Manchester, as Friedrich Engels described it. The material and symbolic center of the Dwořak household is the large loom on which Adalbert Dwořak, a weaver approaching 60 at the time, handcrafts cloth with his sons, which he then hands over to the factory owner in exchange for money – a method of work that has no future, in view of the relentless forward march of machine-produced textiles. The textile industry had a particularly high rate of child labor.⁴³ Upon application, Adalbert's 10-year-old son, Albert, is exempted from compulsory schooling so that he can assist his father. There is also a stove and a bed in this large room, and little Adelheid hides under the bed in fear when her parents quarrel. Her father, who drinks, often brings home too little money for the household budget, and consequently her mother confronts him. "My father had a violent temper, and he would beat

---

40 Popp, *Jugend einer Arbeiterin*, 85–86 and 116–17.
41 Popp, preface to the 4th ed. (1922), 41.
42 Popp, *Jugend einer Arbeiterin*, 43. On the housing conditions in Inzersdorf, see the anthropological research in Iglauer, *Ziegel*, 159–63; on families engaged in home work, see von Saldern, "Im Hause, zu Hause," 283; on the living arrangements of factory workers more generally, see 192–94; with regard to the following, my thanks to Karin M. Hofer for the information.
43 Prager, "Adelheid Popps (fest-)geschriebenes Leben," 30. On the decline of the textile industry in and around Vienna, see Chaloupek, "Industriestadt Wien," 336.

my mother."[44] As a laundry woman, the mother – just like the children – works to help provide for the family's basic needs. The Dwořaks' family life is completely determined by subsistence requirements and the bare necessities of life. First and foremost, the children constitute a workforce.

Fig. 20: Inzersdorf near Vienna, 16–20 Triester Straße, a workers' house prior to demolition in 2016. Source: Karin M. Hofer

In the context of this one-room domesticity among the Inzersdorf *Strassler*, there is no privacy and no separate gender spheres. In one and the same room, people work and argue, are born and die in full view. The emotional relationship young Adelheid has with her mother is much stronger than her relationship with her father, and yet there are ambivalences in the mother–daughter relationship from the very beginning. In the very first lines of her autobiography, Adelheid Popp sums up her childhood as follows: "No point of light, no ray of sunshine, nothing of the comfortable home where maternal love and care would have guided my childhood is known to me." But she immediately adds: "Nevertheless, I had a good, self-sacrificing mother, who did not permit herself an hour of peace and quiet, always driven by necessity and by her own will to bring up her children honestly and to protect them from hunger."[45]

Adalbert Dwořak is a present-yet-absent father of a different sort than the bourgeois fathers who retreat to their studies and thus create distance between themselves and family life. Obviously there are no such opportunities here. His retreat, as in Johann Baumgartner's case, is the masculine conviviality of the pub.

---

44 Popp, *Jugend einer Arbeiterin*, 43. See also 46.
45 Ibid., 43.

Dworak – who, despite his advanced age, has only achieved the rank of journeyman, and who undoubtedly had his own hard life story, about which we know little – is usually impassive and silent in the family circle; when he does express himself, he only knows how to do so through violence. Between Adalbert and Adelheid, his youngest child, there seems to have been no relationship at all. "My whole heart was attached to my mother; I was incurably shy with my father, and I don't remember ever having spoken to him, or that he ever addressed me."[46] Adelheid Popp illustrates the emotional history of her childhood with two scenes: one particular Christmas Eve, and her father's death and burial. In the first scene, her mother wants to show Adelheid, who is not yet 5 years old, and her siblings what Christmas is all about, so she sets aside a few kreuzer over a period of several weeks.[47] They put up and decorate a Christmas tree in their single room. The family wants to light the candles and eat the sugary poppyseed noodles (*Mohnnudeln*), which are a Bohemian-Austrian culinary specialty. But their father is not there. He had wanted to bring some cloth to the factory owner and return home with some money for Christmas presents. They wait for hours and finally go to bed disappointed, without lighting the candles on the tree. Then their father appears – after a stop at the pub – drunk and with less money than their mother had hoped to receive. As Adelheid watches from the bed, "another violent scene" ensues, and her father destroys the decorated tree with a hoe.[48] The next day he has a guilty conscience, and he gives his daughter a few kreuzer to buy something for herself.

When her father dies of cancer in 1875, Adelheid is 6 years old. Her nearness to her father's death also demonstrates that the *Strassler* accommodation is not the appropriate venue in which to search for familial sentimentality. Indeed, it is simply a matter of survival. The medicine does not improve their father's health, but it does devour the family's meager income. "So often was I sent to the pharmacy with a prescription that my mother would complain [and ask] how much longer it was going to take." When the priest finally arrives to hear her father's last confession and give him the last rites, Adelheid sees this as "a major event." Her father dies "without a conciliatory word," and she cannot summon any grief over his death: "when I wore the mourning clothes, the hat, and the veil borrowed from a wealthy family, I felt far more of a sense of satisfaction at being so beautifully dressed for once."[49]

---

46 Ibid., 44.
47 Ibid., 44–45. On the house as an emotional place, see Opitz-Belakhal, "A Space of Emotions"; on the meaning ascribed to Christmas celebrations, see L. Schmidt, *Weihnachtliches Theater*; Baumert, *Bürgerliche Familienfeste*.
48 Popp, *Jugend einer Arbeiterin*, 45.
49 Ibid., 46.

The Dwořak family, headed by a weaver and a washerwoman, constitutes a community of survival to which all members must contribute. In terms of work, this is not a question of housekeeping, providing care, or representing the family by serving tea and entertaining guests, but rather of generating immediate income to provide food for the next day.[50] For this reason the father's death two years after the Vienna stock market crash plunges the family into an even greater existential crisis. The widowed mother is now the sole "breadwinner," responsible for a household that consists of five children.[51] The eldest brother has to leave home and go on the road as a journeyman craftsman. The two middle brothers, aged 13 and 16, are apprenticed. Albert, at 10 years old the youngest boy, continues to attend school but has to earn money as well. The example provided by the Dwořak family indicates that children participated in quite a variety of forms of income generation, besides factory work.[52] As we have already seen above, Adelheid earns a few kreuzer by knitting stockings, sewing, and looking after other children while their parents are at work in the brick factory.

The extra income earned by the children of Inzersdorf points to the simultaneity of traditional, late feudal, and modern practices during the first great economic crisis of the high industrial era. In the rural regions of Lower Austria, seasonal haymaking customs still include a practice in which children and poor people walk through the village and ask for gifts at well-to-do houses by reciting a wish.[53] When the offspring of wealthy families die, children from poorer families can earn some money by participating in the funeral procession. Along with other boys, Adelheid's brother Albert serves as a beater, flushing game during hunts. Adelheid writes a letter to a 'duchess' known for her charitable contributions, asking this lady to graciously grant the girl a pair of shoes so that she can attend school. She is then permitted to come to the castle, where she is given sturdy shoes and a warm winter jacket, as well as money for her mother. With her wooden clogs and thin jacket, the 10-year-old Adelheid wins over the noblewoman to such an extent that she sends her own doctor to examine Adelheid's sick brother, Albert, and hires Anna Dwořak as a gardener the following spring. Before his bone disease (which will eventually prove fatal) takes hold, Albert earns some money during the summer by setting up the bowling pins at local inns on Sundays. Inzersdorf in the 1870s is a place characterized by industrial factories, conventional pre-

---

50 On different forms of domestic work, as previously noted, see Whittle, "A Critique of Approaches to 'Domestic Work,'"; Zucca Micheletto, "Paid and Unpaid Work."
51 Popp, *Jugend einer Arbeiterin*, 46; also on the following.
52 See Papathanassiou, "Kinderarbeit," with further references.
53 Popp, *Jugend einer Arbeiterin*, 49. On the following, see 47–52.

modern customs, and charity, as well as the emerging modern entertainment society.

In addition to premodern rural support practices, the proletarian milieu situated along the main thoroughfare also provides neighborly services. Adelheid's mother is regularly forced to flee her violent father and "to hide out with the neighbors." As Popp reports, should she then fail to reappear for a few days, their scolding father, "whom no one was allowed to approach," would have to take care of the children and the household, which proves to be too much for him. "There wasn't much to eat, so compassionate neighbors helped us."[54] The neighbors eventually also provide soup for 11-year-old Albert as he is wasting away from disease, and try to get him back on his feet by any means possible. The traditional neighborhood tasks also include paying one's respects by being present at key moments over the course of each other's lives. This applies not only to weddings and the initiation of godparent relationships, but also a neighbor's passing away. When the Catholic priest appears at 163 Inzersdorf to administer the last rites to Adalbert Dwořak, it is not only the family who is present: "All the inhabitants of the building knelt in our room, and we with them."[55] Such rituals and neighborly assistance are worth mentioning for several reasons. The Dwořaks often move to different rooms on the main 'street,' which means the household community is always being reconstituted. With regard to the transition to modern society, social history tells us that the relevance of neighborly functions decreased.[56] In the petit bourgeois milieu of Krems, as we have seen, the neighborhood was simply presented as an annoying form of social control. However, many of the migrant women in Inzersdorf came from Bohemian peasant society, as did Anna Dwořak and her first husband, Joseph Kubeschka. They had grown up with the old practices of mutual assistance in the neighborhood as a community of need, which they then took with them to the new world of Inzersdorf.

The nineteenth century was the century of compulsory education, progressive literacy, and educational expansion in Europe.[57] Yet this modern success story is not without its rough patches. Until well into the twentieth century, long periods of schooling for children primarily represented a cost consideration for lower-class families and, as in the case of the Dwořaks, implied the loss of urgently needed income. This is an important issue for Adelheid Popp – and also a point of departure in her relationship with her mother. Although little Adelheid is considered

---

54 All citations taken from ibid., 43–44. On the following, see 48.
55 Ibid., 46.
56 Wrightson, "The 'Decline of Neighbourliness' Revisited"; Cockayne, *Cheek by Jowl*.
57 Osterhammel, *Die Verwandlung der Welt*, chap. 16.

gifted, she is often absent from school, and no excuse for these absences is offered because her mother cannot write. This eventually proves to be the mother's undoing. In 1869 the Austrian education law had introduced eight years of compulsory schooling and abolished school fees.[58] The administration at the elementary school in Inzersdorf files a complaint, and one morning two gendarmes come to take Anna Dwořak away for a 12-hour detention, which she considers a disgrace. She is then summoned to see the head teacher, along with 10-year-old Adelheid's guardian. Adelheid Popp sums up the dilemma in retrospect as follows: "But what good was it to be able to attend school if I had neither clothes nor food"?[59] At the end of the school year, in the summer of 1879, Anna Dwořak and her daughter move to Vienna. Because the child Adelheid is not registered with the police there, no authority notices that the 10-year-old stops attending school. Thus, instead of the legally required eight years, Adelheid attends school for only three. It is not Anna, but rather Adelheid who fills out the official registration form in Vienna, because she knows how to write. She makes no entry in the column for children, because she considers herself "no longer a child [...] I was already a worker"![60] In this way, she anticipates her mother's ideas and desires.

Co-Presence in Chambers and Bedsits

We can pick up our description of the domiciles inhabited by the Dwořak mother and daughter in Vienna immediately where the chapter on the Baumgartners' ever-changing apartments left off. In contrast, however, this account does not mention residences in the Viennese city districts. Anna and Adelheid Dwořak inhabited cheap, dark, poorly heated 'chambers' or one-room 'bedsits' – sometimes just the two of them, sometimes along with one of Adelheid's brothers. These places offered no comfort, privacy, or gender segregation. Compared to the weaver's household in the proletarian quarter of Inzersdorf, however, two differences are worth noting. First, despite a pronounced co-presence, fewer people sleep in the same room; second, at least in principle, work and home life are separated in terms of both time and space. This second difference, however, is evident only to a certain extent. Since her work consists of crocheting wool and cloth, 11-year-old Adelheid takes her work home with her after 12 hours in the workshop so that she can continue working in the evening and through the night.[61]

---

58 Prager, "Adelheid Popps (fest-)geschriebenes Leben," 19.
59 Popp, *Jugend einer Arbeiterin*, 53. On the following, see 55.
60 Ibid., 55.
61 Ibid., 55–56 and 58.

When Adelheid moves to Vienna with her mother in 1879, Albert, the brother who was closest to her in age and with whom she had a close relationship, has already died. Her older brothers are in the military, on a journeyman's tour, and working as an apprentice, respectively. In Vienna, mother and daughter share "a small chamber" with an elderly couple, in which "the couple slept in one bed, my mother and I in the other."[62] The older woman earns money as a fortune teller and, as Popp sees it, tries to persuade Adelheid to engage in prostitution, which motivates the Dwořaks to move out. Their second domicile, which they occupy for several years, is a small room with no windows. Mother and daughter share this room with one of Adelheid's brothers and his work colleague, who both sleep in the same bed. Sometimes a friend of Adelheid's, an unemployed maidservant, also spends the night there. This girl sleeps in the bed next to Adelheid's mother, while Adelheid herself makes a place at the foot of the bed, with a chair pushed up against the bed to accommodate her.[63] Sharing a bed in this way was a known practice in premodern times and is anything but unusual among the lower classes in the nineteenth century. Friedrich Anton Püschmann also reports having done this. In *A History of Private Life* by Philippe Ariès and Georges Duby, *la ruelle* – the niche between the bed and the wall – is considered the only "unambiguously intimate place" available to a broad swathe of the population.[64]

As we have seen in the previous chapter, lodgers and so-called *Bettgeher* who rent rooms or beds by the night are an extremely common phenomenon in Vienna as well as in large German cities at this time. According to one census, 17 percent of small apartments – consisting of one room and a kitchen – in Vienna around 1900 are occupied by six or more people. One-quarter of all households accommodate nightly lodgers or *Bettgeher*.[65] From a bourgeois perspective, sharing a bed and the practice of renting space to nightly lodgers is clearly a deplorable state of affairs, hygienically as well as morally. Adelheid Popp's report confirms this, as the lodger her brother brings into the apartment makes nocturnal advances on 14-year-old Adelheid, which triggers insecurity and anxiety in her. The man is immediately sent away, but Adelheid's anxiety is so strong that she has to see a doctor, who – in the neurasthenic jargon of the time – diagnoses her with "a nervous disorder." A clinical examination also determines that the girls is "extremely mal-

---

62 Ibid., 55.
63 Ibid., 57.
64 Ranum, "Refugien der Intimität," 224. On shared and single beds, see Dibie, *Wie man sich bettet*, 98.
65 The data on Vienna can be found in Haiko, "Wiener Arbeiterwohnhäuser," 30; on nightly lodgers, *Bettgeher*, and subtenants in general, see B. Kuhn, ""Mitwohnen," 373–78; Ehmer, "Wohnen ohne eigene Wohnung"; Brüggemeier and Niethammer, "Schlafgänger."

nourished and anemic."⁶⁶ Later still, after one of her older brothers returns from his military service unemployed, the three of them once again live in a single room. Sharing a bed with her mother is still a matter of course for 16-year-old Adelheid. Nevertheless, their living conditions improve as the economic crisis subsides, and also as a result of work in the cork factory that brings in regular wages: "We had taken a room with two windows, and [my] youngest brother lived with us again, but there were no lodgers. So when I read on Sundays, I could sit by a window, which only opened onto a narrow courtyard, but I was overjoyed nevertheless."⁶⁷ Adelheid Popp does not describe her living conditions in the later phases or her life in any detail. Yet her comments show that it is not the nuclear family model which is common, but rather the 'extended family' model, which includes other family members. For example, mother and daughter later live with one of Adelheid's married brothers, and when Adelheid herself marries, at the age of 24, her mother moves in and manages the couple's household.⁶⁸

The aspect of openness versus privacy in the domestic sphere is clearly different here than in the cases of the Benekes, the Bruckner-Eglingers, or even the village schoolteacher Püschmann. This applies not only to the weaver's household where work takes place in the home, but also to the rented apartments in Vienna. In the winter, the Dwořaks' chamber is effectively uninhabitable during the day, because the wind and snow find their way through the cracks in the doors and the window frames. Using the stove for heat during the day is out of the question because it is too expensive. The mother goes to work at 5:30 in the morning. She gives the girl a piece of bread and a few kreuzer to buy herself something to eat at noon. And so 14-year-old Adelheid wanders through the big city, trying to find some kind of work. "I was on the street almost the entire day." In between, she warms up in churches or in the houses where she asks for work. "I had to find work at all costs."⁶⁹ She changes occupation often. She finds shelter in Vienna's workshops and small factories for a few days or weeks at a time, only to be literally turned back out on the street. In an alley, an "elegant gentleman" approaches her in a suspicious manner. Several times, completely exhausted, she faints. She recovers during a stay in a psychiatric hospital, where she is admitted for observation. There she finally receives good food, even meat, and last but not least: "I had a bed to myself and always had clean laundry."⁷⁰ What is more, at the

---

66 All citations taken from Popp, *Jugend einer Arbeiterin*, 64. On the following, see 71–72 and 90; on neurasthenic discourse, see Radkau, *Das Zeitalter der Nervosität*.
67 Popp, *Jugend einer Arbeiterin*, 89.
68 Ibid., 97 and 126.
69 All citations taken from ibid., 72.
70 Ibid., 81 and 65.

clinic Adelheid has time to pursue her favorite pastime: she reads books that the doctors lend to her.

Obviously the visiting culture typical of bourgeois families in general is not practicable in dark, drafty bedsits. The presence of nightly lodgers, who pay a few kreuzers per night, is purely a material consideration. Domestic co-presence with one's siblings occurs in the context of the family as a community of mutual support. The consequence of all this is an escape to the streets or, for men, to pubs and taverns. Yet despite this extremely limited domesticity, there are also aspects of the adolescent Adelheid Dwořak's life that point beyond materiality or "a mere monetary relation."[71] Jürgen Habermas has identified the eighteenth-century domestic salon as the birthplace of a new kind of discourse – first literary, and later political. For Christopher Clark as well, the Enlightenment in eighteenth-century Prussia began with a culture of conversation, as mentioned above, which took place in the semi-public setting of the home.[72] Adelheid, who is in the process of growing up, is not familiar with visits or with distinguished salon conversation. Yet her story of emancipation also begins in the house, or rather at home, where she sits at the window on Sundays reading and studying books. At first she reads indiscriminately – whatever she can get her hands on or find in the antiquarian bookshops in the suburbs. Later, as she reports with some pride, she reads the classics: Schiller and Goethe.[73] Moreover, this pastime expands beyond her solitary leisure time. The girl is popular as a reader and a storyteller. The master's wife in the house where she works invites her to read aloud. Also "in the building" where she lives with her mother, "the families invited me to tell stories."[74] The second step in her journey takes place thanks to the repeated visits her brother's colleagues pay to the apartment; among them are "some intelligent workers" and social democrats, who not only bring newspapers and books, but also use terms in conversation that are quite new to Adelheid, such as "republic," "anarchism, and socialism."[75] At this point, she is around 20 years old. She does not understand these theoretical treatises immediately, but it is easy for the future Adelheid Popp to relate her own experiences of everyday factory life and the proletarian lower-class milieu to the things she has read. Only after this period of domestic reading, reflection, and discussion – which coincides with her abandoning her infatuation with religion and the aristocracy – does she dare to become politically active in the factory and to attend meetings in the evenings. As editor of the

---

71 Engels and Marx, *The Communist Manifesto*, 11.
72 J. Habermas, *Strukturwandel der Öffentlichkeit*, 107–16; Clark, *Preußen*, 295–99 and 309.
73 Popp, *Jugend einer Arbeiterin*, 58–60; see also 65–66 and 89–90.
74 Ibid., 60.
75 Ibid., 97.

Arbeiterinnen Zeitung, the newspaper for working women, 23-year-old Adelheid imagines that she has arrived at the "promised land."⁷⁶

Another Family Model?

Is the married woman Adelheid Popp's family model different than the domestic environment which caused the young Adelheid Dwořak so much physical suffering? We can certainly assume so. But to what extent do Popp's ideas about marriage and family differ from the normative ideas common within the 'horizon of bourgeois values'? Her autobiography describes two key relationships in her life: the one with her mother, which runs through the entire text, and her marriage to Julius Popp, which she covers in its final pages. The latter presents the reader with a solution to many of the problems associated with growing up in the Inzersdorf proletarian milieu.

The mother–daughter relationship is complex and permeated by intense emotions, in terms of both affection and recurring disputes. At the same time, it is characterized by loyalty and a lifelong commitment that transcends all differences of opinion. This relationship begins in the community of survival in the weaver's rooms in Inzersdorf, where they have to stick together in the face of material hardship and against the violent drunkard who serves as husband and father, respectively. It ends in a combined household with Adelheid's husband, in which mother and daughter have hardly anything to say to one another. Adelheid Popp's text clearly formulates a child's need for and right to maternal love. However, her own mother is not always able to meet this need. After her 14-year-old daughter's psychological breakdown, which led to her being admitted to a clinic, Adelheid's mother "became incredibly tender toward me [...]. My caresses, which she had always rejected in the past, she now accepted [and was] touched."⁷⁷ Even later, when Adelheid the political activist tries to combine her monotonous factory work during the day with assemblies and lectures in the evening, and continues to walk the tightrope of exhaustion and inadequate nutrition, her mother's presence imparts peace of mind: "I felt more secure."⁷⁸ On the other hand, this mother–daughter relationship certainly illustrates Marx and Engels' argument that, "by the action of

---

76 Ibid, 123.
77 Ibid., 66. On mother–daughter relationships in autobiographical texts, see Müller, "Die Beziehung zur Mutter"; on Popp specifically, see 279–81; on the link between childhood and emotionality, see Jarzebowski, *Kindheit und Emotion*; Opitz-Belakhal, "A Space of Emotions."
78 In the original German: "ich fühlte mich geborgener"; Popp, *Jugend einer Arbeiterin*, 121. See also 90.

modern industry, all family ties among the proletarians are torn asunder, and their children transformed into [...] instruments of labour."[79] In other words, family relationships are monetized to a very high degree. Anna Dwořak's non-negotiable expectation is that her daughter has to earn money from an early age. Apparently she insists on this with some ruthlessness. She sees the extended period of compulsory schooling not as an opportunity, but as an encroachment on her parental rights.[80] After Adelheid is released from the clinic, her mother's tone changes abruptly, because she believes her daughter "didn't deserve anything. She severely reproached me and scolded me; because she herself had always understood that she had to earn money, I should also be able to do it."[81] When Adelheid, still only 14 years old, does not want to return to the factory where one of the gentlemen managers had sexually harassed her, and thus brings no money into the household, her mother and her brother scold her. What follows is another ruined Christmas Eve and a deep rift in the family.

The tensions between mother and daughter intensify when the adolescent Adelheid begins to take an interest in social democratic politics. This example shows how a new political movement can have an impact on family relationships and lead to a situation in which members of the same family, even those who share a small suburban apartment, end up living in two different worlds. The mother has no understanding of her daughter's activities or her son's social democratic pursuits. For a long time, Adelheid has to hide the fact that she is attending meetings and giving lectures – which bring in no money – by telling her mother white lies. Adelheid Popp cannot rationalize this family dissent, even with the knowledge that her mother never attended school and instead gave birth to a child every two years while living in very difficult circumstances. She is deeply hurt. Even her husband, Julius Popp, will try over and over again – "for hours" – to make the elderly women "understand what a glorious thing socialism is."[82] Incidentally, the fact that the author admits the futility of these attempts at persuasion proves that her life story is not primarily a matter of propaganda. Seen from the privileged position of the distanced observer, this scene shows that family conflicts can be unintentionally funny. The gap between these two worlds and generations cannot be closed simply by engaging in parlor discussions. One could reasonably call the elderly woman's behavior obstinate, but one could just as easily call her daughter's

---

79 Engels and Marx, *The Communist Manifesto*, 27.
80 Popp, *Jugend einer Arbeiterin*, 47.
81 In the original German: "dieses Mädel verdiente nichts. Sie machte mir schwere Vorwürfe und schalt mich; weil sie selber immer verstanden hatte zu verdienen, sollte auch ich es können"; ibid., 67. On the following, see 76–82.
82 Ibid., 127. See also 115–24.

and son-in-law's attempts at proselytization pigheaded. From an analytical perspective, this confirms the limited power of ideas; on the other hand, it also affirms the continued efficacy of the habitus as the "social made body." As part of his fieldwork, Bourdieu observed that actors who were "endowed with a precapitalist habitus" and "were suddenly uprooted and forcibly thrown into a capitalist cosmos" could "become obsolete and act inopportunely."[83] In plain English: old Anna Dwořak could not escape her own skin. Based on her own life experience, she did not know where to begin with new ideas such as compulsory education, regulations prohibiting child labor, women's political involvement, or even socialism.

This enduring disagreement also finds expression in the elderly woman's initial rejection of her daughter's husband and the manner in which the younger woman conducts her marriage. "She saw marrying and having children as a woman's destiny," Adelheid Popp writes, and thus believed that "a woman belonged in the home."[84] In this way her mother had certainly adopted the bourgeois model of marriage. Julius Popp, whom the factory worker Adelheid Dwořak meets when she goes to buy her social democratic newspaper, festively dressed for the occasion, and whom she marries in 1893, is the antithesis of her own father – that is, of the so-called 'Lumpenproletarian.' Popp is 20 years older than Adelheid and already marked by illness. The grey silk scarf he likes to wear around his neck would probably not have pleased his future mother-in-law. After an apprenticeship as a shoemaker, he joined a trade union and became a member of the executive committee of the Social Democratic Workers' Party in 1886. "With bitter words he spoke of the men who drank or gambled away half of their weekly wages while their wives and children wasted away at home."[85] This remark is certainly also intended as a message to Popp's readers. Adelheid, who soon joined the editorial staff of the *Arbeiterinnen Zeitung*, is impressed by his "wise sagacity and his energetic character."[86] However, it was not a given that this 24-year-old woman would marry and start a family despite the extremely negative family experiences she had endured during her childhood and adolescence. Moreover, the founding fathers of communism had predicted the abolition of the family. Nevertheless, Adelheid Popp does not fundamentally question marriage and the family as institutions, even after she has turned to social democracy. Instead, marital "happiness,"[87] which she explicitly seeks, and which she makes the criterion for marriage

---

83 Bourdieu and Wacquant, An Invitation to *Reflexive Sociology*, 127 and 130.
84 Popp, *Jugend einer Arbeiterin*, 123 and 126.
85 Ibid., 126. On his silk scarf, see 131.
86 Ibid., 131.
87 Ibid., 131–32. See also 126.

– not unlike bourgeois women – is to be reinvented. She is keen to do marriage and family differently. According to her description, Julius Popp is a friend and a sensitive man, "considerate and tender hearted,"[88] who shares her concerns and supports her work with his advice. The work they each do is equally important, and it is clearly about more than making money. Their shared worries include (not least) enduring Adelheid's bitter mother's reproaches in their small apartment, but the older woman also contributes her share to the household by doing the shopping and the cooking. This ultimately reflects a partnership model of marriage, which does not reduce the woman to the role of mother and housewife, and in which family tasks and responsibilities are organized together. When she attends meetings over several days, he is responsible for the children.[89] If we look at the relationship between the genders in the Popps' marriage – again from a critical distance, through the lens of the critique of marriage levelled by the women's movement – then this once again puts a twinkle in the reader's eye here and there. The author reports on everyday life with her husband as follows: "When I left home with him in the morning and had already tidied our room while he sat reading the newspaper, he never took that for granted"![90]

The bourgeois model of marriage is not completely abolished in this case, but is rather redefined as a partnership of equals, with equitable work for husband and wife, and joint care for the children. Adelheid Popp's insistence on morality and her considered distance from the pleasures enjoyed by other young working-class women in the context of the burgeoning entertainment and experience society align with this.[91] There is also another aspect to all this. Adelheid and Julius Popp constitute a new kind of religious couple – with regard to their shared ideological conviction as the basis of and starting point for the relationship – who need not shy away from comparison with Pietist couples. After her political awakening, Adelheid Popp is convinced that "socialism was not only necessary, but would save the world. My belief in it had become unshakable, and when I thought of marriage, I dreamed of a man who would share my ideals." Thus the chosen one is not only a counsellor and an understanding friend, but also a man who "shared my views."[92]

---

[88] Ibid., 128. See also Trepp, *Sanfte Männlichkeit*; on the 'socialist couple,' see Arni, *Entzweiungen*, 261–63.
[89] Popp, *Jugend einer Arbeiterin*, 129–30.
[90] Ibid., 126.
[91] Ibid., 86 and 98; see also Bänziger, *Die Moderne als Erlebnis*. Later in her life, Adelheid Popp is said to have had a penchant for beautiful dresses and 'feminine' accessories; see Hauch, *Frauen bewegen Politik*, 214.
[92] In the original German: "der Sozialismus nicht nur notwendig sei, sondern welterlösend wirken würde. Mein Glaube daran war unerschütterlich geworden, und wenn ich an die Ehe dachte, so

Against the background of the increasing social endogamy prevalent in marriage relationships during the nineteenth century, and analogous to the choice of marriage partners in religious communities, we should also note here that it is hardly likely to be a coincidence that the spouses come from the same political milieu.[93] In contrast, there is little mention of love or romantic companionship in general.

Friedrich Engels, August Bebel, and Adelheid Popp became acquainted at international workers' movement meetings. On the fringes of the meeting of the Second International that took place in Zurich in the autumn of 1892, they also got to know each other on a personal level. The aging Engels must have taken a liking to this committed young woman. In a letter, he refers to her in a slightly macho tone as "a very sweet Viennese factory girl."[94] Popp describes him in retrospect as simply very friendly. But she also tells these leaders of the labor movement about her ongoing problems with her mother and the fact that her mother disapproves of her work for the Social Democratic Party. Thus a cinematic moment ensues: Adelheid Dwořak from Inzersdorf lives with her mother in a small apartment in the Viennese suburbs. One day Engels and Bebel suddenly appear at her door. The reason for their visit is that they want to impress upon Mrs. Dwořak the significance of her daughter's achievements. But the old woman does not understand what is at stake. For her, these two greying men can only be one thing: potential suitors – unsuitable ones, of course – who have come to call on her daughter.

---

träumte ich von einem Manne, der meine Ideale teilen würde"; "meine Gesinnung teilte"; Popp, *Jugend einer Arbeiterin*, 125–26. On p. 130, she speaks of marital happiness, which is "based on complete harmony of views."

93 For an overview of social endogamy, see Gestrich et al., *Geschichte der Familie*, 502; for marriage within particular political milieus, see Guzzi-Heeb, *Passions alpines*, 195–207.

94 In the original German: "ein allerliebstes Wiener Fabriksmädel"; cited in Hauch, *Frauen bewegen Politik*, 210; also in Hamann, "Eine muss immer die Erste sein," 10. On the following, see Popp, *Jugend einer Arbeiterin*, 124–25.

Chapter 10
From a Bourgeois Family to an Artists' Marriage: Paula Becker and Otto Modersohn

Bremen and Worpswede, Germany, and Paris, France (1892–1907)

Despite the cataclysmic effects of industrialization, the social consequences of which forced the bourgeois political model into a defensive stance, we can nevertheless observe the tremendous persistence and ongoing attraction of bourgeois lifestyles in people's everyday lives. This is certainly true when it comes to appreciation for the family and domesticity, which was understood as a private, harmonious retreat. Yet as we have already seen in previous chapters, the domestic reality was often quite different than this ideal. In addition, new challenges arose not only as a result of industrialization and the rise of the labor movement, but also in terms of the accelerated changes that gripped both culture and the social sciences. Thus we can understand the period around 1900 as a second *Sattelzeit* in European modernity. Psychoanalysis and the social sciences, which emerged around the same time as urban mass society, presented radical challenges to familiar perspectives on the world. For example, the bourgeois understanding of the subject, which aspired to sovereignty in every respect, was confronted with Sigmund Freud's widely read study *The Psychopathology of Everyday Life* (*Zur Psychopathologie des Alltagslebens*, first published in 1904, published in English in 1914), the very title of which shook the edifice of liberal ideas. In terms of living space, the aesthetic deluge of historicist interiors, which had replaced the revolutionary simplicity of Biedermeier style in the second half of the nineteenth century, could not drown out the stifling crises and apocalyptic mood, all of which would come to a head prior to the First World War.[1] In the history of emotional culture as well, the period around 1900 is considered an innovative era in which older conventions were overcome.

The decadent attitude to life that characterized the *fin de siècle* was accompanied by a spirit of awakening in art, which broke new ground. 'Secessions' from the official art establishment took place, and artists' colonies were founded outside

---

[1] For an overview, see Blom, *Der taumelnde Kontinent*; on intellectuals, see Giesen, *Die Intellektuellen*, 183–85; on aesthetic modernism, see Reckwitz, *Das hybride Subjekt*, chap. 3, 275–77; on Biedermeier interiors, see Ottomeyer et al., *Biedermeier*; on historicist interiors, see von Saldern, "Im Hause, zu Hause," 173–75; on the following, see Cottier, *Ehre, Subjekt und Kriminalität*; Frevert, "Defining Emotions," 10.

the bourgeois cities. These were places where male and female painters – the latter of which were derided as 'painting wenches' (*Malweiber*) – sought new aesthetic opportunities and were often inspired by ideas about comprehensive life reform (*Lebensreform*).² Furthermore, the first women's movement – with its demands for women's rights, education, and opportunities – was a significant factor contributing to the contemporary crisis of masculinity.³ Despite the aforementioned persistence of bourgeois lifestyles, these phenomena could not simply wash over bourgeois institutions such as marriage and the family without leaving any traces. Criticism of such institutions came not only from outside or from below, as in the case of Adelheid Popp, but was also instigated by actors at the very heart of the bourgeoisie. One did not necessarily have to read Freud or Engels in order to challenge the ingrained conventions of marriage. Moreover, individual action – which brought about the transformation of marital–familial relationships in the medium term – was not always intended as a conscious turning away from the bourgeois family model, at least not from the outset. Yet when actors sought a sense of self and wanted to follow their own paths – and did so in a purposeful, goal-oriented way – then such actions could not help but have political as well as social impacts.⁴

Liberal Habitat and Cultural Capital

Paula Becker was born in Dresden on February 8, 1876, and grew up in the Hanseatic city of Bremen from the age of 12.⁵ She was certainly born into a bourgeois, or more precisely an educated bourgeois family. Born in 1841, her father, Carl Woldemar Becker, was the son of a university lecturer and classical philologist; he studied engineering, and in 1890 he became a Prussian senior civil servant (*Baurat*), working for the Bremen Railroad. His brother, the law student Oskar Becker, attempted to assassinate King Wilhelm of Prussia in 1861. Paula's mother, Mathilde,

---

2 On the idea of life reform, see Barlösius, *Naturgemäße Lebensführung*; on artists generally, see Frevert, "Der Künstler," 311–16; on artists in Worpswede, see Mayer, "Worpswede."
3 On antifeminist discourse, see Planert, *Antifeminismus*; on changes to and the crisis of masculinity, see Arni, *Entzweiungen*, 215–24.
4 On the example of disputed marriage vows around 1800, see Haldemann, *Prekäre Eheschließungen*.
5 On the personal histories of Paula Modersohn-Becker and her family, see the information in both critical editions: Busch and von Reinken, *Paula Modersohn-Becker in Briefen und Tagebüchern* (hereafter abbreviated as: PMB), 9–11 and 602–3; Modersohn and Werner, *Paula Modersohn-Becker and Otto Modersohn* (hereafter abbreviated as: PMB/OM); see also the biography in Stamm, *"Ein kurzes intensives Fest"*; and the essay by Busch, "Paula Modersohn-Becker."

née von Bültzingslöwen, came from an aristocratic family in Thuringia and was an officer's daughter. Paula was the third of seven children. Her brother Kurt, three years her senior, became a doctor. Her sister Bianca Emilie, known as Milly, who was two years older, married a merchant. Her brother Günther, just a year younger, became a merchant in East Asia and Australia. Another brother, Hans, died of pneumonia when he was 2 years old. Then there were the twins, Herma and Henry, born in 1885; Paula's younger sister Herma earned her doctorate and became a high school teacher, and her brother Henry became an officer in the merchant navy. The union of Paula's parents, one from a bourgeois and one from an aristocratic background, was by no means unusual in 1871. This marriage is evidence of the socio-cultural convergence of the bourgeoisie and the nobility in the final decades of the nineteenth century.[6]

Although she only lived to be 31 years old, Paula Becker would go down in art history as an outstanding painter in the early German expressionist movement. Her name is also closely associated with the artists' colony in Worpswede, a peasant village on the moors outside Bremen. However, this chapter is not about Paula Becker's art, which has already been the focus of numerous glossy art books, although her work cannot be excluded from any attempt to understand her as a person. Rather, our focus here is on her agenda and her experiences: first as the daughter of a bourgeois family, and second as one half of an artistic couple, when she became engaged to the Worpswede landscape painter Otto Modersohn in September 1900 and then married him in May 1901. This dual focus on the bourgeois Becker family and the Modersohn-Becker artists' marriage means that this chapter is somewhat longer than the previous ones.

We cannot understand Paula Becker's habitus without insight into the habitat in which she grew up: home and family, kinfolk and milieu.[7] In this context, we must make a distinction with regard to the bourgeoisie. Unlike the von Axens in Hamburg, for example, the Beckers in Bremen do not belong to the long-established urban elite. Their children are not offered customary career paths in the city simply by virtue of their name and family of origin. Paula Becker is no elite daughter to whom the doors of her hometown always stand open and who, equipped with a large dowry, need only wait for a lucrative marriage. As a construction and operations manager for the railroad, her father's financial leeway is limited – especially when he is forced into early retirement in 1895, at the age of only 54, which plunges him into a personal crisis. The family is not particularly wealthy, but nor are they penniless. We note this in contrast to the precarious living con-

---

6 See Kocka, "Das europäische Muster," 46–49; Budde, *Blütezeit des Bürgertums*, 92–93.
7 Here again, see the approach in Bourdieu, *Die feinen Unterschiede*.

ditions that the Baumgartners and the Dvořaks faced. The Beckers rent their living quarters, which until 1899 constitute an official residence on Schwachhauser Chaussee (today Schwachhauser Heerstraße), and thereafter in the house of a merchant family on Wachtstraße, with a view of the Weser river. The years "in our dear old house" in middle-class Schwachhausen have a particular impact on Paula – the house itself is quite presentable, with high-ceilinged rooms in the classicist style, loggia, and a smoker's lounge for the father. At the back of the large garden, 17-year-old Paula, who has learned the new sport of lawn tennis in England and is an enthusiastic player, wants to build a tennis court over the old potato field.[8]

The surviving photos of the family show them carefully dressed and posed in a bourgeois context. The parental home is liberal-cum-conservative, characterized by a general interest in art and literature. The family also takes part in the city's cultural life: concerts, lectures, and festivals put on by the artists' association, not least the exhibitions at the Bremen Kunsthalle. Religion and the church do not play a major role in this culturally Protestant milieu, although Paula later remarks in a letter to Otto Modersohn that she "also loves the Bible."[9] The Becker siblings complete the bourgeois *parcours*, which 21-year-old Paula aptly summarizes in a letter to her 12-year-old sister Herma when she asks: "How are your dancing lessons going? Have they started yet? And how is Latin going? You must tell me about everything."[10] And it does not stop there. The following episode is indicative of the Becker household's openness, in both senses. After a lecture given by the young Nietzsche scholar Ernst Horneffer in Bremen, Paula's mother, Mathilde Becker, spontaneously invites the philosopher to an evening in the immediate family circle. Later the penniless scholar stays with the Beckers for ten days. His ideas on Nietzsche make an impression on the young Paula.[11]

When Paula Becker turns 20 on February 8, 1896, her father recommends that she read Fontane's new novel, *Effi Briest*. Carl Woldemar Becker has a keen sense of the issues of the day. As a liberal, his conversations with Paula include criticism of his painful experiences with the ridiculous German "police state" and the "violent regression" in Wilhelmine politics.[12] His letters also address "women's issues,"

---

[8] Paula to Kurt Becker, April 27, 1895, PMB, p. 82 (citation); on the smoker's lounge (*Fumatorium*), see Mathilde to Paula Becker, December 29, 1896, ibid., p. 105; on the tennis court, see Paula to Kurt Becker, April 26, 1893, p. 76; ibid., April 27, 1895, p. 82.
[9] Paula Becker to Otto Modersohn, December 25, 1900, PMB, p. 292.
[10] Paula to Herma Becker, November 13, 1897, PMB, p. 132.
[11] Paula to Milly Becker, September 21, 1899, PMB, p. 196; see also the note in ibid., p. 662–63.
[12] In the original German: "Polizeiwirthschaft"; "gewaltsame Rückwärtsbewegung"; Carl Woldemar to Paula Becker, February 20, 1898, PMB, p. 145. On *Effi Briest*, see February 6, 1896, ibid., p. 84.

but he is ambivalent on this topic. If Paula wishes to attend the meetings held by these "aunts," it will not do any harm because, as among the social democrats, some of the issues that will be discussed there are "justified. I simply find the egalitarianism repugnant." Paula's father goes on to say that, even if one must consider the women's claims "justifiable from a higher point of view," nevertheless "we will resist them as long as is possible," for "to date no one has voluntarily renounced his rights."[13] Yet he acknowledges that, in terms of education, "English women are superior to ours: they have energetically taken up the fight for existence against men, and they will [...] be the first to establish a new sphere of activity, a new future for themselves."[14] In this sense, he does not see his daughters as destined simply for marriage, but urges them to get an education so they can stand on their own two feet. In a letter to his wife, which he signs "your old misanthrope," he expresses his skepticism that his three daughters will ever marry: "Paula least of all, because she is more critical of others than of herself."[15] The young Paula is prepared for her later life in three ways. First, she earns a teaching certificate at a seminary in Bremen in 1895. However, when she unexpectedly becomes engaged to Otto Modersohn, she is sent to Berlin in January 1901 to attend a two-month culinary course as preparation for her role as a wife and housekeeper. In addition, she attends painting and drawing classes, which her parents understand as the dabbling of a hobbyist with no professional trajectory. Eventually a disagreement will erupt over this. The great importance of cultural capital in this family is also reflected in the fact that Paula is sent to her aunt's estate near London after her confirmation in order to broaden her horizons and learn English. Over the course of this stay, she also takes drawing lessons in London.

The Becker family is a network of constant communication and mutual support. This is evident in Paula's career, beginning with her extended stay at her aunt's home in England; although the 16-year-old breaks off her visit prematurely – after eight months – due to tensions with her aunt, the two nevertheless maintain a familiar correspondence later on.[16] Paula benefits not only from lodging with her uncles and aunts in Dresden and Berlin while she takes painting classes, and from invitations to travel to Norway and Switzerland, but also and repeatedly in a financial sense. When her father wants her to put an end to her painting classes, an inheritance from her godmother and financial support from childless relatives in Dresden, which she is granted for three years in 1898, allows Paula

---

13 All citations taken from Carl Woldemar to Paula Becker, January 26, 1897, PMB, pp. 110–11.
14 Carl Woldemar to Paula Becker, May 11, 1896, PMB, p. 99.
15 Carl Woldemar to Mathilde Becker, July 3, 1896, PMB, p. 102.
16 Paula Becker to Marie Hill, January 14 – May 5, 1893, PMB, pp. 70–78. On uncles and aunts as a factor in professional careers, see Johnson and Sabean, *Sibling Relations*, 19.

to pursue her dream of life as a painter.[17] Grants and payments from relatives also finance the so-called revision (*Korrektur*) period which 22-year-old Paula spends with the Worpswede painter Fritz Mackensen, with her parents' consent, as well as her first stay in Paris, from January to June 1900, where she takes daily lessons at the fine-art academies. Of course we know that this turned out to be an investment in the future! Yet Paula Becker not only receives family support, she also provides it. Of the 1,000-mark dowry her father promises her upon her marriage, she freely gives up 800 marks to support the education of her younger siblings, Herma and Henry.[18]

The Letter-Writing 'I' and the Diary-Keeping 'I'

In this particular case, the sources are simultaneously comprehensive and deficient. The first edition of Paula Modersohn-Becker's letters and diary entries was published as early as 1913, but the original texts of her diaries and numerous letters were lost after they were removed from storage during the Second World War, so that what has survived is often merely excerpts from her self-narratives. Thanks to the edition of letters and diary entries published in 2007, which was expanded with many new discoveries, and a separate 2017 edition of Paula's correspondence with Otto Modersohn, supplemented by his own diary entries, the breadth of source material has improved – especially since quite a number of letters from family and friends are also now available. Nevertheless, all the extant editions contain abridgments and gaps in the text, which are not always explained. A complete annotated edition of all the self-narratives written by the circle of people that centered around Becker and Modersohn remains a desideratum for such research.

Still, thanks to the editions published in 2007 and 2017, the researcher is in the advantageous position of having access to letters and also diaries written by both spouses. The epistolary self and the diaristic self comment on events from different perspectives and in different styles. This is particularly evident in Paula Modersohn-Becker's case, such as when she processes her situation in Paris or her everyday married life in Worpswede in writing. The Becker family participates in a veritable epistolary cult. Receiving letters from relatives on Sundays is both a custom and an obligatory tradition. Mr. Becker describes the ritual of Mrs. Becker reading the letters aloud to the family circle at breakfast on Sunday mornings as follows:

---

[17] PMB, editors' introduction to the years 1892–1896, p. 46; ibid., 1896–1899, p. 90–91.
[18] Paula Becker to Otto Modersohn, February 12, 1901, PMB, p. 331.

> Under the threat of punishment, no one, not even I, may open the letters before she does, because this is her primary pleasure, to cut open the envelope. [...] Therefore everything must wait until the moment when Mother finishes her toilette and appears in her brown robe. First, coffee is carefully poured, and in the meantime the letters are caressed, the twins are admonished to listen quietly, until the right mood is gradually awakened. Then the envelope is neatly opened, with a knife, and coram publico the reading begins.[19]

The children's letters are read aloud in hierarchical order – starting with the eldest son, Kurt – followed by a round of commentary, and finally the mother ceremoniously folds and "lovingly pats" each letter before opening the next. The letters are also passed around the family as a matter of course, a fact of which their authors are well aware. Among the circle of friends in Worpswede, letters are also read aloud. For this reason Paula instructs her husband, Otto Modersohn: "Don't read my letters to anyone, and don't let them out of your hands. I write only for you."[20] The tension between private communication and this family ritual can lead to mishaps and misunderstandings. When Paula visits a raunchy vaudeville show in Paris, which includes a nude scene, with her 20-year-old sister Herma, who is still a minor, she reports the details to her husband with amusement. However, Otto passes the letter on to the family in Bremen, in contravention of the agreement between husband and wife, which promptly leads to an angry reaction from his brother-in-law Kurt, sent to Paula's address.[21]

Although the family considers Paula lazy when it comes to letter writing, numerous letters she wrote to immediate family members, relatives, and friends have survived, as well as long letters – love letters, letters indicating a crisis, farewell letters, and letters attempting to make peace – to Otto Modersohn. As a subject, Paula Modersohn-Becker's letter-writing style is expressive. Naturally the style also depends on the content. In most of her letters she gives the impression of being cheerful, self-confident, not very formulaic, disarmingly open-hearted, and sometimes provocatively direct. The intimate relationships within the Becker family, which I will discuss below, prove to be quite important. Although there are limits to what can be said, especially with regard to sexuality and morality – as we have seen in the case of her visit to the vaudeville theater with her younger sister – Paula's letters nevertheless document a fundamental trust in her parents and siblings, which she presumes will not be betrayed.[22]

---

19 Carl Woldemar to Paula Becker, February 22, 1892, PMB, p. 61. On the following, see ibid., p. 62 (citation); see also Milly to Paula Becker, January 27, 1900, p. 224.
20 Paula to Otto Modersohn, February 17, 1903, PMB, p. 401.
21 Paula to Otto Modersohn, March 6, 1905, PMB, p. 483; editors' note, ibid., p. 720.
22 On "trust communication" (*Vertrauenskommunikation*) as an emblem of modernity, see Frevert, *Vertrauensfragen*, here 15–17.

This epistolary material reveals that Paula Modersohn-Becker had a way with words – that she was a literary artist and has yet to be recognized as such. The judgment handed down by Rainer Maria Rilke, her close friend, decreeing that her written legacy was of poor quality, probably applies to her literary forays in her diary and another book, which are suffused with Art Nouveau longing.[23] But the letters show the young painter, who sets out to overcome convention, as a master of metaphor and (self-)irony. She dubs her fiancé: "My Rex, my king, my sweetheart, dearest, best, only, my knight with a small shirt."[24] She lures her misanthropic father, whom she wants to persuade to model for her work, to Worpswede with the promise: "You won't always have pancakes either, but something decent."[25] She makes insinuations when she writes to her fiancé about the culinary course in Berlin, which she does not enjoy: it is "a cooking school with two natures, simple lunch and roast turkey." She takes Otto's love letter with her in her pocket to this training course for housekeepers, "and he learned to cook baked potatoes and boiled potatoes along with me."[26] The tension between cooking and art, however, will later prove to be a problem in their marriage. The writer of these letters shines brightest when she winks. This includes quotations in Low German, especially things said by the women from the poorhouse in Worpswede who model for her. Sprinklings of colloquial German can also be found in the most surprising places. Impressed by cosmopolitan life in Paris, the 24-year-old reports home, for the purpose of the Sunday ritual of reading aloud: "Do you know, when I walk along the boulevards in the morning, and the sun is shining, and [the streets] are teeming with people, then I say to them in my heart: Folks (*Kinners*), what I have before me is so much more beautiful than what you have between you."[27]

Paula Modersohn-Becker's diaristic self is of a different sort. She uses this type of text to put her problems into words. At the end of April 1900, approximately two weeks after the optimistic, self-confident statement she makes to her family from

---

23 See, for example, Paula Becker, *Tagebuch*, undated, PMB, p. 273: "I came to the land of longing. It was sweet and lovely to look at. The sun looked down from her golden chair in the firmament, and her silky golden hair entwined everything she looked at. It wrapped itself around the tall, gnarled pines. And the old fellows were happy to let her do so". On Rilke's judgment of her work, see Busch, "Paula Modersohn-Becker," 22 and 32.
24 In the original German: "Mein Rex, mein König, mein Trauter, Lieber, Du Bester, Einziger, mein Ritter mit dem Hemdlein"; Paula Becker to Otto Modersohn, December 27, 1900, PMB, p. 294.
25 Paula to Carl Woldemar Becker, March 9, 1899, PMB, p. 183.
26 In the original German: "eine Kochschule beiderlei Gestalt, einfacher Mittagstisch und Puterbraten"; "und er lernte mit mir Pellkartoffeln und Salzkartoffeln kochen"; Paula Becker to Otto Modersohn, January 13, 1901, PMB, p. 307; January 21, 1901, p. 315.
27 Paula Becker to her parents, April 13, 1900, PMB, p. 248.

Paris, the big-city blues strike her down. She notes in her diary: "I have been sad for days, deeply sad and serious. I believe the time of doubt and struggle is coming. It comes in every beautiful life. [...] But I feel so grave and difficult, serious and sad. I walk through this great city, I look into thousands and thousands of eyes. Only rarely do I find a soul there."[28] Yet there is certainly a bridge between the letter discourse and the diary discourse – the two different selves; these two different discourses in two different media do not diverge completely. Thus she also communicates her problems in Paris to her family. Nevertheless, the diary contains very private comments made only for herself. After she returns to Worpswede in the summer of 1900, in an almost prophetic tone, she writes down a stream of thoughts that occurred to her while she was painting. These sentences are well known and have often been quoted: "I know that I shall not live very long. But is that necessarily sad? Is a celebration more beautiful because it lasts longer? And my life is a celebration, a short, intense celebration."[29] The diary also serves as a space for reflection on her crisis-ridden relationships.[30] The first references to Paula Modersohn-Becker's disappointment with her married life are found in her diary, barely a year after her wedding to Otto Modersohn.

Paula Becker's enthusiastic disrespect for authority is expressed not only in bold painting that tends toward the abstract, which her parents and other contemporaries interpret as artistic incompetence, but also in a "mischievousness" that seems to mark her character throughout her life.[31] In this respect, a key scene takes place one month prior to her engagement to Otto Modersohn – that is, her decision to become a wife, a mother, and mistress of a household. Paula reports on the episode in a letter to her mother, in her usual frank manner. At the end of a "rather bland Sunday" in August 1900, the 24-year-old is walking through the village of Worpswede with her friend Clara Westhoff. They would like to go dancing, but no opportunity presents itself. Bored, they pass the village church, which is locked – but the door to the steeple is open. They climb the stairs all the way up to the bell and sit down side by side on a beam. "And there it comes to us. We have to ring the bell. We strike it with the clapper, just once; it sounds too tempting. Then Clara pulls the rope hanging from the big bell, and I [the rope] from the small one, and they swing, and they swing us, high up off

---

28 Paula Becker, *Tagebuch*, end of April 1900, PMB, p. 251.
29 In the original German: "Ich weiß, ich werde nicht sehr lange leben. Aber ist das denn traurig? Ist ein Fest schöner, weil es länger ist? Und mein Leben ist ein Fest, ein kurzes intensives Fest"; Paula Becker, *Tagebuch*, July 26, 1900, PMB, p. 266. See also *Tagebuch*, February 24, 1902, ibid., p. 367.
30 Paula Modersohn-Becker, *Tagebuch*, Easter week, March 1902, PMB, pp. 370–71; March 30, 1902, ibid., p. 371.
31 In the original German: "Schalkhaftigkeit"; Mathilde to Herma Becker, May 10, 1907, PMB, p. 576.

the floor, and it rings and drones and resounds over the Weyerberg until we are tired." The village teacher climbs the stairs to put an end to the commotion. "But," as Paula Becker writes, "when he caught sight of two young maidens dressed all in white, he directed his steps back down again."[32] In the meantime, a large number of people have gathered in front of the church, and the fire engine is getting ready to extinguish the fire in the village, since the unexpected ringing of the bells is intended to announce such an event. In the end, these two bourgeois daughters manage to escape with only a few reprimands and a so-called Canossa visit to the pastor, at which they humbly beg for forgiveness.

Family and Art: Between Familiarity and Departure

We can characterize Paula Becker's relationship to the bourgeoisie as ambivalent. Her parental home is part of the liberal bourgeoisie, which has nevertheless become more conservative over the course of the nineteenth century. She appreciates literary naturalism, Goethe's *Werther*, and Nietzsche's *Zarathustra*, but she dislikes Goethe's later novels and finds Richard Wagner's operas an imposition against which "my nerves bristle."[33] One of the key terms of demarcation she employs is 'philistine.' She loves the post-impressionist paintings by French painters that she sees at the World's Fair in Paris in the summer of 1900: "Next to them, we Germans are somewhat narrow-minded, bourgeois, and philistine."[34] She clearly displays the self-confident habitus of an educated bourgeois daughter. Yet she lives extremely modestly over the months and years she spends in Paris and in the room she rents from the peasant farmer Hermann Brünjes in Worpswede. Paula Modersohn-Becker's identity was not constructed based on a sense of superiority over against the lower classes, but rather in the face of a status-conscious bourgeoisie that placed great value on appearances. In Paris, despite her father's warnings, she enjoys life on the boulevards: "I discovered a crémerie where I dine with all sorts of common people."[35] At the culinary course in Berlin, she takes a liking to

---

32 All citations taken from Paula to Mathilde Becker, August 13, 1900, PMB, p. 268.
33 Paula Becker to Milly Rohland-Becker, December 6, 1905, PMB, p. 511. On readings, see also her letter to her parents, November 25, 1898, ibid., p. 169; see also the diary entries for February 19, 1899 and March 3, 1899, pp. 180–81.
34 In the original German: "Wir Deutschen stehen daneben etwas spießbürgerlich und philisterhaft"; Paula Becker to her parents, c. May 11, 1900, PMB, p. 257 (note: some of the texts lack an exact date).
35 Paula Becker to her parents, January 22, 1900, PMB, p. 223.

the "future cooks, and so they cannot get on my nerves simply because they are being educated in the wrong place." However, she notes that she does not belong in Berlin, "or at least not here, in the elegant district [of Schöneberg]. This is where I fall out of the frame [...] The people around me are pleasant and friendly. But they spend the bulk of their lives in pursuit of superficial things that befit their status."[36] Still, Paula Becker's relationships with the peasant and lower-class actors in the moorland village of Worpswede do not count as friendships. Her interest in the people there is primarily aesthetic and artistic – they seem archaic to her, which makes them interesting as models. Thus after she returns to Worpswede, she emphasizes "their great, biblical simplicity" in contrast to the inhabitants of the metropolises.[37] However, this quasi-anthropological outsider perspective does not entirely exclude proximity and familiarity. When young Paula dances a waltz with the bride's father at a peasant wedding, which she gets herself into rather by accident, they laugh at her. She develops a personal relationship with Anna Dreebeen (literally: three legs), a woman with a walking stick whom she and Modersohn both paint. She likes to listen to what this elderly woman has to say.[38]

Much of what Paula Modersohn-Becker does in her life oscillates between clinging to the familiar and embracing a radical awakening. Her hybrid subjectivity is illustrated by the three locations where she spends several years of her life: first, her open, culturally affiliated parental home and habitat among Bremen's middle class; second, the natural, simple atmosphere of discovery in Worpswede; and third, the dazzling world of the Parisian art metropolis. On closer inspection, two particular cultural affiliations prove to be decisive in 'the making of Paula': the ambivalent bourgeoisie at home, and the intellectual avant-garde in Europe abroad. Like many other artists and intellectuals of the time, she joins in the critique of entrenched conventions and the old, rigid way of life, which in turn is linked to a desire to see the world in a new way – be it artistically, literarily, or scientifically. Thus the actor Paula Modersohn-Becker is characteristic of the *Sattelzeit* around 1900. Her extremely lively circle of friends includes not only the painters in the Worpswede artists' colony, but also a very intimate, fragile relationship

---

36 Paula Becker to Otto Modersohn, January 26, 1901, PMB, p. 320; January 13, 1901, ibid., p. 307. See also her comments in a letter to Herma Becker, November 8, 1905, p. 509: "Hamburg as a city" pleases her, "only the so-called educated [people] make a colossal material impression."
37 Paula Modersohn-Becker, *Tagebuch*, April 1903, PMB, p. 430.
38 Paula to Mathilde Becker, August 20, 1897, PMB, p. 126. On Anna Dreebeen, also Anna Schröder, see esp. Paula Becker to her parents, September 18, 1898, ibid., pp. 160–61; to Mathilde Becker, June 27, 1902, p. 380; to Milly Becker, October 1907, pp. 580–81; Otto Modersohn, *Tagebuch*, June 15, 1902, PMB/OM, p. 175; PMB, figs. 42 and 43.

with the married couple Clara Westhoff and Rainer Maria Rilke, and friendships with the naturalist writer Carl Hauptmann; the sculptor Bernhard Hoetger and his wife, the pianist Helen Hoetger, whom she meets in Paris; and the economist Werner Sombart.[39] This effort to belong in several cultural contexts – which are only conditionally compatible – simultaneously creates tension in the long run. We have already seen this in the cases of Henriette Stettler-Herport and Ferdinand Beneke. In Paula Becker's case, we once again encounter repeated acts of abrupt – though not necessarily final – distancing. One such example concerns her hometown of Bremen. At the end of December 1900, 24-year-old Paula spends Christmas at her parents' house, about which she writes to Rilke in positive terms, but then she also remarks to her fiancé, Otto: "I cannot stand this little town for *so* long now; I'd rather go to Berlin."[40] She makes this statement against the immediate backdrop of her imminent departure to take cooking classes in the German capital, but the context for this is the broader horizons offered by her experiences in Worpswede and Paris.

Does such distancing over the course of an artistic awakening also affect one's family of origin? In Otto Modersohn's case, by his own admission, his relationship with his parents in Münster was not very close. His young wife's contacts with his family were limited to friendly letters and short visits.[41] In contrast, numerous documents detail the Beckers' intra-familial communication. Not only the ritual of reading letters aloud in the family circle on Sundays, but also the fact that letters were preserved down the generations indicates a strong family consciousness. Paula Becker's sense of family is pronounced, and this does not change when she becomes Paula Modersohn, who lives some of the time in Paris, and some of the time in Worpswede. Perhaps it sounds provocative, or even shocking – but the Beckers are an example of a bourgeois family that functions well in many respects.

This can be demonstrated in various ways: from the perspectives of the people concerned; in the sense of ongoing mutual responsibility; as a network in which, despite dissent and tension, follow-up communication is always established; as an emotional and supportive community designed to last. Yet the relationship patterns within the family are not without the potential for conflict; the total absence of conflict would be implausible. From Paula's point of view, the key relationships

---

39 These relationships are traceable in the index to the PMB edition, pp. 782–94.
40 Paula Becker to Otto Modersohn, December 31, 1900, PMB, p. 297 (italics in the original); to Rainer Maria Rilke, Christmas 1900, ibid., pp. 293–94. On her critique of Bremen, see also Paula Becker to Martha Hauptmann, June 5, 1902, ibid., p. 379.
41 Otto to Paula Modersohn-Becker, February 27, 1906, PMB/OM, p. 318; April 17, 1907, ibid., pp. 411–13; Paula to Wilhelm and Luise Modersohn, November 27, 1901, PMB, p. 358; December 31, 1901, p. 360; January 7, 1905, p. 457.

Fig. 21: The Becker family at tea in the garden; the young Paula is second from the left; Mathilde Becker is standing; Carl Woldemar Becker is sitting next to her, holding a cigar. Source: the Paula Modersohn Becker Stiftung, Bremen

are those with her father, her mother, and her older sister, Milly. Kurt is the strict big brother, Herma the beloved little sister. Each of them play a role in Paula's later marital problems with Otto Modersohn. Herma's twin brother, Henry, and Günther, who is traveling in East Asia as a merchant and is rarely mentioned, seem somewhat left out. Carl Woldemar Becker's patience has apparently been considerably strained by his daughter's unprofitable artistic tendencies, which in his estimation offer no future prospects; likewise, Paula is frustrated with him. The pessimistic father is often a burden to his children, not least to Paula. As Milly Becker remarks in a letter to her sister: "I know how [...] father's letters can get on one's nerves, despite his deep love. But of course he only looks at things from his – admittedly grey – perspective, and he also has too little imagination to imagine the impression his written words make on the reader – he writes them as a kind of monologue."[42] Paula Becker's poetic but disarmingly direct advice to her father, conveyed by letter a few years earlier, runs along the same lines: "Father, promise me one thing. Don't sit at your desk and stare into space, or at your father's picture. Then the black troubles will come flying and cover the pinpricks of light in

---

42 Milly to Paula Becker, January 27, 1900, PMB, p. 224.

your soul with their dark wings."[43] Nevertheless, Paula seems to have been her father's daughter in some respects. There is general agreement within the family about the similarities between father and daughter, in terms of both character and physiognomy – and the potential for disruption in everyday family life lay precisely here. After the money she receives from her relatives unexpectedly enables Paula to continue her painting classes, the cash-strapped *Baurat* admonishes his 22-year-old daughter: "Really, you're a lucky girl! Only take some good advice, and don't trust your own stubborn little head too much; you inherited that from me, along with a contrary spirit."[44] In her turn, even years after her father's death, Paula still sees this "similarity" as the "reason our modest father was unsatisfied with me throughout my entire life."[45]

In addition to Paula's lack of professional security, father and daughter's conflicting opinions about the quality of modern art give rise to more or less heated discussions. Mr. Becker does not mince words, and anyone who reads his daughter's letters, with their provocative frankness, may indeed see a case of family resemblance here. Both father and daughter express themselves without regard for the consequences. At the beginning of Paula's training at the Colarossi Academy in Paris, the father tells his daughter in no uncertain terms: "The more you can shake off Worpswede, the less you cling to the silly word modern, the more you will have taken a step forward." He combines this with the hope that, "in any case, your Worpswede potbellies will be replaced by more delicate ones [portraits] at the academy of fine art."[46] Paula's parents are largely united in their opinion of the works produced by the Worpswede artists, especially their daughter's paintings. Nevertheless, there is no question that they will enable and support Paula as long as they are financially able to do so. Paula is "indeed a little depressed"[47] about her father's letters to her in Paris and his lack of confidence in her abilities, but she does not let this deter her in any way. The same is true of her path as an artist generally, as well as her emotional connection to her parents. Although the members of this family do not always get along well, communication never breaks

---

43 Paula to Carl Woldemar Becker, December 17, 1897, PMB, p. 136.
44 In the original German: "Eigentlich bist Du ein Glücksmädel! Nimm nur guten Rath an und vertraue nicht Deinem kleinen Dickkopf zu sehr, den hast Du von mir geerbt, auch den Widerspruchsgeist"; Carl Woldemar to Paula Becker, January 31, 1898, PMB, p. 141. On the physical similarity, see Mathilde to Paula Modersohn-Becker, February 5, 1906, PMB, p. 518.
45 Paula to Mathilde Becker, February 11, 1906, PMB, p. 519.
46 In the original German: "Je mehr Du Worpswede abschütteln kannst, je weniger Du von dem albernen Worte modern an Dir behältst, desto mehr bist Du einen Schritt vorwärtsgekommen"; "Deine Worpsweder Hängebäuche werden jedenfalls durch zierlichere in der Malakademie ersetzt warden"; Carl Woldemar to Paula Becker, January 8, 1900, PMB, p. 215.
47 Paula to Carl Woldemar Becker, January 8, 1900, PMB, p. 220.

off completely; the thread of conversation continues to spin out. Despite the public nature of their Sunday reading ritual, this epistolary conversation is quite direct. Perhaps this is a key ingredient in the family recipe for success. There is no lack of participation and no dearth of expressions of affection. From Berlin, Paula tells her parents: "Even if we didn't have any money, we would have many other things that one simply cannot put a price on. We children have two fine, loving parents who are completely devoted to us."[48] At the same time, the reader must take into account the epistolary style of the time, which tended toward the emphatic. We can expect more distance and neutrality from the perspective of the Beckers' son-in-law. Yet Otto Modersohn turns out to be an avowed fan of the Becker family, and also of Carl Woldemar Becker, whom he describes as an open-minded, 'gentle father.' In this respect, Otto is far less critical than the Becker daughters. After his father-in-law dies on November 30, 1901, with his family gathered around him, Otto Modersohn notes in his private diary (that is, not for public consumption): "The interest he took in everything and everyone in our lives was touching; the joy when we visited him was touching." Moreover, "he had so much understanding and love for all his children; each one had their own relationship with him. This has pleased me so often [...] I am happy that my dear Paula is his daughter."[49] As we have seen, Paula's view is somewhat more nuanced. As a daughter who insists on her own path, she has a different relationship to her father than the welcome son-in-law who supports the daughter and whose landscape paintings are more aligned with the Becker parents' aesthetic tastes than the Worpswede 'potbellies.'

Paula's relationship with her mother is even closer and more intimate than that with her father, which of course does not preclude conflict. We can understand the sovereignty Mathilde Becker exercises over the Sunday ritual of reading letters aloud as an indication of her central role in family life. To say that Mrs. Becker is involved in important decisions is an understatement. Concerning Paula, Mr. Becker reproaches his wife for this: "You started the whole Berlin painting thing without my knowledge. I did not oppose" it.[50] When 30-year-old Paula later celebrates her long-awaited, hard-won first success – the exhibition of some of her paintings at the Bremen Kunsthalle and the gallery director's favorable review in the Bremen newspaper – her mother writes to her in Paris: "I really

---

48 Paula to Carl Woldemar Becker, December 17, 1897, PMB, p. 136.
49 Otto Modersohn, *Tagebuch*, December 5, 1901, PMB, p. 359. See also Otto to Paula Modersohn-Becker, April 17, 1907, PMB/OM, p. 413: "Your whole family is enveloped in a fascinating nimbus."
50 Carl Woldemar to Mathilde Becker, July 3, 1897, PMB, pp. 101–2. This is a reference to Paula Becker's first training at a Berlin painting and drawing school from April 1896, with the painter Jeanne Bauck.

cannot stand the head that has been exhibited, but I'm enormously happy for you."[51] Mrs. Becker sets other priorities in relation to her children than Mr. Becker, who – in what contemporary readers might call a classically paternal vein – demands that they receive a promising education. Above all, Paula's mother is more tolerant. One key comment on the mother–daughter relationship directly from 17-year-old Paula's pen can be found in a letter to her aunt, Marie Hill, in England, a few months after Paula broke off her stay there. Aunt and niece did not get along well, which was ultimately probably the result of an issue with authority. Paula rejects her aunt's accusation that she is selfish, although she does admit that she is "quite used to governing." "In school I also found it quite natural that my word was the definitive one. But does that have anything to do with selfishness?" With regard to her experiences at school, Paula refers to her mother, her aunt's sister-in-law: "Now and previously, Mama almost always praised me, and we took it for granted that I didn't do much that was reprehensible." What is more, "I am, we are all unaccustomed to subordination. I talk to Mama as I would talk to a friend."[52] After reading this letter, one understands why Paula Becker's letter to her mother about the Sunday bell-ringing seven years later is not a confession, but an enthusiastic report.[53] Paula grows up in a free space ruled by indulgence rather than authority. Her relationship with her mother is characterized by astonishing trust and intimacy, by earnestness as well as humor and obstinacy, although the latter does indeed find expression in various ways. Two months after her engagement, Paula outlines her relationship with her fiancé and its positive effect on her temper in a letter to her mother. To her own surprise, she has become a gentler and more indulgent person.[54] In contrast, five years later, in another letter from Worpswede to Bremen, she lets her mother know that she finds her everyday married life unsatisfactory: "I am secretly planning another little trip to Paris, for which I have already saved 50 marks. Otto, on the other hand, feels extremely content. [...] From time to time I have a strong desire to experience something new. The fact that one is so terribly bogged down once one gets married is somewhat difficult."[55] Yet the mother to whom they are addressed does not read these sentences as an announcement of her daughter's imminent separation from Otto Mod-

---

51 Mathilde to Paula Modersohn-Becker, November 11, 1906, PMB, p. 562. One of her first exhibitions, in 1899, had been lambasted by the critic Arthur Fitger, which led to intense discussions, as her father shared Fitger's view; see "Kritik Fitgers," December 20, 1899, PMB, pp. 199–201; Carl Woldemar to Paula Becker, January 8, 1900, ibid., pp. 214–15.
52 All citations taken from Paula Becker to Marie Hill, May 5, 1893, PMB, pp. 77–78.
53 Paula to Mathilde Becker, August 13, 1900, PMB, p. 268.
54 Paula to Mathilde Becker, November 3, 1900, PMB, p. 280.
55 Paula to Mathilde Becker, November 26, 1905, PMB, p. 510.

ersohn. Paula does not request maternal advice on this step, which she understands as her own life decision.

The letters between mother and daughter are full of empathic expressions of sympathy,[56] but even this relationship does not function without boundaries. As the daughter of a bourgeois household, when Paula decides to commit herself to a new understanding of art and a future that is unclear even in its broadest outlines, she is ready for a substantive confrontation with her family. Even before she first leaves for Paris, 23-year-old Paula makes a kind of confession from Worpswede to her sister Milly, with whom she has had a close relationship all her life, which makes everything that has come before seem like mere skirmishing. It is worth quoting the entire paragraph from this letter, dated September 21, 1899:

> I'm currently going through a strange time. Perhaps the most serious of my short life. I see that my goals are becoming more and more removed from yours, that you will approve of them less and less. And despite all this, I must pursue them. I feel that everyone is frightened by me, and yet I must move forward. I cannot go back. I strive onward, just as well as you do, but with my spirit, and in my skin, and according to my judgment.[57]

This statement, formulated like a general declaration of departure on behalf of the young intellectual elite around 1900, is accompanied by a note asking her sister not to pass it on to their parents. This is not suitable for reading aloud at a family breakfast. Yet even in Paula Modersohn-Becker's case, everyday life is less dramatic than this grand announcement. At this point, she has no way of knowing that 16 months later, as someone's fiancée, she will attend a two-month culinary course designed to prepare her for life as a wife. The duration of this training course is a subject of debate, with her mother as well. Paula lives in the Schöneberg district of Berlin with her aunt, Herma Parizot, and her aunt's family, with whom she gets along well. In contrast to her parents, after two months of cooking Paula considers herself sufficiently prepared for married life. Her mother sends a telegram asking her to extend her training in cooking and housekeeping. Paula refuses. She reports to her fiancé, Otto Modersohn, in a staccato style: "I am sitting here with my suitcase packed, restrained by a maternal telegram. I should

---

56 Paula to Mathilde Becker, January 19, 1906, PMB, p. 517: "I lay my head in your lap, from which I came forth, and thank you for my life."
57 In the original German: "Ich verlebe jetzt eine seltsame Zeit. Vielleicht die ernsteste meines kurzen Lebens. Ich sehe, daß meine Ziele sich mehr und mehr von den Euren entfernen werden, daß Ihr sie weniger und weniger billigen werdet. Und trotz alledem muß ich ihnen folgen. Ich fühle, daß alle Menschen sich an mir erschrecken, und doch muß ich weiter. Ich darf nicht zurück. Ich strebe vorwärts, gerade so gut als Ihr, aber in meinem Geist und in meiner Haut und nach meinem Dafürhalten"; Paula to Milly Becker, September 21, 1899, PMB, p. 196.

not return yet, and just keep cooking, cooking, cooking. But I cannot do this anymore, nor do I want to anymore, and so I will not do it anymore. This is demanding more of a person than she can do. It is a waste of a spring."[58] Her letter to her mother makes it clear that this is no trivial matter, but a conflict about Paula's future role as a daughter and a wife. The parents are disgruntled, and the daughter is very angry. Paula, who is now 25 years old, reminds her parents of their agreed-upon plan that the culinary course would last no longer than two months. Now she can no longer stand "this carpet-beating air and these tall buildings [...] I have learned a great deal here about the household. I myself know that I am not perfect," but these conditions are not doing her "soul" any good. "And now she [the soul] demands freedom of me, and I will give it to her." This desire for freedom is underpinned in a culturally appropriate Protestant (*kulturprotestantisch*) manner, by quoting Martin Luther: "Here I stand, I can do no other. Amen."[59]

Engagement: A Culinary Course and 'Social Magic'

This dispute about the culinary course is not an isolated episode. Four weeks earlier, Carl Woldemar Becker had sent his daughter a long letter – which has not been published in its entirety – for her 25th birthday, containing instructions on her future duties as a wife. Written in the style of a sermon, this letter documents the bourgeois model of marriage, including its typical gender roles. At the same time, it is also evidence of the differences between norm and practice that have characterized everyday married life ever since marriage was first held up as an ideal in the Reformation era. According to Mr. Becker, the goal and purpose of marriage is that it should serve as "an eternal source of happiness" for husband and wife. This clearly distinguishes the bourgeois concept of marriage from both Enlightenment and Pietistic concepts, which were primarily concerned with virtuous reason and everyday piety, respectively. On the one hand, Paula's father reminds his daughter of her marital duties, which consist of putting aside her own desires and "selfish thoughts" and, in the spirit of subordination, "merging completely with your future husband." In this respect, it is the wife's "task [...] to exercise forbearance in married life." He also advises the couple against their plan to buy a farmhouse. He certainly does not want to "interfere in your domestic life," and yet his fatherly advice is that Paula should move into Otto's "old home," in

---
58 Paula Becker to Otto Modersohn, March 8, 1901, PMB, p. 340.
59 In the original German: "Ich stehe hier, ich kann nicht anders. Amen"; Paula to Mathilde Becker, March 8, 1901, PMB, pp. 340–41.

which he feels comfortable, and then make it "a place of joy and peace by means of your personality and your industrious creativity." In this context, the domestic sphere is considered the woman's domain. This is the ideal according to the father of the bride, in what is presumably his last letter to his daughter before his death. On the other hand – not least due to his own marriage to a woman with a strong personality, Mathilde née von Bültzingslöwen – the engineer Carl Woldemar Becker also knows that "when two people live together, they must always try to pull together, using both their strength, without one of them trying to dominate too much." He means for his strong-willed daughter to understand this principle of partnership as an appeal. It is clear "that Otto loves you," writes Mr. Becker. "He is perhaps so good natured and, as an artist, also so impractical as to give you complete free rein and to entrust himself to your guidance in many respects, but you must be all the more moderate."[60]

Paula Becker must have had this letter from her father, which reaches her while she is taking the culinary course in Berlin, in the back of her mind when she reacted indignantly to her mother's telegram asking her to continue the course. Yet this disagreement is also evidence of the strength of the Becker family's cohesion. It becomes clear that this dispute – by no means the first she has experienced – is a burden to Paula, and also that family consensus is important to her: "It is so sad that you are annoyed with me. There is also something to be happy about concerning me now and then, I mean apart from my engagement."[61] Moreover, the fact that Paula also gets her way in this case – she leaves the culinary course and returns to Worpswede – does not cause any rift or constriction in the family relationship. Rather than perceiving her father's letter as an affront, she is actually touched by it, as she writes in a letter to Otto.[62]

Why did Paula Becker marry Otto Modersohn? We can reconstruct the stages between getting to know each other and marriage with reference to their letters and diary entries. From the very beginning, art is centrally important to the couple – not as a cultural commodity, but as a practice, a communal and quasi-transcendental experience.[63] Paula Becker first mentions the already well-known painter Modersohn, who lives in Worpswede, in a letter to her brother Kurt after visiting an exhibition at the Bremen Kunsthalle in April 1895.[64] This early Worpswede ex-

---

[60] All citations taken from Carl Woldemar to Paula Becker, February 7, 1901, PMB, pp. 325–26.
[61] Paula to Mathilde Becker, March 8, 1901, PMB, p. 341.
[62] Paula Becker to Otto Modersohn, February 12, 1901, PMB, p. 331.
[63] On the artistic life, see Frevert, "Der Künstler"; on artist couples in the twentieth century, see Berger, *Liebe Macht Kunst*.
[64] Paula to Kurt Becker, April 27, 1895, PMB, pp. 81–83, here p. 83; also published in: PMB/OM, pp. 27–28.

hibition marks the start of this 19-year-old woman from Bremen's enthusiasm for the artists' colony, which leads to her living there for several weeks in the summer of 1897, and then again for a longer period beginning in September 1898, to learn to paint. Her diary entries from this time are enthusiastic. She visits the artists' studios and refers to the artists themselves as the "priests" of Worpswede.[65] She is caught up in an atmosphere of awakening.

At first Paula Becker is drawn to the painter Heinrich Vogeler. However, as she puts it in her diary:

> Then there is Modersohn. I have seen him only once, and this one time unfortunately did not see much and felt nothing at all. I have only a memory of someone tall, in a brown suit, with a reddish beard. He had something soft and amiable in his eyes. His landscapes, which I saw at the exhibitions, had a deep, deep atmosphere in them. Hot, brooding autumn sun, or sweet, mysterious evening. I would like to meet him, this Modersohn.[66]

As of September 1898, Paula Becker is a permanent guest in Worpswede. At a party in Modersohn's studio, where Vogeler plays the guitar and people dance, she enjoys "the feeling of being a woman" and notes that "some people were pleased with me."[67] Mutual affection develops through conversations about art, whereby their roles in terms of experience and expertise are clearly defined at the beginning. As Paula reports on Modersohn in a letter – nota bene, to her father: "He is already so dear to me from his paintings, a subtle dreamer."[68] Modersohn's comments about her are initially detached. The first entry in his diary with reference to the young woman from Bremen simply reads: "Yesterday Miss Becker [spent] all morning with me – talking about every possible subject. Looked at paintings, compositions, studies. Great interest in my compositions."[69] At this time, Otto Modersohn has just married the merchant's daughter Helene Schröder. Paula Becker sets off on her first trip to Paris with Clara Westhoff in January 1900. In the period that follows, Miss Becker and the Modersohn couple write letters to each other. They discuss art and life in Paris. There is hardly anything to indicate a future relationship. But when the Worpswede painters Modersohn, Marie Bock, and Fritz and Hermine Overbeck come to Paris in June 1900 to explore the World's Fair with Paula Becker, Helene Modersohn dies unexpectedly.

---

65 Paula Becker, *Tagebuch*, July 24, 1897, PMB, p. 124; Paula Becker to her parents, August 1897, pp. 125–26: "I am happy, happy, happy" (p. 125); see also the notes in PMB, pp. 89–93.
66 Paula Becker, *Tagebuch*, July 24, 1897, PMB, p. 124; see also PMB/OM, p. 30.
67 Paula Becker, *Tagebuch*, March 30, 1899, PMB, p. 185.
68 Paula to Carl Woldemar Becker, March 9, 1899, PMB, p. 184.
69 Otto Modersohn, *Tagebuch*, December 15, 1899, PMB/OM, p. 37.

After Paula Becker returns to Worpswede in June, something more than affection quickly develops between her and Otto. Only a few months pass before they are engaged, on September 12, 1900. They initially keep their engagement a secret, due to the fact that Helene Modersohn died so recently. Neither his parents nor hers are involved in the decision to marry; it is an autonomous decision that the couple makes on their own. One can observe the growth of their love through the rituals that delimit their relationship from the outside world. The widower Otto visits Paula to read to her when she is sick, in her small room at the Brünjes farm. They invest time in and provide comfort to each other. They begin to write secret letters and messages to each other, which each hides under a stone on the heath for the other to pick up.[70] The events leading up to their engagement are better grasped from the account in Modersohn's diary than from those included in Becker's incomplete estate. The painter, who is eleven years older than Paula, reflects on the young woman's personality, which he cannot do without recourse to her understanding of art. His fascination with this "girl" finds expression in a cascade of attributes, with which he attempts to put his counterpart into words:

> She is lively, full of ideas, stimulating, loves the peculiar, the original, even the picturesque; she has a taste for the finest art (Cottet, Daumier, Velazquez, Rodin). Something feminine, sunny, and cheerful in movement and in speech envelops her, and yet she is very free, very mature and expansive. Like her character, her appearance is fresh and healthy. No one is as close to me as she is. She pleases me most, both inwardly and outwardly, even last year.

In his written soliloquy, Modersohn is remarkably quick to address the question of Paula Becker's suitability for marriage. In this respect he has certain doubts, which correspond to Carl Woldemar Becker's fatherly admonitions. "To be sure, I have a few doubts: 1) She is too free, she knows too much, much more than I do; [...] 2) She would not understand much about housekeeping, but she would be able to take over the management [of a house], and I believe she is also practical and thrifty."[71]

Otto Modersohn's thoughts prior to the engagement already hint at problem areas that will eventually make themselves felt in the marriage. In addition, in this case as well, we see that the road to marriage involves quite a bit of back and forth between attraction and dissociation. Only a day after composing his ode to Paula and recording his initial thoughts about the possibility of marrying her, Modersohn notes: "Yesterday at P. B.'s [Paula Becker's] and since then com-

---

70 See the notes in PMB, p. 208; see also the letters "An Meinen", "Mittwoch-Abend", ibid., pp. 270 and 684.
71 All citations taken from Otto Modersohn, *Tagebuch*, July 26, 1900, PMB/OM, p. 65.

pletely done with her. She is far too ultra-modern, free to the point of excess, overly sophisticated, partly because her parents have had such an effect on her, partly because of her recent life in the cities of art, especially Paris, without which she can no longer imagine living."[72] A few days later, he writes in the same vein: "Yesterday I had the most fruitless conversation with P. B. We are miles apart in our views on life and people."[73] A week before the engagement, however, he notes: "P. B. is attracting me again." Yet doubts remain. Their mutual probing ultimately revolves around the practice of gender relations. The artist and nonconformist once again asks who will do the cooking: "Would she preside over the household as she should, be a housewife, if there were also two servants (for the kitchen and the children)"? Furthermore, even at this stage, it seems impossible to conceive of Paula Becker apart from Paris, her city of dreams: "Wouldn't she be bored with the solitude – without parties, without particular people – without Paris"?[74]

Ultimately any attempt to rationalize personal inclinations from an outsider perspective remains difficult. From a socio-historical perspective, this couple also follows the trend toward endogamy, which was typical of the nineteenth century. Paula Becker is the daughter of a civil servant, and Otto Modersohn is the son of a master builder (*Baumeister*) from Westphalia. His older brother is a lawyer, his younger brother a pastor. So they not only share a passion for art, but also an educated bourgeois upbringing. The sizeable age difference between them is not unusual and is not a topic of discussion.[75] In contrast to endogamy, love is not an academic category, but rather a term employed in the sources. That this relationship is in fact a love relationship, and that it is appropriate to use that label in this case, can be demonstrated on the basis of several diary entries and letters, as well as the couple's self-characterization. Paula writes to Otto after their engagement, alluding to medieval ballads about courtly love (*Minnesang*): "I am yours, you are mine, of that you shall be sure," and she places this missive in their hiding place under the stone.[76] Otto notes in his diary – more prosaically, but more explicitly – "Growing increasingly stronger all on its own, this affection transformed into

---

[72] Ibid., July 27, 1900, p. 65.
[73] Ibid., August 8, 1900, p. 66.
[74] All citations taken from ibid., September 3, 1900, p. 66.
[75] Mr. Becker's questionable assessment, after meeting the Worpswede painters and long before the engagement, is as follows: "Modersohn, a good Westphalian, not at all Semitic, as his name suggests, has a child's soul"; see his letter to Paula Becker, January 11, 1897, PMB, p. 109; see also Paula Becker to Otto Modersohn, March 6, 1901, PMB, p. 339: "My family will receive you with much love and much anticipation."
[76] In the original German: "Ich bin Dein, Du bist mein, des sollst Du gewiß sein"; Paula Becker to Otto Modersohn, sometime after September 12, 1900, PMB, p. 270. See also ibid., p. 684.

the most ardent love."[77] The couple opens a bottle of wine with Heinrich Vogeler to toast their engagement. With Rilke, of course, things have to be a bit grander and more moving. Paula Becker writes to her friend, who as Vogeler's guest during his time in Worpswede is said to have had an inclination toward her: "The one thing for me, the whole, the great, the solid thing for me, is my love for Otto Modersohn and his love for me. And this is something wonderful, which blesses me and overwhelms me, and sings and fiddles around me and in me."[78] This is linked to an offer to make Rilke a godfather, although it remains unclear whether this is meant formally, with a view to their future marriage, or informally, as a friendly invitation to support the couple in their future life together.

Once Paula finishes her culinary course, they plan the wedding. The question of the dowry, as we have seen, is not an issue. Otto Modersohn can make a living by selling his paintings and thus support a family. When the couple marry, Paula becomes stepmother to Otto's daughter Elsbeth from his first marriage. Paula wants to stage the wedding in the Art Nouveau style, namely to travel with her bridegroom from Worpswede on one of the "sad" black peat barges up the little Hamme river to a church two hours away. She already knows the place – which is probably the brick church in Wasserhorst – from her winter ice-skating trips. She plans to sit on the barge "in a white dress, with a green wreath in my hair, and beside me will sit a quiet man, with a red beard and hair, and deep eyes. That will be beautiful."[79] But her father's illness prevents this act of 'social magic' (Bourdieu) from taking place. The couple finally celebrates their wedding on May 25, 1901, at Carl Woldemar Becker's bedside, within the circle of their immediate family. Otto's brother Ernst Modersohn performs the ceremony. No edited report on this even has come down to us.

The Chosen 'Family' as Sacred Friendship

1901 is a year for marriages in Worpswede. In addition to the Becker-Modersohns, Rilke marries Clara Westhoff, a sculptor and the daughter of a merchant from Bremen; Vogeler marries Martha Schröder, the daughter of the Worpswede schoolteacher. Over the course of the year 1900, intense friendships and social inter-

---

77 Otto Modersohn, *Tagebuch*, September 27, 1900, PMB/OM, p. 72.
78 Paula Becker to Rainer Maria Rilke, November 12, 1900, PMB, p. 282. On the inclination between Rilke and Becker, see the notes in PMB, p. 209; on Vogeler, see Paula to Carl Woldemar Becker, October 28, 1900, ibid., p. 277.
79 Paula Becker to Jeanne Bruinier, January 19, 1901, PMB, p. 314. See also Paula Becker to Rainer Maria Rilke, January 10, 1901, PMB, p. 299. On the following, see the notes in PMB, p. 303.

course had developed, although not all the artists in the colony participated in this. The central figures in this network are the three aforementioned couples, who are sometimes joined by Milly Becker, Marie Bock, Carl Hauptmann, and other visitors. What is remarkable is that this circle of friends refer to themselves as 'the family.' As Paula reports to her aunt in England: "On the outside we live as a quiet community: Vogeler and his little bride, Otto Modersohn and me, and Clara Westhoff. We call ourselves: the family."[80] Even when Becker, Westhoff, and Rilke meet in Berlin in 1901, they call themselves "the family." This chosen family meets regularly on Sundays in Worpswede to exchange ideas about art and literature. They read letters and original texts aloud, not least Rilke's poems, accompanied by wine and sometimes music. More mundane entertainment includes bowling evenings, when they meet at the village inn, and joint ice-skating excursions on the Hamme.[81] This aesthetically enriched circle of friends and soulmates is elevated to a type of devotion: "Your Sunday poem made me quiet and devout, and Clara Westhoff read it and remained silent, pondering for quite some time," writes Paula Becker to Rilke.[82]

The extent to which these feelings are authentic is not a topic we can plausibly analyze here. Yet we can say that this 'family' friendship is also a matter of performance. At center stage in the production of Worpswede as a Gesamtkunstwerk stands an imposing house: Heinrich Vogeler's Barkenhoff, where the group meets on Sundays.

Vogeler acquired this farmhouse (named 'Birkenhof' or Birch Farm) with money he inherited in 1894 and rebuilt it over the subsequent years in accordance with his Art Nouveau ideas. When Carl Woldemar Becker advises his daughter against buying a farmhouse, he is thinking of Vogeler's Barkenhoff. Indeed, in her diary before the wedding, Paula imagines a meandering dream house for herself, her husband, and their future children. Similarly, Moderesohn and Vogeler simultaneously draw "our future house" together.[83] Vogeler's Worpswede mise-en-scène, which still resonates with viewers today, also includes his blonde wife, Mar-

---

80 Paula Becker to Marie Hill, December 30, 1900, PMB, pp. 296–97. Rilke was in Berlin at this time. On the following (citation), see Paula Becker to Otto Modersohn, February 3, 1901, ibid., p. 322.
81 Paula Becker to Marie Hill, April 20, 1899, PMB, p. 186; to Herma Becker, November 8, 1905, ibid., pp. 508–9; to Rainer Maria Rilke, January 10, 1901, p. 299.
82 Paula Becker to Rainer Maria Rilke, October 25, 1900, PMB, p. 275. See also *Tagebuch*, September 3, 1900, ibid., p. 269.
83 Paula Becker, *Tagebuch*, c. February 12, 1901, PMB, p. 330; Otto Modersohn to Paula Becker, February 16, 1901, PMB/OM, p. 136 (citation). On artists' houses and home museums, see Holm, "Bürgerliche Wohnkultur," 235–37; on the following, see the comments in Paula Becker, *Tagebuch*, October 18, 1898, PMB, p. 163; on the wife's representative role, see Mettele, "Der private Raum."

Fig. 22: Summer Evening (Concert) at Barkenhoff, by Heinrich Vogeler, 1905; at the garden door stands Martha Vogeler; seated on the left is Paula Modersohn-Becker; fourth from the left is Clara Rilke-Westhoff; and in the background on the left is Otto Modersohn. Source: akg-images

tha, whom he often – "incessantly," according to one of Paula's diary entries – draws or paints in the house or on the terrace. Here we witness not only an Art Nouveau imagination, but also a modern form of staging domesticity, in which the wife is moved to the center as the representative woman. However, in view of such an overload of meaning, one almost expects that this harmonious 'family' community will be short-lived. These self-narratives document a history of euphoric encounters, conflicts and dissonances, drifting apart, and coming together again. As early as April 1902, only a year after all three couples marry, Modersohn notes: "The saddest thing about Worpswede is the social intercourse. All the relationships are short-lived, fluctuation is endless. In one year, everything has changed often. Relationships fall apart in completely inconsistent and inexplicable ways." This applies particularly to the relationship with Rilke and the social "intercourse at the Vogeler house," which had been so "beautiful and rich, natural and innocent." "And today? Not a shadow of [how it was] then."[84] The chosen family based on friendly feeling and congenial artistic sensibility proves to be extremely fragile.

---

84 Otto Modersohn, *Tagebuch*, April 1, 1902, PMB/OM, p. 171.

Marriage as a Crisis-Ridden Communion of Soulmates

How do Paula Becker and Otto Modersohn function as a couple? Their expectations prior to the foundation of the family, which is concretized when Paula moves into Otto's house to live with him and 3-year-old Elsbeth, are exceedingly high. We can describe the couple as lovers who, consistent with Romantic ideals, want to establish a communion of souls founded on intense affection and shared aesthetic experiences.[85] Far more than simply an educated couple, the pair also constitute a working couple and, in a way, a religious couple. Indeed their use of religious vocabulary is striking: "He makes me devout," writes the lovestruck Paula in her diary.[86] For each of them, the encounter with the other is a revival-like experience. Otto Modersohn describes in his diary how love's "infinite power" means that "everything, everything seems changed to me."[87] Striving toward a higher goal through their joint artistic work is characteristic of this couple: together they seek "to approach the eternally regenerating goal."[88] The fact that their opinions about the path to a higher form of existence sometimes differ is not a contradiction. Even among religious and political couples, disputes can and do arise. Thus art brings Paula Becker and Otto Modersohn together, but sometimes it also drives them apart.

How are the couple's feelings translated into everyday married life? In this artists' marriage, the spheres of work and leisure are not separate, nor do separate gender spheres exist. As a couple, Paula and Otto have their own little rituals. In addition to reading art history books together and exchanging ideas about the kind of art they should aspire to – specifically about their own works, and also about paragons such as Böcklin, Cézanne, and Gauguin – the primary ritual is simultaneously painting the same motif or model: landscapes and people in and around the moorland village of Worpswede, not least in the poorhouse that stands directly opposite Modersohn's house. As Paula reports: "Even after supper we rush over to the poorhouse to paint studies in color of the cow, the goat, the three-legged old

---

[85] See Trepp, "Emotion und bürgerliche Sinnstiftung"; and briefly Wienfort, *Verliebt, Verlobt, Verheiratet*, 20–21.
[86] In the original German: "Er macht mich fromm"; Paula Becker, *Tagebuch*, beginning of October 1900, PMB, p. 272.
[87] Otto Modersohn, *Tagebuch*, February 12, 1901, PMB/OM, p. 134.
[88] Paula to Milly Becker, December 6, 1905, PMB, p. 511. On artist couples, see Berger, *Liebe Macht Kunst*.

Fig. 23: Paula Becker and Otto Modersohn on a bench in the garden of their house in Worpswede, 1904. Source: Otto Modersohn Stiftung, Fischerhude

man, and all the poor children."[89] At the end of the day, they set up their studies on the veranda and discuss them together. There are also small pleasures: swimming and enjoying the fresh air in the summer, ice skating on the frozen Hamme river in the winter, as well as social gatherings with their Worpswede 'family' and visitors from Bremen. If one understands the artist couple as a working couple, then it is also worth mentioning that their income is unevenly distributed throughout their marriage. While the older, established artist finds buyers for his paintings, the young, misunderstood artist – who attends fine-art academies in Paris even after she is married – is happy simply to exhibit a painting once. But the marriage also offers her financial security and scope for artistic development. Furthermore, they are a good match in more respects than this. Particularly in the early years, the relationship between Modersohn, who is prone to melancholy, and Paula, who is more sanguine, corresponds to the Pettersson and Findus model. As Otto remarks: "I certainly tend to be serious, brooding; how often I'm like that when I'm alone. Paula is a true balm; she exhilarates, refreshes, invigorates, rejuvenates

---

[89] Paula to Mathilde Becker, June 27, 1902, PMB, p. 380. See the figures in Wölfle, *Kunst & Liebe im Aufbruch*, 74–76; on the three-legged old man, see PMB, figs. 42 and 43; on the following, see Otto Modersohn, *Tagebuch*, November 5, 1905, PMB/OM, p. 306.

– oh tremendous happiness."⁹⁰ But can the couple find a lasting arrangement that takes their individuality and their different quirks into account?

Paula Modersohn-Becker articulates the shock of coming down to earth in everyday married life for the first time barely a year into the marriage. Her diary entry for Easter Sunday 1902 addresses the discrepancy between the expectation of a communion of souls and the realities of everyday life as a married couple, and moreover between her art and the burden of household management, not least in the kitchen:

> In my experience, marriage does not make one happier. It removes the illusion that previously sustained one's entire being: that a soulmate existed. In marriage one feels the lack of understanding doubly, because the whole of one's previous life was oriented toward finding someone who would understand. And indeed, is it not perhaps better [to live] without this illusion, eye to eye with the great, lonely truth? This is what I'm writing in my household accounts book on Easter Sunday 1902, sitting in my kitchen and cooking roast veal.⁹¹

On the evening of the same day, she adds a postscript in which she reflects on the relationship between Böcklin and Titian: a reference to her actual profession. For his part, Otto Modersohn's frustration finds expression three months later. His remarks, which focus more on generalities, correspond to criticisms of the women's movement and the crisis of masculinity around 1900. He accuses his wife of egoism, which he believes ultimately stems from reading Nietzsche.

> That must be the hardest thing for a woman: high-spirited, intelligent, and still fully female. These modern women cannot truly love [...]. They are so far from the truly high goal. [...] With all of their intelligence, they still move farther and farther away from the goal. For their first considerations are egoism, independence, complacency, and that cannot result in a happy marriage.

---

90 In the original German: "Ich neige entschieden zum schweren, grüblerischen, wie oft bin ich so, wenn ich allein bin. Da ist Paula ein wahres Labsal, sie erheitert, erfrischt, belebt, verjüngt – o riesengroßes Glück"; Otto Modersohn, *Tagebuch*, November 26, 1900, PMB, p. 285; see also December 20, 1900, ibid., p. 289. See Sven Nordqvist, Armer Pettersson, www.oetinger.de/buch/armer-pettersson/9783789161735.

91 In the original German: "Es ist meine Erfahrung, daß die Ehe nicht glücklicher macht. Sie nimmt die Illusion, die vorher das ganze Wesen trug, daß es eine Schwesterseele gäbe. Man fühlt in der Ehe doppelt das Unverstandensein, weil das ganze frühere Leben darauf hinausging, ein Wesen zu finden, das versteht. Und ist es vielleicht nicht doch besser ohne diese Illusion, Aug' in Auge einer großen einsamen Wahrheit? Dies schreibe ich in mein Küchenhaushaltebuch am Ostersonntag 1902, sitze in meiner Küche und koche Kalbsbraten"; Paula Modersohn-Becker, *Tagebuch*, March 30, 1902, PMB, p. 371.

Modersohn offers a caricature of the new gender discourse, and he also lets the problems in his own marriage peek through the generalities as he continues:

> If the man expects his wife to do something for him, to live with him, to respond to his concerns, then he is of course caught up in medieval, tyrannical desires. In this way a woman would sacrifice her rights, her personality. This is how they argue, and make themselves and their husbands unhappy.[92]

While such statements of disappointment may read as fatal for the relationship, we must immediately add that the couple writes many letters to each other, both before and after these entries, which testify to great affection, mutual trust, and physical attraction. The same applies to the discourse in the diaries. Despite the ups and down in their emotional states, the parties concerned initially arrive at an arrangement that sustains their marriage for several years. This arrangement is based on the above-mentioned communal rituals, and more so on the principle of time-out from their life as a couple: a temporal–spatial separation over a short or a longer period of time, which then leads to a highly anticipated reunion. Paula Becker and Otto Modersohn begin by organizing the everyday disorder of their lives, dividing their presence between two houses in Worpswede: Otto Modersohn's family home on the one hand, and the studio room at the Brünjes farm on the other. After her marriage, Paula Becker moves into Otto Modersohn's spacious house, but she keeps her room at the Brünjes farm, where she had lived since July 1900, as her studio. The "dear little Brünjes house" becomes her refuge. When her husband goes to visit his father in Münster, she remarks in a letter to her sister Milly: "And I have moved to Brünjes and am playing Paula Becker."[93] On a normal day, Mrs. Modersohn first does some household chores, assisted by the maids – either Bertha or Johanne; then at about 9 o'clock,

---

[92] In the original German: "Das muß das schwerste für ein Frauenzimmer sein: geistig hoch, intelligent u. doch ganz Weib. Diese modernen Frauenzimmer können nicht wirklich lieben [...]. Wie fern sind sie doch vom wirklich hohen Ziele. [...] Mit all' ihrer Intelligenz kommen sie immer weiter vom Ziele ab. – Für das erste halten sie Egoismus, Selbständigkeit, Selbstgefälligkeit u. das kann keine glückl. Ehe warden"; "Der Mann ist natürlich in mittelalterlichen tyrannischen Gelüsten befangen, wenn er erwartet, daß s. Frau ihm zu Liebe etwas thut, mit ihm lebt, auf s. Interesse eingeht. Eine Frau würde da ja ihre Rechte, ihre Persönlichkeit opfern. So argumentieren sie u. machen sich u. ihre Männer unglücklich"; both citations taken from Otto Modersohn, *Tagebuch*, June 28, 1902, PMB, p. 381. See also Planert, *Antifeminismus*; Arni, *Entzweiungen*, 215–24; on "men's fear of women" as a growing problem in the nineteenth century, see Gay, *Erziehung der Sinne*, 187.
[93] Paula to Mathilde Becker, July 6, 1902, PMB, p. 381 (first citation); Paula to Milly Becker, April 15, 1904, ibid., p. 448 (second citation). On Modersohn's house, see Otto to Paula Modersohn-Becker, March 2–3, 1906, PMB/OM, p. 331.

she walks across the Weyerberg meadows to her studio. The family comes together at 1 o'clock for lunch, for which the maid is probably largely responsible, followed by a short nap. Then the afternoon is again devoted to painting.[94] The couple spends the evening alone together or with their Worpswede circle of friends. A situation in which visitors come and go frequently and unexpectedly – as in the cases of the Stettler-Herports, the Benekes, and the Püschmanns – does not obtain here. In this respect, the Modersohn family's version of domesticity gives the impression of greater privacy. We can also speak of separate spheres in this case. However, it is not a matter of separate, gender-specific spaces – with the man out in public and the woman in the house, as is often asserted in academic research – but rather of a very modern-seeming concept of separate work spaces in two different houses, in which the woman and the man each pursue their respective activities.

Paula Modersohn-Becker openly expresses both the fact that these time-outs stabilize the relationship and her own need for a space in which she is free: "How strange that this separation makes our love so jubilant."[95] In a letter to Otto, she compares her feelings at his departure to Münster for a few days with those of 6-year-old Elsbeth when she sees her parents leaving for Bremen "and thinks that she now has a whole day or two ahead of her in which no one will forbid her anything. I felt so divinely free." However, she then adds: "Do you even know, [the fact] that you stand in the background of my freedom is what makes it so beautiful[?] If I were free and did not have you, then it [freedom] would mean nothing to me."[96] The self-narratives that contain the clearest avowals of affection are letters written during periods when the couple is separated: during their engagement, this includes the Christmas holidays Paula spends at her parental home in Bremen and her stay in Berlin; after they are married, this includes several approximately two-month trips to Paris, where Paula goes to study art. Yet these trips are not only about art; they are also an escape from everyday married life and from the narrow world of Worpswede, which no longer inspires her. During her stays in Paris, Paula Modersohn's view of her marriage and family life alters remarkably, as documented in her letters to Otto. For example, on February 12, 1903, she writes: "I think an awful lot of you and Elsbeth, indeed always"; on February 18, she writes: "And despite all this, I am perhaps with you more than

---

[94] See the comments in PMB, p. 303, which are based on an unedited letter written by Herma Becker; on the maidservant Bertha, see Paula to Otto Modersohn, February 14, 1903, PMB, p. 399: "I don't like the hotel food at all and would like to have Bertha here to cook me something nice for once"; on Johanne, see March 2, 1906, PMB, p. 523; June 30, 1906, pp. 547–48; Mathilde to Herma Becker, May 10, 1907, ibid., p. 575.
[95] Paula to Otto Modersohn, November 7, 1902, PMB, p. 387.
[96] Paula to Otto Modersohn, April 15, 1904, PMB, p. 446.

ever"; on February 26: "Tell me, are you still coming? Then you must come soon"; and finally on March 17: "My Red King, I am coming home. All of a sudden I am seized to such a degree that I must return to you and to Worpswede."[97] Among Paula's letters from Paris are also cards sent to little Elsbeth. The ambitious Paula accepts her role as stepmother to her husband's daughter from his first marriage.

Nevertheless, the marriage sails into rough waters. Toward the end of the nineteenth century, the number of couples wanting to separate increased across various milieus. In this respect, the Becker-Modersohn relationship is no exception. By the time Paula Modersohn-Becker leaves for her fourth trip to Paris on February 23, 1906, she is sure that she wants a divorce and consults a lawyer before she leaves – without her husband's consent. However, since the Civil Code (*Bürgerliches Gesetzbuch*) was introduced in 1900, a divorce is no longer so easy to obtain; now divorce must be based on the grounds of fault, especially if – as in this case – both parties do not agree to it.[98] Paula is the driving force, and Otto is the one left behind, the one who does not consent. Yet for her the matter is clear: "Now I have left Otto Modersohn, and I am standing between my old life and my new life. What will the new one be like[?] And what will I be like in the new life?"[99] Why has their marriage fallen into such a serious crisis? It would be overly simplistic to point to differences in their characters, or to Paula's desire for freedom. The fact that she eventually becomes the one who sets the tone in artistic discourse – both practically and theoretically – is something her more-established husband notes with equal parts irritation and fascination.[100] Yet this is not their biggest problem. Compared to Paula's expectations, both Otto Modersohn's considerations and Carl Woldemar Becker's advice prior to the marriage already point to divergent ideas. The dispute over cooking was no exception. On the side stands the bourgeois model of marriage formulated by the two men, which Mathilde Becker probably shares, and which Paula Becker is reluctant to accept from the very beginning in terms of household chores; on the other side stands the ideal of a community of artists

---

97 In order of citation: Paula to Otto Modersohn, February 12, 1903; February 18, 1903; February 26, 1903; March 17, 1903, PMB, pp. 395–427. See also February 23, 1905, ibid., p. 478; on the following, see Paula to Elsbeth Modersohn, February 22, 1903, ibid. pp. 409–10.
98 On divorce law in the German Empire, see Blasius, *Ehescheidung in Deutschland*, 132–33 and 146–54; Wienfort, *Verliebt, Verlobt, Verheiratet*, 244–48.
99 Paula Modersohn-Becker, *Tagebuch*, February 24, 1906, PMB, p. 521 (citation); Paula to Otto Modersohn, February 23, 1906, ibid., p. 520.
100 Otto Modersohn, *Tagebuch*, July 7, 1902, PMB, p. 383; see the more detailed account in PMB/OM, pp. 177–78; see also the ironic remark about Otto's constantly changing reflections on art in Paula to Herma Becker, December 24, 1904, PMB, pp. 454–55.

and a communion of kindred spirits – a goal for which Otto and Paula both strive. For all their liberality, marriage is a social norm for the Becker parents, whereas for their daughter – as of February 1906 – it is a practice which limits the possibilities the world has to offer her. Thus the case of the Modersohn-Beckers touches on a basic problem for many couples, one that is as relevant today as it was then: How can professional-individual and familial-communal identities be reconciled?

Paula's letters to her sister and her mother prior to her separation from Otto address the fact that the couple is drifting apart fairly clearly. The summer of 1905 is already a "prickly time."[101] This dissatisfaction increases during the dark winter months. Paula calls it her "hibernation," whereas Otto, in retrospect, refers to it as his wife's "mental depression."[102] Their lively conversations about art eventually gave way to domestic boredom. In November 1905, Paula writes almost in unison to Herma and Mathilde Becker about her "longing for the world, especially in the long evenings, during which he is very comfortable with a pipe in the corner of a sofa," which is why she was once again secretly planning a trip to Paris.[103] But there is another difficulty, one which is not mentioned in the biographical introductions to the glossy volumes about this artist couple.[104] The husband not only seems to his wife to be comfortably bourgeois, he also has an impotence problem. In a letter to Carl Hauptmann, in whose house in the Silesian town of Schreiberhau a group of intellectuals and artists meet at the end of 1905, Paula Becker – already set on divorce – does not mince words. This is a reckoning with her husband: "I cannot do otherwise. I placed myself *completely* in Otto Modersohn's hands, and it took me five years to get free of him again. I have lived alongside him for five years without him making me his wife; that has been torture." Nor does she want to have a child with him, because "he is a Philistine and is not free in any direction." This accusation culminates in the statement: "My love is truly broken."[105] In another short letter to Hauptmann, probably in response to his inquiry, she confesses that she had an affair with Werner Sombart at the meeting in Silesia,

---

101 Paula to Herma Becker, November 8, 1905, PMB, p. 508.
102 Ibid. See also December 1, 1905, PMB, p. 510; Otto to Paula Modersohn-Becker, March 2–3, 1906, PMB/OM, p. 329.
103 Paula to Herma Becker, November 8, 1905, PMB, p. 508; Paula to Mathilde Becker, November 26, 1905, PMB, p. 510.
104 Cf. the brief mention in Stamm, *"Ein kurzes intensives Fest"*, 185–86.
105 In the original German: " Ich habe 5 Jahre neben ihm gelebt, ohne daß er mich zu seiner Frau machte, das war Tierquälerei"; "Er ist Philister und unfrei nach jeglicher Richtung"; "Meine Liebe ist ja doch kaput"; Paula Modersohn-Becker to Carl Hauptmann, April 22, 1906, PMB, p. 530 (italics in the original).

and that Otto Modersohn knows nothing about it. She asks Hauptmann to "keep silent" about "my private experience" with Sombart.[106]

Apart from the allusion in Barbara Baumgartner's diary, Paula Becker and Otto Modersohn are the first couple presented in this book to write explicitly about eroticism and sexuality. Clearly the limits of what can be said are broader around 1900 than they were when the bourgeois couple Caroline and Ferdinand Beneke were writing – the two talk of love constantly, but do not mention eroticism – and certainly than in diaries inspired by Pietism. If we understand self-narrative along Foucault's lines, as a technology of shaping the self, then it is no longer a matter of Christian principles of morality, renunciation, and containment of lust, but is on the contrary a matter of fulfilled sexuality.[107] It is well known and evident that, in the context of a modern, secularized society, sexuality also becomes a problem in many ways.[108] That this is also the case in the relationship between Paula Becker and Otto Modersohn is surprising, however, once one has read some of their letters. For example, in a letter to Otto as late as March 1905, in which she expresses her joy at his imminent arrival, Paula declares that in Paris "beds are only for shagging in" and signs the letter, "Your little wife."[109] He replies: "My sweet little wife! To thank you for your dear letter, let me first take you and kiss you on the mouth, nose, eyes, the 'belly button,' and the two sweet little holes in the front and the back."[110]

Paula Becker was most likely a virgin when she entered into the marriage, and she alludes to this in a letter during their engagement.[111] Otto Modersohn fathered a daughter with his first wife, Helene. Nevertheless, after Paula and Otto marry, he seems to have a problem that prevents the consummation of the marriage and is apparently not easily resolved.[112] After Paula leaves for Paris a fourth time, at the end of February 1906 – a trip which goes hand in hand with her desire for a di-

---

106 Paula Modersohn-Becker to Carl Hauptmann, June 10, 1906, PMB, p. 546.
107 Foucault, "Technologies of the Self," 16; on the change from the eighteenth century, see ibid., 49; on "the pleasures that are unspoken" – that is, the discourse on sexuality – see Foucault's classic *The History of Sexuality*, 4; on discussions of sexuality in court, which adhered to other principles, see Arni, *Entzweiungen*, 234–46.
108 See Foucault, *The History of Sexuality*; more concretely, see also Bänziger, *Sex als Problem*; on repressed sexuality in the nineteenth century from a psychoanalytic perspective, see Gay, *Die zarte Leidenschaft*, 9–10; and in general, Gay, *Erziehung der Sinne*.
109 Paula to Otto Modersohn, March 20, 1905, PMB, p. 493. See also PMB/OM, p. 295.
110 Otto to Paula Modersohn-Becker, March 23, 1905, PMB/OM, p. 297. This letter is not included in the PMB edition.
111 Paula Becker to Otto Modersohn, February 4, 1901, PMB, p. 323: "it's my virginity that constrains me."
112 See also the metaphorical allusion in Paula to Otto Modersohn, November 7, 1902, PMB, p. 387.

vorce – Otto writes pages and pages of imploring love letters every day in an effort to win her back. In the very first of these letters, he addresses what he sees as the central problems in their marriage: "My Paula! There are two points that have brought about your decision: 1) sexual dissatisfaction, and 2) alienation, not taking part in each other's lives."[113] He then elaborates on both aspects. Concerning "dissatisfaction in love," he refers back to his nervousness: "Without knowing it, I was nervous when I entered into the marriage. Attempts failed, robbed me of my self-confidence on that point, [and] made me anxious." Thus the couple's love life is limited to "small intermezzis."[114] Due to embarrassment and prudishness, as he apologetically states, he took too long to seek advice. Only after three and a half years of marriage, at the end of 1904, does he decide to consult a doctor – namely his brother-in-law Kurt – who simply recommends rest. Otto Modersohn thus blames their marital problems over the course of 1904 on this deficient love life, but he believes that problem has since been solved. Another statement made by the abandoned husband shows how the relationship between the two has changed and even reversed over the course of their marriage: "There is something more in me than the comfortable petite bourgeoisie. Oh, help me; only by your side am I joyful and happy, strong and victorious."[115] This courageous and trusting plea for help blatantly contradicts the prevailing gender hierarchy.

The further correspondence between Paris and Worpswede immediately demonstrates that the separation is not yet definitive; on the one hand, because Otto Modersohn is fighting for his wife and will not agree to the divorce, and on the other hand, because Paula Becker has not planned her new life in advance. With the goal of having a frank discussion, the abandoned husband travels to Paris for a week in June 1906. Paula does not ask her family members for advice directly, but the Beckers are involved in the issue by means of letters and conversations. During the critical discussions in Paris, 21-year-old Herma becomes a witness and mediator in the dispute, which she describes as "very grueling for all

---

113 In the German original: "Meine Paula! Zwei Punkte sind es gewesen, die Deinen Entschluß herbeigeführt haben: 1) die sexuelle Unbefriedigung und 2) die Entfremdung, das nicht in einanderleben"; Otto to Paula Modersohn-Becker, February 27, 1906, PMB/OM, p. 317. See also the account of a crisis conversation about "a lack of true enjoyment in love," which includes the statement: "our life has become too monotonous, philistine"; Otto Modersohn, *Tagebuch*, November 5, 1905, PMB/OM, pp. 305–6.
114 All citations taken from a letter to Paula Modersohn-Becker, February 27, 1906, PMB/OM, pp. 318–19. On the diagnosis of nervousness or 'neurasthenia', which was rampant around 1900, see Radkau, *Das Zeitalter der Nervosität*.
115 In the original German: "In mir ist etwas anderes als gemüthliches Spießerthum. O hilf mir, an Deiner Seite bin ich allein froh u. glücklich, stark u. siegend"; Otto to Paula Modersohn-Becker, February 28, 1906, PMB/OM, p. 322.

three of us." The Beckers' views on the matter fluctuate between understanding for Paula – as their sister or daughter, respectively – and more or less open criticism. In this respect, Paula's older brother Kurt takes the side of his brother-in-law and patient, Otto. The marital conflict illustrates two aspects of the relationship: first, Paula's willpower and charisma, as Herma notes with wonder: "that *someone* is granted such power";[116] and second, the strength of the family's cohesion. After all, Paula's unilaterally formulated wish for a divorce not only plunges the family's beloved brother- and son-in-law into crisis, but also calls into question a fundamental bourgeois value and demonstrates a lack of concern for family honor. The crisis leads to an increase in the number of letters exchanged, as well as conversations and other forms of support: her mother's moral support and attempts to mediate, her older sister's financial support, a trip to Brittany with her younger sister.[117] We can interpret each of the Becker siblings' individual reactions differently. One thing is certain, however: this marital crisis between their sister and brother-in-law does not cause a rift, but rather intensifies communication within the family. The couple's friends in Worpswede, Paris, and Schreiberhau also intervene, writing letters and sometimes taking sides. Ultimately it is abundantly clear that a divorce is not a purely private matter around 1900.

At the beginning of September 1906, it still looks as if the separation will stick. When the couple met in June, they agreed that Otto would come to Paris in the autumn for a longer period of time, more or less on a trial basis. But on September 3, Paula writes to him: "Spare us both this trial period. Give me my freedom, Otto. I don't like having you for a husband. I don't like it. Make your peace with it. Don't torture yourself any longer. Try to put the past behind you."[118] However, Paula has a financial problem. She already ran out of money in March and had to ask her husband to send her some. Now she must ask again: "I have to ask you to send me money for the last time. I ask you for the sum of 500 marks. […] In this period I will take steps to secure my material existence."[119] Yet she takes back this letter –

---

116 Both citations taken from Herma to Mathilde Becker, July 8, 1906, PMB, p. 545 (italics in the original).
117 Exchange of letters between Mathilde and Paula Modersohn-Becker, May 8–10, 1906, PMB, pp. 537–39; Milly to Paula Modersohn-Becker, April 4, 1906, ibid., p. 527; see also May 14, 1906, p. 539; Paula to Otto Modersohn, April 25, 1906, p. 531; Paula to Milly Rohland-Becker, January 29, 1907, p. 566. The crisis ends with a family reunion in Worpswede, including Otto Modersohn and Kurt Becker; see Mathilde to Herma Becker, May 10, 1907, PMB, pp. 575–76.
118 Paula to Otto Modersohn, September 3, 1906, PMB, p. 556. On the following, see March 19, 1906, ibid., p. 526.
119 Paula to Otto Modersohn, September 3, 1906, PMB, pp. 556–57.

which has a devastating impact on Otto Modersohn – just three days later. Paula Modersohn-Becker apologetically explains that she was upset about the account he gave to her family in Bremen of the reason for their marital crisis. In essence, this is also about his impotence problem, because Paula believes she can see in her siblings' letters evidence that "you presented me as the cause of your nervous condition." In this respect, it is clear that a similar problem had already occurred "on your honeymoon with Helene." One key factor in Paula's change of heart is a fulllength sermon she receives from their friend Bernhard Hoetger, who is in Paris at that time. "If you haven't yet given up on me entirely, come here soon so that we can try to find each other again."[120] Incidentally, this is an indication of the importance of friendship as a social context, even around 1900.

Otto Modersohn travels to Paris and stays there the whole winter, while his daughter Elsbeth goes to stay with her grandmother in Bremen. In his travel diary, he briefly notes: "with Paula, everything soon went well."[121] Indeed, the couple succeeds in making a new start during this time, and in March 1907 they return to Worpswede together. Given Paula's strongly expressed dislike for and criticism of her husband's habitus – she refers to him as the "couch potato"[122] – this reversal comes as a surprise. However, her letters from Paris soon after her departure from Worpswede reveal that she had underestimated the difficulties of life on her own. Both objectively and subjectively, she is in a bad way. Paula, who is otherwise so self-confident, admits: "I'm a poor little person, I can't tell which is the right way for me."[123] Specifically she is concerned about the lack of money and the complete uncertainty of her future. Whether sufficient capital would have enabled her to do her thing – colloquially speaking – as she otherwise did in many respects, is simply idle speculation. It is clear that needing to establish an independent existence in the Parisian metropolis was an entirely different matter than a temporary sojourn at a fine-art academy. And there are other reasons for Paula's return, which is suffused with a relatively sober atmosphere. As she explains in a disillusioned tone to Clara Rilke, over the course of the summer she "realized that I am not a woman who can stand alone. Apart from the constant worries about money,

---

120 Paula to Otto Modersohn, September 7, 1906, PMB, pp. 557–58. On Hoetger's intervention, see Paula to Milly Becker-Rohland, September 16, 1906, PMB, p. 558; see also Otto to Paula Modersohn-Becker, September 11, 1906, PMB/OM, pp. 403–4.
121 Otto Modersohn, *Reisetagebuch*, October 1906 – March 1907, PMB/OM, p. 406.
122 In the original German: "Stuben- u. Sophamensch"; this is how Otto repeats Paul's own words back to her in Otto to Paula Modersohn-Becker, April 25, 1906, PMB/OM, p. 354.
123 In the original German: "Ich armes Menschlein, ich fühle nicht welches mein richtiger Weg ist"; Paula to Otto Modersohn, September 7, 1906, PMB, p. 558; see also March 2, 1906, ibid., p. 522: "Of course I'm not doing very well."

it is precisely my freedom that would tempt me to depart from my path." This self-assessment is strongly reminiscent of Caroline Beneke's consent to return from the freedom of her exile in Lübeck to the 'domestic boundaries' of marriage in April 1814. As Paula informs Clara, the decisive factor for her is the prospect of continuous artistic creation without financial concerns "at Otto Modersohn's side."[124] Moreover, Otto has made her pregnant. Her desire to have her own child has fluctuated over the years, and now she is completely in accord with this development. Yet we can certainly not interpret her double return – to her husband and to Worpswede – as an indication that she has chosen "the fulfillment of her human existence as a mother" as her path in life.[125] The summer she and Otto spend together in Worpswede in 1907 is a good time for them as a couple. "I'm doing splendidly," Paula writes to her mother. Nevertheless, she would like to travel to Paris for a week in the final phase of her pregnancy to see a Cézanne exhibition.[126] The couple's new, hard-won consensus on the future of their marriage includes purchasing the Brünjes house and further trips to Paris. Nevertheless, rather than a happy ending, this story ends tragically. On November 2, 1907, Paula gives birth in Worpswede to a healthy daughter whom they name Mathilde, after her grandmother. Eighteen days later, completely out of the blue, Paula Modersohn-Becker dies of an embolism.

Family Trust and the Desire for Freedom

Several aspects of this dual case study of the Becker and the Modersohn-Becker families are particularly interesting and worth summarizing as we close this chapter. Their experiences indicate that the bourgeois family model of an enduring emotional and supportive community can succeed, also and perhaps especially in coping with tensions and conflicts. The Beckers constitute an example of revaluating and cultivating trust relationships within the family as a resource against

---

124 In the original German: "gemerkt, daß ich nicht die Frau bin alleine zu stehn. Außer den ewigen Geldsorgen würde mich gerade meine Freiheit verlocken von mir abzukommen"; "an der Seite Otto Modersohns"; both citations taken from Paula Modersohn-Becker to Clara Rilke, November 17, 1906, PMB, p. 564.
125 Busch, "Paula Modersohn-Becker," 35. On Paula Modersohn-Becker's formulations with regard to her desire to have children, see *Tagebuch*, October 22, 1901, PMB, p. 356; as well as several letters to Otto Modersohn, dated March 10, 1903, ibid., p. 423; April 9, 1906, p. 528; July 14, 1906, p. 550; September 7, 1906, p. 557.
126 Paula to Mathilde Becker, October 2, 1907, PMB, p. 582 (citation); see also October 22, 1907, ibid., p. 585.

the backdrop of increasing uncertainty associated with the modern era.[127] It is not only the immediate family – parents and siblings – which proves to be important, but also broader kinship ties, from which Paula Becker benefits materially as well as immaterially. By 1900, marriage as a prospect for a secure future life is no longer the only option for daughters of the middle class.[128] As a father, Mr. Becker wants his daughters to be able to stand on their own two feet financially and not to be dependent on marriage. Moreover, the openly liberal bourgeois milieu, with its affinity for current discourses, reveals a potential for creativity and innovation, which – in its promotion of the individual habitus – then lobs a grenade at the nineteenth-century ideal of marriage, with its conventions, hierarchies, and gender roles.

The home, houses, and the domestic sphere remain relevant in several respects. Even at the end of the century, 'house' as an alternative term for family has not yet become obsolete. After a good two years of married life, Otto Modersohn notes of his wife: "The household is also going quite well – only the family feeling, the relationship to the house is insufficient."[129] For the artists in Worpswede, the house serves as a place of work, a family sphere, a space for demarcation, and a structural embodiment of self-representation to the outside world. For Paula Becker, however, the domestic sphere also becomes a private prison of boredom on long winter evenings. Apart from the chosen family gathering at Barkenhoff on Sundays, we find no examples of an 'open house' or a visiting culture.

Paula Becker is not a particularly political person. In her younger years she worshipped Otto von Bismarck, but she also made fun of nationalism and the emerging racial doctrine.[130] In the texts that have been edited to date, there is no indication that she engaged with the ideas put forth by the contemporary women's movement. Nevertheless, the reader must attest to her emancipation in praxis, and she does reflect upon this now and then. Considering the much-maligned culinary course as an apprenticeship prior to her marriage, she writes: "It's strange that right from the beginning of marriage, it's we women who are put through our paces. You men can simply remain as you are. Well, I don't hold that against you."[131] As a married woman, Paula Modersohn-Becker lives an eman-

---

127 See Frevert, *Vertrauensfragen*, 213.
128 See B. Kuhn, *Familienstand*.
129 In the original German: "Der Haushalt geht auch ganz gut – nur d. Familiengefühl, d. Verhältniß zum Hause ist zu gering"; Otto Modersohn, *Tagebuch*, September 26, 1903, PMB, p. 439. On the history of this term, see Mathieu, "Domestic Terminologies."
130 Paula to Carl Woldemar Becker, August 7, 1892, PMB, p. 55; see also May 18, 1896, ibid., p. 101; Paula Modersohn to her parents, June 12, 1901, p. 351.
131 Paula Becker to Otto Modersohn, March 6, 1901, PMB, p. 339.

cipated everyday life, and the connection between this and contemporary political discourse is yet to be reflected upon. In some respects, the gender roles in the Modersohn household invert the classic bourgeois model: Otto is a patient, 'gentle man' who values his domesticity and enjoys a pipe on the sofa; the dynamic Paula can no longer stand this domesticity and strives to go out into the world. We can understand this marital crisis as a step on the way to a new understanding of marriage and the family. Toward the end of the century, the divorce rate is rising, despite all legislative and judicial attempts to contain it. The view of the family as a binding norm and social institution is diminishing, but the family has not lost its importance. This may seem paradoxical, but a desire for separation or divorce points not only to the fragility of marriage, but also to the high expectations both women and men had with regard to family life.[132] The ideal of a life with one's soulmate, which Romanticism introduced to the world, poses a challenge to every relationship when it comes to daily life. "The subject's expressive individuality," as Reckwitz puts it,[133] which stems from Romanticism and is further developed by the avant-garde around 1900, is another source of this fragility. Paula Modersohn-Becker's subjectivity is mixed, combining her bourgeois origins with her artistic individualism. The fact that she commutes between Worpswede or Bremen and Paris points to the two ideals she is trying to reconcile: a strong sense of family and aesthetic freedom.

---

[132] The divorce rate in Switzerland was comparatively high; see Arni, *Entzweiungen*, 24; on Germany, see Blasius, *Ehescheidung in Deutschland*, 152–53; on the shift in expectations, see Schneider, "Familie in Westeuropa," 21–23; Nave-Herz, "Unkenrufe," 993–94.
[133] Reckwitz, *Das hybride Subjekt*, 30.

Chapter 11
The Family: Decline or Resilience?

Now that we have explored these various self-narratives from different milieus, the first impression we are left with is an immense diversity of living conditions. However, when we look more closely, we can identify specific challenges and responses exemplified by the actors in these family contexts. The task of this final chapter is to separate the exemplary from the incidental, which we will do on the basis of selected criteria. Since the period from 1750 onward constituted an era of tremendous change and upheaval, one might assume that everyday life in the domestic microcosm also experienced fundamental changes. Yet we should beware of the temptations of modernization theory and the tendency to presume anthropological constants when it comes to research on the nature of the family. The nineteenth century was certainly a century of the family. But what does this mean concretely?

Thomas Mann's *Buddenbrooks*

In the context of the *fin de siècle* mood around 1900, Thomas Mann wrote the novel *Buddenbrooks*, which he subtitled: *The Decline of a Family.* In this famous work, the author allows his main characters – members of a respected merchant family in Lübeck, who thus embody both bourgeois pride and professional success – to fail one after the other. One of the two Buddenbrook brothers dies, and the other is committed to a mental institution. Their sister, Tony – with whom the novel begins and ends, as the last remaining guardian of the family tradition – divorces twice. Hanno – the eldest son and intended heir, the future head of the company – is musically gifted but has no interest in business matters. He dies before he reaches adulthood. The company is liquidated, which causes the family both consternation and relief. The rise and fall of the House of Buddenbrook is metaphorically linked to concrete residential buildings: their acquisition, construction, and sale, as well as processes of moving in and moving out. Ironically the family's biggest professional competitor acquires their ancestral home: the "godly patrician house," the "parents' home," "our Mother's house!" on Mengstraße.[1] Clearly Thomas Mann has his

---

[1] Mann, *Buddenbrooks*, 2: 242 and 1: 201. On the decline and fall of the family from the perspective of literary studies, see Koschorke et al., *Vor der Familie*, 12–14; on the family as a theme in *Buddenbrooks*, see Grugger, "Familie"; Schmiedt, "Paarbeziehungen."

finger on the pulse of his time with this novel, in several respects. He addresses a number of themes that are also conspicuous in the family stories presented in the previous ten chapters here: marriages based on love or convenience, sibling love and rivalry, and the tense relationship between the family sphere and the artistic world, to name just three such topics.

The broad reception and ongoing success of Mann's family saga, even up to the present day, demonstrates not least that the theme of the family provokes strong imaginative reactions – wishful thinking as well as the fear of loss – across epochs. With the motif of decline, Mann refers to the bourgeoisie of the late nineteenth century and takes aim at its citadel: the family. Seen from a social and cultural-historical perspective, Mann's view of the bourgeoisie is broadly correct. They did indeed face new challenges over the course of the nineteenth century. The dynamics of industrialization marginalized the early liberal concept of the *Bürger*, pulverized the livelihoods of many families, and paved the way for new professions and new classes of upwardly mobile people who could care less about Romanticism, morality, or domestic literary circles. New discourses countered the bourgeois understanding of the subject, which emphasized independence and sovereignty. Widespread urbanization opened the door not only to modern mass society, but also to a culture focused on consumption and experience, which then ushered in the twentieth century. The extent to which the bourgeoisie continued not simply to exist after the *Sattelzeit* around 1900, but to represent a model of a life worth striving for – at least in some respects – is another question.[2]

From the perspective of the history of the family, the point of view presented in Thomas Mann's *Buddenbrooks* is problematic. Even in the novel itself, the Hagenströms – who play a supporting role – provide an example of a family that behaves more dynamically and achieves more success than the merchant family in bourgeois garb, which is on a downward spiral. Leaving literary imagination aside, there is ample evidence to demonstrate that the family is enormously fragile in individual cases, as we have seen in previous chapters, but nevertheless resilient overall. The period around 1900 is one – though certainly not the only – era of rupture in the family.[3] Nevertheless, as a social institution, the family has proven to be resilient, flexible, and more adaptable in the modern era.[4] Changes to the political system, crises, and challenges of various kinds have not brought

---

[2] On modernity as experience, see Bänziger, *Die Moderne als Erlebnis*; for a discussion of the topicality of *Bürgerlichkeit*, see the contributions in Bude et al., *Bürgerlichkeit*; Pyta and Kretschmann, *Bürgerlichkeit*; and above all Reckwitz, "Wie bürgerlich ist die Moderne?".

[3] See Arni, *Entzweiungen*.

[4] On the concept of resilience from a sociological perspective, see Blum et al., "Soziologische Perspektiven," 152; Endreß and Maurer, "Einleitung," 7.

an end to the family, but have instead prompted changes and increasing diversity while still preserving the family's core components. The model of a (married) couple with one or more children as a long-term community of care continues to enjoy a high socio-cultural status and is obviously an attractive model for many people. In more abstract terms, the family seems to offer a framework within which one can muddle through ambivalences, tensions, and conflict – in short, everyday disorder – among people who enjoy an emotionally close, relatively permanent relationship, thus making such challenges bearable and negotiable even as circumstances change. The families presented in this book, who lived in the long nineteenth century, reveal this continuous community of care in several variations: as a community of emotion, support, conflict, and survival – a community which includes more people than simply the members of the nuclear family.

Matchmaking and Society

In contrast to the basic idea of the freedom to marry, members of the lower classes without financial resources were subject to marriage restrictions until the second half of the nineteenth century. Hence not everyone could hope for a marriage license. The connubial relationships of both the main and the secondary characters in the self-narratives in this book display a distinct pattern of endogamy. There is not a single case in which social boundaries are effectively crossed in marriage. Within the couple's milieu, however, we can certainly discern inequalities between the partners. On closer inspection, two types of marriage can be distinguished across classes: first, social consolidation through marriage, according to the 'like with like' principle (as in the Stettler-Herport, Bruckner-Eglinger, and Dworak-Kubeschka cases); second, social advancement through (attempted) marriage into a family situated on a higher level of the same social milieu (as in the Bräker, Beneke, Püschmann, and Baumgartner cases). The second type would also include the bourgeois engineer Carl Woldemar Becker's marriage to the aristocratic officer's daughter Mathilde von Bültzingslöwen. In individual cases, the relative social positioning of the people involved is open to debate. From a socio-historical perspective, these findings are not surprising. Yet it is surprising that there is not a single case of cousin marriage among our samples. From the perspective of new kinship research, the increase in the number of marriages between cousins as well as the intensification of sibling relationships after 1800 is an indicator of the emergence of new social classes, particularly the bourgeoisie, by means of the establishment of exclusive kinship networks.[5] However, this thesis may apply primarily to social contexts that were already closed or in the process of closing – for example, in kinship marriage among the aristocracy and the urban patriciate, within religious communities, or in precisely those new bourgeois families that pursued a strategy of consolidating property and power by means of kinship alliances. In contrast, the self-narratives presented here suggest more openness and freedom to act when it comes to the marriage relationship. Thus when we trace the kinship ties between Henriette Herport and Rudolf Stettler back in time, their bloodlines do not meet until the sixteenth century. Both the Benekes in Hamburg and the Beckers in Bremen are newcomers who are not related to the old city elite by marriage, but they nevertheless strive to establish marital relations within the bourgeoisie. For Paula Becker as well as for Adelheid Dwořak, however, the decision to marry is motivated by considerations other than social equality. It is true that these two women also marry men from either the same or a comparable social class. Yet there are clearly other criteria – and indeed these are the primary, decisive criteria – that make Otto Modersohn and Julius Popp attractive marriage partners.

The aim and purpose of marriage was to link the inclination known as love with aspects of security and permanence. From the end of the eighteenth century, a new 'emotional regime' came to be regarded as the trademark of family relationships.[6] The bourgeoisie – along with the Pietists and the Romantics – are generally considered to have played a pioneering role in this shift. Yet the liaisons between Henriette Herport and Rudolf Stettler in the patrician context, and Ulrich Bräker and Anna Lüthold in the peasant context – characterized as they are by affection, physical attraction, and explicit reference to 'love' – cast doubt on the pioneering role played by the bourgeoisie. Coincidentally, both of these premarital relationships take place in 1755 – some time before Romanticism emerged, and prior to the establishment of the new bourgeoisie in German-speaking Central Europe. In Bräker's case, this effort at matchmaking ultimately fails; in the case of the Stettler-Herports, it succeeds. On the one hand, the difference lies in the social prospects associated with the marriage; on the other, it has to do with the reactions to the potential union in the family environment. Unlike a marriage to the son of a patrician family who has career prospects in the city-state of Bern, marriage between a poor peasant and an innkeeper's daughter offered no prospect of a sta-

---

[5] See the essential research in Sabean, *Kinship in Neckarhausen*, chap. 22; see also Johnson, "Das 'Geschwister Archipel'"; Sabean, "Kinship and Class Dynamics," and "Kinship and Issues of the Self"; Johnson and Sabean, *Sibling Relations*; but cf. the skeptical summary of the contemporary state of the field in Fertig, *Familie*, 55–60.

[6] For an overview, see Opitz-Belakhal, "A Space of Emotions"; on the following, see esp. Trepp, "Emotion und bürgerliche Sinnstiftung."

ble, economically successful household. The decisive factor in both cases was parental consent – or more precisely, the fathers' consent – to the marriage. At the end of the *ancien régime*, many couples who wanted to marry went to court in an attempt to obtain a license to marry despite parental prohibitions and various other obstacles to marriage.[7] It is easy to understand the actors' subjective sense of obstinacy in opposition to outmoded constraints as a rebellion against the principles of the old estate-based society.

However, concepts of status and honor, stability and self-sufficiency were also cultivated in the bourgeois nineteenth century, albeit in a different way. The bourgeois subject and family conceived of themselves in terms of their cross-generational reputation and the establishment of tradition.[8] This is why diary writing took on such significance during this period, and why the end of the *Buddenbrooks* story is so tragic – beyond the demise of individual family members. Yet we can also identify a shift exemplified in the concrete examples here. The marriages that took place prior to the mid-nineteenth century share a connection beyond the themes of individual affection and the goal of establishing a household – they have a task, one could even say a mission. For Pietists, it is a matter of establishing a 'pious house'; in Romantic contexts, it is about becoming truly human through the experience of love and finding a 'soul mate'; and in the context of liberalism, there is a drive to shape the nucleus of a new, associative society of free, educated, 'moral' subjects. This tendency to overload marriage and domesticity with meaning later recedes into the background. Friedrich Anton Püschmann and Wetti Teuschl, later known as Barbara Baumgartner, simply hope to achieve earthly happiness through marriage. In addition to advice and admonitions, Carl Woldemar Becker expresses to his engaged daughter, Paula, the wish that "your marriage may also become an everlasting source of happiness for you and your husband."[9] However, modernity also seeds movements that run counter to the expectation of happiness as an end in itself. For Adelheid Dvořak, her marriage to Julius Popp is not least a politically relevant model of a new type of partnership; for Paula Modersohn-Becker, marriage establishes a mutually inspiring artistic community. She does not think in terms of economic independence, but rather of artistic freedom – even if, as it turns out, the one is difficult to achieve without the other.

---

7 See Lanzinger, *Verwaltete Verwandtschaft*; more recently, advancing the research with a convincing thesis, see Haldemann, *Prekäre Eheschließungen*.
8 See Reckwitz, *Das hybride Subjekt*, 161–63.
9 Carl Woldemar to Paula Becker, 7 February 1901, PMB, p. 326.

The question of whom a man or a woman marries seems quite simple, but is in fact complex and subject to historical change. With regard to the somewhat different question of whom a man or a woman falls in love with, Pierre Bourdieu's concept of habitus is helpful in combining the subjective and the collective: one's counterpart does not appear simply as an individual, but as "the embodied social."[10] Thus Ferdinand Beneke recognizes a future *Bürgerin* in the habitus of the young Caroline von Axen, while Adelheid Dworak sees the sickly, sympathetic Julius Popp with his silk scarf as the antithesis of her taciturn, violent father. The degree of social control exercised over the matchmaking process seems to have been particularly rigorous in the small-town atmosphere of Krems. The practices that can end up leading to marriage are remarkably variable and varied: the exchange of glances or an interaction that may well be called flirting by today's standards; promenading through the streets as a couple; reading to each other; paying visits to each other's homes; the hopeful man approaching the potential bride's parents; arrangements made by the parents without the knowledge of the bride-to-be; even unexpected marriage proposals out of the blue. This last point does not necessarily imply the renunciation of love as a goal. Instead, it reflects a contemporary notion that love and happiness can develop even after the marriage vows have been made, as it did in Ursula Eglinger's case. In 1788, Mr. Stettler tells his unhappy 16-year-old daughter that the principle of convenience must be followed; 113 years later, the author of *Buddenbrooks* is still referring to this principle, although Tony Buddenbrook's marriage to the merchant Grünlich – which they entered into, or which was forced upon them, purely for reasons of convenience – famously goes very wrong. Contrary to what Thomas Mann's family saga suggests, the self-narratives we have studied here provide evidence that the importance of parental consent waned over the course of the nineteenth century. However, this is likely to be true primarily for families in which there was not much capital to distribute. Paula Becker comes from a middle-class family that nevertheless has limited financial resources, as her father was forced to retire early and there are six children to support. Her parents are simply informed of her engagement to Otto Modersohn. In cases in which the parents take an active role in matters of matchmaking, we can discern a gender-specific division of roles and labor. Mothers usually take the stage first, as the more understanding parent and confidante, whereas fathers appear later – more strict, more distant, and more concerned with the dictates of status and wealth. The fact that the parents do not always agree on these matters points to both the importance and the fragility of the business.

---

10 Bourdieu and Wacquant, *Reflexive Anthropologie*, 161.

In contrast to the custom of the early modern period, the nineteenth-century wedding is not a grand event staged before a large audience. With the exception of the wedding in Krems, one looks in vain for a couple who parades through the streets, for playful or even serious *charivari* rituals on the wedding night, or for dissolute festivities.[11] In 1807 the socially well-connected Beneke, who adhered to the cult of friendship, found himself in a dispute with his future parents-in-law when he insisted on a "preferably silent wedding," in which only the witnesses and close family members would participate.[12] For Wetti Teuschl, the festivities on her wedding night in 1872 seem like "some happy family celebration."[13] The importance of getting married in church, which had been laboriously enforced by the authorities over the course of the early modern period, also declined during the nineteenth century – at least from the point of view of those who were getting married, although there were still major differences between Catholic states such as Austria on the one hand, where civil marriage was not provided for, and Protestant regions and Pietist communities on the other. Nevertheless, a wedding is still an act of 'social magic' accompanied by intense emotions. The choice to exclude neighbors, guild mates, distant relatives, and friends (among others) has something programmatic about it. A celebration on such a small scale corresponds to an imagined goal: the desire for privacy and intimacy in marriage. In contrast, domesticity as it was actually practiced in society was quite different.

Relationship Patterns and Gender

Contemporary descriptive models were based on the presumption of different 'gender characters' and of a natural hierarchy between men and women. Diaries and other self-narratives offer the advantage of viewing family relationships from the practical, everyday perspectives of the hybrid subjects who were themselves involved as actors in the events they described. In recent research on such self-narratives, the picture that has emerged to date is markedly removed from the 'horizon of bourgeois values.'[14] We will take up this thread here.

---

11 On premodern rituals, see Lischka, *Liebe als Ritual*, chap. C; on wedding rituals, see Roper, "Going to Church and Street"; van Dülmen, "Fest der Liebe."
12 Beneke, *Tagebücher*, Caroline von Axen to Ferdinand Beneke, 14 April 1807, vol. 2.5, p. 262.
13 Langreiter 2010, entry for 3 June 1872, p. 57. On the southern German bourgeoisie, see R. Habermas, *Frauen und Männer*, 399; on large wedding celebrations and 'cousin marriage' in France, see Johnson, "Das 'Geschwister Archipel,'" 65.
14 On the German bourgeoisie, see esp. Trepp, *Sanfte Männlichkeit*; R. Habermas, *Frauen und Männer*; and B. Kuhn, *Familienstand*. On the Swiss bourgeoisie, see Tanner, *Arbeitsame Patrioten*. See

Our sources reveal many facets of the married couple: relationships in which the woman and the man constitute a loving couple, an educated couple, a working couple, a religious couple, and an artistic couple. We can identify both continuities and differences. Emotional inclination plays a role throughout, even when this is only expressed discreetly, in the intention and style of the text, as in the cases of Püschmann and Popp. The significance of love as an argument in favor of marriage, as one among many considerations in this decision, obviously differs drastically from couple to couple – especially since love must first be explored and established as such by those in the relationship, which is not always easy. Whether the emotionalization of family relationships is related to the formation of the bourgeois private sphere, as scholars often assume, is open to question: Does Adelheid Dwořak, in her one-room apartment in Inzersdorf, have no emotional relationship with her mother? Her text suggests the opposite. Although the young Püschmann leaves his parental home at the age of 14, he maintains a close, trusting relationship with his brother Ernst and his father. If we do not equate emotion exclusively with the feeling of love, then Ulrich Bräker and Salome Ambühl as well as Adelheid Dwořak's parents also conduct decidedly emotional marriages. Yet the language of Romanticism changed the expectations of married life permanently. Around 1800, the older model of companionship was replaced by the idea of friendship.[15] The spouses' companionship was legally set in stone in the early modern period and could only be effectively dissolved in very specific cases, such as adultery or 'malicious desertion' – and then only in Protestant territories. Faithful companionship found daily expression in joint work and housekeeping as well as spiritual communion, but nevertheless existed in some tension with the legal hierarchy between husband and wife. After 1800, marriage – understood as friendship – could continue the older companionship model while also emphasizing a felt kinship of soul and spirit. It meant more than loyalty – it was based on reciprocity. More than companionship, marriage in the sense of friendship accentuated empathy and inwardness (*Innerlichkeit*). This understanding of marriage can be found across all social classes in the relationships we have examined here. Bräker's plans for marriage still correspond to the older companionship model, while the Stettler-Herport's pietistically inflected concept of a harmonious marriage and familial inwardness already point beyond this horizon.

---

also the overview of the state of the field from an international perspective in Eibach and Lanzinger, *The Routledge History of the Domestic Sphere*.

15 See, e.g., Reckwitz, *Das hybride Subjekt*, 152: "The classic bourgeois marriage *is* friendship," which Reckwitz nevertheless equates with a "community of 'companions'" (ibid.); see also ibid., 145–66. On the idea of friendship as the basis of marital relations among the Bernese patriciate, see Wittwer Hesse, *Die Familie von Fellenberg*, 30–31.

As forms of relationship, friendship and love share the aspect of fragility. Looking at the Benekes as a loving, educated couple, and again at the Modersohn–Beckers almost one hundred years later as a loving, artistic couple, we can see that the more emphatically love is invoked, the more vulnerable it seems to be. In the case of Caroline and Ferdinand Beneke, this precipitates a delicate episode; in the cause of Paula and Otto Modersohn, their high standards almost bring down the marriage. Hegel was already aware of love's fragility: in his *Elements of the Philosophy of Right*, published in 1820, he counsels against the "contingency of passion" as a basis for marriage, since this would run counter to the vaunted principles of morality.[16]

We should not be surprised to find examples of both hierarchy and equality between the sexes in marriage relationships. However, if we take the contemporary gender model at the time as a foil, it is striking how often male dominance is challenged and countered in everyday marital life. Salome Ambühl, Caroline Beneke, Barbara Baumgartner, Anna Dwořak, Adelheid Popp, Mathilde Becker, and Paula Modersohn-Becker are all strong women in very different ways. At the same time, Ferdinand Beneke, Julius Popp, Carl Woldemar Becker, and Otto Modersohn make up a gallery of sensitive husbands and fathers. We know little about Adelheid Popp's spouse, but it is probably no coincidence that a sensitive masculinity coupled with a melancholic subjectivity found particular expression in the era around 1800, and then again around 1900 – that is, at both the beginning and the end of classic bourgeois modernity, when new concepts of gender identity were being discussed under the auspices of Romanticism and the avant-garde. This finding is all the more worthy of emphasis because, both in the period of the Napoleonic Wars and in the period just before the First World War, a completely different concept of masculinity – the 'military man' – came to dominate the field.[17]

Research on the subject has often been critical of the notion of newly separated spheres in everyday life – men in public, women in the home – as characteristic of the bourgeois nineteenth century. In fact, the everyday radius of even pietistically oriented women was by no means limited to the 'pious house' or otherwise domesticated. Indeed, among the educated middle class, pastors and lawyers as well as artists and intellectuals worked at home. Apart from gainful employment performed in the home, domesticity was also an important value for men.[18] Factory work, which the bourgeois Engels criticized, in fact frequently led to a reversal of the gender hierarchy in the household. However, we should not overlook the

---

16 Hegel, *Elements of the Philosophy of Right.* par. 163.
17 On 'gentle men,' see Trepp, *Sanfte Männlichkeit*; see also (briefly) Johnson, "Das 'Geschwister Archipel,'" 51; for essential research on hegemonic masculinity, see Connell, *Masculinities*.
18 See Tosh, *A Man's Place*; Sarti, "Men at Home."

fact that a functional as well as a spatial domestic order for men and for women did exist, and it corresponded to certain patterns in terms of gender roles. For example, Beneke's diary omits any mention of household activities – an eloquent silence that stands in striking contrast to the records kept by women, from Henriette Stettler-Herport to Paula Modersohn-Becker, who make everyday household stress a theme in their diaries. Bourgeois men had studies or libraries at home, and in the context of bourgeois domesticity they often had a gentleman's room or a smoker's lounge to which they could retire. Thus men who were physically present in the house were not always actually present – that is, not emotionally or attentively available. In terms of participating in intra-family communication, mothers – who were present at all times – could be distinguished in their roles from fathers, who were simultaneously quasi-present and absent. The second category includes not only the stay-at-home fathers upstairs in their studies, but also the 'sullen' fathers, like Baumgartner and Dvořak, who did not participate in conversation or sought refuge in the pub in the evening. However, one can also understand their wives' complaints about this behavior in another way: fathers had difficulty gaining access to the family communication networks of mutual trust in which dominant mothers like Luise von Axen, Anna Dvořak, and Mathilde Becker occupied the central role.

The nineteenth century was a century characterized by kinship and sibling relationships. It is true that one cannot always speak of trust and affection in such relationships, let alone love. Among siblings and in-laws there were (and still are) black sheep like Christoph Eglinger, love–hate relationships like that between Barbara Baumgartner and Maria Stawinoha, or those who simply lost track of each other. On the other hand, sisters and brothers, along with cousins, are almost universally among the most important contacts for our writing subjects and are prioritized accordingly. It was not only marriage, but also the (favored) sibling relationship that followed a model of friendship, with the necessary ingredients of emotionality and vulnerability. The pastor's wife Ursula Bruckner-Eglinger's inclination toward her younger brother Emanuel is strikingly pronounced. Ferdinand Beneke's relationship with his sister Regine, who lives in the same house, appears less intense. At the age of 17, Paula Becker sends a letter to her brother Kurt, who is three years older and with whom she would later engage in heated disputes: "But now here is a kiss, and another one, and imagine yourself properly, sisterly squeezed. If only I had you here, really, I would kiss you to my heart's content."[19]

---

[19] Paula to Kurt Becker, 26 April 1893, PMB, p. 75. On sibling relationships in the seventeenth century, see Ruppel, *Verbündete Rivalen*; in the nineteenth century, see Davidoff, *Thicker than Water*; and more recently, Kaufmann, "Gel(i)ebte Geschwister." On the following, see Sabean, "Kinship and Issues of the Self," 223.

Whether the 'family revolution' that took place around 1800 arose out of such emotionalized, borderline incestuous relationships between siblings, and whether they developed a new kind of language of love, is not a matter we can adjudicate in this chapter due to the small number of such case studies in this book. In this aspect as well, Paula Modersohn-Becker impresses the reader with her exceptional, teasingly playful openness.

The relationship between parents and their growing children also changed at the historical juncture when the children were no longer sent out of the house to take up an apprenticeship or enter into servitude at the age of 14. In this older mode, a child's early detachment from his or her parents meant that the family avoided some of the problems that arise in a new guise in the modern family as a community of care, provoked as they are by continued responsibility and dependence. In none of the families we have considered here is the communication between parents and children uniformly harmonious and untroubled. Nevertheless, it is striking that in most cases, follow-up communication does take place. Even the 'prodigal son' Christoph Eglinger is brought back into the family fold as a godfather. Paula Modersohn-Becker's attempt to break out of the normative bourgeois understanding of marriage leads to an all-the-more intense family exchange, with everyone sitting down at the same table again in the end. Just as there were favorite and problem siblings, so there were also favorite and problem children – who may in fact be one and the same person, like Theophil Bruckner, who sometimes plays one role, and sometimes the other. Family harmony was considered extremely important, and dissonant episodes that disturbed this harmony were perceived as serious and stressful.

Throughout and across classes, these self-narratives show that children were eminently important creators of meaning. At the same time, the aims of education shifted over time. For Henriette Stettler-Herport, education is still primarily a matter of raising godly, humane children who shun the vanities of the world. Fifty years later, her sister-in-faith Ursula Bruckner-Eglinger is already concerned with a bourgeois habitus: neat clothing, success at school, and individual achievement. Another fifty years later, despite the fact that her entries have become increasingly rare, Barbara Baumgartner considers her Hansi's triumphs at school as well as his piano lessons worth a mention in her diary. But we should not imagine that the bourgeois nineteenth century was monotonous and frozen in time. Around 1900, the Becker parents wanted their daughters to be independent and to receive professional training, so that they did not have to depend on securing an advantageous marriage.

Diaries and letters also shed light on the changing relationship between the family and their servants. Both the 'pious houses' at the end of the *ancien régime* and the Becker-Modersohn artist couple after 1900 have several maids – or at least one – to help them with the housekeeping. The number of servants in the household decreased over time. Both the housemother in the parsonage and the educated couple in the house on Holländischer Brook still maintain a personal relationship with their domestic servants, which in the first case is characterized by tense competition when it comes to raising children and the housemother's duty to exercise social control, and in the second case by a well-meaning sense of responsibility. One searches in vain for such a relationship in later self-narratives. We have to read some of the late nineteenth-century diaries very closely indeed to determine whether or not a maid is present at all. Püschmann's diary entries provide an interesting shift in perspective. For the journeyman craftsman, family ties with his landlords and sharing a meal at the same table with them are no longer desirable goals.

Small Rituals and Time-Outs

What is it that stabilized families as such, in the sense of reaffirmation and self-assurance, both externally and internally? When reading these sources, one comes across recurring practices that can be described as small rituals or rituals of interaction. As a rule, such rituals are not a type of 'grand spectacle' in which strictly standardized procedures are intended to have an effect on society at large, as is typical of social rituals in the face-to-face societies (*Anwesenheitsgesellschaften*) of the premodern era, but are rather characteristic practices charged with various meanings, which in this respect constitute more than simply a routine.[20] The concrete execution of such rituals is context dependent. In the muddle of everyday domestic life, the necessary dose of flexibility in carrying out such common or out-of-the-ordinary rituals is significant when it comes to their effectiveness. Here we must distinguish not only between rituals with more or less pronounced degrees of formalization, but also between domestic practices with a high degree of inwardness and those that involve the non-domestic public sphere as a stage. On the one hand, we could consider wedding celebrations that include promenading through the streets to church, organized entertainment for large companies, and Sunday outings; on the other hand, we could think of praying together as a family, table fellowship, or reading family letters together on Sundays.

It is easy to identify several types of meaning in these small rituals. Concerning the couple's image of themselves as a couple, activities such as praying together or even the father of the house preaching a sermon refer back to their shared

---

20 For a definition, see Stollberg-Rilinger, *Rituale*, esp. 9–14 and 45–47.

faith; joint reading sessions early in the morning or late in the evening indicate the educated couple; taking walks in the garden or around the ramparts symbolizes companionship; painting the same motif as one's spouse reflects an artistic communion of souls. The family as such comes together every day for meals, but also to exchange family news or to sing, in addition to special rituals at Christmas and birthdays. Sunday is 'family day' and is usually associated with sharing a meal – which, in the case of the pastor's wife in Basel, can be a source of stress. A number of other practices are closely related to modeling a particular habitus: table manners and conversational styles, as well as literary and musical literacy. This list undoubtedly reads as quite bourgeois. However, we should also consider the importance of Christmas and of bidding farewell to the deceased father in the proletarian Dwořak household, or of Püschmann's fellow apprentices reading aloud to each other in their shared living quarters. In 1848 the apprentices at the Grimma printworks politicized themselves not least by means of reading and discussion in their domestic sphere. Reading, singing, and making music together in the home were widespread practices far beyond the bourgeois milieu.

Rituals tied to access to the house correspond with power and status: Who has access, and who is allowed to be present? This question proves relevant not only when it comes to issuing invitations or establishing friendship, but also in sounding out marriage candidates. The preening merchant from Hamburg who wants to marry Tony Buddenbrook needs the express consent of her parents as his ticket into the house, and this consent is granted. This is not simply a matter of literary imagination. Ferdinand Beneke only sets eyes on his future bride, Caroline von Axen, because he has access to her parents' house as a friend. In Krems, the shop assistant Johann Baumgartner gains a decisive advantage over his competitors for the coachman's daughter Wetti Teuschl's hand when he repeatedly and visibly gains admittance to Anton Teuschl's home in full view of the small-town public. Particularly in the matchmaking process, not only structured, semi-private rituals of structured togetherness, but also playful practices publicly staged – such as promenading, holding hands, and escorting someone home for the evening – played an important role.

But were marriage, family, and domesticity consolidated only by means of rituals that cemented community and initiated identity? We might expect this to be so, yet in the light of these self-narratives, we can see that this was not the case. If we look at the other side of the balance sheet, we can even identify a kind of flanking maneuver in which time-outs were important for a couple. As we have already seen, larger houses offered spaces of retreat, and where these were lacking, husbands went to the pub, while wives visited their female friends. A time-out is understood here as a spectrum of possibilities for temporally limited distancing. Ulrich Bräker takes refuge from his wife's punitive sermons in his daughter-in-law's parlor, in the annex of his own house. Barbara Baumgartner moves back in with her parents for the foreseeable future. Caroline Beneke goes on a summer vacation with her children for a few weeks. Paula Modersohn-Becker follows a different, innovative path in the longer term. Apart from her repeated stays in Paris, each of which clearly consolidates her marriage emotionally, she also insists on having her own studio – a workspace separate from her husband's house – as a small kingdom unto herself.

This temporal distance in all its facets does not alter the importance of the small rituals mentioned above, but rather opens a space of further possibility for ritualized interaction at the moment of coming together again. The significance of communal practices for marriage and family relationships can be seen not least in the fact that deviant behavior on the part of the actors was perceived as very problematic. This applies to disturbances in everyday scenarios, such as loud arguments at the table, or absence or even exclusion from table fellowship, as well as to extraordinary events. Christmas is clearly so charged with meaning – not only in middle-class families, but also among the petite bourgeoisie and in working-class households – that quarrels during the festivities are remembered as particularly painful. If the reconciliation foreseen in dramaturgy does not occur at the father's deathbed, as in the Eglingers' case, then this constitutes a catastrophe. Meaningful rituals could and did become burdensome. After his wedding, the lawyer Beneke in Hamburg is so irritated by the fact that he is suddenly expected to sleep in a bed next to and with his young bride that he cannot sleep at all. After three nerve-wracking, sleepless nights, his wife suggests that he return to his old bed: "What a confounded beginning to my marriage."[21] In fact, this wedding night, which was primarily experienced as a very tiring event, was not associated with any kind of 'social magic.'

Work and Leisure

These self-narratives reveal that even in the bourgeois era, the house constitutes a multifunctional sphere and a venue in which very different practices take place. A clear separation between work and leisure is only discernible in the journeyman Püschmann's diary. As a young factory worker, Adelheid Dvořak has to take work home in the evening to earn extra money. On the whole, the domestic sphere in the

---

[21] Beneke, *Tagebücher*, entry for 12 June 1807, vol. 2.2, pp. 473–74. See also the letter that mentions Modersohn's 'nervousness' about sexual intercourse after the wedding: Paula to Otto Modersohn, 7 September 1906, PMB, pp. 557–58.

nineteenth century was less a place of leisure and recreation than a scene of work, industrious housekeeping, and hectic activity. For the Pietist bailiff's wife Henriette Stettler-Herport, 'work' is a key concept, although her activities cannot be described as gainful employment. The question of whether and to what extent the home was a workplace ultimately depends on the definition of work. Feminists have rightly pointed out that an overly narrow concept of work as paid labor excludes and devalues the informal work performed by women, which took place not least in the home.[22] In a broader sense, from the perspective of research on the subject, we can distinguish several types of work: first, paid labor; second, production and subsistence work; third, housekeeping practices; and fourth, educational and care work. Evidence of each of these four categories of work can be found in the self-narratives considered in this book. Notably, the majority of men's gainful employment was also tied to the domestic sphere. In contrast, paid labor among women is found only among women from the petite bourgeoisie and the lower classes. Farming as an economic sideline was an issue for a surprisingly long time: as late as 1893, Paula Becker reported on a potato field in the garden behind her parents' villa. Performing household chores, educating children, and caring for sick family members were tasks for which women, mothers, and wives – with the assistance of maidservants – were responsible. Unlike the working couple in the early modern period, however, bourgeois women and men generally no longer worked side by side in the same profession. This is an important difference. The overall picture of labor practices in the home broadens even further when we add status and representational practices, as I have suggested in previous chapters. Of course, representational work in the salon is a very different kind of labor than work performed at home (*Heimarbeit*) in the weaver's household. However, as the example of the patrician bailiff's wife shows, this work is still linked to effort and toil, and it requires a big time commitment, for which she has little motivation. This form of unpaid labor as a hostess and a representative wife led to an increase in social contacts and an expansion of the family network, which could then be directly translated into career opportunities for the husband. Such facets and shifts must be considered when we contrast an early modern 'two-supporter' model with a modern 'male-breadwinner' model.

    Home and family are widely regarded as the genuine sphere of the modern 'intimate subject' (*Intimitätssubjek*t; Reckwitz). Indeed, the trappings of an upscale home included not only a parlor, but also a study and a small library for intellec-

---

[22] See Whittle, "A Critique of Approaches to 'Domestic Work'"; Zucca Micheletto, "Paid and Unpaid Work"; Flather, "Space, Place, and Gender"; R. Habermas, *Frauen und Männer*, 395–96; and the contributions in Ågren, *Making a Living*.

tual work, reflection, and self-reflection – not least for writing entries in one's diary. Hours which the couple spends alone as a couple are predominantly described as happy, and only sometimes as boring or unsatisfying. In any case, such hours were relatively rare in the course of the day. A claim to 'quality time' as a couple is consistently formulated as a criterion of a good marriage, from the *ancien régime* to the period just prior to the First World War. Yet leisure and intimacy were not a permanent condition; in the majority of cases, they could be found only situationally. Wives and husbands who shared one-room households with children or tiny apartments with subtenants and nightly lodgers had to do without leisure and intimacy almost entirely. Thus the young Adelheid Dworak loved the few precious hours on Sundays that she spent with a book by the window in her one-room apartment in Vienna, which was occupied by three people.

Habitat as an Actor

Winston Churchill is said to have once remarked: "We shape our buildings and afterward buildings shape us."[23] Buildings are planned and constructed by people. But once the construct is a material reality, it has considerable repercussions for the everyday lives of the actors within it. This applies directly, to social relationships along a spectrum from openness to closure, and indirectly in a symbolic sense, as a message to outsiders about the material and cultural capital that a building's owners and residents have invested. In contrast to the topography of social interaction in premodern cities, the nineteenth century saw a greater differentiation between residential neighborhoods. Needless to say, it made a big difference whether one grew up in a working-class suburb or in a district filled with villas. Yet early photographs of Holländischer Brook in Hamburg, for example, show that middle-class living and older houses with modest furnishings were not yet effectively separated at that time. This habitat certainly suited the habitus of Ferdinand Beneke, who did not feel very comfortable in elite society, with its stilted conversational style. If we look at the history of housing in a broader perspective, we can identify long-term processes of segregation and differentiation of living space from as early as the late Middle Ages. Nevertheless, in the nineteenth century it is still true that the chance to demarcate a private sphere was not least a question of wealth and the means at one's disposal. An elaborate visiting culture presupposed a cost-intensive level of domestic comfort – or at least a parlor that was clearly separated from the sleeping quarters. The large house on Holländisch-

---

23 Cited in Gieryn, "What Buildings Do," 35.

er Brook finally afforded the Benekes the opportunity to socialize and to entertain larger groups. Those who did not have the opportunity to receive visitors and friends at home were at a disadvantage in terms of developing and maintaining a social network. It is striking to note that, across social boundaries and classes, all the families in this book that could be called successful had a network that manifested in a more or less continuous practice of visits and return visits.

One's residence and place of residence made – and still make – a statement about the respective actor. This is not a particularly bold assertion.[24] Nevertheless, we can point to several features specific to the period under investigation here. Rapid and frequent changes in rented accommodation, as in the case of the Baumgartners and of Mrs. Dworak and her daughter in Vienna, contradicted the bourgeois values of permanence and independence. The free citizen and the economically independent *Bürger* were best served by a detached house. A move to the poor suburbs of the expanding cities signaled a social decline. The referential function of one's house and domesticity – real as well as symbolic – is striking. For Bräker the peasant's son, having his own house was even a condition for his marriage, and only the house on the Hochsteig, the construction of which sent him into massive debt, made him a full human being in the eyes of his bride. In a different, namely moral way, the parsonage – constructed as a stately baroque building at the gates of 'pious Basel' – became a burden for the pastor's family. And what did a proletarian habitat such as that inhabited by the Inzersdorf *Strassler* do to a young person? The young girl Adelheid's recurring anxieties led to her stay in a psychiatric institution. A completely different symbolism emanated from Heinrich Vogeler's Barkenhoff around 1900. His imagination, concretized in the form of an elaborately converted farmhouse in the Art Nouveau style, remains emblematic of the Worpswede artists' colony today. The house provided this chosen family with a public image.

The subject must somehow relate to their house and habitat – but neither constitutes an irrevocable fate. None of the four sons raised at the Binningen parsonage later took up their father's profession. Adelheid Dworak became Adelheid Popp, an assertive politician with a penchant for bourgeois feminine accessories. The Worpswede 'family' and the marriages of the closely associated artist couples who participated in the colony quickly plunged into crisis, and so Vogeler changed the concept. After the First World War, he turned his Art Nouveau Barkenhoff into a commune, and later into a Rote Hilfe (International Red Aid) children's home.

---

[24] On the connection between habitus and lifestyle, see once again Bourdieu, *Die feinen Unterschiede*, chap. 5.

Between Privacy and Openness

Can we characterize the nineteenth century as the golden age of privacy? The discrepancy between the ideal and actual domestic practice remains striking. We cannot deny that intimacy was something people imagined and longed for – hence the weddings celebrated in intimate circles. It is true that around 1800, both the married couple's relationship and the housekeeping itself were domesticated in many respects. Yet we can also observe domestication in characteristic practices of sociability. Thus the result was not ultimately an increase in intimacy. The more self-narratives one reads, the more evidence emerges of the actual openness of home and family in practice. Here co-residence must be distinguished from co-presence: on the one hand, we have relatives who lived with the family permanently, servants, tenants, subtenants, and nightly lodgers; on the other hand, there were a variety of visitors who, for various reasons, gained access to the domestic interior for a short period of time. It was not only the writing subjects who participated in this visiting culture, but also the numerous people of both sexes mentioned in their diaries and letters. Among them one can identify close relatives, close friends, clients and colleagues, friends of the family at the table, and ladies visiting for tea. In contrast, compared to the 'open house' of the early modern period, neighbors – and thus the rituals of neighborly interaction – are absent. Neighborliness – that social, close-knit space – no longer carried the same importance it had in the centuries before 1800.[25] This is especially true for the urban living environment. In village contexts, female neighbors remained relevant and present as social contacts. The example of the workers' settlement at the gates of Vienna, to which the women who migrated from Bohemian rural society brought the traditional neighborly support practices of their place of origin, is impressive. The example of visiting practices in small towns and villages in the Erz Mountains around the middle of the century shows that visiting culture was certainly not limited to the elite bourgeois milieu. There were favored days and times for visits, particularly Sundays, but in principle visitors could turn up at the door on any day, at any time in the afternoon or evening. Mornings were reserved for professional or household business. Although gender-specific forms and occasions – such as coffee circles (*Kaffeekranz*) and voluntary associations (*Freundeverein*) – can be distinguished, in general women as well as men took part in the various forms of open domesticity.

---

25 For further details, see Eibach, "Das Haus in der Moderne," 31–34; Eibach, "From Open House to Privacy?," 358–59; for an overview, see Wrightson, "The 'Decline of Neighbourliness' Revisited."

From the perspective of the lower classes, the question of privacy obviously arose in a different way. The women of Inzersdorf cooked and kept house in communal kitchens in the newly built residences. A bed of one's own was not a given. In dormitories like the one at the Grimma printworks and on the journeymen's travels, people were used to sharing rooms and places to sleep. As long as the roommate was a trusted comrade, companion, or cousin, then no further privacy was sought. Even in bourgeois houses, the function of the rooms often changed, and this speaks against the idea that the rooms were designed for particular purposes or designated for particular individuals. The need for demarcation was more of a factor when it came to landlords and 'innkeepers' (*Wirtsleute*). Overall these domestic actors complained surprisingly little about co-presence and the lack of privacy. The elaborate *parcours* of paying and receiving visits was simply part of everyday life. From the perspective of the history of communication, we must bear in mind that the society described here got by without telephones or other more modern communication tools. We should not underestimate this fact: if a person wanted something from a client, a friend, or an acquaintance, they either had to write a letter or go there in person and knock on the door. In the examples we have seen from rural society, it is worth noting that many people took long journeys to pay a visit without knowing for sure whether they would actually manage to meet the person in question.

In addition to the broad acceptance of open domesticity, we can also observe attempts to regulate domestic openness. These include the introduction of visiting hours for clients during the workday and the way in which socializing was increasingly concentrated on regular events, such as family days or *jour fixes* with family friends. Thus we cannot speak of a permanent openness. In this sense, social selection mechanisms, which were already being imparted to children in the domestic environment, also had an effect on socializing. Over the course of the nineteenth century, the tendency toward exclusion and closure seems to have increased. The most impressive examples of repeated, elaborate visiting practices involving numerous people can be found in the self-narratives written in the time between the end of the *ancien régime* and about 1830. To this we must add the network consisting of the village schoolteacher Püschmann's relatives and neighbors at the beginning of the 1850s. By the end of the century, the Becker family's social life was dominated by long-distance kinship relations and short-term reciprocal visits.

In the end, the various pieces of the puzzle reveal an image of a distinct epoch of family history: the era of open domesticity. The families I have described here functioned differently than households in the early modern period, and also differently than families in the second heyday of the bourgeois nuclear family, after 1945 and even today. The different ways in which people dealt with privacy and openness in the domestic sphere are striking. Communication and various other aspects of everyday life provided reasons for this open domesticity. We can certainly observe some practices that were carried over from the early modern period, although – in contrast to the 'open house' model in the period prior to 1800 – other characteristic aspects are missing from the picture. This is true of the bourgeois milieu – less so among the lower classes – when it comes to female work performed collectively and public housekeeping among women; it is also true across social groups when it comes to the old shaming rituals used as social control mechanisms to regulate matchmaking and marriage.[26] The contrast between the ideal of respectable domesticity and the actual practice of everyday domesticity remains striking. The openness of the domestic microcosm around and after 1800 cannot be explained simply as a functional logic of everyday life, nor as a habit handed down from the early modern period. Instead, the ways of doing and living home and family that we have observed throughout this book corresponded to the basic idea of the new society as a free association of citizens engaging with one another. This utopian socialization program was linked to domestic sociability between friends.[27] Therefore it makes sense that social milieus such as the bourgeoisie were established and shaped in this era, and that horizontal networks became increasingly important. Open domesticity combined the new cult of the family with the bourgeois public sphere, and this openness certainly included women.

---

26 For further details, see Eibach, "Das offene Haus"; on hospitality in the premodern period, see Jancke, *Gastfreundschaft*.
27 For an overview, see Sting, "Freundschaft als soziale Utopie," 61; on Hamburg as an example, see Trepp, *Sanfte Männlichkeit*, 370–72; on the following, see Weckel, *Zwischen Häuslichkeit und Öffentlichkeit*; Sabean, "Kinship and Class Dynamics."

List of Figures

Chapter 1

Fig. 1: The Forester Wilhelm Heinrich Seyd and Family (1845), by Joseph Hartmann. Source: Hessisches Landesmuseum, Darmstadt, Germany

Chapter 3

Fig. 2: Ulrich Bräker and Salome Ambühl. Source: Bernisches Historisches Museum, Bern, Switzerland

Fig. 3: Bräker's House with the Extension, Hochsteig, near Wattwil, by Heinrich Thomann. Source: Toggenburg Museum, Lichtensteig, Switzerland

Chapter 4

Fig. 4: Henriette Stettler-Herport's Tally Sheet of Transgressions, Pastimes, and States of Mind, April 1774. Source: Journal de mes actions, Burgerbibliothek Bern, FA Stettler 12.4

Fig. 5: Henriette Stettler-Herport's Tally Sheet of Transgressions, Pastimes, and States of Mind, January–June 1786. Source: Journal de mes actions, Burgerbibliothek Bern, FA Stettler 12.5

Fig. 6: Henriette Stettler-Herport (artist unknown). Source: Journal de mes actions, Burgerbibliothek Bern, FA Stettler 12.4

Fig. 7: Official Residence of the Frienisberg Bailiwick (Bern), c. 1670. Source: Bernisches Historisches Museum, Bern

Chapter 5

Fig. 8: The Beneke Family, daguerreotype dated 1844. Source: Museum für Hamburgische Geschichte, Hamburg, Germany

Fig. 9: The Beneke Family Home (right-hand side), 67 Holländischer Brook, Hamburg. Source: Otto Beneke, Liederkranz zum Andenken an das alte Beneke'sche Haus, Hamburg 1849

Fig. 10: The view down Holländischer Brook to the west; Beneke's house was on the left-hand side. Source: Bernd Nasner

Chapter 6

Fig. 11: Castle and Parsonage (No. 3), Binningen 1738, by Emanuel Büchel. Source: Staatsarchiv Basel-Stadt, Bild_Falk._Fb_2.7

Fig. 12: Binningen Parsonage 1842 (artist unknown). Source: Kantonsmuseum Baselland, Liestal, Switzerland

Chapter 7

Fig. 13: Friedrich Anton Püschmann in his old age. Source: Matthias John

Fig. 14: The former printworks building on Frauenstraße in Grimma, as it appears today. Source: Wikimedia Commons

https://doi.org/10.1515/9783111081700-013

Chapter 8

Fig. 15: Johann and Barbara Baumgartner's wedding photo, 1872. Source: Private collection
Fig. 16: The Baumgartners' (formerly the Teuschls') house on 7 Herzogstraße in Krems, with the store on the ground floor, 1901. Source: Private collection
Fig. 17: The Baumgartner Family, c. 1885. Source: Private collection

Chapter 9

Fig. 18: Adelheid Popp, née Dwořak. Source: Wikimedia Commons
Fig. 19: A brickmaking family in Vösendorf, barefoot at work. Source: Historical archive of the Wienerberger company
Fig. 20: Inzersdorf near Vienna, 16–20 Triester Straße, a workers' house prior to demolition in 2016. Source: Karin M. Hofer

Chapter 10

Fig. 21: The Becker family at tea in the garden. Source: Paula Modersohn Becker Stiftung, Bremen
Fig. 22: Summer Evening (Concert) at Barkenhoff, by Heinrich Vogeler, 1905. Source: akg-images
Fig. 23: Paula Becker and Otto Modersohn on a bench in the garden of their house in Worpswede, 1904. Source: Otto Modersohn Stiftung, Fischerhude

Bibliography

Primary Sources: Unpublished

[Bruckner-Eglinger, Ursula], Universitätsbibliothek Basel, Lebenslauf & Leichenrede von Frauen; Respinger, Johann Rudolf. July 2, 1876, Fz. 251: 1876 Bruckner-Eglinger.
Burgerbibliothek Bern, Stettler-Herport, Henriette. Journal de mes actions, 5 vols. FA Stettler 12 (1–5).
Kirchenbücher Gemeinde Hartenstein (Saxony), "Taufen," 1832, pp. 427–28; "Trauungen," 1856, pp. 507–08; 1859, pp. 543–44.

Primary Sources: Published

Allgemeines Landrecht für die Preußischen Staaten. June 1, 1794, part 2, first title, "Von der Ehe." opinioiuris.de/quelle/1623.
Beneke, Ferdinand. *Die Tagebücher*. Edited by Frank Hatje and Ariane Smith. 4 series (3 published to date). Göttingen: Wallstein, 2012–2019.
Bräker, Ulrich. *Lebensgeschichte und Natürliche Ebentheuer des Armen Mannes im Tockenburg*. Edited by H. H. Füßli. In *Ulrich Bräker, Sämtliche Schriften*, vol. 4: *Lebensgeschichte und vermischte Schriften*, edited by Andreas Bürgi et al., 355–557. Munich: C. H. Beck, 2000.
Bräker, Ulrich. *Tagebücher*. In *Ulrich Bräker, Sämtliche Schriften*, 3 vols., edited by Andreas Bürgi et al. Munich: C. H. Beck, 2000.
Engels, Friedrich. *The Condition of the Working Class in England in 1844*. Cambridge: Cambridge University Press, 2010.
Engels, Friedrich, and Karl Marx. *The Manifesto of the Communist Party*. New York: International Publishers, 1948.
Freund, Georg. *Inzersdorf am Wienerberge. Historisch-topografische Darstellung des Ortes und seiner Bestandtheile vom Ursprunge bis in die neueste Zeit*. Inzersdorf am Wienerberge: n. p., 1882.
[Görnandt, Antonie]. *Die von der Tochter verfasste Lebensskizze F. A. Püschmanns: "Vom Schriftsetzer zum Lehrerbildner: Friedrich Anton Püschmann."* In Püschmann, Friedrich Anton, *Das Tagebuch des Buchdruckerlehrlings Friedrich Anton Püschmann während der Revolution von 1848/49 und der Restaurationsepoche von 1850 bis 1856*, edited by Matthias John, 3:841–52. Berlin: trafo, (1920) 2015.
Gotthelf, Jeremias. *Wie fünf Mädchen im Branntwein jämmerlich umkommen. Eine merkwürdige Geschichte*. Bern: Wagnersche Buchhandlung, 1838.
Hagenbuch, Bernadette, ed. *"Heute war ich bey Lisette in der Visite." Die Tagebücher der Basler Pfarrersfrau Ursula Bruckner-Eglinger, 1816–1833*. Basel: Schwabe, 2014.
Hegel, G. W. F. *Elements of the Philosophy of Right*. Edited by Allen W. Wood. Translated by H. B. Nisbet. Cambridge: Cambridge University Press, 1991.
John, Matthias, ed. *Das Tagebuch des Buchdruckerlehrlings Friedrich Anton Püschmann während der Revolution von 1848/49 und der Restaurationsepoche von 1850 bis 1856*. 3 vols. Berlin: trafo, 2015.
Krünitz, Johann Georg. *Oekonomische Encyklopädie, oder allgemeines System der Staats-, Stadt-, Haus- und Landwirthschaft in alphabetischer Ordnung, 1773–1858*. www.kruenitz1.uni-trier.de/.

Langreiter, Nikola, ed. *Tagebuch von Wetti Teuschl (1870–1885)*. L'Homme Archiv, vol. 4. Cologne: Böhlau, 2010.

Mann, Thomas. *Buddenbrooks. Verfall einer Familie*. Edited by Eckhard Heftrich. Frankfurt am Main: Fischer, (1901) 2002. Published in English as: *Buddenbrooks. The Decline of a Family*, Lowe-Porter, H.T., 1922.

Modersohn-Becker, Paula. *Paula Modersohn-Becker in Briefen und Tagebüchern [PMB]*. Edited by Günter Busch and Liselotte von Reinken. Frankfurt am Main 2007

Modersohn-Becker, Paula, and Otto Modersohn. *Paula Modersohn-Becker and Otto Modersohn: Der Briefwechsel [PMB/OM]*. Edited by Antje Modersohn and Wolfgang Werner. Berlin: Insel, 2017.

Popp, Adelheid. *Jugend einer Arbeiterin*. Edited by Sibylle Hamann. Vienna: Picus (1909) 2019. Published in English as: *The Autobiography of a Working Woman*. Translated by F. C. Harvey. London: T. Fisher Unwin, 1912.

Riehl, Wilhelm Heinrich. *Die Naturgeschichte des Volkes als Grundlage einer deutschen Social-Politik*, vol. 3: *Die Familie*. 6th ed. Stuttgart: Cotta, (1855) 1862.

Rotteck, Carl von. "Familie, Familienrecht (natürliches)." In *Staats-Lexikon oder Encyclopädie der Staatswissenschaften*, edited by Carl von Rotteck and Carl Welcker, 5:385–408. Altona: Hammerich, 1837.

Selected Research Literature

Ågren, Maria. "Lower State Servants and Home Office Work." In *The Routledge History of the Domestic Sphere in Europe: 16th to 19th Century*, edited by Joachim Eibach and Margareth Lanzinger, 120–33. London: Routledge, 2020.

Ågren, Maria, ed. *Making a Living, Making a Difference: Gender and Work in Early Modern European Society*. Oxford: Oxford University Press, 2016.

Ariès, Philippe. *Geschichte der Kindheit*. 8th ed. Munich: dtv, 1988. Published in English as: *Centuries of Childhood*. Harmondsworth: Penguin, 1979.

Ariès, Philippe, and Georges Duby, eds. *Geschichte des privaten Lebens*, vol. 4: *Von der Revolution zum Großen Krieg*. Augsburg: S. Fischer, 1999. Published in English as: *A History of Private Life*, vol. 4: *From the Fires of Revolution to the Great War*. Cambridge, MA: Belknap, 1994.

Arni, Caroline. *Entzweiungen. Die Krise der Ehe um 1900*. Cologne: Böhlau, 2004.

Aschmann, Birgit, and Rebekka Habermas, eds. *Durchbruch der Moderne? Neue Perspektiven auf das 19. Jahrhundert*. Frankfurt am Main: Campus, 2019.

Bänziger, Peter-Paul. *Die Moderne als Erlebnis. Eine Geschichte der Konsum- und Arbeitsgesellschaft, 1840–1940*. Göttingen: Wallstein, 2020.

Bänziger, Peter-Paul. "Jenseits der Bürgerlichkeit: Tagebuch schreiben in den Konsum- und Arbeitsgesellschaften des 20. Jahrhunderts." In *Selbstreflexionen und Weltdeutungen. Tagebücher in der Geschichte und der Geschichtsschreibung des 20. Jahrhunderts*, edited by Janosch Steuwer and Rüdiger Graf, 186–206. Göttingen: Wallstein, 2015.

Bänziger, Peter-Paul. *Sex als Problem. Körper und Intimbeziehungen in Briefen an die 'Liebe Marta'*. Frankfurt am Main: Campus, 2010.

Barlösius, Eva. *Naturgemäße Lebensführung. Zur Geschichte der Lebensreform um die Jahrhundertwende*. Frankfurt am Main: Campus, 1997.

Baumert, Susan. *Bürgerliche Familienfeste im Wandel. Spielarten privater Festkultur in Weimar und Jena um 1800*. Frankfurt am Main: Peter Lang, 2014.

Baur, Esther. "'Sich schreiben.' Zur Lektüre des Tagebuchs von Anna Maria Preiswerk-Iselin (1758–1840)." In *Von der dargestellten Person zum erinnerten Ich. Europäische Selbstzeugnisse als historische Quelle (1500–1850)*, edited by Kaspar von Greyerz et al., 113–34. Cologne: Böhlau, 2001.
Beck, Rainer. "Frauen in Krise. Eheleben und Ehescheidung in der ländlichen Gesellschaft Bayerns während des Ancien régime." In *Dynamik der Tradition. Studien zur historischen Kulturforschung IV*, edited by Richard van Dülmen, 137–212. Frankfurt am Main: S. Fischer, 1992.
Beck, Rainer. "Illegitimität und voreheliche Sexualität auf dem Land. Unterfinning, 1671–1770." In *Kultur der einfachen Leute*, edited by Richard van Dülmen, 112–50. Munich: C. H. Beck, 1983.
Berger, Renate, ed. *Liebe Macht Kunst. Künstlerpaare im 20. Jahrhundert*. Cologne: Böhlau, 2000.
Bischoff, Lucas. "Der Himmel über Hamburg. Die Wetteraufzeichnungen in Ferdinand Benekes Tagebüchern zwischen 1811 und 1816." Masters thesis, University of Bern, 2018.
Blasius, Dirk. *Ehescheidung in Deutschland 1794–1945*. Göttingen: Vandenhoeck & Ruprecht, 1987.
Blom, Philipp. *Der taumelnde Kontinent. Europa 1900–1914*. Munich: Hanser, 2009. Published in English as: *The Vertigo Years: Change and Culture in the West, 1910–1914*. New York: Basic Books, 2010.
Blum, Sabine, et al. "Soziologische Perspektiven." In *Multidisziplinäre Perspektiven der Resilienzforschung*, edited by Rüdiger Wink, 151–78. Wiesbaden: Springer, 2016.
Bödeker, Hans-Erich. "Die 'gebildeten Stände' im späten 18. und frühen 19. Jahrhundert: Zugehörigkeit und Abgrenzungen, Mentalitäten und Handlungspotentiale." In *Bildungsbürgertum im 19. Jahrhundert*, vol. 4: *Politischer Einfluss und gesellschaftliche Formation*, edited by Jürgen Kocka, 21–52. Stuttgart: Klett-Cotta, 1989.
Böning, Holger. "Der lesende Bauer aus dem Toggenburg." *Schweizer Monatshefte. Zeitschrift für Politik, Wirtschaft, Kultur* 87 (2007): 62–64.
Böning, Holger. *Ulrich Bräker. Der Arme Mann aus dem Toggenburg – Eine Biographie*. Zürich: Orell Fuessli, 1998.
Böth, Mareike. "'Ich handele, also bin ich.' Selbstzeugnisse praxeologisch lesen." *Geschichte in Wissenschaft und Unterricht* 69 (2018): 253–70.
Borscheid, Peter. "Geld und Liebe. Zu den Auswirkungen des Romantischen auf die Partnerwahl im 19. Jahrhundert." In *Ehe, Liebe, Tod. Zum Wandel der Familie, der Geschlechts- und Generationsbeziehungen in der Neuzeit*, edited by Peter Borscheid and Hans Jürgen Teuteberg, 112–34. Münster: Coppenrath, 1983.
Bourdieu, Pierre. "Das Haus oder die verkehrte Welt." In *Entwurf einer Theorie der Praxis*, edited by Pierre Bourdieu, 48–65. 3rd ed. Frankfurt am Main: Suhrkamp, 2012.
Bourdieu, Pierre. *Die feinen Unterschiede. Kritik der gesellschaftlichen Urteilskraft*. Frankfurt am Main: Suhrkamp, 1987. Published in English as: *Distinction: A Social Critique of the Judgement of Taste*. London: Routledge, 2015.
Bourdieu, Pierre. "Ökonomisches Kapital, kulturelles Kapital, soziales Kapital." In *Soziale Ungleichheiten*, edited by Reinhard Kreckel, 183–98. Göttingen: Otto Schwartz, 1983.
Bourdieu, Pierre, *Outline of a Theory of Practice*. 18th ed. Cambridge: Cambridge University Press, 2004.
Bourdieu, Pierre, and Loïc Wacquant. *Reflexive Anthropologie*. 4th ed. Frankfurt am Main: Suhrkamp, 2017. Published in English as: *An Invitation to Reflexive Sociology*. Cambridge: Polity Press, 1992.
Brändle, Fabian, et al. "Texte zwischen Erfahrung und Diskurs. Probleme der Selbstzeugnisforschung." In *Von der dargestellten Person zum erinnerten Ich. Europäische Selbstzeugnisse als historische Quelle (1500–1850)*, edited by Kaspar von Greyerz et al., 3–31. Cologne: Böhlau, 2001.

Breit, Stefan. *"Leichtfertigkeit" und ländliche Gesellschaft. Voreheliche Sexualität in der frühen Neuzeit.* Munich: Oldenbourg, 1991.

Brüggemeier, Franz Josef, and Lutz Niethammer. "Schlafgänger, Schnapskasinos und schwerindustrielle Kolonie. Aspekte der Arbeiterwohnungsfrage im Ruhrgebiet vor dem Ersten Weltkrieg." In *Fabrik – Familie – Feierabend. Beiträge zur Sozialgeschichte im Industriezeitalter*, edited by Jürgen Reulecke and Wolfhard Weber, 135–75. Wuppertal: Hammer, 1978.

Brunner, Otto. "Das 'ganze Haus' und die alteuropäische 'Ökonomik.'" In *Neue Wege der Verfassungs- und Sozialgeschichte*, edited by Otto Brunner, 103–27. 2nd ed. Göttingen: Vandenhoeck & Ruprecht, 1968.

Budde, Gunilla-Friederike. *Auf dem Weg ins Bürgerleben. Kindheit und Erziehung in deutschen und englischen Bürgerfamilien 1840–1914.* Göttingen: Vandenhoeck & Ruprecht, 1994.

Budde, Gunilla-Friederike. *Blütezeit des Bürgertums. Bürgerlichkeit im 19. Jahrhundert.* Darmstadt: wbg Academic, 2009.

Budde, Gunilla-Friederike. "Das Dienstmädchen." In *Der Mensch des 19. Jahrhunderts*, edited by Ute Frevert and Heinz-Gerhard Haupt, 148–75. Essen: Magnus, 2004.

Budde, Gunilla-Friederike, ed. *Bürgertum nach dem bürgerlichen Zeitalter. Leitbilder und Praxis seit 1945.* Göttingen: Vandenhoeck & Ruprecht, 2010.

Bude, Heinz, et al., eds. *Bürgerlichkeit ohne Bürgertum. In welchem Land leben wir?* Munich: Wilhelm Fink, 2010.

Bürgi, Andreas. "Das Reisen, die Schlacht. Zu einer Voraussetzung von Ulrich Bräkers Tagebuch." In *Schreibsucht. Autobiografische Schriften des Pietisten Ulrich Bräker (1735–1798)*, edited by Alfred Messerli and Adolf Muschg, 116–28. Göttingen: Vandenhoeck & Ruprecht, 2004.

Burghartz, Susanna. *Zeiten der Reinheit – Orte der Unzucht. Ehe und Sexualität in Basel während der Frühen Neuzeit.* Paderborn: Schöningh, 1999.

Burghartz, Susanna. "Zwischen Integration und Ausgrenzung. Zur Dialektik reformierter Ehetheologie am Beispiel Heinrich Bullingers." *L'Homme* 8 (1997): 30–42.

Burguière, Andrè, and Francois Lebrun. "Die Vielfalt der Familienmodelle in Europa." In *Geschichte der Familie*, vol. 3, edited by André Burguière et al., 13–118. Frankfurt am Main: Campus, 1997. Published in English as: *A History of the Family*. Cambridge, MA: Belknap, 1996.

Burkart, Günter. *Familiensoziologie.* Konstanz: UTB, 2008.

Busch, Günther. "Paula Modersohn-Becker, ihre Briefe und Tagebücher und ihre Kunst." In *Paula Modersohn-Becker in Briefen und Tagebüchern*, edited by Günther Busch and Liselotte von Reinken, 19–41. Frankfurt am Main: S. Fischer, 2007.

Butler, Judith. *Das Unbehagen der Geschlechter.* 17th ed. Frankfurt am Main: Suhrkamp, 2014. Published in English as: *Gender Trouble*. New York: Routledge, 1990.

Capp, Bernard. *When Gossips Meet. Women, Family and Neighbourhood in Early Modern England.* Oxford: Oxford University Press, 2003.

Chaloupek, Günther. "Industriestadt Wien." In *Wien Wirtschaftsgeschichte 1740–1938*, part 2: *Dienstleistungen*, edited by Günther Chaloupek et al., 267–484. Vienna: Jugend & Volk, 1991.

Clark, Christopher. *Preußen. Aufstieg und Niedergang 1600–1947.* 7th ed. Munich: DVA, 2007. Published in English as: *Iron Kingdom: The Rise and Downfall of Prussia, 1600–1947*. London: Penguin, 2007.

Claudon, Francis. "Hausmusik." In *Deutsche Erinnerungsorte*, vol. 3, edited by Étienne François, 138–53. Munich: C. H. Beck, 2001.

Cockayne, Emily. *Cheek by Jowl: A History of Neighbours.* London: Bodley Head, 2012.

Connell, Robert W. *Masculinities.* Berkeley: University of California Press, 1995.

Conrad, Christoph, et al., eds. *Wohnen und die Ökonomie des Raums*. Schweizerisches Jahrbuch für Wirtschafts- und Sozialgeschichte 28. Zürich: Chronos, 2014.
Cottier, Maurice. *Ehre, Subjekt und Kriminalität am Übergang zur Moderne. Das Beispiel Bern 1868–1941*. Konstanz: UVK, 2017.
Csáky, Moritz. *Das Gedächtnis der Städte. Kulturelle Verflechtungen – Wien und die urbanen Milieus in Zentraleuropa*. Vienna: Böhlau, 2010.
Darnton, Robert. *Das große Katzenmassaker. Streifzüge durch die französische Kultur vor der Revolution*. Munich: Carl Hanser, 1989. Published in English as: *The Great Cat Massacre: And Other Episodes in French Cultural History*. London: Penguin Books, 1991.
Davidoff, Leonore. *Thicker than Water. Siblings and their Relations, 1780–1920*. Oxford: Oxford University Press, 2012.
Davidoff, Leonore, and Catherine Hall. *Family Fortunes. Men and Women of the English Middle Class 1780–1850*. Chicago: University of Chicago Press, 1991.
De Capitani, François, and Brigitte Schnegg. "Die Oberschicht der Hauptstadt als gesellschaftliche Kerngruppe." In *Berns goldene Zeit. Das 18. Jahrhundert neu entdeckt*, edited by André Holenstein, 142–53. Bern: Stämpfli, 2008.
De Certeau, Michel. *Kunst des Handelns*. Berlin: Merve, 1988.
De Certeau, Michel. *The Practice of Everyday Life*. Berkeley: University of California Press, 1988.
Deines, Stefan, et al., ed. *Historisierte Subjekte – Subjektivierte Historie. Zur Verfügbarkeit und Unverfügbarkeit von Geschichte*. Berlin: De Gruyter, 2003.
Dellsperger, Rudolf. "Der Pietismus in der Schweiz." In *Geschichte des Pietismus*, vol. 2, edited by Martin Brecht et al., 588–616. Göttingen: Vandenhoeck & Ruprecht, 1995.
Dellsperger, Rudolf. *Die Anfänge des Pietismus in Bern*. Göttingen: Vandenhoeck & Ruprecht, 1984.
Dellsperger, Rudolf. "Pietismus." *Historisches Lexikon der Schweiz*. October 19, 2010. hls-dhs-dss.ch/de/articles/011424/2010-10-19/.
Dejung, Christof, et al. "Worlds of the Bourgeoisie." In *The Global Bourgeoisie. The Rise of the Middle Classes in the Age of Empire*, edited by Christof Dejung, et al., 1–40. Princeton: Princeton University Press, 2019.
Dibie, Pascal. *Wie man sich bettet. Die Kulturgeschichte des Schlafzimmers*. Stuttgart: Klett-Cotta, 1989.
Dirlmeier, Ulf, ed. *Geschichte des Wohnens*, vol. 2: *500–1800, Hausen, Wohnen, Residieren*. Stuttgart: DVA, 1998.
Dober, Birgit, et al. "Strittige Scheidungen vor dem Wiener Zivilmagistrat (1786–1850). Ein Projektbericht." *Frühneuzeit-Info* 30 (2019): 188–95.
Dobson, Miriam. "Letters." In *Reading Primary Sources: The Interpretation of Texts from Nineteenth- and Twentieth-Century History*, edited by Miriam Dobson and Benjamin Ziemann, 57–73. London: Routledge, 2009.
Dorgerloh, Annette. "Beseelung der Bilderscheinung. Porträt und Selbstbildnis im 19. Jahrhundert." In *Geschichte der bildenden Kunst in Deutschland*, vol. 7: *Vom Biedermeier zum Impressionismus*, edited by Hubertus Kohle, 433–53. Darmstadt: Prestel, 2008.
Dubler, Anne-Marie. "Landesherrschaft und Landesverwaltung." In *Berns goldene Zeit. Das 18. Jahrhundert neu entdeckt*, edited by André Holenstein, 446–52. Bern: Stämpfli, 2008.
Dülmen, Richard van. *Die Entdeckung des Individuums 1500–1800*. Frankfurt am Main: S. Fischer, 1997.
Dülmen, Richard van. "Fest der Liebe. Heirat und Ehe in der Frühen Neuzeit." In *Gesellschaft der frühen Neuzeit: Kulturelles Handeln und sozialer Prozess*, edited by Richard van Dülmen, 194–235. Vienna: Böhlau, 1993.

Dülmen, Richard van. "Freundschaftskult und Kultivierung der Individualität um 1800." In *Entdeckung des Ich. Die Geschichte der Individualisierung vom Mittelalter bis zur Gegenwart*, edited by Richard van Dülmen, 267–86. Cologne: Böhlau, 2001.
Dülmen, Richard van, ed. *Entdeckung des Ich. Die Geschichte der Individualisierung vom Mittelalter bis zur Gegenwart*. Cologne: Böhlau, 2001.
Ehmer, Josef. "Ehekonsens." *Enzyklopädie der Neuzeit*, 3:60–62. Stuttgart: J. B. Metzler, 2006.
Ehmer, Josef. "Wohnen ohne eigene Wohnung. Zur sozialen Stellung von Untermietern und Bettgehern." In *Wohnen im Wandel. Beiträge zur Geschichte des Alltags in der bürgerlichen Gesellschaft*, edited by Lutz Niethammer, 132–50. Wuppertal: Hammer, 1979.
Eibach, Joachim. "Das Haus in der Moderne." In *Das Haus in der Geschichte Europas. Ein Handbuch*, edited by Joachim Eibach and Inken Schmidt-Voges, 19–37. Berlin: De Gruyter, 2015.
Eibach, Joachim. "Das offene Haus. Kommunikative Praxis im sozialen Nahraum der europäischen Frühen Neuzeit." *Zeitschrift für historische Forschung* 38 (2011): 621–64.
Eibach, Joachim. "Der Kampf um die Hosen und die Justiz – Ehekonflikte in Frankfurt im 18. Jahrhundert." In *Kriminalität in Mittelalter und Früher Neuzeit. Soziale, rechtliche, philosophische und literarische Aspekte*, edited by Sylvia Kesper-Biermann and Diethelm Klippel, 167–88. Wiesbaden: Harrassowitz, 2007.
Eibach, Joachim. "Die Schubertiade. Bürgerlichkeit, Hausmusik und das Öffentliche im Privaten." *Themenportal Europäische Geschichte*. 2008. www.europa.clio-online.de/essay/id/fdae-1462.
Eibach, Joachim. "From Open House to Privacy? Domestic Life from the Perspective of Diaries." In *The Routledge History of the Domestic Sphere in Europe: 16th to 19th Century*, edited by Joachim Eibach and Margareth Lanzinger, 347–63. London: Routledge, 2020.
Eibach, Joachim. "The *Everyday Life:* Still a Challenge for Historians?" In *Körper – Macht – Geschlecht. Einsichten und Aussichten zwischen Mittelalter und Gegenwart. Festschrift für Claudia Opitz*, edited by Anna Becker et al., 99–110. Frankfurt am Main: Campus, 2020.
Eibach, Joachim, and Margareth Lanzinger, eds. *The Routledge History of the Domestic Sphere in Europe: 16th to 19th Century.* London: Routledge, 2020.
Eibach, Joachim, and Inken Schmidt-Voges, eds. *Das Haus in der Geschichte Europas. Ein Handbuch.* Berlin: De Gruyter, 2015.
Eigner, Peter. "Mechanismen urbaner Expansion: Am Beispiel der Wiener Stadtentwicklung 1740–1938." In *Wien Wirtschaftsgeschichte 1740–1938*, part 2: *Dienstleistungen*, edited by Günther Chaloupek et al., 623–756. Vienna: Jugend & Volk, 1991.
Endreß, Martin, and Andrea Maurer. "Introduction." In *Resilienz im Sozialen. Theoretische und empirische Analysen*, edited by Martin Endreß and Andrea Maurer, 7–14. Wiesbaden: Springer, 2015.
Ernst, Katharina. *Krankheit und Heiligung. Die medikale Kultur württembergischer Pietisten im 18. Jahrhundert*. Stuttgart: Kohlhammer, 2003.
Fahrmeir, Andreas. "Das Bürgertum des 'bürgerlichen Jahrhunderts': Fakt oder Fiktion?" In *Bürgerlichkeit ohne Bürgertum. In welchem Land leben wir?*, edited by Heinz Bude et al., 23–32. Munich: Wilhelm Fink, 2010.
Farge, Arlette. *"Das brüchige Leben." Verführung und Aufruhr im Paris des 18. Jahrhunderts*. Berlin: Wagenbach, 1989. Published in English as: *Fragile Lives: Violence, Power and Solidarity in Eighteenth-Century Paris*. Cambridge, MA: Harvard University Press, 1993.
Fertig, Christine. *Familie, verwandtschaftliche Netzwerke und Klassenbildung im ländlichen Westfalen (1750–1874)*. Stuttgart: Lucius & Lucius, 2012.

Fertig, Christine. "Rural Society and Social Networks in Nineteenth-Century Westphalia: The Role of Godparenting in Social Mobility." *Journal of Interdisciplinary History* 39, no. 4 (2009): 497–522.
Fertig, Christine. "Social Networks and Class Formation in the Rural Society. A Comparative Micro-Analysis (Westphalia, 1750–1874)." *Archiv für Sozialgeschichte* 54 (2014): 25–53.
Flather, Amanda. "Space, Place, and Gender: The Sexual and Spatial Division of Labor in the Early Modern Household." *History and Theory* 52 (2013): 344–60.
Foucault, Michel. *Sexualität und Wahrheit 1: Der Wille zum Wissen*. Frankfurt am Main: Suhrkamp, 1983. Published in English as: *The History of Sexuality 1. The Will to Knowledge*. New York: Pantheon Books, 1978.
Foucault, Michel. "Technologies of the Self." In *Technologies of the Self: A Seminar with Michel Foucault*, edited by Luther H. Martin et al., 16–49. Amherst: University of Massachussetts Press, 1988.
Frevert, Ute. "Defining Emotions: Concepts and Debates over Three Centuries." In *Emotional Lexicons: Continuity and Change in the Vocabulary of Feeling 1700–2000*, edited by Ute Frevert and Thomas Dixon, 1–31. Oxford: Oxford University Press, 2014.
Frevert, Ute. "Der Künstler." In *Der Mensch des 19. Jahrhunderts*, edited by Ute Frevert and Heinz-Gerhard Haupt, 292–323. Essen: Magnus, 2004.
Frevert, Ute. *Mächtige Gefühle. Von A wie Angst bis Z wie Zuneigung. Deutsche Geschichte seit 1900*. Frankfurt am Main: S. Fischer, 2020.
Frevert, Ute. *Mann und Weib, und Weib und Mann, Geschlechter-Differenzen in der Moderne*. Munich: Beck, 1995.
Frevert, Ute. *Vertrauensfragen. Eine Obsession der Moderne*. Munich: C. H. Beck, 2013.
Frey, Manuel. *Der reinliche Bürger. Entstehung und Verbreitung bürgerlicher Tugenden, 1760–1860*. Göttingen: Vandenhoeck & Ruprecht, 1997.
Frühwirth, Hans. *Die Doppelstadt Krems-Stein. Ihre Geschichte von 1848–2000*. Krems: Kulturamt, 2000.
Füssel, Marian. "Die Rückkehr des 'Subjekts' in der Kulturgeschichte. Beobachtungen aus praxeologischer Perspektive." In *Historisierte Subjekte – Subjektivierte Historie. Zur Verfügbarkeit und Unverfügbarkeit von Geschichte*, edited by Stefan Deines et al., 141–59. Berlin: De Gruyter, 2003.
Gailus, Manfred. *Straße und Brot. Sozialer Protest in den deutschen Staaten unter besonderer Berücksichtigung Preußens, 1847–1849*. Göttingen: Vandenhoeck & Ruprecht, 1990.
Gall, Lothar. *Vom alten zum neuen Bürgertum. Die mitteleuropäische Stadt im Umbruch 1780–1820*. Munich: Oldenbourg, 1991.
Gall, Lothar. *Von der ständischen zur bürgerlichen Gesellschaft*. Munich: Oldenbourg, 1993.
Gall, Lothar, ed. *Stadt und Bürgertum im Übergang von der traditionalen zur modernen Gesellschaft*. Munich: Oldenbourg, 1993.
Gay, Peter. *Die zarte Leidenschaft. Liebe im bürgerlichen Zeitalter*. Munich: C. H. Beck, 1987. Published in English as: *The Tender Passion, The Bourgeoise Experience: Victoria to Freud*. New York: Norton, 1999.
Gay, Peter. *Erziehung der Sinne. Sexualität im bürgerlichen Zeitalter*. Munich: C. H. Beck, 1986. Published in English as: *Education of Senses: Sexuality in the Bourgoise Age*, New York: Norton, 1999.
Gerber-Visser, Gerrendina. *Die Ressourcen des Landes. Der ökonomisch-patriotische Blick in den Topographischen Beschreibungen der Oekonomischen Gesellschaft Bern*. Zürich: Hier & Jetzt, 2012.
Gestrich, Andreas. "Ehe, Familie, Kinder im Pietismus. Der 'gezähmte Teufel.'" In *Geschichte des Pietismus*, edited by Martin Brecht et al., 4:498–521. Göttingen: Vandenhoeck & Ruprecht, 2004.

Gestrich, Andreas. *Geschichte der Familie im 19. und 20. Jahrhundert.* Munich: Oldenbourg, 1999.
Gestrich, Andreas, et al. *Geschichte der Familie.* Stuttgart: Kröner, 2003.
Giddens, Anthony. *Wandel der Intimität: Sexualität, Liebe und Erotik in modernen Gesellschaften.* Frankfurt am Main: S. Fischer, 1993. Published in English as: *The Transformation of Intimacy: Sexuality, Love and Eroticism in Modern Societies.* Stanford: Stanford University Press, 1992.
Gieryn, Thomas F. "What Buildings Do." *Theory and Society* 31 (2002): 35–74.
Giesen, Bernhard. *Die Intellektuellen und die Nation*, vol. 2: *Kollektive Identität.* Frankfurt am Main: Suhrkamp, 1999. Published in English as: *Intellectuals and the German Nation: Collective Identity in an Axial Age.* Translated by Nicholas Levis and Amos Weisz. Cambridge: Cambridge University Press, 1998.
Gleixner, Ulrike. "Familie, Traditionsstiftung und Geschichte im Schreiben von pietistischen Frauen." In *Frauen in der Stadt. Selbstzeugnisse des 16. bis 18. Jahrhunderts*, edited by Daniela Hacke, 131–63. Sigmaringen: Jan Thorbecke, 2004.
Gleixner, Ulrike. *Pietismus und Bürgertum. Eine historische Anthropologie der Frömmigkeit. Württemberg 17. bis 19. Jahrhundert.* Göttingen: Vandenhoeck & Ruprecht, 2005.
Gleixner, Ulrike. "Zwischen göttlicher und weltlicher Ordnung. Die Ehe im lutherischen Pietismus." *Pietismus und Neuzeit* 28 (2002): 147–85.
Götte, Gisela. "In der Grundanschauung verwandt – in den Äußerungen verschieden." In *Paula Modersohn-Becker. Otto Modersohn. Der Briefwechsel*, edited by Antje Modersohn and Wolfgang Werner, 9–20. Berlin: Insel, 2017.
Goffman, Erving. *Interaktionsrituale. Über Verhalten in direkter Kommunikation.* Frankfurt am Main: Suhrkamp, 2010. Published in English as: *Interaction Ritual. Essays in Face-to-Face Behavior.* New York: Routledge, 2017.
Greiffenhagen, Martin, ed. *Das evangelische Pfarrhaus. Eine Kultur- und Sozialgeschichte.* Stuttgart: Kreuz, 1984.
Greyerz, Kaspar von. "Observations on the Historiographical Status of Research on Self-Writing." In *Mapping the "I." Research on Self-Narratives in Germany and Switzerland*, edited by Claudia Ulbrich et al., 34–57. Leiden: Brill, 2015.
Greyerz, Kaspar von. *Passagen und Stationen. Lebensstufen zwischen Mittelalter und Moderne.* Göttingen: Vandenhoeck & Ruprecht, 2010.
Griesebner, Andrea. "Marriage Jurisdiction in the Habsburg Monarchy. Transition from Ecclesiastical to Secular Courts and Gender-Related Implications." *Annales de Démographie Historique* 140 (2020): 21–51.
Griesebner, Andrea. "Property, Power, Gender. Conflicts and Agency of a 'Merchantess' in the Archduchy of Austria below the Enns in the Eighteenth Century." In *Negotiations of Gender and Property through Legal Regimes (14th–19th Century): Stipulating, Litigating, Mediating*, edited by Margareth Lanzinger et al., 345–374. Leiden: Brill, 2021.
Grießinger, Andreas. *Das symbolische Kapital der Ehre. Streikbewegungen und kollektives Bewußtsein deutscher Handwerksgesellen im 18. Jahrhundert.* Frankfurt am Main: Ullstein, 1981.
Grießinger, Andreas, and Reinhold Reith. "Lehrlinge im deutschen Handwerk des ausgehenden 18. Jahrhunderts. Arbeitsorganisation, Sozialbeziehungen und alltägliche Konflikte." *Zeitschrift für historische Forschung* 13 (1986): 149–99.
Gröwer, Karin. *Wilde Ehen im 19. Jahrhundert. Die Unterschichten zwischen städtischer Bevölkerungspolitik und polizeilicher Repression.* Berlin: Reimer, 1999.
Grugger, Helmut. "Familie." In *Buddenbrooks-Handbuch*, edited by Nicole Mattern and Stefan Neuhaus, 117–25. Stuttgart: Springer, 2018.

Gutkas, Karl. "Die Städte Niederösterreichs im 19. Jahrhundert – Ihre Entwicklung zu zentralen Orten." *1000 Jahre Krems*. Special issue, *Jahrbuch für Landeskunde von Niederösterreich* 60/61 (1994/1995): 43–64.

Guzzi-Heeb, Sandro. *Le sexe, l'impôt, les cousins. Une histoire sociale et politique de la sexualité moderne (1450–1850)*. Paris: CNRS Editions, 2021.

Guzzi-Heeb, Sandro. *Passions alpines. Sexualité et pouvoirs dans les montagnes suisses (1700–1900)*. Rennes: Presses universitaires de Rennes, 2014.

Guzzi-Heeb, Sandro. "Sexuality and Intimacy." In *The Routledge History of the Domestic Sphere in Europe: 16th to 19th Century*, edited by Joachim Eibach and Margareth Lanzinger, 286–304. London: Routledge, 2020.

Habermas, Jürgen. *Strukturwandel der Öffentlichkeit. Untersuchungen zu einer Kategorie der bürgerlichen Gesellschaft*. Frankfurt am Main: Suhrkamp, 1990. Published in English as: *The Structural Transformation of the Public Sphere: An Inquiry into a Category of Bourgeois Society*. Cambridge: Polity Press, 1992.

Habermas, Rebekka. "Bürgerliche Kleinfamilie – Liebesheirat." In *Entdeckung des Ich. Die Geschichte der Individualisierung vom Mittelalter bis zur Gegenwart*, edited by Richard van Dülmen, 287–310. Cologne: Böhlau, 2001.

Habermas, Rebekka. *Frauen und Männer des Bürgertums. Eine Familiengeschichte 1750–1850*. Göttingen: Vandenhoeck & Ruprecht, 2000.

Habermas, Rebekka. "Spielerische Liebe oder: Von der Ohnmacht der Fiktionen. Heinrich Eibert Merkel und Regina Dannreuther (1783–1785)." In *Ungleiche Paare. Zur Kulturgeschichte menschlicher Beziehungen*, edited by Eva Labouvie, 152–74. Munich: C. H. Beck, 1997.

Hacke, Daniela. "Selbstzeugnisse von Frauen in der Frühen Neuzeit. Eine Einführung." In *Frauen in der Stadt. Selbstzeugnisse des 16. bis 18. Jahrhunderts*, edited by Daniela Hacke, 9–39. Sigmaringen: Jan Thorbecke, 2004.

Hämmerle, Christa. "Diaries." In *Reading Primary Sources: The Interpretation of Texts from Nineteenth- and Twentieth-Century History*, edited by Miriam Dobson and Benjamin Ziemann, 141–58. London: Routledge, 2009.

Häusler, Eric. *Ökonomisches Scheitern. Solidarische Praktiken in Bern, 1750–1900*. Bielefeld: transcript, 2023.

Hahn, Philip. "Trends der deutschsprachigen historischen Forschung nach 1945: Vom 'ganzen Haus' zum 'offenen Haus.'" In *Das Haus in der Geschichte Europas. Ein Handbuch*, edited by Joachim Eibach and Inken Schmidt-Voges, 47–63. Berlin: De Gruyter, 2015.

Haiko, Peter. "Wiener Arbeiterwohnhäuser 1848–1934." *Kritische Berichte. Zeitschrift für Kunst- und Kulturwissenschaft* 5 (1977): 26–50.

Haldemann, Arno. *Prekäre Eheschließungen. Eigensinnige Heiratsbegehren und Bevölkerungspolitik in Bern, 1742–1848*. Munich: UVK, 2021.

Hamann, Sibylle. "Adelheid Popp und wir." In *Adelheid Popp, Jugend einer Arbeiterin*, edited by Sibylle Hamann, 135–57. Vienna: Picus, 2019.

Hamann, Sibylle. "Eine muss immer die Erste sein." In *Adelheid Popp, Jugend einer Arbeiterin*, edited by Sibylle Hamann, 9–14. Vienna: Picus, 2019.

Hammer-Tugendhat, Daniela. "Dutch Paintings of Interiors and the Invention of a Bourgeois Identity." In *The Routledge History of the Domestic Sphere in Europe: 16th to 19th Century*, edited by Joachim Eibach and Margareth Lanzinger, 527–53. London: Routledge, 2020.

Hammer-Tugendhat, Daniela. "'Familie! Familie?' Kunstwissenschaftliche Betrachtungen." In *Family Matters. Ausstellungskatalog*, edited by Johanna Schwanberg, 56–76. Vienna: Birkhäuser, 2019.

Hanisch, Ernst. "Arbeiterkindheit in Österreich vor dem Ersten Weltkrieg." *Internationales Archiv für Sozialgeschichte der deutschen Literatur* 7 (1982): 109–47.
Hardwick, Julie. "Sexual Violence and Domesticity." In *The Routledge History of the Domestic Sphere in Europe: 16th to 19th Century*, edited by Joachim Eibach and Margareth Lanzinger, 237–54. London: Routledge, 2020.
Hatje, Frank. "Aus dem Leben eines Diaristen." In *Ferdinand Beneke (1774–1848). Die Tagebücher, Begleitband I zur ersten Abteilung "Bürger und Revolutionen,"* edited by Frank Hatje et al., 58–100. Göttingen: Wallstein, 2012.
Hatje, Frank. "Die private Öffentlichkeit des Hauses im deutschen und englischen Bürgertum des 18. und 19. Jahrhunderts." In *Das Haus in der Geschichte Europas. Ein Handbuch*, edited by Joachim Eibach and Inken Schmidt-Voges, 503–23. Berlin: De Gruyter, 2015.
Hatje, Frank. "Domestic Sociability and the Emergence of the Bürgertum." In *The Routledge History of the Domestic Sphere in Europe: 16th to 19th Century*, edited by Joachim Eibach and Margareth Lanzinger, 174–96. London: Routledge, 2020.
Hatje, Frank. "Ferdinand Beneke und seine Zeit. Der Kosmos eines Tagebuchs und die Geschichte des Bürgertums zwischen Aufklärung und Romantik." *Jahrbuch der patriotischen Gesellschaft von 1765. Von der Bürgerlichkeit zur Zivilität* (2014): 19–29.
Hatje, Frank. "Leben und Ansichten des Ferdinand Beneke, Dr." In *Ferdinand Beneke (1774–1848). Die Tagebücher. Begleitband zur dritten Abteilung. "Leben und Ansichten,"* edited by Frank Hatje et al., 5–111. Göttingen: Wallstein, 2016.
Hatje, Frank. "Tagebücher und Korrespondenzen." In *Ferdinand Beneke (1774–1848). Die Tagebücher, Begleitband I zur ersten Abteilung "Bürger und Revolutionen,"* edited by Frank Hatje et al., 5–35. Göttingen: Wallstein, 2012.
Hauch, Gabriella. *Frauen bewegen Politik. Österreich 1848–1938.* Innsbruck: Studien, 2009.
Haupt, Heinz-Gerhard, and Geoffrey Crossick. *Die Kleinbürger. Eine europäische Sozialgeschichte des 19. Jahrhunderts.* Munich: C. H. Beck, 1998. Published in English as: *The Petite Bourgeoisie in Europe 1780–1914: Enterprise, Family and Independence.* London: Routledge, 1995.
Hausen, Karin. "Der Aufsatz über die 'Geschlechtscharaktere' und seine Rezeption. Eine Spätlese nach dreißig Jahren." In *Geschlechtergeschichte als Gesellschaftsgeschichte*, edited by Karin Hausen, 83–108. Göttingen: Vandenhoeck & Ruprecht, 2012.
Hausen, Karin. "Die Polarisierung der Geschlechtscharaktere – Eine Spiegelung der Dissoziation von Erwerbs- und Familienleben." In *Sozialgeschichte der Familie in der Neuzeit Europas*, edited by Werner Conze, 363–93. Stuttgart: Ernst Klett, 1976.
Hausen, Karin. "Öffentlichkeit und Privatheit. Gesellschaftspolitische Konstruktionen und die Geschichte der Geschlechterbeziehungen." In *Frauengeschichte – Geschlechtergeschichte*, edited by Heide Wunder, 81–88. Frankfurt am Main: Campus, 1992.
Hebeisen, Erika. *Leidenschaftlich fromm. Die pietistische Bewegung in Basel 1750–1830.* Cologne: Böhlau, 2005.
Heer, Peter W., et al., eds. *Vom Weissgerber zum Bundesrat. Basel und die Familie Brenner, 17.–20. Jahrhundert.* Basel: Christoph Merian, 2009.
Hein, Dieter, and Andreas Schulz, eds. *Bürgerkultur im 19. Jahrhundert. Bildung, Kunst und Lebenswelt.* Munich: C. H. Beck, 1996.
Heling, Antje. *Zu Haus bei Martin Luther. Ein alltagsgeschichtlicher Rundgang.* Wittenberg: Stiftung Luthergedenkstätte, 2003.
Hettling, Manfred. "Die persönliche Selbständigkeit. Der archimedische Punkt bürgerlicher Lebensführung." In *Der bürgerliche Wertehimmel. Innenansichten des 19. Jahrhunderts*, edited by

Manfred Hettling and Stefan-Ludwig Hoffmann, 57–78. Göttingen: Vandenhoeck & Ruprecht, 2000.
Hettling, Manfred, and Stefan-Ludwig Hoffmann, eds. *Der bürgerliche Wertehimmel. Innenansichten des 19. Jahrhunderts.* Göttingen: Vandenhoeck & Ruprecht, 2000.
Heyl, Christoph. *A Passion for Privacy. Untersuchungen zur Genese der bürgerlichen Privatsphäre in London (1660–1800).* Munich: Oldenbourg, 2004.
Hill, Paul B., and Johannes Kopp. *Familiensoziologie. Grundlagen und theoretische Perspektiven.* 5th ed. Wiesbaden: Springer, 2013.
Hill, Paul B., and Johannes Kopp. "Familiensoziologie: Zum Stand der Dinge." In *Handbuch Familiensoziologie*, edited by Paul B. Hill and Johannes Kopp, 9–17. Wiesbaden: Springer, 2015.
Hobsbawm, Eric. *The Age of Revolution. Europe 1789–1848.* London: Weidenfeld & Nicolson, 1962.
Hochstrasser, Olivia. *Ein Haus und seine Menschen 1549–1989. Ein Versuch zum Verhältnis von Mikroforschung und Sozialgeschichte.* Tübingen: Tübinger Vereinigung für Volkskunde, 1993
Holenstein, André. *Mitten in Europa. Verflechtung und Abgrenzung in der Schweizer Geschichte.* Baden: Hier & Jetzt, 2014.
Holm, Christiane. "Bürgerliche Wohnkultur im 19. Jahrhundert." In *Das Haus in der Geschichte Europas. Ein Handbuch*, edited by Joachim Eibach and Inken Schmidt-Voges, 233–53. Berlin: De Gruyter, 2015.
Iglauer, Erika. *Ziegel – Baustoff unseres Lebens.* Vienna: Berger, 1974.
Jancke, Gabriele. *Gastfreundschaft in der frühneuzeitlichen Gesellschaft. Praktiken, Normen und Perspektiven von Gelehrten.* Göttingen: Vandenhoeck & Ruprecht, 2013.
Jancke, Gabriele, and Daniel Schläppi, eds. *Die Ökonomie sozialer Beziehungen: Ressourcenbewirtschaftung als Geben, Nehmen, Investieren, Verschwenden, Haushalten, Horten, Vererben, Schulden.* Stuttgart: Franz Steiner, 2015.
Jancke, Gabriele, and Claudia Ulbrich. "Vom Individuum zur Person. Neue Konzepte im Spannungsfeld von Autobiographietheorie und Selbstzeugnisforschung." *Querelles. Jahrbuch für Frauen- und Geschlechterforschung* 10 (2005): 7–27.
Jarzebowski, Claudia. "Kindheit." *Enzyklopädie der Neuzeit*, 6:570–79. Stuttgart: J. B. Metzler, 2007.
Jarzebowski, Claudia. *Kindheit und Emotion. Kinder und ihre Lebenswelten in der europäischen Frühen Neuzeit.* Berlin: De Gruyter Oldenbourg, 2018.
Jarzebowski, Claudia, and Thomas Max Safely, eds. *Childhood and Emotion: Across Cultures 1450–1800.* London: Routledge, 2014.
Johnson, Christopher H. "Das 'Geschwister Archipel': Bruder-Schwester-Liebe und Klassenformation im Frankreich des 19. Jahrhunderts." *L'Homme* 13 (2002): 50–67.
Johnson, Christopher H. "Siblinghood and the Emotional Dimensions of the New Kinship System, 1800–1850. A French Example." In *Sibling Relations and the Transformations of European Kinship, 1300–1900*, edited by Christopher H. Johnson and David W. Sabean, 189–220. New York: Berghahn, 2011.
Johnson, Christopher H., and David W. Sabean. *Sibling Relations and the Transformations of European Kinship, 1300–1900.* New York: Berghahn, 2011.
Joris, Elisabeth. "Gender Implications of the Separate Spheres.", In *The Routledge History of the Domestic Sphere in Europe: 16th to 19th Century*, edited by Joachim Eibach and Margareth Lanzinger, 364–80. London: Routledge, 2020.
Joris, Elisabeth. *Liberal und eigensinnig: Die Pädagogin Josephine Stadlin – die Homöopathin Emilie Paravicini-Blumer. Handlungsspielräume von Bildungsbürgerinnen im 19. Jahrhundert.* Zürich: Chronos, 2010.

Jütte, Daniel. *The Strait Gate. Thresholds and Power in Western History.* New Haven: Yale University Press, 2015.

Kaspar, Fred. "Das mittelalterliche Haus als öffentlicher und privater Raum." In *Die Vielfalt der Dinge. Neue Wege zur Analyse mittelalterlicher Sachkultur,* 207–35. Vienna: Verlag der österreichischen Akademie der Wissenschaften, 1998.

Kaufmann, Amanda. "Gel(i)ebte Geschwister. Bürgerlich-patrizische Geschwisterbeziehungen in Bern im 18. und 19. Jahrhundert am Beispiel der Familie Zeerleder." Masters thesis, University of Bern, 2021.

Kaufmann, Jean-Claude. *Schmutzige Wäsche. Zur ehelichen Konstruktion von Alltag.* Konstanz: UVK, 1994. Published in English as: *Dirty Linen: Couples and Their Laundry.* Translated by Helen Alfrey. London: Middlesex University Press, 1998.

Keppler, Angela. *Tischgespräche. Über Formen kommunikativer Vergemeinschaftung am Beispiel der Konversation in Familien.* Frankfurt am Main: Suhrkamp, 1994.

Kessel, Martina. *Langeweile. Zum Umgang mit Zeit und Gefühlen in Deutschland vom 18. bis zum frühen 20. Jahrhundert.* Göttingen: Wallstein, 2001.

Kocka, Jürgen. *Bourgeois Society in Nineteenth-Century Europe.* Edited by Allan Mitchell. Translated by Gus Fagan. Oxford: Berg, 1994.

Kocka, Jürgen. "Das europäische Muster und der deutsche Fall." In *Bürgertum im 19. Jahrhundert. Deutschland im europäischen Vergleich,* edited by Jürgen Kocka, 1:9–75. Göttingen: Vandenhoeck & Ruprecht, 1995.

Kormann, Eva. *Ich, Welt, Gott. Autobiographik im 17. Jahrhundert.* Cologne: Böhlau, 2004.

Koschorke, Albrecht, et al. *Vor der Familie. Grenzbedingungen einer modernen Institution.* Konstanz: Konstanz University Press, 2010.

Kühner, Christian. "Geschichte der Freundschaft." In *Freundschaft heute. Eine Einführung in die Freundschaftssoziologie,* edited by Janosch Sobin et al., 79–94. Bielefeld: transcript, 2016.

Kuhn, Bärbel. *Familienstand: ledig. Ehelose Frauen und Männer im Bürgertum (1850–1914).* Cologne: Böhlau, 2000.

Kuhn, Bärbel. "Mitwohnen im 19. und frühen 20. Jahrhundert." In *Das Haus in der Geschichte Europas. Ein Handbuch,* edited by Joachim Eibach and Inken Schmidt-Voges, 373–88. Berlin: De Gruyter, 2015.

Kuhn, Thomas K. "Basel." In *Handbuch Pietismus,* edited by Wolfgang Breul and Thomas Hahn-Bruckart, 239–44. Tübingen: Mohr Siebeck, 2021.

Kuhn, Thomas K. "Basel – ein 'Liebling Gottes.' Die Stadt am Rhein als Ort der Erweckungsbewegung." *Theologische Zeitschrift* 56 (2000): 165–85.

Kuhn, Thomas K. "Das Haus im Protestantismus: Historisch-theologische Perspektiven." In *Das Haus in der Geschichte Europas. Ein Handbuch,* edited by Joachim Eibach and Inken Schmidt-Voges, 725–42. Berlin: De Gruyter, 2015.

Labouvie, Eva. *Andere Umstände. Eine Kulturgeschichte der Geburt.* Cologne: Böhlau, 1998.

Labouvie, Eva, ed. *Schwestern und Freundinnen. Zur Kulturgeschichte weiblicher Kommunikation.* Cologne: Böhlau, 2009.

Langreiter, Nikola. "Nachbemerkungen – Wetti Teuschls Tagebuch als kulturwissenschaftliches und historisches Material." In *Tagebuch von Wetti Teuschl (1870–1885),* edited by Nikola Langreiter, 151–94. Cologne: Böhlau, 2010.

Lanzinger, Margareth. "Schwestern-Beziehungen und Schwager-Ehen. Formen familialer Krisenbewältigung im 19. Jahrhundert." In *Schwestern und Freundinnen. Zur Kulturgeschichte weiblicher Kommunikation,* edited by Eva Labouvie, 263–82. Cologne: Böhlau, 2009.

Lanzinger, Margareth. "Spouses and the Competition for Wealth." In *The Routledge History of the Domestic Sphere in Europe: 16th to 19th Century*, edited by Joachim Eibach and Margareth Lanzinger, 61–78. London: Routledge, 2020.

Lanzinger, Margareth. *Verwaltete Verwandtschaft. Eheverbote, kirchliche und staatliche Dispenspraxis im 18. und 19. Jahrhundert*. Vienna: Böhlau, 2015.

Laslett, Peter. "Die europäische Familie der Gegenwart: Einzigartig in der Geschichte?" In *Historische Familienforschung. Ergebnisse und Kontroversen*, edited by Josef Ehmer et al., 39–56. Frankfurt am Main: Campus, 1997.

Laslett, Peter. "Introduction: The History of the Family." In *Household and Family in Past Time*, edited by Peter Laslett and Richard Wall, 1–89. Cambridge: Cambridge University Press, 1972.

Latour, Bruno. *Eine neue Soziologie für eine neue Gesellschaft. Einführung in die Akteur-Netzwerk-Theorie*. 3rd ed. Frankfurt am Main: Suhrkamp, 2014. Published in English as: *Reassembling the Social: An Introduction to Actor-Network Theory*. Oxford: Oxford University Press, 2005.

Lenger, Alexander et al. "Pierre Bourdieus Konzeption des Habitus." In *Pierre Bourdieus Konzeption des Habitus. Grundlagen, Zugänge, Forschungsperspektiven*, edited by Alexander Lenger et al., 13–41. Wiesbaden: Springer, 2013.

Lenger, Friedrich. *Industrielle Revolution und Nationalstaatsgründung (1849–1870er Jahre)*. Stuttgart: Klett-Cotta, 2003.

Lenger, Friedrich. *Metropolen der Moderne. Eine europäische Stadtgeschichte seit 1850*. Munich: C. H. Beck, 2023.

Lenger, Friedrich. *Sozialgeschichte der deutschen Handwerker seit 1800*. Frankfurt am Main: Suhrkamp, 1988.

Lenger, Friedrich. *Zwischen Kleinbürgertum und Proletariat. Studien zur Sozialgeschichte der Düsseldorfer Handwerker 1816–1878*. Göttingen: Vandenhoeck & Ruprecht, 1986.

Lindström, Dag, et al. "Working Together." In *Making a Living, Making a Difference. Gender and Work in Early Modern European Society*, edited by Maria Ågren, 57–79. New York: Oxford University Press, 2017.

Lischka, Marion. *Liebe als Ritual. Eheanbahnung und Brautwerbung in der frühneuzeitlichen Grafschaft Lippe*. Paderborn: Schöningh, 2006.

Löw, Martina. *Raumsoziologie*. Frankfurt am Main: Suhrkamp, 2001. Published in English as: *The Sociology of Space: Materiality, Social Structures, and Action*. New York: Palgrave Macmillan, 2016.

Lorenz, Angelika. *Das deutsche Familienbild in der Malerei des 19. Jahrhunderts*. Darmstadt: Wissenschaftliche Buchgesellschaft, 1985.

Lüdtke, Alf. *Eigen-Sinn. Fabrikalltag, Arbeitererfahrungen und Politik vom Kaiserreich bis in den Faschismus*. Hamburg: Ergebnisse, 1993.

Lüdtke, Alf. "People Working: Everyday Life and German Fascism." *History Workshop Journal* 50 (2000): 75–92.

Luhmann, Niklas. *Die Gesellschaft der Gesellschaft*. 2 vols. Frankfurt am Main: Suhrkamp, 1997. Published in English as: *Theory of Society*. 2 vols. Stanford: Stanford University Press, 2012.

Luhmann, Niklas. *Liebe als Passion. Zur Codierung von Intimität*. Frankfurt am Main: Suhrkamp, 1994. Published in English as: *Love as Passion: The Codification of Intimacy*. Translated by Jeremy Gaines and Doris L. Jones. Cambridge: Polity Press, 1986.

Maderthaner, Wolfgang, and Lutz Musner. *Die Anarchie der Vorstadt. Das andere Wien um 1900*. Frankfurt am Main: Campus, 1999.

Martschukat, Jürgen, and Steffen Patzold. "Geschichtswissenschaft und 'performative turn': Eine Einführung in Fragestellungen, Konzepte und Literatur." In *Geschichtswissenschaft und "perfor-

mative turn". Ritual, Inszenierung und Performanz vom Mittelalter bis zur Neuzeit, edited by Jürgen Martschukat and Steffen Patzold, 1–32. Cologne: Böhlau, 2003.

Mathieu, Jon. "Domestic Terminologies: House, Household, Family." In *The Routledge History of the Domestic Sphere in Europe: 16th to 19th Century*, edited by Joachim Eibach and Margareth Lanzinger, 25–42. London: Routledge, 2020.

Mathieu, Jon. "Temporalities and Transitions of Family History in Europe: Competing Accounts." *Genealogy* 3 (2019): doi.org/10.3390/genealogy3020028.

Matz, Klaus-Jürgen. *Pauperismus und Bevölkerung. Die gesetzlichen Ehebeschränkungen in den süddeutschen Staaten während des 19. Jahrhunderts*. Stuttgart: Klett-Cotta, 1980.

Maurer, Michael. *Die Biographie des Bürgers. Lebensformen und Denkweisen in der formativen Phase des deutschen Bürgertums (1680–1815)*. Göttingen: Vandenhoeck & Ruprecht, 1996.

Mayer, Pia. "Worpswede – eine Künstlerinnenkolonie?" In *Kunst & Liebe im Aufbruch. Paula & Otto. Ausstellungskatalog*, edited by Sylvia Wölfle, 30–36. Lindau: Kunstmuseum Lindau, 2020.

Maynes, Mary Jo. "Class Cultures and Images of Proper Family Life." In *The History of the European Family*, vol. 2: *Family Life in the Long 19th Century (1789–1913)*, edited by David I. Kertzer and Marzio Barbagli, 195–228. New Haven: Yale University Press, 2002.

Medick, Hans. "Einführung: Kulturelle Mehrfachzugehörigkeiten." In *Selbstzeugnis und Person. Transkulturelle Perspektiven*, edited by Claudia Ulbrich et al., 181. Cologne: Böhlau, 2012.

Messerli, Alfred. "Der papierene Freund. Literarische Anregungen und Modelle für das Tagebuchführen." In *Von der dargestellten Person zum erinnerten Ich. Europäische Selbstzeugnisse als historische Quelle (1500–1850)*, edited by Kaspar von Greyerz et al., 299–320. Cologne: Böhlau, 2001.

Messerli, Alfred, and Adolf Muschg, eds. *Schreibsucht. Autobiografische Schriften des Pietisten Ulrich Bräker (1735–1798)*. Göttingen: Vandenhoeck & Ruprecht, 2004.

Mettele, Gisela. "Der private Raum als öffentlicher Ort. Geselligkeit im bürgerlichen Haus." In *Bürgerkultur im 19. Jahrhundert. Bildung, Kunst und Lebenswelt*, edited by Dieter Hein and Andreas Schulz, 155–69. Munich: C. H. Beck, 1996.

Mettele, Gisela. *Weltbürgertum oder Gottesreich. Die Herrnhuter Brüdergemeine als globale Gemeinschaft 1727–1857*. Göttingen: Vandenhoeck & Ruprecht, 2009.

Mitterauer, Michael, and Reinhard Sieder. *Vom Patriarchat zur Partnerschaft. Zum Strukturwandel der Familie*. 4th ed. Munich: C. H. Beck, 1991. Published in English as: *The European Family: Patriarchy to Partnership from the Middle Ages to the Present*. Oxford: Blackwell, 1982.

Möhle, Sylvia. *Ehekonflikte und sozialer Wandel: Göttingen 1740–1840*. Frankfurt am Main: Campus, 1997.

Möhring, Maren. "Das Haustier: Vom Nutztier zum Familientier." In *Das Haus in der Geschichte Europas: Ein Handbuch*, edited by Joachim Eibach and Inken Schmidt-Voges, 389–406. Berlin: De Gruyter, 2015.

Müller, Heidy Margrit. "Die Beziehung zur Mutter in autobiographischer Erzählprosa von Marie von Ebner-Eschenbach, Hedwig Dohm und Adelheid Popp." In *Mutter und Mütterlichkeit. Wandel und Wirksamkeit einer Phantasie in der deutschen Literatur*, edited by Irmgard Roebling and Wolfram Mauser, 271–84. Würzburg: Königshausen & Neumann, 1996.

Nave-Herz, Rosemarie. "Der Wandel der Familie zum spezialisierten gesellschaftlichen System im Zuge der allgemeinen gesellschaftlichen Differenzierung unserer Gesellschaft." In *Familiensoziologie. Ein Lehr- und Studienbuch*, edited by Rosemarie Nave-Herz, 1–26. Berlin: De Gruyter Oldenbourg, 2014.

Nave-Herz, Rosemarie. "Unkenrufe. Ist die Familie ein 'Auslaufmodell'?" *Forschung & Lehre* 12 (2015): 992–94.

Niggl, Günter. *Geschichte der deutschen Autobiographie im 18. Jahrhundert. Theoretische Grundlegung und literarische Entfaltung.* Stuttgart: J. B. Metzler, 1977.
Opitz-Belakhal, Claudia. "A Space of Emotions." In *The Routledge History of the Domestic Sphere in Europe: 16th to 19th Century*, edited by Joachim Eibach and Margareth Lanzinger, 271–85. London: Routledge, 2020.
Opitz-Belakhal, Claudia. *Geschlechtergeschichte.* Frankfurt am Main: Campus, 2010.
Opitz-Belakhal, Claudia, and Sandro Guzzi-Heeb. "Family, Community and Sociability." In *A Cultural History of Education*, vol. 4: *The Age of Enlightenment*, edited by Daniel Tröhler, 91–109. London: Bloomsbury, 2020.
Orland, Barbara. *Wäsche waschen. Technik- und Sozialgeschichte der häuslichen Wäschepflege.* Reinbek bei Hamburg: Deutsches Museum/Rowohlt, 1991.
Osterhammel, Jürgen. *Die Verwandlung der Welt. Eine Geschichte des 19. Jahrhunderts.* Munich: C. H. Beck, 2009. Published in English as: *The Transformation of the World: A Global History of the Nineteenth Century.* Translated by Patrick Camiller. Princeton: Princeton University Press, 2014.
Ottomeyer, Hans, et al., eds. *Biedermeier. Die Erfindung der Einfachheit.* Ostfildern: Hatje Cantz, 2006.
Papathanassiou, Maria. "Kinderarbeit." *Enzyklopädie der Neuzeit*, vol. 6:553–57. Stuttgart: J. B. Metzler, 2006.
Perrot, Michelle. "Einleitung." In *Geschichte des privaten Lebens*, vol. 4: *Von der Revolution zum Großen Krieg*, edited by Philippe Ariès and Georges Duby, 7–11. Augsburg: S. Fischer, 1999. Published in English as: "Introduction." In *A History of Private Life*, vol. 4: *From the Fires of Revolution to the Great War*, edited by Philippe Ariès and Georges Duby, 1–4. Cambridge, MA: Belknap Press, 1990.
Piller, Gudrun. "Private Körper. Schreiben über den Körper in Selbstzeugnissen des 18. Jahrhunderts." In *Selbstzeugnisse in der Frühen Neuzeit. Individualisierungsweisen in interdisziplinärer Perspektive*, edited by Kaspar von Greyerz, 45–60. Munich: Oldenbourg, 2007.
Piller, Gudrun. *Private Körper. Spuren des Leibes in Selbstzeugnissen des 18. Jahrhunderts.* Cologne: Böhlau, 2007.
Planert, Ute. *Antifeminismus im Kaiserreich. Diskurs, soziale Formation und politische Mentalität.* Göttingen: Vandenhoeck & Ruprecht, 1998.
Prager, Katharina. "Adelheid Popps (fest-)geschriebenes Leben." In *Adelheid Popp, Jugend einer Arbeiterin*, edited by Sibylle Hamann, 15–32. Vienna: Picus, 2019.
Przyrembel, Alexandra. "Friedrich Engels, Die Lage der arbeitenden Klasse in England nach eigenen Anschauungen und authentischen Quellen, Leipzig 1845." *Themenportal Europäische Geschichte.* 2011. www.europa.clio-online.de/essay/id/fdae-1540.
Pyta, Wolfram, and Carsten Kretschmann, eds. *Bürgerlichkeit. Spurensuche in Vergangenheit und Gegenwart.* Stuttgart: Franz Steiner, 2016.
Radkau, Joachim. *Das Zeitalter der Nervosität. Deutschland zwischen Bismarck und Hitler.* Munich: Carl Hanser, 1998.
Ranum, Orest. "Refugien der Intimität." In *Geschichte des privaten Lebens*, vol. 3: *Von der Renaissance zur Aufklärung*, edited by Philippe Ariès and Georges Duby, 213–68. Augsburg: S. Fischer, 1999.
Reckwitz, Andreas. *Das hybride Subjekt. Eine Theorie der Subjektkulturen von der bürgerlichen Moderne zur Postmoderne.* Berlin: Suhrkamp, 2020.
Reckwitz, Andreas. "Wie bürgerlich ist die Moderne? Bürgerlichkeit als hybride Subjektivierungsform." In *Bürgerlichkeit ohne Bürgertum. In welchem Land leben wir?*, edited by Heinz Bude et al., 169–87. Munich: Wilhelm Fink, 2010.
Reiter, Roswita. *Adelheid Popp – Biografie einer bewegenden Sozialdemokratin.* Berlin: Miramonte, 2010.

Reulecke, Jürgen, ed. *Geschichte des Wohnens*, vol. 3: *1800–1918: Das bürgerliche Zeitalter*. Stuttgart: Deutsche Verlagsanstalt, 1997.

Ricker, Julia. "Evangelische Pfarrhäuser: Zwischen Himmel und Erde – Vom Leben protestantischer Pfarrfamilien." *Monumente* 27, no. 2 (2017): 8–15.

Roper, Lyndal. *Das fromme Haus. Frauen und Moral in der Reformation*. Frankfurt am Main: Campus, 1995. Published in English as: *The Holy Household: Women and Morals in Reformation*. Oxford: Oxford Clarendon, 1989.

Roper, Lyndal. "Going to Church and Street: Weddings in Reformation Augsburg." *Past & Present* 106 (1985): 62–101.

Rosenbaum, Heidi. *Formen der Familie. Untersuchungen zum Zusammenhang von Familienverhältnissen. Sozialstruktur und sozialem Wandel in der deutschen Gesellschaft des 19. Jahrhunderts*. Frankfurt am Main: Suhrkamp, 1996.

Ruppel, Sophie. *Verbündete Rivalen. Geschwisterbeziehungen im Hochadel des 17. Jahrhunderts*. Cologne: Böhlau, 2006.

Sabean, David W. "Kinship and Class Dynamics in Nineteenth-Century Europe." In *Kinship in Europe, Approaches to Long-Term Development (1300–1900)*, edited by David W. Sabean et al., 301–13. New York: Berghahn, 2007.

Sabean, David W. "Kinship and Issues of the Self in Europe around 1800." In *Sibling Relations and the Transformations of European Kinship, 1300–1900*, edited by Christopher H. Johnson and David W. Sabean, 221–38. New York: Berghahn, 2011.

Sabean, David W. *Kinship in Neckarhausen, 1700–1870*. Cambridge: Cambridge University Press, 1998.

Sabean, David W. *Property, Production, and Family in Neckarhausen, 1700–1870*. Cambridge: Cambridge University Press, 1990.

Sabean, David W. "Social Background to Vetterleswirtschaft: Kinship in Neckarhausen." In *Frühe Neuzeit – Frühe Moderne? Forschungen zur Vielschichtigkeit von Übergangsprozessen*, edited by Rudolf Vierhaus et al., 113–32. Göttingen: Vandenhoeck & Ruprecht, 1992.

Sabean, David W., et al., eds. *Kinship in Europe: Approaches to Long-Term Development, 1300–1900*. New York: Berghahn, 2007.

Saldern, Adelheid von. "Im Hause, zu Hause. Wohnen im Spannungsfeld von Gegebenheiten und Aneignungen." In *Geschichte des Wohnens*, vol. 3: *1800–1918: Das bürgerliche Zeitalter*, edited by Jürgen Reulecke, 145–332. Stuttgart: DVA, 1997.

Sandgruber, Roman. *Die Anfänge der Konsumgesellschaft. Konsumgüterverbrauch, Lebensstandard und Alltagskultur in Österreich im 18. und 19. Jahrhundert*. Munich: Oldenbourg, 1982.

Sarasin, Philipp. *Stadt der Bürger. Bürgerliche Macht und städtische Gesellschaft: Basel 1846–1914*. 2nd ed. Göttingen: Vandenhoeck & Ruprecht, 1997.

Sarti, Raffaella. *Europe at Home. Family and Material Culture 1500–1800*. New Haven: Yale University Press, 2002.

Sarti, Raffaella. "Men at Home: Domesticities, Authority, Emotions and Work (Thirteenth-Twentieth Centuries)." *Gender & History* 27 (2015): 521–58.

Sarti, Raffaella, et al., eds. "Open Houses in Early-Modern Europe: Contexts and Approaches." Special issue, *European History Quarterly* 51, no. 4 (2021).

Sarti, Raffaella, et al., eds. *What is Work? Gender at the Crossroads of Home, Family, and Business from the Early Modern Era to the Present*. New York: Berghahn, 2018.

Saurer, Edith. *Liebe und Arbeit, Geschlechterbeziehungen im 19. und 20. Jahrhundert*. Edited by Margareth Lanzinger. Vienna: Böhlau, 2014.

Scarpatetti, Beat von, et al., eds. *Binningen – die Geschichte*. Liestal: Baselland, 2004.

Schillig, Anne. *Hausgeschichten. Materielle Kultur und Familie in der Schweiz (1700–1900)*. Zürich: Chronos, 2020.

Schläppi, Daniel. "Logiken der Subsistenz in historischer Perspektive: Der wirtschaftlich tragfähige Haushalt als gesellschaftliche und politische Leitgröße der Vormoderne." In *Strategien der Subsistenz. Neue prekäre, subversive und moralische Ökonomien*, edited by Kerstin Poehls et al., 31–47. Berlin: Panama, 2017.

Schlögl, Rudolf. "Vergesellschaftung unter Anwesenden. Zur kommunikativen Form des Politischen in der vormodernen Stadt." In *Interaktion und Herrschaft. Die Politik der frühneuzeitlichen Stadt*, edited by Rudolf Schlögl, 9–62. Konstanz: UVK, 2004.

Schmidt, Heinrich R. *Dorf und Religion. Reformierte Sittenzucht in Berner Landgemeinden der Frühen Neuzeit*. Stuttgart: Gustav Fischer, 1995.

Schmidt, Laura. *Weihnachtliches Theater. Zur Entstehung und Geschichte einer bürgerlichen Fest- und Theaterkultur.* Bielefeld: transcript, 2017.

Schmidt-Voges, Inken, ed. *Ehe – Haus – Familie. Soziale Institutionen im Wandel 1750–1850*. Cologne: Böhlau, 2010.

Schmidt-Voges, Inken. *Mikropolitiken des Friedens. Semantiken und Praktiken des Hausfriedens im 18. Jahrhundert*. Berlin: De Gruyter Oldenbourg, 2015.

Schmiedt, Helmut. "Paarbeziehungen." In *Buddenbrooks-Handbuch*, edited by Nicole Mattern and Stefan Neuhaus, 126–33. Stuttgart: Springer, 2018.

Schnegg, Brigitte. "Soireen, Salons, Sozietäten. Geschlechterspezifische Aspekte des Wandels städtischer Öffentlichkeit im Ancien régime am Beispiel Berns." In *Frauen in der Stadt*, edited by Anne-Lise Head-König and Albert Tanner, 163–83. Zürich: Chronos, 1993.

Schnegg, Brigitte. "Tagebuchschreiben als Technik des Selbst. Das Journal ‚de mes actions' der Bernerin Henriette Stettler-Herport (1738–1805)." In *Frauen in der Stadt. Selbstzeugnisse des 16. bis 18. Jahrhunderts*, edited by Daniela Hacke, 103–30. Sigmaringen: Jan Thorbecke, 2004.

Schneider, Norbert F. "Familie in Westeuropa, Von der Institution zur Lebensform." In *Handbuch Familiensoziologie*, edited by Paul B. Hill and Johannes Kopp, 21–53. Wiesbaden: Springer, 2015.

Schnell, Rüdiger. *Sexualität und Emotionalität in der vormodernen Ehe*. Cologne: Böhlau, 2002.

Scholz-Löhnig, Cordula. "Eheauflösung." *Enzyklopädie der Neuzeit*, 3:52–57. Stuttgart: J. B. Metzler, 2006.

Schorn-Schütte, Luise. "'Gefährtin' und 'Mitregentin'. Zur Sozialgeschichte der evangelischen Pfarrfrau in der Frühen Neuzeit." In *Wandel der Geschlechterbeziehungen zu Beginn der Neuzeit*, edited by Heide Wunder and Christina Vanja, 109–53. Frankfurt am Main: Suhrkamp, 1991.

Schroers, Fritz D. *Lexikon deutschsprachiger Homöopathen*. Stuttgart: Karl F. Haug, 2006.

Schulze, Winfried, ed. *Ego-Dokumente. Annäherung an den Menschen in der Geschichte*. Berlin: Akademie, 1996.

Schweizer, Jürg. "Die Landvogteischlösser im 18. Jahrhundert." In *Berns goldene Zeit. Das 18. Jahrhundert neu entdeckt*, edited by André Holenstein, 446. Bern: Stämpfli, 2008.

Seidel Menchi, Silvana, ed. *Marriage in Europe, 1400–1800*. Toronto: University of Toronto Press, 2016.

Shoemaker, Robert. *Gender in English Society, 1650–1850: The Emergence of Separate Spheres?* London: Routeldge, 1998.

Shorter, Edward, *Die Geburt der modernen Familie*. Reinbek bei Hamburg: Rowohlt, 1983. Published in English as: *The Making of the Modern Family*. New York: Basic Books, 1977.

Spohn, Thomas, ed. *Pfarrhäuser in Nordwestdeutschland*. Münster: Waxmann, 2000.

Spohn, Thomas. "Verdichtung und Individualisierung. Bauen und Wohnen." In *Westfalen in der Moderne 1815–2015: Geschichte einer Region*, edited by Karl Ditt et al., 601–24. Münster: Aschendorff, 2015.

Stamm, Rainer. *"Ein kurzes intensives Fest": Paula Modersohn-Becker. Eine Biographie*. 3rd ed. Stuttgart: Reclam, 2007.

Steinbrecher, Aline. "Dogs as Domestic Animals in the Eighteenth Century." In *The Routledge History of the Domestic Sphere in Europe: 16th to 19th Century*, edited by Joachim Eibach and Margareth Lanzinger, 495–508. London: Routledge, 2020.

Steiner, Gustav. "Das 'alte' Binninger Pfarrhaus 1708–1938." *Basler Stadtbuch* (1939): 142–69.

Sting, Stephan. "Freundschaft als soziale Utopie. Zur Entstehung bürgerlicher Gesellungsformen im 18. Jahrhundert." In *Die Kultur der Freundschaft. Praxen und Semantiken in anthropologisch-pädagogischer Perspektive*, edited by Meike Sophia Baader et al., 60–69. Weinheim: Beltz, 2008.

Stollberg-Rilinger, Barbara. *Rituale*. 2nd ed. Frankfurt am Main: Campus, 2019.

Streissler, Agnes. "Die Inzersdorfer Ziegelarbeiter. Eine sozialstatistische Fallstudie zur Industrialisierung im Raum Wien." Diplom thesis, University of Vienna, 1991.

Studer, Brigitte. "Familialisierung und Individualisierung. Zur Struktur der Geschlechterordnung in der bürgerlichen Gesellschaft." *L'Homme* 11 (2000): 83–104.

Suter, Mischa. *Rechtstrieb. Schulden und Vollstreckung im liberalen Kapitalismus 1800–1900*. Konstanz: Konstanz University Press, 2016. Published in English as: *Bankruptcy and Debt Collection in Liberal Capitalism: Switzerland 1800–1900*. Ann Arbor: University of Michigan Press, 2021.

Tadmor, Naomi. *Family and Friends in Eighteenth-Century England. Household, Kinship and Patronage*. Cambridge: Cambridge University Press, 2001.

Tadmor, Naomi. "The Concept of the Household Family in Eighteenth-Century England." *Past & Present* 151 (1996): 111–40.

Tanner, Albert. *Arbeitsame Patrioten – Wohlanständige Damen. Bürgertum und Bürgerlichkeit in der Schweiz 1830–1914*. Zürich: Orell Füssli, 1995.

Teuteberg, Hans-Jürgen. "Von der Hausmutter zur Hausfrau: Küchenarbeit im 18. / 19. Jahrhundert in der zeitgenössischen Hauswirtschaftsliteratur." In *Die Revolution am Esstisch. Neue Studien zur Nahrungskultur im 19. / 20. Jahrhundert*, edited by Hans-Jürgen Teuteberg, 101–22. Stuttgart: Franz Steiner, 2004.

Tolkemitt, Brigitte. "Knotenpunkte im Beziehungsnetz der Gebildeten." In *Die gemischte Gesellligkeit in offenen Häusern der Hamburger Familien Reimarus und Sieveking*, edited by Ulrike Weckel et al., 167–202. Göttingen: Wallstein, 1998.

Tosh, John. *A Man's Place. Masculinity and the Middle-Class Home in Victorian England*. New Haven: Yale University Press, 1999.

Tosh, John. *Manliness and Masculinities in Nineteenth-Century Britain. Essays on Gender, Family and Empire*. Harlow: Pearson, 2005.

Trepp, Anne-Charlott. "Anders als sein 'Geschlechtscharakter.' Der bürgerliche Mann um 1800 – Ferdinand Beneke (1774–1848)." *Historische Anthropologie* 4 (1996): 57–77.

Trepp, Anne-Charlott. "Emotion und bürgerliche Sinnstiftung oder die Metaphysik des Gefühls: Liebe am Beginn des bürgerlichen Zeitalters." In *Der bürgerliche Wertehimmel. Innenansichten des 19. Jahrhunderts*, edited by Manfred Hettling and Stefan-Ludwig Hoffmann, 23–55. Göttingen: Vandenhoeck & Ruprecht, 2000.

Trepp, Anne-Charlott. "Männerwelten privat: Vaterschaft im späten 18. und beginnenden 19. Jahrhundert." In *Männergeschichte – Geschlechtergeschichte. Männlichkeit im Wandel der Moderne*, edited by Thomas Kühne, 31–50. Frankfurt am Main: Campus, 1996.

Trepp, Anne-Charlott. *Sanfte Männlichkeit und selbstständige Weiblichkeit. Frauen und Männer im Hamburger Bürgertum zwischen 1770 und 1840*. Göttingen: Vandenhoeck & Ruprecht, 1996.
Trepp, Anne-Charlott. "Zwischen Ungleichheit, Unterordnung und Selbstbehauptung: Handlungsspielräume von Frauen in bürgerlichen Paarbeziehungen um 1800." In *Handlungsspielräume von Frauen um 1800*, edited by Julia Frindte, 91–118. Heidelberg: Winter, 2005.
Ulbrich, Claudia, et al. "Selbstzeugnis und Person. Transkulturelle Perspektiven." In *Selbstzeugnis und Person. Transkulturelle Perspektiven*, edited by Claudia Ulbrich, 1–19. Cologne: Böhlau, 2012.
Vickery, Amanda. *Behind Closed Doors: At Home in Georgian England*. New Haven: Yale University Press, 2009.
Vickery, Amanda. "Golden Age of Separate Spheres? A Review of the Categories and Chronology of English Women's History." *The Historical Journal* 36 (1993): 383–414.
Vickery, Amanda. *The Gentleman's Daughter. Women's Lives in Georgian England*. New Haven: Yale University Press, 1998.
Wadauer, Sigrid. *Die Tour der Gesellen. Mobilität und Biographie im Handwerk vom 18. bis zum 20. Jahrhundert*. Frankfurt am Main: Campus, 2005.
Wall, Richard. "Ideology and Reality of the Stem Family in the Writings of Frédéric Le Play." In *The Stem Family in Eurasian Perspective*, edited by Antoinette Fauve-Chamoux and Emiko Ochiai, 53–80. Bern: Peter Lang, 2009.
Weckel, Ulrike. *Zwischen Häuslichkeit und Öffentlichkeit. Die ersten deutschen Frauenzeitschriften im späten 18. Jahrhundert und ihr Publikum*. Tübingen: Max Niemeyer, 1998.
Wegelin, Peter, ed. *Ulrich Bräker. Die Tagebücher des Armen Mannes im Toggenburg als Geschichtsquelle*. Neujahrsblatt 118. St. Gallen: Historischen Verein des Kantons St. Gallen, 1978.
Wehler, Hans-Ulrich. *Deutsche Gesellschaftsgeschichte*, vols. 1–3. Munich: C. H. Beck, 1987–1995.
Weiß, Stefan. "Otto Brunner und das Ganze Haus oder die zwei Arten der Wirtschaftsgeschichte." *Historische Zeitschrift* 273 (2001): 335–69.
Westphal, Siegrid, et al., eds. *Venus und Vulcanus. Ehen und ihre Konflikte in der Frühen Neuzeit*. Munich: Oldenbourg, 2011.
Whittle, Jane. "A Critique of Approaches to 'Domestic Work': Women, Work and the Pre-Industrial Economy." *Past & Present* 243 (2019): 35–70.
Whittle, Jane. "Gender and Consumption in the Household Economy." In *The Routledge History of the Domestic Sphere in Europe: 16th to 19th Century*, edited by Joachim Eibach and Margareth Lanzinger, 199–217. London: Routledge, 2020.
Widmer, Eric D. *Family Configurations. A Structural Approach to Family Diversity*. Farnham: Routledge, 2010.
Wienfort, Monika. *Verliebt, Verlobt, Verheiratet. Eine Geschichte der Ehe seit der Romantik*. Munich: C. H. Beck, 2014.
Wischermann, Clemens. "Mythen, Macht und Mängel; Der deutsche Wohnungsmarkt im Urbansierungsprozeß." In *Geschichte des Wohnens*, vol. 3: *1800–1918: Das bürgerliche Zeitalter*, edited by Jürgen Reulecke, 333–502. Stuttgart: Deutsche Verlagsanstalt, 1997.
Wittwer Hesse, Denise. "Die Bedeutung der Verwandtschaft im bernischen Patriziat." In *Berns goldene Zeit. Das 18. Jahrhundert neu entdeckt*, edited by André Holenstein, 149–53. Bern: Stämpfli, 2008.
Wittwer Hesse, Denise. *Die Familie von Fellenberg und die Schulen von Hofwyl. Erziehungsideale, "häusliches Glück" und Unternehmertum einer bernischen Patrizierfamilie in der ersten Hälfte des 19. Jahrhunderts*. Bern: Hier & Jetzt, 2002.

Wölfle, Sylvia. "Kunst & Liebe im Aufbruch – Paula Modersohn-Becker und Otto Modersohn." In *Kunst & Liebe im Aufbruch. Paula & Otto. Ausstellungskatalog*, edited by Sylvia Wölfle, 12–27. Lindau: Kunstmuseum Lindau, 2020.

Wölfle, Sylvia, ed. *Kunst & Liebe im Aufbruch. Paula & Otto. Ausstellungskatalog*. Lindau: Kunstmuseum Lindau, 2020.

Wrightson, Keith. "The 'Decline of Neighbourliness' Revisited." In *Local Identities in Late Medieval and Early Modern England*, edited by Norman Jones and Daniel Woolf, 19–49. New York: Springer, 2007.

Wunder, Bernd. *Vom Dorfschulmeister zum Staatsbeamten. Die Verbeamtung der badischen Lehrerschaft im 19. Jahrhundert*. Bühl: Konkordia, 1993.

Wunder, Heide. *"Er ist die Sonn', sie ist der Mond." Frauen in der Frühen Neuzeit*. Munich: C. H. Beck, 1992. Published in English as: *He Is the Sun, She Is the Moon: Women in Early Modern Germany*. Translated by Thomas Dunlap. Cambridge, MA: Harvard University Press, 1998.

Wydler, Andreas. "'Wie könnte ich euch vergessen, euch, die ihr mir alles seyd!' Die Entstehung eines neuen Typus von Freundschaft in der Sattelzeit und dessen Bedeutung für Franz Schubert." Masters thesis, University of Bern, 2019.

Zeeb, Annette. "Hartmann, Joseph, (1812)." *Allgemeines Künstlerlexikon – Internationale Künstlerdatenbank* 69 (2010): 511.

Zimmermann, Clemens. "Wohnen als sozialpolitische Herausforderung. Reformerisches Engagement und öffentliche Aufgaben." In *Geschichte des Wohnens*, vol. 3: *1800–1918: Das bürgerliche Zeitalter*, edited by Jürgen Reulecke, 503–636. Stuttgart: Deutsche Verlagsanstalt, 1997.

Zucca Micheletto, Beatrice. "Husbands, Masculinity, Male Work and Household Economy in Eighteenth-Century Italy: The Case of Turin." *Gender & History* 27 (2015): 752–72.

Zucca Micheletto, Beatrice. "Paid and Unpaid Work." In *The Routledge History of the Domestic Sphere in Europe: 16th to 19th Century*, edited by Joachim Eibach and Margareth Lanzinger, 101–19. London: Routledge, 2020.

Zurbuchen, Simone. *Patriotismus und Kosmopolitismus. Die Schweizer Aufklärung zwischen Tradition und Moderne*. Zürich: Chronos, 2003.

Index of Persons

Adler, Emma   190
Adler, Victor   190-191
Ambühl, Johann Ludwig   23
Ambühl, Salome   30-31, 33-36, 252
Anna (maid in Hamburg)   75, 94
Ariès, Philippe   198
Axen, Caroline von (*see* Beneke, Caroline)
Axen, Ida von   80
Axen, Luise von   84-87, 254
Axen, Otto von   19, 70, 81–83, 85-87, 101

Bänziger, Peter-Paul   132
Barbel (maid in Basel)   120
Baumann, Traugott Heinrich   146
Baumgartner, Barbara (née Teuschl)   153-180, 191, 197, 209, 238, 247, 249, 251, 253–258, 261, 266
Baumgartner, Elisabeth   160
Baumgartner, Hans (Johann, Hansi)   155, 167, 174-175, 255
Baumgartner, Johann   153-180, 193, 197, 209, 247, 254, 257, 261
Baumgartner, Sebastian   160, 173
Bebel, August   190-191, 205
Becker, Bianca Emilie (Milly)   208, 218, 222, 229, 234
Becker, Carl Woldemar   207-211, 213, 218–220, 223–226, 228-229, 236, 243, 247, 249, 253
Becker, Günther   208, 218
Becker, Hans   208
Becker, Henry   208, 211, 218
Becker, Herma   208-209, 211-212, 218, 237-240
Becker, Kurt   208, 212, 218, 224, 239-240, 254
Becker, Mathilde (née von Bültzingslöwen)   207-210, 214, 218-221, 224, 237, 242, 247, 253-254
Becker, Oskar   207
Becker, Paula (*see* Modersohn-Becker-, Paula)
Beer, Christof   164, 176-177
Beer, Henriette (Betti)   160, 164, 176-177
Beilig, Johanna   136

Beneke, Caroline (née von Axen)   68-103, 108, 150, 157, 175, 178, 199, 235, 238, 242, 247-250, 253, 257-258, 261, 265
Beneke, Emma   73, 93, 96
Beneke, Ferdinand   19, 68-103, 108, 123, 125, 131, 133, 139, 141, 150, 157, 162, 175, 178-179, 199, 217, 235, 238, 247-254, 257-261
Beneke, Johann Friedrich (Fritz)   75
Beneke, Justine Dorothea   74-75, 83-84
Beneke, Minna   73, 75, 93-94, 98
Beneke, Otto Adalbert   71-73, 75, 77, 93
Beneke, Regine   74-75, 84, 254
Bennigsen, Levin August von   73, 93
Bert & Ernie (characters on *Sesame Street*)   141
Bertha (maid in Worpswede)   234
Bismarck, Otto von   243
Bochmann (plumber in Stollberg)   150
Bock, Marie   225, 229
Böcklin, Arnold   231, 233
Bourdieu, Pierre   12, 15, 17, 89, 203, 228, 250
Bräker, Johannes   22, 28, 35
Bräker, Michel   30
Bräker, Salome (*see* Ambühl, Salome)
Bräker, Ulrich   22-37, 84, 87, 179, 247-248, 252, 257, 261
Briest, Effi (character in Fontane's novel)   209
Bruckner, (Wilhelm) Eduard   19, 118-120
Bruckner, Abraham   19, 104-126, 142, 150, 199, 247
Bruckner, Carl Gustav   118, 120
Bruckner, Emil Albert   118, 120, 122
Bruckner, Theophil   118-120, 255
Bruckner, Wilhelm   119
Bruckner-Eglinger, Ursula   19, 104-126, 150, 175, 178, 199, 247, 254-255
Brünjes, Hermann   216, 226, 234, 242
Brunner, Mr. (landlord in Zürich)   139
Brunner, Mrs. (landlord in Zürich)   139
Brunner, Otto   9
Brust, Alexander   138
Brust (married couple in Hamburg)   138-140
Buddenbrook, Hanno (character in Thomas Mann's novel)   245

Index of Persons

Buddenbrook, Tony (character in Thomas Mann's novel) 83, 245, 250, 257
Bullinger, Heinrich 45
Burns, Mary 184
Burrowes, William 77, 93, 95, 103

Cervantes, Miguel de 24
Cézanne, Paul 231, 242
Chaufepié, Charlotte de (married name Rambach) 80, 85
Chaufepié, Jean Henri de 79-80, 101
Churchill, Winston 260
Clark, Christopher 11, 200
Cottet, Charles 226

Dachselhofer, Carl Gottlieb 57
Darnton, Robert 134
Daumier, Honoré 226
Don Quixote (character in Cervantes' novel) 24
Dotzauer (apprentice printer) 140
Dreebeen, Anna (a.k.a. Anna Schröder) 216
Duby, Georges 198
Dulcinea (character in Cervantes' novel) 24, 32
Dworak, Adalbert 186-188, 192-196, 247, 250, 254, 257
Dworak, Adelheid (*see* Popp, Adelheid)
Dworak, Albert 192, 195-198
Dworak (Kubeschka), Anna 186–188, 192–197, 201-205, 247, 252-253

Eglinger, Christoph 121-122, 254-255
Eglinger, Emanuel 108, 117, 121-122, 254
Eglinger, Maria (née Weber) 121
Eglinger, Simon 108, 116, 122
Eglinger, Susanna (Susette) 108, 121
Eglinger, Ursula (*see* Bruckner-Eglinger, Ursula)
Ehrenstein, Sophia Emilia von 98
Eimbcke, Johanna Charlotte 81, 89
Elseli (maid in Frienisberg) 52
Engels, Friedrich 3, 181–188, 191-192, 201–202, 205, 207, 253
Escher, Alfred 139

Farge, Arlette 3
Fischer (wife of an army major) 63
Fontane, Theodor 209

Foucault, Michel 15, 18, 40, 72, 85, 132, 156, 238
Frederking, Johann Friedrich 70
Freud, Sigmund 206-207
Friederike (maid in Hamburg) 75
Füßli, Johann Heinrich 23

Gauguin, Paul 231
Gerstl, Betti 155
Gerstl, Karl 155
Gessler, Rosine 122-123
Giddens, Anthony 28
Gleixner, Ulrike 60
Goethe, Johann Wolfgang von 24, 27, 71, 99, 132, 200, 215
Goffman, Erving 26
Gotthelf, Jeremias 28
Grouber (bailiff in Buchsee) 63
Grünlich, Bendix (character in Thomas Mann's novel) 83, 86, 250
Gutensohn, Joseph 75-76

Habermas, Jürgen 100, 200
Habermas, Rebekka 4
Hagenbuch, Bernadette 106
Hartmann, Joseph 1–3
Haselgruber, Franz 156
Hatje, Frank 73
Hauptmann, Carl 217, 229, 237-238
Hausen, Karin 9, 99
Haydn, Joseph 119, 146
Hegel, Georg Wilhelm Friedrich 2, 68, 253
Heineken, Minna (Hermanna) 75
Henriette (nanny in Basel) 118, 120
Hermann, Johanna Maria 77
Herport, Henriette (*see* Stettler-Herport, Henriette)
Herport, Johann Anton 38, 55
Herzfeld, Jakob 81
Herzfeld, Karoline 81
Hill, Marie 221
Hoetger, Bernhard 217, 241
Hoetger, Helene 217, 241
Horneffer, Ernst 209
Hudtwalcker, Johann Michael 79

Im Hoof, Margaritha 38

Jacobi, Bertha   144-146
Jacobi, Emilie   144–146
Jacobi, Friedrich August   145, 150
Jacobi (tradeswoman in Hartenstein)   145, 150
Jänisch, Johann Joachim   81
Jean Paul   71, 89, 91, 97, 128
Jean (servant in Frienisberg)   52
Johann (king of Saxnony)   133
Johanne (maid in Worpswede)   234
John, Matthias   134
Joseph II (emperor)   41
Julie (character in Rousseau's novel)   27
Jung-Stilling, Johann Heinrich   24

Kant, Immanuel   23, 189
Kätchen (Ulrich Bräker's friend)   30, 32–34
Kleist, Heinrich von   71
Klopstock, Friedrich Gottlieb   65
Kohl (teacher trainer in Thalheim)   139
Krüger, Franz   134
Kubeschka, Anna (see Dvořak, Anna)
Kubeschka, Joseph   186, 196
Kuniß, Auguste   143
Kunze (neighbor in Mitteldorf)   151

La Motte Fouqué, Friedrich de   71, 97
La Roche, Sophie von   65
Lamm (journeyman printer and roommate)   139–142, 147
Langhans, Sigmund Ludwig   56
Langreiter, Nikola   154, 157
Laslett, Peter   9
Lavater, Johann Caspar   24, 40
Le Play, Frédéric   9
Lisgen von K. (Ulrich Bräker's friend)   30
Luhmann, Niklas   11, 28, 160
Luther, Katharina (née von Bora)   112
Luther, Martin   4, 45, 112, 223
Lüthold, Anna (Ännchen)   26-34, 36-37, 84, 248

Mackensen, Fritz   211
Mann, Thomas   71, 83, 86, 245–246, 250
Maria Wutz (character in Jean Paul's novel)   128
Mariannchen (Ulrich Bräker's friend)   30
Marie (cook in Hamburg)   75
Marie (publisher's daughter in Waldenburg)   144

Mariechen (Ulrich Bräker's friend)   30
Marion (maid in Frienisberg)   52
Marx, Karl   185–186, 201
Meier (admirer in Krems)   156
Meister, Wilhelm (character in Goethe's novel)   132
Meyer (pastor in Basel)   108
Miers (book printer)   140
Mitterauer, Michael   9
Modersohn, Elsbeth   228, 231, 235–236, 241
Modersohn, Ernst   228
Modersohn, Helene (née Schröder)   225–226, 238
Modersohn, Otto   206–244, 248, 250, 253, 255
Modersohn-Becker, Paula   206–244, 248–250, 253–255, 258–259

Napoleon I, Bonaparte   69
Nielsen (book printer)   140
Nietzsche, Friedrich   209, 215, 233

Ott (roommate in Basel)   140
Overbeck, Fritz   225
Overbeck, Hermine   225

Pammer, Max   162
Parizot, Herma   222
Pettersson & Findus (comic book characters)   232
Pfeifer (widow in Stuttgart)   140
Philippi, Ferdinand Carl   131, 135
Popp, Adelheid (née Dvořak)   181–205, 207, 248–250, 252–253, 257–258, 260–261
Popp, Julius   190, 201–204, 248–250, 253
Püschmann, Agnes   147
Püschmann, Antonie   143
Püschmann, Ernst   127, 143, 145, 147, 149–150, 252
Püschmann, Friedrich Anton   127–152, 175, 198–199, 235, 247, 250, 252, 256–258, 263
Püschmann, Johann Gottfried   127, 147–151, 199, 252, 263
Püschmann, Pauline   143, 145, 147, 149
Püschmann, Wilhelm   127, 147, 149
Püschmann, Wilhelmine   147
Püschmann (schoolteacher's wife in Mitteldorf)   145–148

Rambach, Charlotte (see Chaufepié, Charlotte de)
Rambach, Johann Jakob 80, 103, 142
Reckwitz, Andreas 15-18, 21, 23, 89, 129, 244, 246, 259
Richardson, Samuel 65
Riehl, Wilhelm Heinrich 2, 9, 139
Rilke, Rainer Maria 213, 217, 228-230
Rilke-Westhoff, Clara (see Westhoff, Clara)
Rodin, Auguste 226
Roeck, Carl Ludwig 97-99
Roper, Lyndal 161
Rosina (Ulrich Bräker's friend) 30
Rotteck, Carl von 68
Rousseau, Jean-Jacques 24, 27
Ruther (baker in Stollberg) 150

Sabean, David 11, 100
Salchli (collector in Frienisberg) 51
Salome (nanny in Basel) 118
Sandberg, Johann Christian 76
Scheiffler (servant in Hamburg) 75
Scheuchzer, Johann Jakob 65
Schiller, Friedrich 92, 120-121, 200
Schlingemann, Johann Andreas 95, 101, 142
Schnegg, Brigitte 40
Schober (bridegroom in Krems) 158, 179
Schorn-Schütte, Luise 104
Schuchmacher, Johann Diedrich 79, 101
Seyd, Wilhelm Heinrich 1
Shakespeare, William 23, 92
Sieder, Reinhard 9
Sombart, Werner 217, 237-238
Spener, Philipp Jacob 46
Stähelin, Balthasar 105, 117
Stawinoha, Maria (née Baumgartner) 162, 167, 173, 254
Stawinoha, Wenzel 162, 167
Steiner (admirer in Krems) 156
Stettler, Albert Friedrich (Frizli) 50, 56, 65-66
Stettler, Anna Maria (Marianne) 56-58
Stettler, Bernhard Albrecht (Brechtli) 49

Stettler, Henriette 50, 56, 64-65
Stettler, Rudolf 38-67, 175, 178, 235, 247-248, 250, 252
Stettler-Herport, Henriette 24, 38-67, 91, 100, 105-106, 113-114, 125, 217, 235, 247-248, 252, 254-255, 259
Stettler-Wyttenbach, Johanna Catharina 52
Stockmann, Julie 135

Teuschl, Anna Maria 155, 158-160, 169, 174
Teuschl, Anton 154-155, 159, 168-169, 173, 175, 177, 257
Teuschl, Wetti (Barbara, Betti; see Baumgartner, Barbara)
Therese (maid in Grimma) 144
Titian 233
Trepp, Anne-Charlott 4, 73

Ursel (Ulrich Bräker's friend) 30

Velazquez, Eugenio 226
Vogeler, Heinrich 225, 228-230, 261, 266
Vogeler, Martha (née Schröder) 228, 230
Vogl, Lori 158, 160, 179

Wagner, Richard 215
Weber, Max 8
Wehner, Christoph Johann 79
Wehner, Sophie Dorothea 79
Werther (character in Goethe's novel) 27, 99, 215
Weseloh, Marie (married name Gutensohn) 75
Westhoff, Clara (married name Rilke) 214, 217, 225, 228-230, 241
Westphalen, Johann Ernst 79, 95
Wilhelm I (king of Prussia) 207
Wunder, Heide 4

Zarathustra (character in Nietzsche's work) 215
Zschau (lady in Grimma) 133

Index of Subjects

bourgeoisie (*Bürgertum; Bürgerlichkeit*)   3, 13, 16, 21, 68-69, 81-82, 88, 100, 102, 104, 119-120, 127, 129, 131, 142, 149-150, 154, 182, 189, 192, 207-208, 215-216, 246–248, 251, 264
– horizon of bourgeois values   68, 88, 201, 251
– petite bourgeoisie (*Kleinbürgertum*)   129, 153-154, 239, 258-259

childcare (*see also* childrearing; nanny)   50, 111
childhood   21, 24, 38, 40, 105, 147, 155, 176, 189–191, 193-195, 201, 203
child-rearing / development (*see also* childcare; nanny)   61, 65, 94, 117, 170
co-presence   13, 51, 102, 120, 139, 141, 151, 171, 176, 197, 200, 262-263
cousin marriage   55, 247, 251

divorce / marital separation   4, 8-9, 35-36, 170, 178, 236-237, 239-240, 244-245
domestication   114, 122, 262
domesticity (*Häuslichkeit*; *see also* open domesticity; domestication)   5, 10, 12, 14, 21, 26, 39, 46, 49, 68, 80, 90, 100, 102, 127, 133, 167, 172, 174, 176, 179, 192-193, 200, 206, 230, 235, 244, 249, 251, 253-254, 257, 261, 264
dowry   55, 86, 88, 116, 161, 208, 211, 228

educated bourgeoisie (*Bildungsbürgertum*)   20, 27, 91-92, 104, 142, 154, 207, 215, 227
educated classes (*gebildete Stände*)   68-69
elite / urban elite (*Stadtbürgertum*)   28, 37–40, 55-56, 62, 64, 69, 82, 87-88, 102, 104-105, 120, 123, 146, 149, 208, 222, 248, 260, 262
endogamy   55, 57-58, 88, 109, 125, 205, 227, 247
engagement to marry / promise to marry   26, 30, 55, 80, 87-88, 108, 145, 214, 221-228, 235, 238, 250
Enlightenment, the   6, 10, 13, 18, 23-24, 31, 39, 42, 46, 48-49, 69-70, 96, 181, 189, 200, 223

ethics / values   8, 60, 68-69, 88, 129, 201, 244, 251, 261
extended family   75, 100, 199

family as (*see also* nuclear family; extended family)
– bourgeois   1–3, 9, 39, 65–69, 83, 94, 98, 119, 124-125, 133, 137, 185, 200, 206–209, 217, 242, 248
– community of care   170, 247, 255
– community of conflict   169, 247
– community of emotion   118, 169, 247
– community of support   153, 172-173, 247
– community of survival   195, 201, 247
family, fragility of   3, 8, 96, 173, 244, 250, 253
friendship   16, 75, 80, 89, 103, 123, 141-142, 176, 217, 228-229, 241, 251–254, 257

gender character   9, 90, 96, 99, 116, 132, 136, 251
gender hierarchy / models / relations   2, 9, 12, 16, 19, 21, 30, 34, 54–56, 60-61, 68, 72, 74, 77, 88, 99, 103, 115, 121, 123, 138-139, 147, 151, 153, 165, 178, 183-184, 210, 216, 227, 239, 248, 251–253, 263
gender roles / norms   5, 9, 11, 20, 41, 54, 91, 97, 103, 115-116, 126, 178, 184-185, 223, 243-244, 254

habitat   12, 17, 81-82, 88, 207-208, 216, 260-261
habitus   3-4, 11-12, 14–18, 21, 27, 37, 49, 68-69, 81, 89, 123, 126, 131, 146, 160, 203, 208, 215, 241, 243, 250, 255, 257, 260-261
housefather   2, 59, 69, 75, 78, 99, 116-117, 135, 139
housekeeping / household economy / family economy   6, 34, 41, 46, 52-53, 61, 91, 112–114, 116-117, 189, 195, 222, 226, 252, 256, 259, 262, 264
housemother   11, 51-52, 54, 59, 62-65, 67, 114–116, 118, 120, 122, 125, 256
housewife / mistress of the household   91, 109-110, 113-114, 117, 155, 204, 214, 227

https://doi.org/10.1515/9783111081700-016

Index of Subjects

intimacy / intimate sphere / intimate relationships / intimate communication   13–16, 26, 32, 37, 66-67, 116, 125, 142, 144, 212, 221, 251, 260, 262
inwardness (*Innerlichkeit*)   4, 106, 252, 256

kitchen / cooking   49, 52-53, 80, 110, 114, 116, 135-136, 163, 165–167, 176, 185, 192, 198, 204, 213, 217, 222-223, 227, 233, 236, 263

liberalism / liberals   2, 4, 6, 13, 70, 99, 181, 249
living room / parlor   1, 35, 49, 76, 80, 110, 136, 141, 144, 176, 202, 258–260
love   4, 7, 20–22, 26–29, 31-32, 36–37, 55, 57, 66, 68, 80, 83–85, 87-88, 92–94, 96–99, 109, 115, 118, 120, 122, 130, 143-144, 147, 156–160

maid / maidservant (*see also* nanny)   51-52, 66, 75, 91, 94, 110, 112–114, 116–120, 122, 124, 128, 139, 144, 155, 163, 165, 169, 176, 186, 198, 234-235, 255–256, 259
male breadwinner   164, 172, 195, 259
marital crisis   153-154, 156, 240-241, 244
marriage
– agreement to / consent to / contract   25, 31, 34-35, 55-57, 86-87, 108, 159, 161-162, 249-250, 257
– as companionship / companionate   35, 54, 58-59, 115-116, 205, 252, 257
– as friendship   16, 89, 162, 216, 252-254
– as partnership   9, 60, 99, 204, 224, 249
– ban / restriction / permission   143, 247
– bourgeois   11, 65–72, 89, 91, 93, 177–178, 252
– convenience as a motivation for   20, 36, 88, 246, 250
– hierarchy in   2, 54, 58, 60, 99, 115-116, 135, 178, 239, 251-253
– promise of (*see* engagement)
– proposal of   57, 82, 85, 107-109, 250
married couple / spouses
– as educated couple (*Bildungspaar*)   4, 32, 89, 91, 231, 252-253, 256-257
– as loving couple (*Liebespaar*)   4, 252
– as religious couple (*Glaubenspaar*)   204, 231, 252
– as working couple (*Arbeitspaar*)   4, 35, 171-172, 231-232, 252, 259
matchmaking   20, 25-29, 34, 36, 54-58, 82–85, 87, 109, 125, 137, 153, 157-158, 177, 247-248, 250, 257, 264
members of the household (*Hausgenossen*)   75, 79, 104, 113
men / masculinity
– gentle / sensitive: 73, 94, 116, 136, 204, 220, 244, 253
middle class (*Bürgertum*; *see also* bourgeoisie)   1-3, 5, 16, 20–21, 27, 37, 39, 68, 90, 154, 216, 243, 253
morals / morality   2, 15, 21, 34, 40, 46, 52, 67, 104, 144, 184, 204, 212, 238, 246, 253
music at home / in the house   64-65, 106, 119-120, 150-151, 229, 257

nanny (*see also* childcare; childrearing; maid)   75, 110, 118, 120
neighbors / neighborliness / neighborhood   25, 31, 53, 62, 76, 78-79, 93, 103, 123, 128, 139, 149-151, 164, 177, 181, 188, 196, 251, 260-263
nightly lodger (*Bettgeher*)   13, 166, 176, 198, 200, 260, 262
nuclear family (*see also* family, bourgeois)   2, 5, 8, 13, 51, 66, 74, 100-101, 120, 122, 124, 127, 133, 135, 141, 148-149, 151, 155, 199, 247, 263

obstinacy   24, 45, 60, 98-99, 115, 221, 249
open house / open domesticity   13, 21, 62, 64, 67-68, 102-103, 120, 122, 124, 139, 149-150, 175, 183, 243, 262–264

Pietism / Pietist (*see also* pious house)   4, 6, 13, 18, 24, 39–43, 45–46, 49, 53–56, 58, 60, 64, 67, 105, 107, 109, 118-119, 123, 180, 204, 238, 248-249, 251, 259
pious house / family / household (*see also* Pietism)   46, 53, 112, 125, 178, 249, 253, 255
privacy / private sphere   13-14, 21, 49, 62, 64, 91, 100-103, 110, 123, 135, 137, 140-141, 149, 151, 176, 193, 197, 199, 235, 251-252, 260, 262-263

resilience   80, 157, 167, 245-246
Romantic / Romanticism   4, 6, 13, 15-16, 18, 20, 27-28, 37, 69, 71-72, 88, 142, 157, 162, 180, 205, 231, 244, 246, 248-249, 252-253

salon / salon culture   59, 67, 162-163, 167–169, 171, 173-176, 179, 200, 259
separate spheres   12, 20-21, 54, 59, 90-91, 122, 235
servants (*see also* maid)   1-2, 11, 13, 16, 41, 44, 49, 51–53, 59, 61, 67, 75, 80, 92, 100, 102, 106, 113, 163, 227, 255-256, 262
sexuality / sex   25–27, 30, 37, 60, 84-85, 179, 212, 238-239, 258
sibling relationships / love   6, 13, 21, 121, 147, 246-247, 254
subject
– hybrid subject, subjectivity   15, 23, 129, 251
– subject culture   15-16, 21

technology of the self   15, 18, 40, 72, 156, 238
tenant / landlord / subtenant   22, 78, 138–140, 150-151, 155, 164, 166, 176-177, 198, 256, 260, 262-263

trust / familiarity (*see also* intimacy)   7, 78, 100, 103, 116, 118, 122, 125, 142-143, 212, 215-216, 219, 221, 234, 242, 254
two-supporter model   172, 259

visiting culture / visiting practice / conviviality (*see also* visits)   43–45, 59–63, 102, 123, 128, 149–151, 175-176, 193, 200, 243, 260, 262-263
visits / soiree (*see also* visiting culture)   42, 44–46, 50, 59, 61–65, 67, 71, 83-84, 90, 92, 100–102, 106, 108-109, 114, 123, 125, 132, 145-146, 148, 150-151, 166, 170, 175, 200, 212, 217, 225-226, 250, 261–263

wedding / wedding day   30, 35, 55-58, 75-76, 80, 87, 106, 108-109, 112, 118, 122, 150-151, 157–163, 172, 179, 196, 214, 216, 228-229, 251, 256, 258, 262, 266
women's movement   10, 190, 204, 207, 233, 243
work in the house / household   4, 51-55, 62-64, 66-67, 90-94, 102, 111-114, 132, 151, 171-172, 188-193, 195, 199, 204, 231, 235, 243, 252, 258-260, 264